THE LOGIC OF TYPED FEATURE STRUCTURES

T0210652

Cambridge Tracts in Theoretical Computer Science

Managing Editor   Professor C. J. van Rijsbergen, Department of Computing Science, University of Glasgow

Titles in the series

THE LOGIC OF TYPED FEATURE STRUCTURES

With Applications to Unification Grammars, Logic Programs and Constraint Resolution

Bob Carpenter

Computational Linguistics Program
Philosophy Department
Carnegie Mellon University

CAMBRIDGE
UNIVERSITY PRESS

CAMBRIDGE UNIVERSITY PRESS
Cambridge, New York, Melbourne, Madrid, Cape Town, Singapore, São Paulo

Cambridge University Press
The Edinburgh Building, Cambridge CB2 2RU, UK

Published in the United States of America by Cambridge University Press, New York

www.cambridge.org
Information on this title: www.cambridge.org/9780521419321

© Cambridge University Press 1992

First published 1992
This digitally printed first paperback version 2005

A catalogue record for this publication is available from the British Library

Library of Congress Cataloguing in Publication data

Carpenter, Bob.
The logic of typed feature structures with applications to
unification grammars, logic programs and constraint resolution / Bob
Carpenter.
    p.   cm. – (Cambridge tracts in theoretical computer science:
32)
Includes bibliographical references and index.
ISBN 0–521–41932–8
1. Data structures (Computer science) 2. Logic programming.
I. Title. II. Series.
QA76.9.D35C37 1992
005.7'3–dc20   91–39777
                                                   CIP

ISBN-13 978-0-521-41932-1 hardback
ISBN-10 0-521-41932-8 hardback

ISBN-13 978-0-521-02254-5 paperback
ISBN-10 0-521-02254-1 paperback

Contents

Acknowledgments

This project could not have been completed without the encouragement, enthusiasm, and careful eye for detail of Carl Pollard. He not only contributed valuable insights and references so that I could absorb the state of the art on feature structures, but also provided feedback and comments on the original results reported here as they were developing. Almost all of the innovations presented here were directly inspired by the HPSG grammar formalism of Pollard and Sag (1987). Most of the well known and published results concerning feature structures came out of two projects: the PATR-II project at SRI international, with contributions by Lauri Karttunen, Fernando Pereira, and Stu Shieber, and by the group at the University of Michigan including Bob Kasper, Drew Moshier, and Bill Rounds. The basic approach and some of the more sophisticated results and techniques upon which this work was based were developed by Carl Pollard and Drew Moshier. Another major source of inspiration was the work of Gert Smolka (1988, 1989), in particular with respect to the connections between feature algebras and feature structures.

An early source of inspiration was the Unification Categorial Grammar project at the University of Edinburgh, involving Ewan Klein, Mike Reape, Jo Calder, and Henk Zeevat. It was in the context of this project, and in Ewan Klein's introduction to GPSG, that I was first exposed to feature structures. An unpublished paper by Mike Reape was partially responsible for the treatment of extensionality, and Jo Calder's development of typed feature structures was always in the back of my mind.

This research has also benefited from presentations at the International Workshop on Inheritance in Natural Language Processing hosted by the University of Tilburg, at Carnegie Mellon University, at the Second International Workshop on Parsing Technology in Cancun and at the 29th Association for Computationl Linguistics meeting in Berkeley. The first draft of this monograph was provided for students at the Second European Summer School for Language, Logic and Information at Leuven. It was this group that made me realize that the audience for results in the theory of feature structures was much larger than I had previously imagined, and cemented my resolve to finish this monograph sooner rather than later. In particular, some comments of Gert Smolka's during the Summer School led me to change the way in which I thought of his and Mark Johnson's work. This in turn led to a general rewriting of all of the criticisms and comparisons between the logical/algebraic approach and the feature-structure-based approaches. I now hope that this monograph can help to reconcile some of the apparent differences between the algebraic, logical and graph-based approaches. It was Gert Smolka who first demonstrated the connection between the two approaches, bringing with it a view of feature structures as representations of normal-form descriptions.

I originally began thinking about inheritance while working with Rich Thomason at the University of Pittsburgh. It was with his encouragement that I tried to work out connections between knowledge representation formalisms and unification-based linguistic grammar formalisms. Unfortunately, many of the comparisons and contrasts between the inheritance-based feature structure logics presented here and terminological knowledge representation systems such as KL-ONE still remain unclear. Hopefully, this avenue of exploration can be taken up in the future by myself and others. Another task waiting in the wings is the integration of non-monotonic inheritance into the feature structure framework. Recently, foundational work on non-monotonic inheritance has progressed enormously, in part due to the work of the NSF funded LINKUP project involving Dave Touretzky at Carnegie Mellon University, Rich Thomason at the University of Pittsburgh, and Jeff Horty at the University of Maryland.

The ideas presented here originally developed in the context of an HPSG interest group at Carnegie Mellon University consisting of myself, Carl Pollard, Alex Franz, Sondra Ahlèn, and Andreas Kathol. Many fruitful discussions took place among various subsets of this group, and during these meetings we forced ourselves to clarify issues and come up with concrete proposals. Many of our false starts, negative results, and alternative proposals are not reported here for the sake of readability, continuity, and conciseness.

Finally, I would like to thank a number of people for comments on early drafts of this work. In particular, Bob Kasper, Carl Pollard, and Andreas Kathol, who worked their way through a late draft and provided detailed technical and stylistic comments. I would also like to thank Robert Dale for providing invaluable editorial and stylistic comments from the point of view of someone who was not a full-time feature structure researcher. Gerald Penn then carefully read and made significant comments on the penultimate draft. Thanks also to Kathy Baker and Rob Lefferts, who also read parts of the final draft. Last but not least, I would like to thank Katharita Lamoza, a production editor at Cambridge University Press, for her stylistic advice and attention to detail.

The text was composed and typeset by the author in LaTeX with an HP 370 workstation and a DEC 5200 workstation, part of the facilities of the Laboratory for Computational Linguistics at Carnegie Mellon University.

Chapter 1

Introduction

In this monograph we motivate and provide theoretical foundations for the specification and implementation of systems employing data structures which have come to be known as *feature structures*. Feature structures provide a record-like data structure for representing partial information that can be expressed in terms of features or attributes and their values. Feature structures are inherently associative in nature, with features interpreted as associative connections between domain objects. This leads to natural graph-based representations in which the value of a feature or attribute in a feature structure is either undefined or another feature structure. Under our approach, feature structures are ideally suited for use in unification-based formalisms, in which unification, at its most basic level, is simply an operation that simultaneously determines the consistency of two pieces of partial information and, if they are consistent, combines them into a single result. The standard application of unification is to efficient hierarchical pattern matching, a basic operation which has applications to a broad range of knowledge representation and automated reasoning tasks.

Our notion of feature structures, as well as its implications for processing, should be of interest to anyone interested in the behavior of systems that employ features, roles, attributes, or slots with structured fillers or values. We provide a degree of abstraction away from concrete feature structures by employing a general attribute-value logic. We extend the usual attribute-value logic of Rounds and Kasper (1986, Kasper and Rounds 1986) to allow for path inequations, but do not allow general negation or implication of the sort studied by Johnson (1987, 1988), Smolka (1988), or King (1989). On the other hand, we extend the axiomatization of Rounds and Kasper to account not only for path inequations, but also type inclusion, appropriateness, and extensionality specifications.

Feature structures, as presented here, have immediate applications to linguistic formalisms based on unification, including the basic phrase structure formalisms, Functional Unification Grammar (FUG) (Kay 1979, 1985) and Parse and Translate II (PATR-II) (Shieber et al. 1983, Shieber 1984), equation-based formalisms such as Lexical Functional Grammar (LFG) (Kaplan and Bresnan 1982), and also constraint-based formalisms such as Head-driven Phrase Structure Grammar (HPSG) (Pollard and Sag 1987, in press). For a general introduc-

1

tion to feature structures in linguistic theories, see Shieber (1986). Because our feature structures provide a natural generalization of first-order terms, they also have applications to the more traditional logic grammar formalisms, which are based on the unification of first-order terms (Pereira and Warren 1980, Pereira and Shieber 1987). Another obvious application is to logic programming languages themselves, in which feature structures can replace first-order terms as the data structure out of which definite clauses are constructed (Aït-Kaci and Nasr 1986, Höhfeld and Smolka 1988). Our notion of feature structures is related to the tree-based data structures used in Prolog II (Colmerauer 1984, 1987) and Prolog III (Guenthner 1987, Lehner in press). Finally, we believe that our feature structures also have applications to the so-called *terminological* knowledge representation systems such as KL-ONE (Brachman and Schmolze 1985) and its descendants, especially LOOM (Mac Gregor 1988, 1990) and CLASSIC (Borgida et al. 1989, Brachman et al.1991). These terminological formalisms are themselves descendants of the more procedurally oriented frame-based representation systems (Minsky 1975). The basis of the terminological components of these systems is an inheritance network of concepts defined in terms of their features and values. It is often argued that it is the associative nature of inheritance and frame-based representation systems and their facility for pattern-matching that leads to their efficiency (see Brachman (1979) for a summary of associative network reasoning systems).

We introduce a number of new and borrowed notions that have not been previously considered in the context of feature structure unification systems. These extensions form a proper generalization of both the more commonly found feature structure unification systems used in linguistic formalisms and the term representations found in logic programming languages. We consider these extensions in turn in an attempt to place our system in the perspective of previous studies of feature structures and unification.

Many researchers have chosen to study algebraic models of attribute-value logics, in which features are interpreted as partial functions over a domain of objects (for instance, Smolka 1988, Johnson 1988, King 1989). We feel free to restrict our attention to feature structures in our formal development, as Smolka (1988, 1989) has shown that they play a canonical role as models for attribute-value logics in much the same way that initial algebras play a canonical role with respect to a collection of first-order equational axioms (Cohn 1965, Goguen et al. 1978, Goguen 1988).

We choose to impose a particular kind of object-oriented type discipline on the collection of feature structures. We incorporate an ordered notion of types organized into a multiple inheritance hierarchy based on type inclusion. We also impose appropriateness conditions that specify the features which are appropriate for each type and the admissible types of their values. The benefits of typed programming languages are well known (see Cardelli and Wegner 1985). In particular, they allow for compile- and run-time error detection and efficient memory management. The benefits of multiple inheritance in type systems is especially prominent in reasoning systems, in which a significant amount of information can be efficiently coded in terms of the types, which eliminates a large degree of redundancy and allows information to be encoded at the appropriate level of abstraction.

We contrast two different forms of typing, one of which is more restrictive than the other. In the weaker version, a feature structure is well-typed if all of its features and their values are appropriate; in the stronger, the converse must also hold: every appropriate feature must be defined. The weaker version is well suited to the representation of sparse feature structures, while the strong approach lends itself well to efficient precompilation.

Both the strong and weak versions of our type system are well behaved in that they admit straightforward type inference algorithms. More precisely, we can define an effective procedure which takes a feature structure with underspecified types and extends it to a unique minimal well-typed feature structure if it is typable. Type inference is necessary to show that unification is well defined; we want to maintain a system in which two pieces of partial information represented by feature structures can always be combined into a single unified whole. The general picture of unification in our typed setting amounts to a standard process of unification followed by a type inference operation. For the unification portion of this process, Aït-Kaci (1984) and Moshier (1989) have shown how to modify an efficient (quasi-linear) term unification algorithm (Martelli and Montanari 1982, Jaffar 1984) to deal with type ordering information.

We also show how to efficiently (linearly) compute the subsumption or information containment relation between feature structures. This operation is often employed in linguistic applications relying on chart parsing techniques. Subsumption also plays a fundamental role in knowledge representation formalisms in the KL-ONE family, in which it is applied to both reasoning and knowledge acquisition tasks (Brachman and Schmolze 1985, Schmolze and Lipkis 1983, Mac Gregor 1988).

We study the conditions on type specifications under which a static type discipline can be maintained. A type system is said to be *static* if all of the type checking and type inference operations can be computed at compile time. The standard way to show that a type system is static is to define a type inference procedure and then show that all of the basic operations of the system preserve well-typedness. In our particular case, to achieve a fully static notion of typing, we need to ensure that the unification of two well-typed feature structures results in a well-typed feature structure. If well-typedness is preserved by unification, then all of the necessary type inference can be carried out at compile time.

An additional benefit of ordering our types into a multiple inheritance hierarchy surfaces at run time. Information which might otherwise be encoded by inference steps, or even in terms of feature structure unification, can be recast in terms of efficient inheritance operations. This factorization of inheritance, structural unification, and inference allows many expensive unification and inference steps to be reduced to table look-ups and has proved invaluable in automatic theorem proving systems (Walther 1985, Cohn 1987) and hybrid reasoning systems such as KRYPTON (Brachman et al. 1983), KL-TWO (Vilain 1985), BACK (Luck et al. 1987, Nebel 1988), CLASSIC (Borgida et al. 1989, Brachman et al. 1991), and LOOM (Mac Gregor 1988, 1990).

In addition to a type discipline, we allow a specialized form of negation that can be expressed by means of path inequations. Our inequations are the feature structure analogues of the inequations found in Prolog II (Colmerauer 1987). The intuition is that two feature structures can be explicitly constrained to be non-identical even if they do not contain conflicting information. In terms of our motivating application to natural language grammar formalisms, inequality provides a natural interpretation for disjoint reference conditions imposed by non-reflexive pronouns (Pereira 1987). What separates this brand of negation from others that have been applied to feature structures, with the notable exceptions of the intuitionistic approach of Moshier and Rounds (1987) and the three-valued approach of Dawar and Vijay-Shanker (1989), is that it preserves the monotonicity of the model theory. More specifically, if a feature structure models a description, then every informational extension of the feature structure also models the description. A further benefit of our version of negative information is that it allows the unification of two consistent feature structures to result in a unique well-defined feature structure, which is absolutely crucial if we want to base our systems on a notion of efficient unification (Pereira 1987). In Prolog II and Prolog III, it has been found that many of the practical applications of negation, including the cut operation, can be cast in terms of inequations rather than highly problematic forms of predicate negation (Colmerauer 1987).

One of the major differences between feature structures and logical terms is in the notion of identity. In logic programming systems, two terms are taken to be identical if they have the same function or relation symbol and all of their arguments are identical. Somewhat surprisingly, this is not the natural notion of identity that is applicable to feature structures or terminological knowledge representation systems. It has been almost universally assumed (for example, by Pereira and Shieber 1984, Aït-Kaci 1984, Kasper and Rounds 1986, Pollard and Moshier 1990, Johnson 1987, and Smolka 1988) that two feature structures can have an identical type and have identical values for all of their features without themselves being identical, thus building a fair degree of intensionality into feature structure systems. Pollard and Sag (1987) argue for an intensional treatment of identity in which token identity cannot be inferred from type identity in feature structures. Concepts in terminological knowledge representation systems are also assumed to be intensional in the sense that structural isomorphism is not enough to derive token identity (Brachman et al. 1991). We generalize the treatment of identity in both first-order terms and feature structures by requiring each type to be identified as either extensional or intensional. Two feature structures of the same extensional type are identified if they have identical values for all of their features. On the other hand, there is no way to derive identities between feature structures of an intensional type. The distinction between token identity and type identity is similar to the distinction between the predicates *EQ* and *EQUAL* in the Lisp programming language; the

EQ relations holds between two objects only if they occupy the same location in memory, whereas *EQUAL* checks to see if they have identical structure componentwise. A similar distinction is made in Prolog, in which the predicate == tests for true equality in the underlying representation rather than alphabetic variance. It is interesting to note that there is no built-in check for alphabetic variance in Prolog, as it is much more difficult to compute than ==, which can be determined by simply chasing pointers.

Another aspect of our feature structures that is worth mentioning is that we allow cycles. Thus it is possible to have a feature structure whose value for some non-empty sequence of features is itself. In Prolog II, cyclic terms are allowed and are identified semantically by their infinite, albeit rational, tree unfoldings. The rational tree representation is not adequate for our purposes, as it assumes that the types are all extensional. On the other hand, when we consider extensionality, we show how to represent both Prolog and Prolog II terms as a special case of typed feature structures. One of the major processing benefits of cyclic terms is that they arise naturally during unification and the so-called *occurs check* that would rule them out turns practical quasi-linear unification algorithms into quadratic ones (Martelli and Montanari 1982, Jaffar 1984). For the sake of completeness, we also present a treatment of acyclic feature structures, in which a single additional axiom scheme completely characterizes the notion of acyclicity.

The informational content of a term in a logic programming language can be characterized uniquely by the set of its instances which are ground terms (terms without variables). Two terms are alphabetic variants (informationally identical) if and only if they can be instantiated to exactly the same set of ground terms. Ground terms are informationally maximal in the sense that there are no terms that properly extend them. A ground feature structure would have a subsumption-maximal type (that is, a type with no proper subtypes) and a ground value for each of its features and would furthermore specify the identity or inequality of each of its substructures. What is interesting is that it is only with the addition of typing and inequality that the notion of ground feature structure begins to make sense. In the standard treatments of feature structures without inequality or types, maximal feature structures require maximal amounts of structure sharing; a feature structure could always be extended informationally to a properly more specific feature structure by unifying two compatible substructures. With inequality, a feature structure can be extended by either unifying two substructures or explicitly adding an inequality between them. Without a notion of typing, maximal feature structures must provide values for every feature, even those not intended to occur together in the application. A similar problem arises in Prolog with inappropriate values. Mycroft and O'Keefe (1984) point out that the standard program for *append* admits *append*(*nil*, 3, 3) as a solution, where *append* was clearly only intended to be applied to lists. Even in our extended setting, it is quite difficult to characterize feature structures in terms of their maximal or ground extensions; the interaction of inequations, extensional types and finite type hierarchies leads to subtle inconsistencies which neither our logic nor our models are powerful enough to detect. For instance, we later see that there are some feature structures which cannot be extended to any ground feature structure.

After considering the status of maximal feature structures and the nature of partial information in our representational system, we go on to consider two "extensions" to the system, of which one enriches the description language, and the other generalizes the class of models in an algebraic direction. However, it turns out that neither of these moves truly adds any power to the system, which is why they are put off until after our study of feature structures and Rounds-Kasper-like description language. First, we consider the addition of variables to the description language, along with equations and inequations between variables. We then go on to axiomatize the enlarged collection of descriptions with variables. This allows us to prove a normal form theorem which shows how descriptions involving variables can be eliminated in favor of path equations and inequations. After variables, we tackle the problem of providing more general algebraic models of our description language. In particular, we consider a class of models consisting of an arbitrary collection of domain objects and treat features as partial functions over this domain. It is straightforward to cast the collection of feature structures as an instance of this extended model scheme. We next define satisfaction and other logical notions for these models and see that our description logic is sound over the extended interpretations. Soundness, in turn, allows us to prove, following Smolka (1988, 1989), that the feature structure model is canonical in the sense that logical equivalence, satisfiability and validity are the same notions when defined over the whole class of models as when restricted solely to the feature structure model.

The primary difference between the general algebraic models and the feature structure models of our description language is that the algebraic models have a degree of infiniteness that is not present in the feature structures. Thus our final step in characterizing the logic of feature structures is to consider the class of feature structures with possibly infinite sets of nodes. This is standard in the logical treatments of Johnson (1987) and Smolka (1988), and was originally treated in the feature structure case by Pereira and Shieber (1984), who provided a denotational semantics of PATR-II. Our treatment follows Moshier (1988) and Pollard and Moshier (1990), who make connections to the description language we employ and study the type inheritance situation. Just as in the algebraic case, this extension does not affect our logical notions, such as satisfiability and logical equivalence, because our infinite feature structure models form a particular algebraic model. The purpose of studying countably infinite feature structures is that the collection of them forms a domain in the denotational semantics sense (see Gunter and Scott in press). In fact, the collection of possibly infinite feature structures modulo alphabetic variance form a Scott domain (that is, arbitrary consistent joins and arbitrary meets are well-defined). One nice property of this domain model is that the finite or compact domain elements correspond to the finite feature structures; infinite feature structures can be treated as the limits of their finite approximations. Another nice point about the domain-theoretic model is that it allows solutions to be constructed that correspond to non-terminating computations in the finite case.

Finally, following Pollard and Moshier (1990), we show how to apply the upper powerdomain construction of Smyth (1978) to model disjunction in our logic.

After completing our study of feature structures, we provide three applications to phrase structure grammars, definite clause programs and general constraint resolution systems. Our treatment of phrase structure grammars generalizes context-free grammars to allow feature structures to act as categories. This is the standard treatment of unification grammars in the feature structure literature and dates back to Kay's (1979) Functional Unification Grammar, Kaplan and Bresnan's (1982) Lexical Functional Grammar and the generic PATR-II formalism of Shieber et al. (1983). Because our feature structures can be used to model first-order terms, our treatment of phrase structure grammars also provides a generalization of the logic grammars, which originated with Colmerauer's (1970, 1978) Metamorphosis Grammars. The treatment of logic grammars we provide is most like Pereira and Warren's (1980) Definite Clause Grammars (also see Pereira and Shieber 1987, Gazdar and Mellish 1989, and sources cited therein). We later show that the phrase structure formalism is able to characterize arbitrary recursively enumerable languages, and is thus undecidable. We also consider restrictions put forward by Kaplan and Bresnan (1982), which ensure decidability.

Our second application is to definite clause programs. In this application, we treat feature structures much like the logical terms of a definite clause logic programming language like Prolog (Lloyd 1984, Sterling and Shapiro 1986). In fact, because our feature structures can be used to model logical terms and even Prolog II terms with cycles and inequations, our treatment of definite clause programs reduces to Prolog and Prolog II in the relevant cases. Our treatment does not quite fall into the constraint logic programming paradigm put forward by Jaffar and Lassez (1987) and applied to feature structures by Höhfeld and Smolka (1988). In a constraint logic programming approach, we would take our feature structure description language to provide the constraints. This was the approach adopted by Aït-Kaci and Nasr (1986) in their definite clause programming language LOGIN. Instead of defining definite relations using our attribute-value description language, we treat feature structures as terms themselves. Thus we do not have an analogue of relations at all. Rather, our treatment is much more similar to that of Mukai (1985, 1987, in press, Mukai and Yasukawa 1985), which simply replaces first-order terms with feature structures. The only real difference is that we allow a much more general notion of typed feature structure with inequations and extensionality than was considered by Mukai. We provide the standard analysis of both the operational and denotational semantics of our definite clause programming language (van Emden and Kowalski 1976, Jaffar and Lassez 1987). We show that our system is Turing-complete in the sense that any Turing-computable function can be captured by a definite clause program over the feature structures. The primary benefit of our definite clause system is that it allows inheritance-based reasoning as well as logical reasoning by means of definite clause. It shares this property with LOGIN (Aït-Kaci and Nasr 1986) and also the order-sorted logical programming language developed by Smolka (1988b). The benefit of adding inheritance-based reasoning to a logic programming language is the same as that of augmenting first-order the-orem provers with inheritance (Walther 1985, 1988); expensive inference steps that might otherwise be carried out by structural unification or chains of logical inferences can be replaced by efficient inheritance operations. This partition-ing of information between inheritance and logic has become commonplace in artificial intelligence applications of terminological reasoning, beginning with KRYPTON (Brachman et al. 1983).

Our final application, which is to constraint solving, is one that we believe is unique to feature structure-based approaches and is based on the KBL knowl-edge representation system of Aït-Kaci (1984, 1986) and on the HPSG system of Pollard and Sag (1987). More specifically, our approach is based directly on the denotational semantics of Pollard and Moshier (1990), which formalizes a restricted version of Pollard and Sag's (1987) informal presentation of the mechanisms underlying HPSG. Pollard and Moshier's system is a generaliza-tion of Aït-Kaci's KBL system to possibly cyclic structures, and they clean up Aït-Kaci's semantics to the point where their system can be proven complete. We generalize Pollard and Moshier's treatment by allowing types, extensionality specifications, and inequations. The motivation for constraint-based grammars is the overwhelming trend in theoretical linguistics toward grammar formalisms which eschew rule-based analyses of individual constructions, as in a phrase structure grammar, in favor of interacting collections of general constraints, as in Chomsky's (1981, 1988) Government-Binding theory or in HPSG. In the present context, a system of constraints is realized as a set of descriptions of the admissible objects of each type. These descriptions are culled from our general attribute-value descriptive language. A feature structure is a solution to a con-straint system if all of its substructures satisfy the constraints placed on their types and supertypes. One nice feature of the constraint system we present is that it can be smoothly integrated with the inheritance hierarchy so that con-straints can be placed at the appropriate level of generalization. In some ways, our constraints are similar to the rules in terminological knowledge represen-tation systems such as LOOM (Mac Gregor 1988, 1990) or CLASSIC (Brachman et al. 1991). Rules in these systems correspond to implicational constraints be-tween a concept and a concept description; if an object is determined to match a concept, all of the rules matching the concept are fired in a forward-chaining fashion and their consequences added to the object description. The reason that rules are separated from the other constraints in CLASSIC is that they lead to systems in which classification (subsumption checking) is not only intractable, but undecidable. The type theory we present restricts the well-formed objects of a given type in a very weak way and is easily decidable. Allowing arbitrary descriptions to be attached to types which might involve disjunction, structure sharing, and type restrictions at arbitrary depths in a structure, leads to a sys-tem in which arbitrary recursively enumerable languages can be represented. On the other hand, we are able to show how to effectively generate the collec-tion of solutions to an arbitrary constraint system using a method similar to the SLD-resolution technique employed for enumerating the solutions to a query with respect to a definite clause logic program (van Emden and Kowalski 1976).

Part I

Basics

Chapter 2

Types and Inheritance

From the outside, our feature structures look much like the Ψ-terms of Aït-Kaci (1984, 1986) or the feature structures of Pollard and Sag (1987), Moshier (1988) or Pollard and Moshier (1990). In particular, a feature structure is modeled by a possibly cyclic directed graph with labels on all of the nodes and arcs. Each node is labeled with a symbol representing its type, and the arcs are labeled with symbols representing features. We think of our types as organizing feature structures into natural classes. In this role, our types are doing the same duty as concepts in a terminological knowledge representation system (Brachman and Schmolze 1985, Brachman, Fikes, and Levesque 1983, Mac Gregor 1988) or abstract data types in object-oriented programming languages (Cardelli and Wegner 1985). Thus it is natural to think of the types as being organized in an inheritance hierarchy based on their generality. Feature structure unification is then modified so that two feature structures can only be unified if their types are compatible according to the primitive hierarchy of types.

In this chapter, we discuss how type inheritance hierarchies can be specified and the restrictions that we impose on them that allow us to define an adequate notion of type inference, which is necessary during unification. These restrictions were first noted by Aït-Kaci (1984) in his unification-based reasoning system. The polymorphism allowed in our type system is based on inheritance in which a subtype inherits information from all of its supertypes. The possibility of more than one supertype for a given type allows for multiple inheritance.

Type Inheritance Hierarchies

To begin with, we assume that we are dealing with a finite set Type of types ordered according to their specificity, and we think of a type τ as being more specific than another type σ if τ inherits information from σ. We write $\sigma \sqsubseteq \tau$ for types $\sigma, \tau \in$ Type, if τ inherits from σ and say that σ *subsumes* or is more *general* than τ (or inversely, τ is subsumed by or more *specific* than σ). If $\sigma \sqsubseteq \tau$, then σ is a *supertype* of τ, or inversely, τ is a *subtype* of σ.

The standard procedure for specifying subsumption in inheritance-based approaches to knowledge representation has been to allow the specification of a finite number of so-called ISA arcs which link subtypes to supertypes. The full subsumption relation is then inferred as the transitive and reflexive closure of the relation determined by the ISA links. The result of such an operation is a pre-order in general, but we require much stricter conditions on our inheritance hierarchies. Even so, an inheritance hierarchy is still fully determined by the transitive and reflexive closure of its set of basic ISA links, so that the basic ISA-style presentations of inheritance can be used in implementations.

A standard restriction on inheritance hierarchy specifications is that they do not contain inheritance loops. More specifically, it is not possible to follow a chain of ISA links from a type back to itself. The lack of cycles ensures that the transitive reflexive closure of the ISA relation is a partial order. We require our inheritance hierarchies to be much more well behaved; specifically, they have to admit a well-defined unification operation. We are taking feature structures to be ordinary feature structures in which each node has been typed. The unification of two consistent feature structures must itself be given a type which is determined by the types of its inputs. This restriction is necessary to ensure that unification is well defined and can assign a type to every node in the resulting feature structure. Pereira (1987) pointed out the crucial role in unification-based formalisms of finding a unique most general unifier for every pair of consistent feature structures. We also want to make sure that the type of the resulting feature structure is more specific than the types of the feature structures being unified, so that information is not lost during unification. To satisfy these requirements, the same restriction was derived by those working from an order-sorted algebraic perspective (Meseguer et al. 1987, Walther 1988, Gallier and Isakowitz 1988) and those employing ordered feature structure unification (Aït-Kaci 1984, 1986, Smolka and Aït-Kaci 1989, Pollard and Moshier 1990). The restriction is that the type of the unifying result had to be the most general type more specific than the types of the feature structures being unified. The condition on inheritance hierarchies is that there must be a unique most general type more specific than any two consistent types.

As we said earlier, in the process of unifying feature structures we are forced to find most general subtypes for pairs of types labeling them. But remember that two feature structures are only unifiable if their types are consistent. The definition of feature structure consistency follows from that of type consistency. A set T of types is said to be *consistent* or *bounded* if they share a common subtype or *upper bound* σ such that $\tau \sqsubseteq \sigma$ for every $\tau \in T$. This subtype or upper bound contains all of the information that is represented by the types in the set for which it is an upper bound. What we require of our inheritance hierarchies is that every consistent subset of types has a most general subtype (which is a least upper bound in the subsumption ordering). Least upper bounds are usually referred to as *joins*. Recall that the *join* or *least upper bound* $\bigsqcup S$ of a set of S is defined so that $x \sqsubseteq \bigsqcup S$ for every $x \in S$, and $\bigsqcup S \sqsubseteq y$ for every y such that $x \sqsubseteq y$ for every $x \in S$. We see below that the join of the empty set of types, which is always consistent, yields a most general or *universal* type $\bot$, read "bottom," such that $\bot \sqsubseteq \tau$ for every type τ. We could relax our conditions on inheritance hierarchies so that least upper bounds only need to exist for non-empty bounded sets of types, and so that there need not be a most general or universal type, but it makes a number of arguments more straightforward to assume that there is such a universal type. A least type can always be added to an inheritance specification, and many inheritance network formalisms provide some reserved universal concept "thing" to which every object belongs and from which every other concept inherits information. The existence of consistent joins and a most general type simply amounts to assuming that our inheritance hierarchy is a bounded complete partial order (sometimes referred to as a consistent complete partial order). In general, a partial order is a *bounded complete partial order* (BCPO) just in case for every (possibly empty or infinite) set of elements with an upper bound there is a least upper bound or join. A BCPO always has a least element, which we write $\perp$ and refer to as the *bottom* element. We can define $\perp$ as the join of the empty set $\emptyset$, which is always consistent:

(1) $\quad \perp = \bigsqcup \emptyset$

Thus, $\perp$ must be the least element that is greater than every element in $\emptyset$, and hence the least element in the ordering, because every element is greater than every element in $\emptyset$. Also note that in a BCPO, arbitrary non-empty greatest lower bounds, known as *meets*, exist and can be expressed by:

(2) $\quad \bigsqcap X = \bigsqcup \{y \mid y \leq x \text{ for every } x \in X\}$

We are thus ready to state our assumptions about the inheritance hierarchy formally:

Definition 2.1 (Inheritance Hierarchy)

An inheritance hierarchy *is a finite bounded complete partial order* $\langle \text{Type}, \sqsubseteq \rangle$.

As it turns out, a finite BCPO is nothing more nor less than a finite meet semilattice, but it is more natural to provide a characterization in terms of joins, since joins correspond to unifications, which we take as our primitive operation. It would also be possible to allow infinite inheritance hierarchies, but we choose to restrict our attention to the finite case, as it suffices for the applications that we have in mind.

The simplest kind of partial order that is guaranteed to meet the BCPO condition is a simple tree. In the case of a tree-structured inheritance hierarchy, the only way in which $\sigma \sqcup \tau$ can be defined is if $\sigma \sqsubseteq \tau$ or $\tau \sqsubseteq \sigma$, in which case the result of the join is the more specific of the two concepts. The usual way to depict a partial order is in terms of a *Hasse Diagram*, which depicts the subsumption relation graphically (see Grätzer 1971:13). Contrary to standard practice in artificial intelligence, we follow the lead of domain theory (see Stoy 1977 or Gunter and Scott, in press) and draw our inheritance hierarchies with the most general elements toward the bottom. This is because we treat the subsumption ordering as an informational ordering; if $\sigma \sqsubseteq \tau$, then σ is less than or equal to τ in terms of information content. For instance, Figure 2.1 illustrates a rather artificial inheritance network which we suppose arises from a grammarian for whom the second person has fallen into disfavor. Although

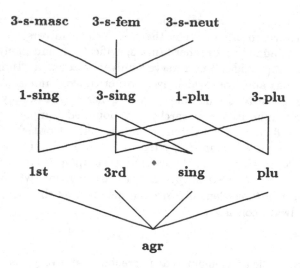

Figure 2.1. Simple Inheritance Network.

1st ⊓ 3rd = 1st ⊓ plu = sing ⊓ plu = agr
3-sing ⊓ 3-plu = 3-s-masc ⊓ 3-plu = 3rd
3rd ⊔ sing = 3-sing
1-plu ⊔ agr = 1-plu ⊔ plu = 1-plu
1-plu ⊓ agr = agr
3-sing ⊔ 1-plu   *is undefined*
3-s-masc ⊔ 3-s-neut   *is undefined*

Figure 2.2. Examples of Joins and Meets.

it is not sophisticated, it contains just enough interesting structure to illustrate the major points about inheritance.

Some examples of joins and meets are as given in Figure 2.2. It can be seen from this figure that not all joins need to exist. But the existence of consistent joins rules out a situation such as the one depicted in Figure 2.3. In this case, σ and σ' are consistent because both τ and τ' are upper bounds for σ and σ'. The problem is that there is no least upper bound; the upper bounds τ and τ' are incomparable. Allowing the kind of inheritance hierarchy depicted in Figure 2.3 would lead to situations in which there was no unique type that could be attached to the result of unifying a type σ feature structure with one of type σ'. Another problem faced by the partial order shown in Figure 2.3 is that there is no join for the empty set, and hence no least or bottom element. Both σ and σ' are minimal upper bounds for $\emptyset$, but there is no unique least upper bound. In general, it would be possible to relax our strict bounded

$$\tau \qquad \tau'$$

$$\sigma \qquad \sigma'$$

Figure 2.3. Partial Order Failing Consistent Joins Condition.

completeness condition on inheritance hierarchies, for instance to SFP domains, 2/3 SFP domains, or even to complete partial orders (see Vickers 1989, Gunter and Scott in press), but this would lead to non-determinism in the unification process. For instance, the example in Figure 2.3, with the addition of a bottom element, is a complete partial order and, if we were to allow it, the unification of σ and σ' would have to be defined non-deterministically to produce both τ and τ' as possible results. Just this kind of non-determinism arises naturally in the context of *universal unification* (Siekmann 1989), where first-order terms are unified with respect to some equational theory. The same kind of non-determinism can also stem from certain notions of set-valued feature structures (Pollard and Moshier 1990).

Returning to our example of an acceptable inheritance hierarchy in Figure 2.1, there are a few points at which the join and meet operations may provide unexpected results. For instance, consider the combinations of joins and meets in:

(3) **3-s-neut = (3-s-masc ⊓ 3-s-fem) ⊔ 3-s-neut**

  ≠ (3-s-masc ⊔ 3-s-neut) ⊓ (3-s-fem ⊔ 3-s-neut)

Thus it should be obvious that meets do not correspond to disjunctions, as can also be seen from the first example in Figure 2.2. The disjunction of the masculine and feminine type and consequent conjunction of the neuter type would lead to an inconsistency. In the case of taking meets and then joins, the result is not only consistent, but the neuter type. In lattice theory terms, this is because our partial orders are *not* required to be distributive (and in fact, are not even required to be modular):

(4)   • $\sigma \sqcup (\tau \sqcap \rho) = (\sigma \sqcup \tau) \sqcap (\sigma \sqcup \rho)$ (Distributivity)

    • $\sigma \sqcap (\tau \sqcup \rho) = (\sigma \sqcap \tau) \sqcup (\sigma \sqcap \rho)$ (Distributivity)

On the other hand, we do think of joins as corresponding to conjunctions, and we include an axiom to this effect in due time. A thorough study of the relation between meets and disjunction in the context of feature structures can be found in Pollard and Moshier (1990). Their treatment is based on Smyth's (1978) domain-theoretic characterization of finitely branching non-determinism, which shows how to construct a distributive domain that allows disjunctions to

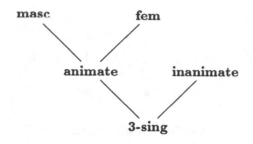

Figure 2.4. Animacy Type Hierarchy.

be represented as meets. In the resulting domain, meets approximate disjunctions in the sense that the meet of two types is more general than their disjunction, and thus possibly loses information, as was the case in (4). A similar study was carried out by Aït-Kaci (1984), but arguably using the wrong construction of a distributive domain (Pollard personal communication). An interesting reason for not requiring distributive lattices has to do with the sparseness of the concept hierarchy with respect to the possible numbers of concepts which can be created by disjunction and conjunction over the basic concepts. Borgida and Etherington (1989) argue that the sparseness of the concept hierarchy and its non-distributive nature and ability to approximate disjunctions with meets is well motivated when considering the relative ease of human conceptual reasoning as opposed to logical reasoning. The concepts that are employed as types in feature structures tend to be natural or useful categorizations of the domain for which information is being encoded. For instance, consider again the inheritance hierarchy in Figure 2.1. It would be possible to add an additional type standing for animate gender to provide a common supertype for the masculine and feminine genders that is not a supertype of the neuter gender. The result is illustrated in Figure 2.4. These kinds of decisions about the structure of the inheritance hierarchy determine the way that information is encoded using the primitive concepts, and in this particular case, the ease with which certain kinds of agreement phenomena could be modeled. For instance, the animate type might be handy for classifying the distinction between the relative pronouns *who* and *which*.

It should be pointed out that our inheritance networks allow a simple kind of reasoning about inconsistency. The fact that there is no type which is consistent with (more specific or informative than) both the types **sing** and **plu** encodes the fact that they are incompatible. Any attempts to unify a feature structure of type **sing** with one of type **plu** simply fails. Some authors (Aït-Kaci 1984, Smolka 1988) choose to append a top element ⊤ to their inheritance hierarchies which represents an inconsistent concept or necessarily empty type. The benefit of this is that consistent complete join semilattices become lattices when a top element is inserted: previously inconsistent types now have ⊤ as their join. The benefit of primitive reasoning about inconsistency in the type hierarchy is that

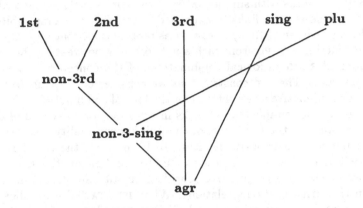

Figure 2.5. Non-Third-Singular Type Hierarchy.

it allows early pruning of useless branches in a search space. To do this, it is necessary to detect inconsistencies in a simple and efficient manner. Just this kind of early inconsistency detection was the motivation for Walther's (1985) and Cohn's (1987) addition of sort checking to first-order logic and Aït-Kaci and Nasr's (1986) addition of sort consistency to their programming language LOGIN, which is based on definite clauses over feature structures. Detecting inconsistencies as early as possible avoids the creation of expensive structural copies or binding frames that have to be restored upon backtracking.

Consider the possibility of adding a single type that stood for non-third-singular agreement to the inheritance hierarchy in Figure 2.1. This type would have to be placed into the hierarchy between the bottom type **agr** and the types for **1st** and **plu**. This is because the only way to be non-third-singular is to be either first person or plural. Of course, this placement is rather ad hoc and rests on the assumption that there is no type for second person. Consider what would have to be done to simultaneously add a type for second person and a type for non-third-singular. The lower part of the resulting type hierarchy is illustrated in Figure 2.5. Of course, the type for non-third-person could be eliminated without jeopardizing the non-third-singular/third-singular distinction. The upper portion of this herarchy, which is omitted in Figure 2.5, is similar to the upper portion of Figure 2.1, with the obvious extension to the second person case.

Constructing Inheritance Hierarchies

In this section we consider a number of techniques which can be used for taking more familiar structures, such as ISA networks, and constructing inheritance hierarchies which meet our bounded completeness condition. In particular, we consider two alternatives for generating inheritance hierarchies from inheritance networks of the variety often found in artificial intelligence applications. We consider both networks with simple ISA links to express inclusion and also networks that include ISNOTA links to express disjointness or incompatibility. We think of the nodes in an IS(NOT)A network as representing concepts. Our methods for constructing a BCPO from such a network rely on treating the elements of the generated BCPO as logical combinations of the concepts in the original IS(NOT)A network. The two constructions we consider correspond to taking a disjunctive or conjunctive interpretation of the logical combinations of concepts. The constructions for simple ISA networks in both the conjunctive and disjunctive case are based on the finite case of the well-known duality between partial orders and bounded distributive lattices. In both cases, the result is a finite distributive lattice. In addition to the conjunctive and disjunctive ISA constructions, we also consider a conjunctive construction with additional information supplied in the form of ISNOTA relations. When ISNOTA links are allowed, the generated BCPO is not guaranteed to be either bounded or distributive. We only discuss networks which are monotonic in the sense that they allow full transitive (and reflexive) reasoning. The final part of this section is devoted to a demonstration that three proposals for handling inheritance information in linguistics can be captured by techniques developed for general IS(NOT)A hierarchies. In particular, we consider King's (1989) method of modeling partial information about grammatical objects in the HPSG grammar formalism by partitioning the empirical domain into disjoint (maximally informative) types. We then turn to Pollard and Sag's (1987) method for generating lexical and grammatical inheritance hierarchies in HPSG. Finally, we show how Pollard and Sag's inheritance hierarchy specifications are simply a notational variant of the systemic networks of Halliday (Kress 1976).

Before seeing how to construct bounded complete partial orders, we first review the treatment of monotonic semantic networks (we drop the adjective *monotonic* from now on). The standard assumption, which we also make, is that there is a finite set Conc of primitive concepts or properties. These concepts should be thought of as categorizing the empirical domain being modeled into natural and useful classes. We then assume that there is a relation ISA specified between the concepts in Conc expressing class inclusion relationships. We use infix notation for ISA and read p ISA q as saying that all ps are qs. The following kinds of reasoning are allowed in networks for arbitrary concepts $p, q, r \in$ Conc:

(5)   • p ISA p (Reflexivity)

        • p ISA r if p ISA q and q ISA r (Transitivity)

It is also usually assumed that there are no cycles in the ISA specification, which can be formally stated as the condition:

(6)   if p ISA q and q ISA p, then $p = q$ (Anti-Symmetry)

This simply amounts to:

Definition 2.2 (ISA Network)
A finite partial order $\langle$Conc, ISA$\rangle$ *is said to be an* ISA *network.*

Brachman (1979) provides a comprehensive survey of the development of inheritance networks and their application to cognitive psychology and artificial intelligence.

Disjunctive Type Construction

We base the first method we consider for developing bounded complete partial orders from ISA networks on the upper powerdomain construction due to Smyth (1978). The upper powerdomain was developed to model the behavior of finitely branching non-deterministic programming languages (Smyth 1978, Gunter and Scott in press). It turns out that since we are considering only finite ISA networks, the upper powerdomain construction is equivalent to (the dual of) Birkhoff's (1933) original construction of bounded distributive lattices from partial orders (see Davey and Priestley 1990). Our types correspond to partial disjunctive (or non-deterministic) information that we can express about objects using our ISA network. We take our collection Type of types to be sets of pairwise incomparable elements of Conc. We thus assume:

Definition 2.3 (Disjunctive Types)

The set Type *of disjunctive types is such that $\sigma \in$ Type if and only if:*

- $\sigma \subseteq$ Conc

- *there are no $p, q \in \sigma$ such that $p \neq q$ and p ISA q*

The intuition here is that the information that an object is of type $\sigma \subseteq$ Conc is taken to mean that it belongs to (at least) one of the basic concepts in σ. Thus the information conveyed by asserting that an object is of the type $\{p_0, p_1, \ldots, p_{n-1}\}$ is that the object is a p_i for some $i < n$. To borrow an example from Gunter and Scott (in press), consider a simple ISA network dealing with fruit and vegetables. A type over this network might be something like {**fruit, red-vegetable, green-vegetable**}. Asserting that a particular object was of this type would mean that it was either a fruit, a red vegetable, or a green vegetable. The reason that we assume that the basic concepts are pairwise ISA-incomparable is that the type {**fruit, yellow-fruit, banana, potato**} would tell us that an object was either a fruit, a yellow fruit, a banana or a potato. The type {**fruit, potato**} would give us exactly the same information about an object. There is simply no point to adding more specific concepts to a set describing disjunctive possibilities. This example should point to the way in which we can define what it means for one type to be more specific than another; a more specific type provides strictly more specific concepts than a more general type. Thus the type {**lemon, banana, red-vegetable**}, which states than an object is either a lemon, a banana or a red vegetable would provide strictly more information than the type {**yellow-fruit, vegetable**}, which would simply tell us that an object was either a yellow fruit or a vegetable. The intuition when dealing with information containment between disjunctions is that a more specific type rules out more possibilities than a more general type. Formally, we take:

Definition 2.4 (Disjunctive Type Subsumption)

For disjunctive types σ and τ, we assume $\sigma \sqsubseteq \tau$ if and only if for every $q \in \tau$ there is some $p \in \sigma$ such that q ISA p.

We define a top and bottom element in the disjunctive type ordering by:

(7)   • $\top = \emptyset$

   • $\bot = Min_{\text{ISA}}(\text{Conc})$
       $= \{p \in \text{Conc} \mid \text{no } q \in \text{Conc is such that } q \neq p \text{ and } p \text{ ISA } q\}$

The top element represents inconsistency because it is interpreted as the empty disjunction. The bottom element is slightly more interesting and consists of the most general classes in Conc. In general, we let $Min_{\leq}(S)$ be the set of $\leq$-minimal elements of S. We have $\bot \sqsubseteq \sigma$ for every $\sigma \in$ Type because every element p of σ must be such that there is some $q \in \bot$ such that p ISA q; every concept is at least as specific as some maximally general concept.

We can define meets for types Type as the maximally general elements of their union. Thus the assertion that an object is of type $\sigma \sqcap \tau$ is equivalent to stating that it is either of the type σ or of the type τ. This holds just in case it belongs to one of the basic concepts in σ or one of the ones in τ and thus one of the basic concepts in their union. As we saw before, we can simply discard the non-maximal elements of the union to arrive at a collection whose elements are pairwise incomparable. We thus set:

(8) $\sigma \sqcap \tau = Min_{\text{ISA}}(\sigma \cup \tau)$
      $= \{p \in \sigma \cup \tau \mid \text{no } q \in \sigma \cup \tau \text{ is such that } p \neq q \text{ and } p \text{ ISA } q\}$

This provides arbitrary meets; the meet of the empty set is given to be the top element $\top$ and non-empty meets can be defined iteratively by:

(9)   • $\bigsqcap \emptyset = \top$

   • $\bigsqcap\{p_1, p_2, \ldots, p_n\} = p_1 \sqcap (\bigsqcap\{p_2, \ldots, p_n\})$

Consequently, we can define joins in terms of meets by setting:

(10) $\sigma \sqcup \tau = \bigsqcap\{\gamma \mid \sigma \sqsubseteq \gamma \text{ and } \tau \sqsubseteq \gamma\}$

The meet of all of the upper bounds of two types is the most general type which is more specific than both of them.

A consequence of the duality that Birkhoff proved between finite partial orders and finite distributive lattices tells us that our construction of Type from the partially ordered set Conc results in a complete distributive lattice (see Davey and Priestley 1990).

Theorem 2.5

If $\langle \text{Conc}, \text{ISA} \rangle$ is a finite pre-order, then the disjunctive types $\langle \text{Type}, \sqsubseteq \rangle$ form a complete distributive lattice.

Proof: Before proving this result, we consider an alternative representation of Type in terms of upper-closed subsets of concepts. We say a subset $X \subseteq \mathsf{Conc}$ is *upper-closed* if $x \in X$, and if $y \in \mathsf{Conc}$ is such that y ISA x, then $y \in X$. Let $Upper(\mathsf{Conc})$ be the collection of upper-closed subsets of Conc. First note that every type $\sigma \in \mathsf{Type}$ generates a unique upper-closed set by:

$$Up(\sigma) = \{t \in \mathsf{Conc} \mid s \in \sigma, \, t \text{ ISA } s\}$$

Furthermore, the function $Up: \mathsf{Type} \rightarrow Upper(\mathsf{Conc})$ is an isomorphism from the ordering $\langle \mathsf{Type}, \sqsubseteq \rangle$ to $\langle Upper(\mathsf{Conc}), \supseteq \rangle$. Simply note that if $\sigma \sqsubseteq \tau$, then:

$$Up(\sigma) = \{t \mid s \in \sigma, \, t \text{ ISA } s\} \supseteq \{t \mid s \in \tau, \, t \text{ ISA } s\} = Up(\tau)$$

What is important about this construction is that if X and Y are upper closed, then so are $X \cup Y$ and $X \cap Y$. Thus the operations of union and intersection correspond to meet and join respectively in $\langle Upper(\mathsf{Conc}), \supseteq \rangle$. Since union and intersection distribute over one another, we know that $\langle Upper(\mathsf{Conc}), \supseteq \rangle$ is distributive, and hence $\langle \mathsf{Type}, \sqsubseteq \rangle$ is distributive. $\square$

Of course, every complete lattice is a bounded complete partial order. If we discard the empty set (as Smyth did), we are left with a bounded complete partial order because bounded joins still exist. A further consequence of Birkhoff's representation theorem is that every finite distributive lattice can be constructed as the collection of types generated by a finite ISA hierarchy. In fact, the result is even stronger in that the correspondence set up between finite distributive lattices and partial orders is one-to-one. This one-to-oneness is expressed by the uniqueness condition in the following theorem.

Theorem 2.6

If $\langle D, \leq \rangle$ is a finite distributive lattice, then there is a unique finite ISA network $\langle \mathsf{Conc}, \mathsf{ISA} \rangle$ such that the derived BCPO $\langle \mathsf{Type}, \sqsubseteq \rangle$ is isomorphic to $\langle D, \leq \rangle$.

Proof: See Davey and Priestley (1990:171) for a full proof. If we have a finite distributive lattice $\langle D, \leq \rangle$, then the partial order $\langle \mathsf{Conc}, \mathsf{ISA} \rangle$ that generates $\langle D, \leq \rangle$ is formed by taking Conc to be the set of meet-irreducible elements of $\langle D, \leq \rangle$, where an element is said to be *meet-irreducible* if it is not the top element of the order or if it cannot be expressed as the meet of two elements neither of which is identical to itself. The ordering ISA is simply the restriction of $\leq$ defined over all of D to $\mathsf{Conc} \subseteq D$. Meet-irreducible elements can be easily identified as the elements which are covered by fewer than two other elements (in our diagrams, this means that they have less than two lines drawn up from them). $\square$

Thus we can construct an arbitrary finite distributive lattice from a finite partial order. The full duality result of Stone (which generalizes Birkhoff's result for the finite case) shows that the category of distributive lattices (of arbitrary cardinality) with top and bottom elements under top and bottom preserving homomorphisms is dual to the category of partial orders under order preserving

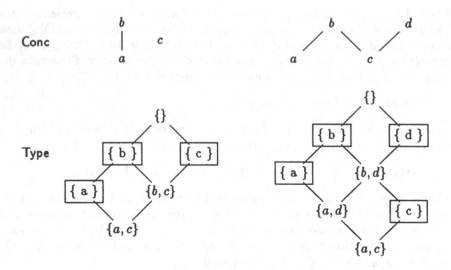

Figure 2.6. Examples of Disjunctive Type Construction.

maps. This establishes not only a connection between the appropriate partial
orders, but also between the appropriate structure preserving maps (see Davey
and Priestley 1990 for proofs). Very simple examples of the construction of a
finite partial order from the meet-irreducible elements of a distributive lattice
are given in Figure 2.6 and Figure 2.7. In these diagrams, we have displayed
both the concept partial ordering and the derived distributive lattice. To illustrate the significance of the meet-irreducible elements, we have enclosed them
in boxes. Notice that the suborders of the type hierarchies consisting of meet
irreducible elements is isomorphic to the concept hierarchy from which the type
hierarchy is defined. The finite portion of Stone's (1936) representation theorem for boolean algebras tells us that arbitrary finite boolean algebras can be
generated using flat partial orders (those in which none of the elements are
comparable) as seen in Figure 2.7 (see Davey and Priestley 1990:164).

Our disjunctive construction shows how to derive a complete distributive
lattice (and hence a BCPO) representing disjunctive information about class
membership from a simple ISA network. A degenerate application of this construction was put forward by King (1989:42) in his formalization of the HPSG
grammar formalism. In particular, King started with a set of so-called *species*
(borrowing terminology from biology) that represent the partitioning of the
objects in the empirical domain into disjoint classes. This would correspond
to an ISA network in which the concepts were the species and the ISA relation
was simple identity, so that p ISA q if and only if $p = q$. Applying the upper
powerdomain construction to this degenerate ISA network results in the types
defined by King, which are simply arbitrary sets of species because every set of
species is pairwise incomparable. Thus a set $\sigma \in$ Type of species was meant to
signal a disjunction of species. Of course, in this case, the resulting complete

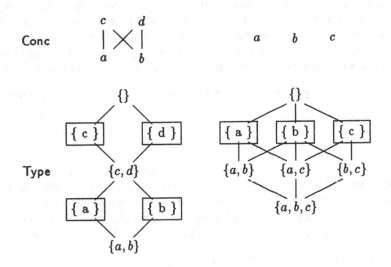

Figure 2.7. Further Examples of Disjunctive Type Construction.

lattice is a boolean algebra, as it is (the dual of) a simple powerset algebra; joins correspond to intersections and meets correspond to unions, with the top and bottom elements being the empty set and complete set of species respectively. This results in a system in which every possible disjunction of species information is represented by a type. Of course, there are 2^n types derived from King's construction if there are n species, which is a worst-case scenario for the upper powerdomain construction.

Conjunctive Type Construction

We now turn our attention to an alternative technique for constructing bounded complete partial orders from ISA networks which also uses sets of concepts to represent types. The difference is that the sets in this case are interpreted conjunctively rather than disjunctively. The method we use is a modified version of the lower powerdomain construction (Gunter and Scott in press), which is sometimes called the Hoare powerdomain (not because Hoare invented it, but because it has applications to the characterization of the partial correctness of programs). As far as the ISA components of our networks go, the lower powerdomain construction is simply the dual of the upper powerdomain construction; it generates the dual of the lattice generated by the upper powerdomain construction. Without the ISNOTA links, we are able to construct arbitrary distributive lattices from partial ISA orderings just as before, because the dual of a distributive lattice is also distributive. We think of the ISNOTA links as then carving out some of the derived concepts as being incoherent. But when the construction is modified to cope with ISNOTA information, the BCPO which is generated might be neither bounded nor distributive.

Before going on to provide the conjunctive BCPO construction, we expand our notion of ISA network to include ISNOTA links. Like ISA, ISNOTA is defined as a binary relation between the concepts in Conc. The usual idea is that p ISNOTA q is to be read as ps are not qs, or as no ps are qs. This leads to the following rules concerning the behavior of ISNOTA on concepts $p, q \in$ Conc:

(11) • p ISNOTA q if and only if q ISNOTA p (Symmetry)

  • not p ISNOTA p (Anti-Reflexivity)

  • if p ISA q and q ISNOTA r, then p ISNOTA r (Chaining)

These rules for ISA and ISNOTA are discussed more fully by Carpenter and Thomason (1989). In an implementation or user specification, the fact that **fruit** ISNOTA **vegetable** could be asserted directly and then **lemon** ISNOTA **tomato** could be inferred (see Carpenter and Thomason 1989). We thus require an IS(NOT)A network to be closed under inheritance.

Definition 2.7 (IS(NOT)A Network)

An IS(NOT)A network *is a finite relational structure* $\langle$Conc, ISA, ISNOTA$\rangle$ *where* ISA *is a partial ordering of* Conc *and* ISNOTA *is a symmetric relation over* Conc *such that if p* ISA q *and q* ISNOTA r, *then p* ISNOTA r.

Our types are again modeled as sets of pairwise ISA-incomparable concepts. This time we are interpreting a set of concepts conjunctively so that the information conveyed about an object by stating that it is of type $\{p_0, \ldots, p_{n-1}\} \in$ Type is that it belongs to each of the concepts p_i for $i < n$. Returning to our fruit example, the type {**fruit, yellow**} could be used to describe objects that were yellow fruits. We restrict our attention again to pairwise ISA-incomparable sets of concepts, as more general concepts add nothing to our information. For instance, the type {**fruit, yellow-fruit**} would state that an object is both a fruit and a yellow fruit, which is the same information as is conveyed by the type {**yellow-fruit**}. This time, less specific concepts can be discarded from types without loss of information. With our conjunctive interpretation of types, we want to exclude the situation in which there are ISNOTA conflicts in a type; it is simply not possible for an object to belong to both of the concepts p and q if p ISNOTA q. For instance, if we had **fruit** ISNOTA **vegetable**, then we would not want a type like {**fruit, vegetable**}, which would state of an object that it was both a fruit and a vegetable. This leads us to the following definition of types:

Definition 2.8 (Conjunctive Types)

The set Type *of conjunctive types is such that $\sigma \in$* Type *if and only if:*

  • $\sigma \subseteq$ Conc

  • *if $p, q \in \sigma$ and $p \neq q$, then not p* ISA q

  • *no $p, q \in \sigma$ are such that p* ISNOTA q

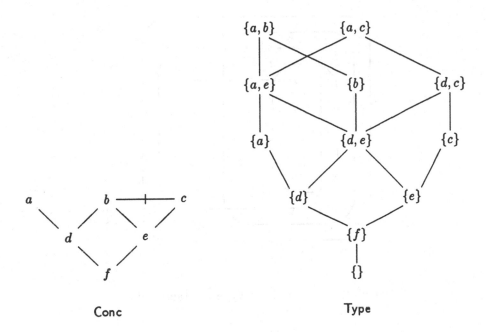

Figure 2.8. Example of Conjunctive Type Construction.

This representation of partial information in terms of pairwise compatible but incomparable sets of concepts is also employed in KL-ONE-like languages such as LOOM (Mac Gregor 1988). We now turn to the natural informational ordering placed on such representations and see that the result is a BCPO. It is this fact that justifies the use of the representations found in LOOM.

With the conjunctive interpretation of types, we can derive a natural informational ordering on our types which is simply the restriction of the lower powerdomain ordering to sets of pairwise compatible concepts:

Definition 2.9 (Conjunctive Type Subsumption)

$\sigma \sqsubseteq \tau$ *if and only if for every* $s \in \sigma$ *there is a* $t \in \tau$ *such that* t ISA s.

An example of the conjunctive type hierarchy construction with ISNOTA links is shown in Figure 2.8. Note that there is no top element due to the fact that the types $\{a, b\}$ and $\{a, c\}$ are inconsistent. Also note that the resulting type hierarchy is not distributive. For a graphic depiction of the classes of objects that can be picked out using the type hierarchy generated in Figure 2.8, see the Euler diagram in Figure 2.9. In this diagram, each concept in Conc is displayed as a region. The conjunctive types correspond to the intersections of various regions. It is important to note that not every region in Figure 2.9 can be picked out by means of a type; only those which correspond to intersections of basic concepts can. This highlights the conjunctive nature of our construction.

By very similar reasoning to that used for the disjunctive or upper powerdo-

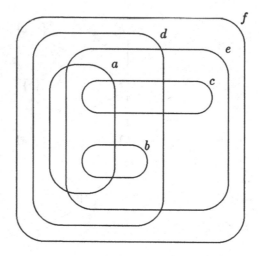

Figure 2.9. Example of Type Containments.

main construction, it can be shown that the lower or conjunctive powerdomain construction produces a bounded complete partial order. In fact, Carl Pollard has pointed out (personal communication) that concrete representations of domains by Scott's (1970) information systems can be used to prove this result immediately (see Davey and Priestley 1990 for an introduction to information systems). For those familiar with information systems, it should be apparent that:

Theorem 2.10 (Information System Representation)

The type hierarchy generated by the IS(NOT)A network $\langle \text{Conc}, \text{ISA}, \text{ISNOTA} \rangle$ is isomorphic to the domain $\langle Con, \subseteq \rangle$ of elements generated by the information system $\langle A, Con, \vdash \rangle$, in which:

- $A = \text{Conc}$

- $X \in Con$ *if and only if* $X \subseteq A$ *and there are no* $p, q \in X$ *such that* p ISNOTA q

- $t \vdash s$ *if and only if* t ISA s

Instead of relying on information systems, we show directly that a conjunctively generated type hierarchy forms a finite bounded complete partial order. In the conjunctive construction, there is not a top element if there are two concepts related by ISNOTA. The bottom element or least informative type corresponds to the empty set; in symbols, $\perp = \emptyset$. This is plausible given our conjunctive reading of sets of concepts; asserting that an object is of the type $\emptyset$ is not asserting anything about the concepts to which it belongs, and thus provides no information. Rather than taking meets as primitive as we did with the disjunctive construction, it is simpler to carry out the dual construction and first define joins by:

$$(12) \quad \sigma \sqcup \tau = \begin{cases} Max_{\text{ISA}}(\sigma \cup \tau) & \text{if no } p \in \sigma, q \in \tau \text{ have } p \text{ ISNOTA } q \\ \text{undefined} & \text{otherwise} \end{cases}$$

Thus taking joins corresponds to taking a union and discarding all the concepts in the result which are not maximally specific. It should be fairly obvious that $\sigma \sqcup \tau$ is the least specific type that is more specific than σ and τ if σ and τ are consistent; consistency in this situation simply amounts to not containing any concepts related by ISNOTA. The empty join is given by $\bigsqcup \emptyset = \perp$. This is enough to show that:

Theorem 2.11

If $\langle$Conc, ISA, ISNOTA$\rangle$ *is an* IS(NOT)A *network, then the conjunctive types* $\langle$Type, $\sqsubseteq$$\rangle$ *form a bounded complete partial order.*

The construction of bounded complete partial orders from IS(NOT)A networks has two immediate applications for linguistic representations: systemic networks (Kress 1976, Winograd 1983) and HPSG inheritance specifications (Pollard and Sag 1987). Both systemic grammars and HPSG place a great deal of emphasis on the hierarchical classification of linguistic objects. We consider these applications together because their mechanisms for specifying inheritance information are notational variants.

Systemic grammar (Kress 1976) has found many applications in linguistic grammar processing. An especially popular combination is that of systemic network classifications and case-based grammar formalisms (Winograd 1983), which produces a representational system strikingly similar to the typed feature structures we present here. More recently, Mellish (1988) and Kasper (1986, 1988, 1989) have investigated the connections between systemic grammar formalisms and unification-based formalisms. Mellish examines the connection of systemic classification to Prolog unification in terms of representational power, and Kasper argues that adding inheritance-based reasoning to feature-structure systems leads to the kind of speed-up that is attained by adding inheritance to a reasoning system based on unordered types. An example of a systemic network, using the notation of Mellish (1988), can be found in Figure 2.10. The systemic network in Figure 2.10 is meant to capture the same hierarchical information as was expressed in our inheritance hierarchy in Figure 2.1. Before we can see that this is indeed the case, we introduce the traditional interpretation of systemic networks. In general, a systemic network is constructed from nodes and connectives. The nodes in the network in Figure 2.10 are the elements occurring in bold face, such as **plu**, **sing**, **masc**, and **first**. The connectives are traditionally written as }, {, and |, but we have avoided the curly brackets in our diagrams. The { and | connectives are labeled with names in the standard Roman font, but these names actually have no significance as far as the information conveyed by the network is concerned. We consider the connectives in turn. The | connective, of which there are three in Figure 2.10 (for

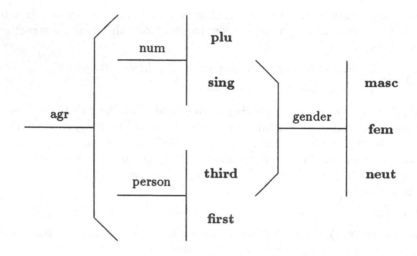

Figure 2.10. Systemic Inheritance Network Notation.

number, person, and gender), is intended to signal choices, and is thus referred to as the *choice* connective. Thus the choices for number are **plu** and **sing** and the choices for gender are **masc**, **fem**, and **neut**. Formally speaking, to fully specify a gender, one of the choices must be made, and similarly for number and person. Furthermore, the choices provided by a choice connective are taken to be pairwise incompatible; it is not possible for a number to be given as both plural and singular or a gender to be given as both neuter and feminine. The { connective, of which there is one for agreement in Figure 2.10, signals a conjunctive choice. To fully specify an agreement it is necessary to specify both a number and a person. Conjunctive choices correspond to orthogonal classifications; the choices for number and person are independent. The final connective we consider, }, of which there is one in the network leading into the gender choice system, is intended to signal necessary preconditions for a choice. In the case of Figure 2.10, the } connective is meant to signal that a choice for gender is made only if the choice made for number was singular and for person was third. In general, every choice system | connective may have a *precondition* (also known as an *entry condition*) associated with it, where a precondition consists of one or more nodes or choices that need to be made for the choice system in question to be applicable. We should point out that we have not chosen to model the fourth systemic network connective], which signals disjunctive preconditions. If we had replaced } with] in our diagram as a precondition for the gender choice, then we would make a choice for gender only if the choice of either singular for number or third for person had been made. Further discussion of systemic networks can be found in Mellish (1988) and Winograd (1983:290–294).

In general, the only restriction placed on systemic networks is that no paths

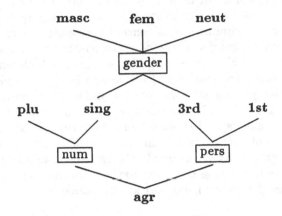

Figure 2.11. HPSG Inheritance Network Notation.

link a node back to itself through a chain of connectives. Thus it is possible
to have } connectives operating across objects of different depths. Similarly,
there are no restrictions against multiple choice systems with the same preconditions. For instance, if we need a choice for case on a third-singular pronoun,
another } connective could be added covering the nodes for third and singular and attaching to the choice system for case. Of course, another possibility
would be to use the combination }{ rather than two uses of }|.

Before formalizing the systemic network formalism, we consider the HPSG
inheritance formalism. Head-driven Phrase Structure Grammar also depends
heavily on a hierarchical organization of linguistic objects. It is this organization that allows universal and language-specific constraints or principles to be
expressed at the proper level of abstraction (Pollard and Sag 1987, Pollard in
press). In particular, there is an emphasis on lexical organization in the HPSG
framework, which is where the greatest use of inheritance-based organization is
made (see Pollard and Sag 1987, Flickinger et al. 1985, Flickinger 1987). An
example of an HPSG inheritance hierarchy, expressed in the notation of Pollard
and Sag (1987), is given in Figure 2.11. The diagram in Figure 2.11 also represents the same hierarchical information as the simple inheritance hierarchy in
Figure 2.1 and the systemic diagram in Figure 2.10. The interpretation of the
diagram in Figure 2.11 is similar to that of the systemic network diagram in
Figure 2.10. The boxed items correspond directly to the choice systems, and
are referred to as *partitions*. The choices for each boxed item are connected by a
line directly above the box. For instance, the choices for gender are masculine,
feminine, or neuter and the choices for person are first or third, just as in the
systemic diagram in Figure 2.10. The lines running from the box containing
gender back down to the nodes representing singular and third are meant to
indicate that a choice for gender is made only if the object is already known
to be third person and have singular number. In the case of Figure 2.11, rep-

resentational power would not be lost by eliminating the node **agr**, as we see when we make our informal presentation precise; we ignore the node **agr** in what follows. Along a similar line, a concept for gender could be introduced below the partition for gender in the diagram without seriously affecting the information content. This choice is similar to the one between using two }| connectives as opposed to using one }{ connective in systemic networks.

To formalize the systemic network notation and HPSG inheritance formalism, we show how to turn either of these notations into an IS(NOT)A network in an information-preserving way. First we present the formal details at a level that abstracts the relevant information from the particular notations employed in the respective diagrams. At the heart of both systems is a finite collection Conc of concepts, just as in the case of the IS(NOT)A networks. The concepts in the diagrams in Figure 2.10 and Figure 2.11 are the same:

(13) Conc = {**plu**, **sing**, **3rd**, **1st**, **masc**, **fem**, **neut**}

In both cases, these primitive concepts or classes are organized into partitions or choice systems. In general, we suppose that there is a finite collection Part = $\{\Pi_0, \ldots, \Pi_{n-1}\}$ of subsets of Conc such that:

(14)   • Conc = $\bigcup_{i<n} \Pi_i$

           • $\Pi_i \cap \Pi_j = \emptyset$ if $i \neq j$

Thus the collection of Π_i truly partition the primitive concepts. The Π_i can be thought of as representing the choice systems in the systemic case where $p \in \Pi_i$ if and only if p is one of the choices for the system Π_i. In the HPSG case, we have $p \in \Pi_i$ if there is a line from p down to Π_i in the network diagram. For the case we have been considering, we have:

(15)   • Π_0 = num = {**plu**, **sing**}

           • Π_1 = pers = {**3rd**, **1st**}

           • Π_2 = gender = {**masc**, **fem**, **neut**}

It only remains to capture the preconditions and we do this by requiring every partition Π_i to specify a set of concepts on which it is dependent. We take the preconditions to be a relation *PreCond* $\subseteq$ Conc × Part. We have *PreCond*(p, Π_i) if the choice p is a necessary precondition for the choice system Π_i. In the HPSG inheritance diagrams, this corresponds to there being a line from the partition Π_i down to the node p. Of course, just as in HPSG or systemic grammar, we require the combination of the partitions and the preconditions to not have any loops. To this end, we first define a relation *Dep* $\subseteq$ Conc × Conc between concepts that captures the notion of *dependence*. We want it to be such that *Dep*(p, q) if and only if to be classified as being a q requires being classified as a p. In the concrete example of the HPSG network in Figure 2.11, we have *Dep*(p, q) just in case it is possible to follow a path from q down to p

through partitions and concepts. We define this relation formally by:

(16)   • $Dep(p, q)$ if some Π_i is such that $PreCond(p, \Pi_i)$ and $q \in \Pi_i$

       • $Dep(p, p)$

       • $Dep(p, r)$ if $Dep(p, q)$ and $Dep(q, r)$ for some $q \in$ Conc

For instance, in the HPSG diagram in Figure 2.11, we have $Dep(\mathbf{fem}, \mathbf{sing})$ because **fem** $\in$ gender and $PreCond(\mathbf{sing}, \text{gender})$, and we have $Dep(\mathbf{1st}, \mathbf{agr})$ for the same reason. The second clause in the definition of Dep tells us that we have $Dep(\mathbf{plu}, \mathbf{plu})$, and the third clause allows transitive reasoning so that we have $Dep(\mathbf{neut}, \mathbf{agr})$ because $Dep(\mathbf{neut}, \mathbf{sing})$ and $Dep(\mathbf{sing}, \mathbf{agr})$. The acyclicity condition then amounts to the requirement that Dep is an anti-symmetric relation:

(17)   if $Dep(p, q)$ and $Dep(q, p)$, then $p = q$ (Anti-Symmetry)

This anti-symmetry condition is equivalent to the requirement that there is no sequence $p_0, \Pi_0, p_1, \Pi_1, \ldots, p_{n-1}, \Pi_{n-1}, p_n$ of concepts and partitions such that $PreCond(p_i, \Pi_i)$ and $p_{i+1} \in \Pi_i$ for $i < n$. This latter statement of acyclicity more closely corresponds to the requirement that we cannot trace a non-empty path from a node back to itself. Thus we model a systemic network or HPSG inheritance hierarchy by a partition system, which is defined as follows:

Definition 2.12 (Partition System)

$\langle$Conc, Part, $Dep\rangle$ *is a* partition system *if* Conc *is a finite set of concept choices,* Part *is a partition of* Conc *and* $PreCond \subseteq$ Conc $\times$ Part *is a precondition relation such that* Dep *is anti-symmetric.*

We can define an IS(NOT)A network from our partition system by taking the same set of concepts and taking Dep as our ISA relation; we set p ISA q if and only if $Dep(p, q)$. We know that it is a partial ordering because we have assured that it is transitive and reflexive with the second and third clauses of (16) and anti-symmetry follows from (17). We next define ISNOTA in the natural way according to the partitions by assuming that:

(18)   • p ISNOTA q if there is a partition $\Pi \in$ Part such that $p, q \in \Pi$

       • p ISNOTA q if some $r \in$ Conc is such that p ISA r and r ISNOTA q

By definition we are guaranteed that the ISNOTA is symmetric and also respects the ISA hierarchy. For instance, the first condition gives us **plu** ISNOTA **sing** while the second provides **fem** ISNOTA **1st**.

Finally, we use the consistent conjunctive (modified lower powerdomain) construction to generate a BCPO from $\langle$Conc, ISA, ISNOTA$\rangle$. The elements of **Type** generated in this way from the systemic and HPSG networks in Figure 2.10 and Figure 2.11 are:

(19) **Type** $= \{\{\}, \{\mathbf{masc}\}, \{\mathbf{fem}\}, \{\mathbf{neut}\}, \{\mathbf{plu}\}, \{\mathbf{sing}\}, \{\mathbf{3rd}\}, \{\mathbf{1st}\},$
          $\{\mathbf{1st}, \mathbf{plu}\}, \{\mathbf{1st}, \mathbf{sing}\}, \{\mathbf{3rd}, \mathbf{plu}\}, \{\mathbf{3rd}, \mathbf{sing}\} \}$

The way in which these types are ordered in the conjunctive construction results in a structure that is isomorphic (by the obvious mapping) to the inheritance hierarchy given explicitly in Figure 2.1.

In addition to using our general method for constructing bounded complete partial orders in terms of IS(NOT)A networks, we can informally explain how to construct BCPOs from HPSG or systemic networks directly. In terms of the systemic networks, elements of the BCPO correspond to sets of choices where each set of choices must include all dependent choices and must not include two distinct choices from the same choice system. In terms of the HPSG diagrams, elements of the derived BCPO consist of downward closed sets of concepts which do not contain any two distinct elements from any partition. In either of these cases, the subsumption ordering simply corresponds to the subset relation among the sets; more information corresponds to having fixed more choices. Consistent joins correspond to unions and non-empty meets are given by intersections. Inconsistency is signaled by the presence of two distinct elements from the same partition or choice system. The bottom element is the empty set, and there is not a top element if there is at least one two-element partition. It should be obvious that the result of this construction is isomorphic to the construction given more formally in terms of the modified lower powerdomain construction over the IS(NOT)A networks.

A final alternative that is worth considering is a construction due to Ahlèn (1989) and employed in her HPSG parser. Ahlèn's idea is to use an HPSG inheritance hierarchy of the variety found in Figure 2.11 to generate a type hierarchy using the conjunctive type construction. She then takes the maximal types that are generated by this process and applies King's strategy of constructing all of the possible disjunctive types that can be formed from these. Since all of the maximal types are pairwise incomparable, it follows from Stone's (1936) representation theorem that the result of applying the disjunctive construction is a boolean algebra. This method provides a very extensive set of disjunctive types, but is very large in general. It also suffers from the problem that if there are unary branches in the original hierarchy, they are lost in the resulting hierarchy. For instance, in the extremely simple HPSG hierarchy illustrated in Figure 2.11, the resulting BCPO contains 64 elements, one for each subset of the maximal types given in Figure 2.1. The increase in number of types is quite dramatic when new elements of partitions are added. For instance, if a second-person element were added to the person partition, as in Figure 2.5, the resulting structure would have 256 types. Ahlèn's implementation strategy has been to represent the resulting structures in terms of bit vectors. A bit is provided for each maximal type with a 1 signaling that it is a possibility and a 0 signaling that it is not. This is the natural and efficient representation for powerset algebras, as joins correspond to the bitwise logical *and* operation, and meets correspond to the bitwise logical *or* operation. An issue remains as to how fine grained the inheritance hierarchy should be in representing disjunctive possibilities, as the logic we introduce is geared toward providing a general notion of disjunction following Kasper and Rounds (1986).

Chapter 3

Feature Structures

With our definition of inheritance, we have a notion of consistency and unification for our smallest conceptual unit, the type. We now turn to the task of developing structured representations that can be built out of the basic concepts, which we call *feature structures*. The reason for the qualifier is that even though feature structures are defined using our type symbols, they are not typed, in the sense that there is no restriction on the co-occurrence of features or restrictions on their values. We introduce methods for specifying appropriateness conditions on features and a notion of well-typing only after studying the ordered notion of feature structures. We also hold off on introducing inequations and extensionality conditions. Before introducing these other topics, we concentrate on fully developing the notion of untyped feature structure and the logical notions we employ. Most of the results that hold for feature structures can be immediately generalized to well-typed feature structures by application of the type inference mechanism.

Our feature structures are structurally similar to the more traditional form of feature structures such as those used in the PATR-II system and those defined by Rounds and Kasper. The next major development after these initial systems was introduced by Moshier (1988). The innovation of Moshier's system was to allow atomic symbols to label arbitrary nodes in a feature structure. He also treated the identity conditions for these atoms fully intensionally. Both PATR-II and the Rounds and Kasper systems treated feature structures intensionally, but enforced extensional identity conditions on atoms. The interpretation that we give these structures extends the unordered treatment of Moshier to the ordered case introduced by Pollard and Moshier (1990) and axiomatized by Pollard (in press).

An independent line of development was pursued by Aït-Kaci, beginning with his dissertation (1984). He introduced a notion of Ψ-terms, which were taken to represent partial information about features and structured values. He employed a feature-structure-like representation in which identity conditions were given intensionally, and primitive conceptual class information, like the types in our type hierarchy, could be placed on arbitrary nodes. Furthermore, he allowed a partial order to be placed on these conceptual classes that resulted in a system remarkably similar to that developed by Pollard and Moshier, especially when considering the abstract feature structures introduced by Moshier (1988). The main differences between the approach of Aït-Kaci and that of Pollard and Moshier shows up in the extension of the finite structures to distributive domains. Smolka and Aït-Kaci (1989) discuss the relation of Aït-Kaci's Ψ-terms to terms in order-sorted algebras.

It should also be noted that our feature structures are quite similar to the frame-based representations found in artificial intelligence knowledge representation systems. This similarity is even more striking when considering the current trend of terminological knowledge representation systems exemplified by KL-ONE and its descendants. The primary distinction between the structures employed in these systems and our feature structures is that frame-based representations, in general, allow features to have more than one value, thus leading to a relational rather than functional interpretation of attributes or features. Often in these relational systems, restrictions can be placed on the cardinality of the set of values for a feature. One of the main reasons we are keen to keep a simple notion of functional role filler is that the existence of multiple role fillers was the key to the undecidability of KL-ONE subsumption, as was shown by Schmidt-Schauß (1989). With functional roles, subsumption is as easy to decide as unification, which is linear in theory, and near-linear in practical applications (Jaffar 1984). Rounds (1988) and then Pollard and Moshier (1990) introduced notions of *set-valued* feature structures in which a feature can be associated with a set of values. Rounds employed well known powerdomain constructions to model sets, while Pollard and Moshier introduce a new powerdomain construction in which only upper bounds can be placed on the number of values that are present. Linguistic motivation for this move is provided by Pollard and Moshier, who claim that it is necessary for a proper treatment of unbounded dependencies, in which the collection of gaps associated with a constituent is most naturally modeled as a set, and in anaphora resolution, in which the set of discourse referents can also be modeled by sets. In both of these cases, elements of the sets may become identified, but new elements can only be added explicitly. These representations are employed in recent treatments of HPSG (Pollard and Sag in press). The Pollard and Moshier set-valued system is decidable, but its non-determinism leads to an exponential number of results in the worst case.

Our feature structures are like ordinary feature structures in the sense that they can be represented by directed finite labeled attribute-value graphs. In the HPSG system (Pollard and Sag 1987, Pollard and Moshier 1990, Pollard in press), the way in which feature structures are used to model partial information about empirical objects is made specific by the so-called *modeling convention*. According to this convention, the nodes of a feature structure are taken to represent objects, and we assume that every node is labeled with a type symbol which represents the most specific conceptual class to which the object is known to belong. Furthermore, arcs come labeled with feature symbols, and an arc between two nodes indicates that the object represented by the source node has a feature, represented by a feature symbol, which has a value represented by the target node. Structure sharing is taken to model identity. That is, two arcs pointing to the same node indicate that the objects represented by the sources of the arcs have identical values for the features represented by the arcs.

What is interesting about feature structures as object representations is that, in general, they provide only partial information about types and features. Thus it is possible to model what is known about an object at some intermediate computation stage with very general types and features until more specific information becomes available. It is also possible to represent the fact that two nodes model identical objects before the exact identity of these objects is determined. For instance, we know in an arbitrary sentence that the person feature of the head verb and the subject must be identical before we know what the exact value is. We should point out that this notion of feature structures as representing partial information is very different from the notion of feature structure developed by Johnson (1988), Smolka (1988) and King (1989). They interpret feature structures as total objects and introduce a logical language in which to express partial information about these total objects.

One thing to keep in mind about our feature structures is that they allow for the possibility of cycles. A cycle arises when following a non-empty sequence of features out of a node leads back to that node. Moshier (1988) was the first to consider cyclic feature structures from a unification point of view, but it should be noted that the attribute-value logics of Johnson (1987, 1988) and Smolka (1988) allowed cycles. Cyclic representations of these kinds seem crucial for the finite modeling of common knowledge (Barwise 1985) and for dealing with self-referential anaphora of the variety found in the liar sentence *this sentence is false*, which denies its own truth (Barwise and Etchemendy 1987). To take a more mundane example, we could model a self-employed person by using a node with a feature that represents the employer and points back to itself. Pollard and Moshier (1990) and Moss (1990) show how non-well-founded sets (Aczel 1988) can be partially represented by cyclic set-valued feature structures. In terms of implementation, it turns out to be more expensive to eliminate cycles than to allow them. The reason for this is that cycles crop up naturally during the unification process and it is expensive to perform the so-called *occurs check* to filter them out. Thus efficient unification algorithms such as that described by Jaffar (1984) allow for cycles. For the same reason, Prolog II (Colmerauer 1984, 1987) has incorporated cyclic terms which can arise from the unification of acyclic terms, as is the case with $f(X,Y) = f(g(X),b)$ or $f(X,X) = f(g(Y),Y)$.

In the unification-based systems PATR-II, FUG, and LFG and in Rounds and Kasper's treatment of feature structures, instead of allowing types to label arbitrary nodes, a set of atoms was taken to label only *terminal* nodes, which are those nodes without any features defined. Even more significant was the fact that these atoms were *uncopyable* in that only one node in a feature structure could be labeled by any given atom. If more than one feature had to have the value **first** or **john**, then these features had to point to the same node. We call this behavior *extensional* because the fact that two nodes have the same atomic type forces them to be identified. The only incompleteness in the equational characterization of feature structures presented by Kasper and Rounds

(1986, 1990) was that they failed to equate any two paths that led to the same atom. Pereira and Shieber (1984) included an axiom to this effect in their logical characterization of PATR-II as an information system. Rather than adding this additional axiom (which we exactly characterize when we come to treat extensionality), Moshier relaxed the restrictions on copyability and labeling. In particular, he allowed atoms to label arbitrary nodes in feature structures rather than just terminal ones. Second, and more significantly, Moshier treated nodes intensionally by allowing copies of the same atom to show up on two distinct nodes in a feature structure. Thus true identity could only be determined by structure sharing and not by any equivalence in terms of information content. Smolka (1988), in developing his models for attribute-value logics, allowed the possibility of specifying whether or not a given atom was copyable. What Smolka did for atoms is just a special case of the intensionality specifications we introduce later. For the time being, we follow the lead of Moshier and allow arbitrary types to be copied.

Feature Structures

In what follows, we assume that a finite set **Feat** of features and an inheritance hierarchy $\langle \text{Type}, \sqsubseteq \rangle$ have been specified.

Definition 3.1 (Feature Structure)

A feature structure over **Type** *and* **Feat** *is a tuple* $F = \langle Q, \bar{q}, \theta, \delta \rangle$ *where:*

- Q : *a finite set of* nodes *rooted at* $\bar{q}$ *(see below)*

- $\bar{q} \in Q$: *the* root *node*

- $\theta\colon Q \to$ **Type** : *a total node* typing *function*

- $\delta\colon$ **Feat** $\times Q \to Q$: *a partial* feature value *function*

Let $\mathcal{F}$ *denote the collection of feature structures.*

The usual way to conceptualize a feature structure is as a labeled rooted directed graph where Q is the set of nodes, θ determines the labels on the nodes and where there is an arc from q to q' labeled by f, which we write as $q \xrightarrow{f} q'$ if $\delta(f, q) = q'$. In general, we write:

(1) $q : \sigma \xrightarrow{f} q' : \sigma'$

if there is an arc labeled with f from q to q', and the type assigned to q is σ and to q' is σ', or more formally, when $\delta(f, q) = q'$, $\theta(q) = \sigma$ and $\theta(q') = \sigma'$. Smolka (1989) presents a formal definition of feature structures in which these arcs are taken as primitive. The analogy between our feature structures and frame-based representations comes from associating frames with each node, where the features on arcs represent slot labels, and the arcs themselves point to their fillers. The fact that we model our arcs using a partial function δ naturally enforces the unique-value restriction on features.

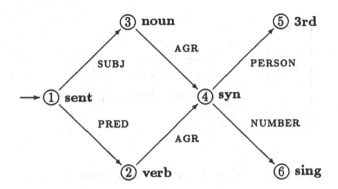

Figure 3.1. Feature Structure: Graph Notation.

In general, we are interested in traversing more than one feature at a time, so we allow the transition function to be composed. A *path* is a sequence of features and we let Path = Feat* be the collection of paths. We let ϵ be the *empty path* containing no features. We then extend δ to paths so that $\delta(\pi, q)$ is the node that is reached by following the features in the path π from q. Of course, $\delta(\pi, q)$ is not defined for every π in every feature structure so that δ is still only a partial function. More formally, we set:

(2)   • $\delta(\epsilon, q) = q$

        • $\delta(f\pi, q) = \delta(\pi, \delta(f, q))$

Graphically, if $\pi = f_1 \cdots f_n$, then $\delta(\pi, q_0) = q_n$ if $q_0 \xrightarrow{f_1} q_1 \xrightarrow{f_2} q_2 \cdots \xrightarrow{f_n} q_n$. The set $\{\delta(\pi, q) \mid \pi \in \mathsf{Path}\}$ is the collection of nodes *reachable* from q by some path. A feature structure is said to be *rooted* at $\bar{q}$ if every node is reachable from the root node $\bar{q}$. More precisely, we require:

(3) $Q = \{\delta(\pi, \bar{q}) \mid \pi \in \mathsf{Path}\}$

We now see how feature structures can be depicted graphically. The diagrams in Figure 3.1 and Figure 3.2 depict the same feature structure. The diagram in Figure 3.1 is the standard graphical notation for feature structures where its automata-like and graph-like character are most apparent. The nodes are enclosed in circles with the arrow pointing at the root, while types appear in bold face next to their nodes and the features in small caps label the arcs. Unfortunately, it becomes very difficult both to set typeset and understand feature structures in this notation when they become complicated. Thus a more standard notation is the frame-like *attribute-value matrix* (AVM) notation used in Figure 3.2. In this notation, each bracketed entry represents a node and the type of the node is written at the top left of the frame. Re-entrancy (structure sharing) is indicated by *tags* such as ④. The slots are the features and their values are written next to them. We conserve space when using this notation and do not duplicate the information if it is shared. Thus the value of the path

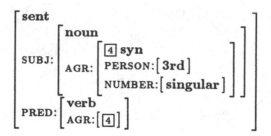

Figure 3.2. Feature Structure: AVM Notation.

SUBJ AGR is the same as the path PRED AGR and its structure is only displayed once; in the second occurrence only the tag is explicitly displayed. Similarly, we only use tags when there is explicit structure sharing, though we could just as easily have tagged each AVM, which would bring out the correspondence with the graph diagrams by making the nodes explicit. Aït-Kaci modeled the attribute value matrices and their tagging and showed how a Ψ-term corresponds to such a matrix. The main thing to keep in mind is that the actual set from which the nodes are drawn is not important nor is the identity of the tags. We are only interested in feature structures up to the renaming of their nodes (or equivalently, their tags). The important information is which features lead to which types and which paths lead to identical structures. Both Aït-Kaci (1984) and Moshier (1988) explicitly considered equivalence classes of structures under such renamings.

As we mentioned earlier, we have not ruled out cyclic structures. A cyclic feature structure is one for which a non-empty path leads from a node back to that node.

Definition 3.2 (Cyclicity)

A feature structure $F = \langle Q, \bar{q}, \theta, \delta \rangle$ is said to be cyclic *if there is a node $q \in Q$ and a non-empty path π such that $\delta(\pi, q) = q$.*

An instance of such a structure is given in (5), which we think of as representing the liar sentence:

(4)   This sentence is false.

(5) $\begin{bmatrix} \boxed{1}\,\textbf{false} \\ \text{ARG:}\big[\boxed{1}\big] \end{bmatrix}$

It is interesting to note that this feature structure supplies a value for an infinite number of paths, namely those in the sequence $\epsilon, \text{ARG}, \text{ARG ARG}, \ldots$.

It should be evident at this point that feature structures can be thought of as assigning feature structures as the values of paths. To make this more precise, we let $F \mathbin{\text{\small@}} \pi$ be the value of the feature structure F at some path π for which it is defined, where the root of $F \mathbin{\text{\small@}} \pi$ is given by the node that is reached by following π from the root of F, the nodes are those that are reachable from the new root, and the transition and type functions are the appropriate restrictions to the new set of nodes.

Definition 3.3 (Path Value)

If $F = \langle Q, \bar{q}, \theta, \delta \rangle$ and $\delta(\pi, \bar{q})$ is defined, then:

$$F @ \pi = \langle Q', \bar{q}', \delta', \theta' \rangle$$

where:

- $\bar{q}' = \delta(\pi, \bar{q})$

- $Q' = \{\delta(\pi', \bar{q}') \mid \pi' \in \mathsf{Path}\} = \{\delta(\pi\pi', \bar{q}) \mid \pi' \in \mathsf{Path}\}$

- $\delta'(f, q) = \delta(f, q)$ *if $q \in Q'$*

- $\theta'(q) = \theta(q)$ *if $q \in Q'$*

It should be obvious that if F is a feature structure, then $F @ \pi$ is also a feature structure for any path π for which F is defined. We can thus think of every feature or path as determining a partial function from feature structures to feature structures. This approach was adopted by Johnson (1987), Smolka (1988) and King (1989). This highlights the intensional nature of our representations; substructures of a feature structure which supply the same value for all of their features are not necessarily identified. We can define the set of *substructures* of a feature structure $F = \langle Q, \bar{q}, \theta, \delta \rangle$ as the set:

(6) $Sub(F) = \{F @ \pi \mid \delta(\pi, \bar{q}) \text{ is defined}\}$

There is exactly one substructure for each node in the feature structure. Thus even for cyclic feature structures such as (5) for which there are an infinite number of paths defined, there are only a finite number of substructures, just as for the infinite rational trees of Prolog II (Colmerauer 1984). It should be pointed out, though, that unlike the case of Prolog II, we have true cyclicity in that a feature structure is not wholly determined by the type that occurs at the end of each path, as in the representation of cyclic terms as their infinite tree unfoldings that was given by Colmerauer (1984). In fact, the feature structure in (8) represents the proposition asserting the falsehood of the liar sentence:

(7)   It is false that [[this sentence]$_i$ is false]$_i$

The subscripts indicate that the anaphoric *this sentence* is taken to refer to the embedded sentence (see Barwise and Etchemendy 1987 for a number of related examples). The sentence in (7) can be represented as:

(8) $\begin{bmatrix} \mathbf{false} \\ \text{ARG:} \begin{bmatrix} \boxed{1}\,\mathbf{false} \\ \text{ARG:} [\,\boxed{1}\,] \end{bmatrix} \end{bmatrix}$

The corresponding representations in Prolog II, namely the results for X and Y in (9), have the same unfoldings into infinite trees and thus can be taken to be identical:

(9) $X = false(X), \quad Y = false(X)$

The solutions for X and Y above would also be identical to the solution for Z in $Z = false(false(Z))$.

We later see that we can recover the Prolog II behavior where it is desirable by asserting that certain types are extensional. For instance, in the case of (8) and (5), there are two nodes, namely, the root node $\bar{q}$ and the argument given by $\delta(\text{ARG}, \bar{q})$, which have token identical values (due to structure sharing) for all of their features (which is only ARG in this case) but are not identified.

Subsumption

The primary goal in constructing our feature structures is to allow for the representation of partial information. We do not think of a feature structure as representing all that can be known about a domain object, but rather what is known at some particular stage in a computation. When dealing with partial information it is important to be able to tell when one piece of partial information is more informative or specific than another. In this section, we extend the subsumption ordering on types to provide a subsumption ordering of the feature structures. Due to the fact that two feature structures can differ in the identity of their nodes, while not differing in their information content, we see that distinct feature structures can represent exactly the same information. There is an analogous situation in the term representations used in logic programming, in which the terms $f(X, g(Y), X)$ and $f(W, g(Z), W)$ represent the same information, but differ in the variables that they use to express it. We are not interested in the difference between feature structures that represent identical information. Thus we formalize a notion of alphabetic variance that is similar to the notion of alphabetic variance used in logic programming semantics. This allows us to abstract away from differences that arise from programs that only vary in the names assigned to their variables. It also allows us to abstract away from notational details in a feature structure and recover the underlying information content in a representation-neutral fashion.

We base our notion of subsumption on the definitions of Rounds and Kasper (1986), Moshier (1988), and its extension to the ordered case by Pollard and Moshier (1990). The intuitive idea is that a feature structure F subsumes another feature structure F' if and only if every two paths which are shared in F are also shared in F', and every type assigned by F to a path subsumes the type assigned to the same path in F' in the type ordering. The formal definition of subsumption is based on a modification of the standard definition of morphisms between automata (see Holcombe 1982). A morphism for us is a mapping from the node set of one feature structure to the node set of another that preserves the transitions and sorts in the appropriate way. Our morphisms differ from the usual notion of automata morphism in that they have

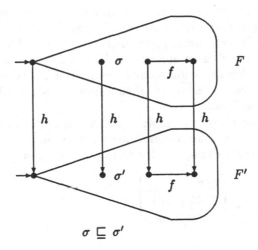

$$\sigma \sqsubseteq \sigma'$$

Figure 3.3. Generic Morphism Diagram.

to account for type information, but also are different in that they do not allow the renaming of features. Formally, it is a morphism because the collection of feature structures forms a category with the arrows as morphisms, as should be obvious from our Lemma 3.5 below, though category-theoretic characterizations of unification are beyond the scope of the present study (but see Goguen 1988).

We now present our formal definition of subsumption. Throughout this section, we suppose that we are dealing with feature structures defined over a fixed inheritance hierarchy $\langle \text{Type}, \sqsubseteq \rangle$ and finite set **Feat** of features.

Definition 3.4 (Subsumption)
$F = \langle Q, \bar{q}, \theta, \delta \rangle$ *subsumes* $F' = \langle Q', \bar{q}', \theta', \delta' \rangle$, $F \sqsubseteq F'$, *if and only if there is a total function* $h: Q \to Q'$, *called a* morphism *such that:*

- $h(\bar{q}) = \bar{q}'$

- $\theta(q) \sqsubseteq \theta'(h(q))$ *for every* $q \in Q$

- $h(\delta(f, q)) = \delta'(f, h(q))$ *for every* $q \in Q$ *and feature* f *such that* $\delta(f, q)$ *is defined*

In terms of arcs, the last condition can be restated as requiring that:

(10) if $q \xrightarrow{f} q'$, then $h(q) \xrightarrow{f} h(q')$

A diagram for an arbitrary morphism is given in Figure 3.3. The intended interpretation of this diagram is that if the situation pictured holds in the upper diagram of F, then it should hold in the lower diagram of F'.

Thus we see that one feature structure subsumes another just in case the nodes of the first can be mapped onto the nodes of the second so that the initial node is preserved, every node is mapped onto a node whose type is at least as specific, and all transitions are preserved. In particular, this last condition implies that if there is structure sharing in the more general feature structure, then the same structure sharing appears in the more specific feature structure (and possibly more). We show this formally as part of Theorem 3.9 below. An alternative algebraic characterization of subsumption is provided later in the chapter on feature algebras.

It turns out that deciding subsumption is quite efficient. In fact, determining whether or not $F \sqsubseteq F'$ can be accomplished in time linear in the size of F.

We now provide some examples illustrating the subsumption relation:

$$(11) \quad \begin{bmatrix} \textbf{agr} \\ \text{PERS}: \begin{bmatrix} \textbf{1st} \end{bmatrix} \end{bmatrix} \sqsubseteq \begin{bmatrix} \textbf{agr} \\ \text{PERS}: \begin{bmatrix} \textbf{1st} \end{bmatrix} \\ \text{NUM}: \begin{bmatrix} \textbf{sing} \end{bmatrix} \end{bmatrix}$$

$$(12) \quad \begin{bmatrix} \textbf{sign} \\ \text{AGR}: \begin{bmatrix} \textbf{agr} \\ \text{PERS}: \begin{bmatrix} \textbf{1st} \end{bmatrix} \end{bmatrix} \end{bmatrix} \sqsubseteq \begin{bmatrix} \textbf{phrase} \\ \text{AGR}: \begin{bmatrix} \textbf{agr} \\ \text{PERS}: \begin{bmatrix} \textbf{1st} \end{bmatrix} \\ \text{NUM}: \begin{bmatrix} \textbf{sing} \end{bmatrix} \end{bmatrix} \end{bmatrix}$$

iff **sign** $\sqsubseteq$ **phrase**

$$(13) \quad \begin{bmatrix} \textbf{sign} \\ \text{SUBJ}: \begin{bmatrix} \textbf{agr} \\ \text{PERS}: \begin{bmatrix} \textbf{1st} \end{bmatrix} \end{bmatrix} \\ \text{PRED}: \begin{bmatrix} \textbf{agr} \\ \text{PERS}: \begin{bmatrix} \textbf{1st} \end{bmatrix} \end{bmatrix} \end{bmatrix} \sqsubseteq \begin{bmatrix} \textbf{sign} \\ \text{SUBJ}: \begin{bmatrix} \boxed{1}\,\textbf{agr} \\ \text{PERS}:\textbf{1st} \end{bmatrix} \\ \text{PRED}: \begin{bmatrix} \boxed{1} \end{bmatrix} \end{bmatrix}$$

$$(14) \quad \begin{bmatrix} \textbf{prop} \\ \text{ARG}1: \begin{bmatrix} \textbf{prop} \\ \text{ARG}1: \begin{bmatrix} \textbf{prop} \end{bmatrix} \end{bmatrix} \end{bmatrix} \sqsubseteq \begin{bmatrix} \boxed{1}\,\textbf{prop} \\ \text{ARG}1: \begin{bmatrix} \boxed{1} \end{bmatrix} \end{bmatrix}$$

$$(15) \quad \begin{bmatrix} \textbf{false} \\ \text{ARG}: \begin{bmatrix} \boxed{1}\,\textbf{false} \\ \text{ARG}: \begin{bmatrix} \boxed{1} \end{bmatrix} \end{bmatrix} \end{bmatrix} \sqsubseteq \begin{bmatrix} \boxed{1}\,\textbf{false} \\ \text{ARG}: \begin{bmatrix} \boxed{1} \end{bmatrix} \end{bmatrix}$$

All of these subsumptions are proper in the sense that the inverse subsumptions do not hold. It is important to note that subsumption is not a substructure relationship, so that, for instance, we have:

$$(16) \quad \begin{bmatrix} \textbf{agr} \\ \text{PERS}: \begin{bmatrix} \textbf{1st} \end{bmatrix} \end{bmatrix} \not\sqsubseteq \begin{bmatrix} \textbf{sign} \\ \text{AGR}: \begin{bmatrix} \textbf{agr} \\ \text{PERS}: \begin{bmatrix} \textbf{1st} \end{bmatrix} \end{bmatrix} \end{bmatrix}$$

The subsumption relation over feature structures, as we have defined it, is transitive and reflexive, but not anti-symmetric, because it is possible to have two distinct feature structures that mutually subsume each other. We state this as:

Lemma 3.5 (Feature Structure Pre-ordering)

The subsumption relation $\sqsubseteq$ is a pre-ordering on the collection $\mathcal{F}$ of feature structures.

Proof: Reflexivity follows from the fact that the identity map is a morphism. Transitivity can be verified by checking that the composition of two morphisms is again a morphism.   □

When two feature structures mutually subsume one another, we say that they are *alphabetic variants*. We state this formally as:

Definition 3.6 (Alphabetic Variants)

If F and F' are feature structures such that $F \sqsubseteq F'$ and $F' \sqsubseteq F$, then we write $F \sim F'$ and say that they are alphabetic variants.

The reason that we call this an alphabetic variant relation is that two feature structures can only be alphabetic variants if there is a one-to-one mapping of the nodes in one onto the nodes of the other that preserves all of structure present. That is, every alphabetic variant of a feature structure arises from replacing the nodes in the original feature structure under an arbitrary one-to-one mapping. It should be obvious that alphabetic variance determines an equivalence relation. The fact follows directly from Lemma 3.5.

Lemma 3.7

The alphabetic variance relation $\sim$ over the collection of feature structures is an equivalence relation.

We are not concerned with the differences between feature structures which are alphabetic variants. Of course, we cannot replace arbitrary substructures of a feature structure with alphabetic variants because structure sharing is determined by the actual identity of the nodes in a substructure. Thus we can proceed as if we were working in the quotient set of feature structures modulo alphabetic variance.

Abstract Feature Structures

Moshier and Rounds (1987) provide an elegant representation of equivalence classes in this ordering, the details of which can be found in Moshier (1988). This representation was extended to the ordered case by Pollard and Moshier (1990). The construction of abstract feature structures by Moshier is similar in its approach to Aït-Kaci's (1984) characterization of Ψ-terms. The main difference is that Aït-Kaci's definition included explicit information about tags and could contain inconsistent sorts, which then had to be factored out. We first present the definition of abstract feature structures.

Definition 3.8 (Abstract Feature Structure)

If $F = \langle Q, \bar{q}, \theta, \delta \rangle$ is a feature structure, then $Abs(F) = \langle \Theta_F, \approx_F \rangle$ is an abstract feature structure *where:*

- $\Theta_F : \mathsf{Path} \to \mathsf{Type}$ *is a partial function defined by* $\Theta_F(\pi) = \theta(\delta(\pi, \bar{q}))$

- $\approx_F \subseteq \mathsf{Path} \times \mathsf{Path}$ *is such that* $\pi \approx_F \pi'$ *if and only if* $\delta(\pi, \bar{q}) = \delta(\pi', \bar{q})$

The value of $\Theta_F(\pi)$ is the type that is assigned to the node at the end of path π by the feature structure F. Since all of the nodes in F are reachable from the root, Θ_F represents all of the typing information provided by F. We have $\pi \approx_F \pi'$ if and only if the paths π and π' lead to the same node from the root in F. Moshier includes a third component in an abstract feature structure for the set of paths, which is defined by:

(17) $\mathcal{P}_F = \{\pi \mid \delta(\pi, \bar{q}) \text{ defined}\}$

This component is not strictly necessary as we can recover $\mathcal{P}_F$ from either Θ_F or $\approx_F$, by noting that:

(18) $\mathcal{P}_F = \{\pi \mid \pi \approx_F \pi\} = \{\pi \mid \Theta_F(\pi) \text{ defined}\}$

Moshier also provides a definition of abstract feature structures which is independent of their being generated from concrete feature structures, but we do not need an independent characterization here.

Moshier's fundamental insight was that the information in an abstract feature structure is enough to uniquely characterize a feature structure up to isomorphism. We can order arbitrary partial functions $\Theta, \Theta' : \mathsf{Path} \to \mathsf{Type}$ pointwise by putting $\Theta \sqsubseteq \Theta'$ if and only if whenever $\Theta(\pi)$ is defined, $\Theta'(\pi)$ is also defined, and furthermore $\Theta(\pi) \sqsubseteq \Theta'(\pi)$. Also note that if we have arbitrary relations $\approx, \approx \subseteq \mathsf{Path} \times \mathsf{Path}$, then we have $\approx \subseteq \approx'$ if and only if $\pi \approx \pi'$ implies $\pi \approx' \pi'$. The following proof is adapted with only minor variations from Moshier (1988).

Theorem 3.9 (Abstract Subsumption)

$F \sqsubseteq F'$ if and only if $\Theta_F \sqsubseteq \Theta_{F'}$ and $\approx_F \subseteq \approx_{F'}$.

Proof: Suppose that $F \sqsubseteq F'$ so that there is a morphism $h : Q \to Q'$. Then we have $\theta(\delta(\pi, \bar{q})) \sqsubseteq \theta'(\delta'(\pi, h(\bar{q}))) = \theta'(\delta'(\pi, \bar{q}'))$ and thus $\Theta_F \sqsubseteq \Theta_{F'}$. Now if $\delta(\pi, \bar{q}) = \delta(\pi', \bar{q})$, then $\delta'(\pi, h(\bar{q})) = \delta'(\pi', h(\bar{q}))$ so that $\delta'(\pi, \bar{q}') = \delta'(\pi', \bar{q}')$. Consequently, $\approx_F \subseteq \approx_{F'}$.

To show the converse, we explicitly construct a morphism $h : Q \to Q'$ by setting $h(\delta(\pi, \bar{q})) = \delta'(\pi, \bar{q}')$. This is a total function from Q to Q' because of our rootedness condition and the fact that if Θ_F is defined on a path, then so is $\Theta_{F'}$ if $\Theta_F \sqsubseteq \Theta_{F'}$. It is well defined because if $\delta(\pi, \bar{q}) = \delta(\pi', \bar{q})$, then $\delta'(\pi, \bar{q}') = \delta'(\pi', \bar{q}')$ because $\approx_F \subseteq \approx_{F'}$. To see that it is a homomorphism, first consider the fact that the root is preserved because $h(\bar{q}) = h(\delta(\epsilon, \bar{q})) = \delta'(\epsilon, \bar{q}') = \bar{q}'$. Next, we know that if $q = \delta(\pi, \bar{q})$, then $h(q) = \delta'(\pi, \bar{q}')$ so that $\theta(q) = \Theta_F(\pi) \sqsubseteq \Theta_{F'}(\pi) = \theta'(h(q))$. Finally, we need to show that $h(\delta(f, q)) = \delta'(f, h(q))$. So suppose $q = \delta(\pi, \bar{q})$. We then have $h(\delta(f, q)) = h(\delta(f, \delta(\pi, \bar{q}))) = h(\delta(\pi f, \bar{q})) = \delta'(\pi f, \bar{q}') = \delta'(f, \delta'(\pi, \bar{q}')) = \delta'(f, h(q))$. □

An immediate corollary to this result tells us that the abstract feature structures provide a representation of the equivalence classes of feature structures modulo alphabetic variance.

Corollary 3.10 (Abstract Equivalence)

$F \sim F'$ *if and only if* $Abs(F) = Abs(F')$.

Proof: Suppose $F \sim F'$ so that $F \sqsubseteq F'$ and $F' \sqsubseteq F$. It then follows that $\Theta_F \sqsubseteq \Theta_{F'}$ and $\Theta_{F'} \sqsubseteq \Theta_F$ from which we can conclude that $\Theta_F = \Theta_{F'}$. Similarly, if $\approx_F \subseteq \approx_{F'}$ and $\approx_{F'} \subseteq \approx_F$, then $\approx_F = \approx_{F'}$. □

This result tells us that all of the information provided by a feature structure F is conveyed by its abstract counterpart $Abs(F)$, which determines the paths that are shared and the types assigned to paths.

Unification

Now that we have defined a subsumption ordering on feature structures based on their informational content, we are able to define a unification operation. Just like the situation with type unification, the unification of two feature structures is a feature structure representing neither more nor less information than is contained in the feature structures being unified. Thus we again take unification to be a simple least upper bound operation with respect to the subsumption ordering. To see that this operation is sensible, we have to show that any pair of consistent feature structures can be unified to produce a unique result modulo alphabetic variance. The fact that our feature structures admit a unification operation is crucial to their efficient application to the representation of conjunctive information (Pereira 1987). By applying unification, information from a number of distinct sources can be combined into a unique representative (again modulo alphabetic variance). Unification only fails when it is applied to feature structures that, when taken together, provide inconsistent information. In the case of feature structures, inconsistency can only arise from attempting to unify two structures that assign incompatible types (in the type ordering) to the same path. When we consider appropriateness conditions, extensionality, and inequations in later chapters, we see other ways in which inconsistencies can surface.

We provide a constructive definition of an operation that unifies two feature structures, which is a minor generalization to types of the definition provided by Moshier (1988:53). The proof that the result is indeed a least upper bound is rather technical, but the actual definition of unification itself is straightforward. It is easiest to conceptualize unification procedurally. We start by identifying the root nodes of the two feature structures and labeling the result with the unification of their types. We then recursively identify nodes that are values of identical features of nodes which have been identified, each time replacing the type of the identified nodes with the join of their types before identification. We simply continue to carry out this node identification process until we have reached closure. If at any stage we try to identify nodes with inconsistent types, then we fail; the feature structures we were trying to unify were not consistent. In the formal definition, we represent collections of nodes that have been identified by equivalence classes. Recall that an equivalence relation is a transitive, reflexive, and symmetric relation. If $\equiv$ is an equivalence relation over X we use the standard notation for *equivalence classes*:

(19) $[x]_{\equiv} = \{y \in X \mid y \equiv x\}$

and also for the *quotient set of X modulo $\equiv$*:

(20) $X/_{\equiv} = \{[x]_{\equiv} \mid x \in X\}$

Thus an equivalence class consists of a maximal set of $\equiv$-equivalent objects. The quotient is then just the set of all such classes and thus partitions X. We represent the intuitive identification of nodes by making them equivalent, so that the feature structure that results from the unification process has nodes which are equivalence classes.

Definition 3.11 (Unification)

Suppose $F, F' \in \mathcal{F}$ are feature structures such that $F \sim \langle Q, \bar{q}, \theta, \delta \rangle$ and $F' \sim \langle Q', \bar{q}', \theta', \delta' \rangle$ are such that $Q \cap Q' = \emptyset$. We define an equivalence relation $\bowtie$ on $Q \cup Q'$ as the least equivalence relation such that:

- *$\bar{q} \bowtie \bar{q}'$*

- *$\delta(f, q) \bowtie \delta(f, q')$ if both are defined and $q \bowtie q'$*

The unification *of F and F' is then defined to be:*

$$F \sqcup F' = \langle (Q \cup Q')/_{\bowtie}, [\bar{q}]_{\bowtie}, \theta^{\bowtie}, \delta^{\bowtie} \rangle$$

where:

$$\theta^{\bowtie}([q]_{\bowtie}) = \bigsqcup \{(\theta \cup \theta')(q') \mid q' \bowtie q\}$$

and

$$\delta^{\bowtie}(f, [q]_{\bowtie}) = \begin{cases} [(\delta \cup \delta')(f, q)]_{\bowtie} & \textit{if } (\delta \cup \delta')(f, q) \textit{ is defined} \\ \textit{undefined} & \textit{otherwise} \end{cases}$$

if all of the joins in the definition of $\theta^{\bowtie}$ exist. $F \sqcup F'$ is undefined otherwise.

We begin the unification process defined above by choosing alphabetic variants of F and F' that do not share any nodes. The reason for this is to avoid unwanted clashes. For instance, we want $\theta \cup \theta'$ to be a well-defined function. As we have said before, unification is a process of information conjunction, and we consider alphabetic variants to represent identical information. The definition of $\bowtie$ is just a formalization of our intuitive explanation of node identification, so that $q \bowtie q'$ just in case the nodes q and q' are identified at some stage of the unification process. The definition of $\theta^{\bowtie}$ on the resulting equivalence classes, which represent sets of identified nodes, then simply takes the join of the types of the nodes that have been identified. This is why the result of unification is undefined if we cannot produce such a join for some equivalence class.

Before going on to show that unification does indeed represent information conjunction in the sense that it produces least upper bounds in the information ordering, we pause to verify that the result of unification is in fact a feature structure.

Lemma 3.12

If $F \sqcup F'$ is defined, then $F \sqcup F' \in \mathcal{F}$ is a feature structure.

Proof: First of all, the quotient set $(Q \cup Q')/_{\bowtie}$ is finite because both Q and Q' are finite. $\theta^{\bowtie}$ is obviously total as $F \sqcup F'$ is defined if and only if $\theta^{\bowtie}$ produces a value for each member of $(Q \cup Q')/_{\bowtie}$. It remains to show that $\delta^{\bowtie}$ is in fact well defined and roots $(Q \cup Q')/_{\bowtie}$ at $[\bar{q}]_{\bowtie}$. We need to show that the definition of $\delta^{\bowtie}(f, [q]_{\bowtie})$ does not depend on the representative $q \in Q \cup Q'$ we choose. So suppose $q' \bowtie q$. It follows that $\delta^{\bowtie}(f, [q]_{\bowtie}) = \delta^{\bowtie}(f, [q']_{\bowtie})$ by the definition of $\bowtie$. To see that $F \sqcup F'$ is rooted, simply note that if $q \in Q$ and $\delta(\pi, \bar{q}) = q$, then $\delta^{\bowtie}(\pi, [\bar{q}]_{\bowtie}) = [q]_{\bowtie}$, and if $q \in Q'$ and $q = \delta'(\pi, \bar{q}')$, then $\delta^{\bowtie}(\pi, [\bar{q}]_{\bowtie}) = \delta^{\bowtie}(\pi, [\bar{q}']_{\bowtie}) = [q]_{\bowtie}$. $\square$

We now provide a generalization to type inheritance of Moshier's (1988:54) proof that unification produces least upper bounds. The only details that have been modified are to deal with ordered types.

Theorem 3.13 (Unification)

$F \sqcup F'$ is the least upper bound of F and F' in $\langle \mathcal{F}, \sqsubseteq \rangle$ if F and F' have an upper bound.

Proof: Suppose that $F'' = \langle Q'', \bar{q}'', \theta'', \delta'' \rangle$ is an upper bound of F and F' so that $F \sqsubseteq F''$ and $F' \sqsubseteq F''$, and there are morphisms $h: Q \rightarrow Q''$ and $h': Q' \rightarrow Q''$. We then define a total function $h^*: (Q \cup Q') \rightarrow Q''$ by:

$$h^*(q) = \begin{cases} h(q) & \text{if } q \in Q \\ h'(q) & \text{if } q \in Q' \end{cases}$$

We also need the partial function $\delta^*: (Q \cup Q') \times \mathsf{Feat} \rightarrow (Q \cup Q')$ defined by:

$$\delta^*(f, q) = \begin{cases} \delta(f, q) & \text{if } q \in Q \\ \delta'(f, q) & \text{if } q \in Q' \end{cases}$$

Finally, we define a total function $\theta^*: (Q \cup Q') \rightarrow \mathsf{Type}$ by:

$$\theta^*(q) = \begin{cases} \theta''(h(q)) & \text{if } q \in Q \\ \theta''(h'(q)) & \text{if } q \in Q' \end{cases}$$

The equivalence relation $\equiv_{h^*}$ induced on $Q \cup Q'$ by h^* is given in the usual way by setting $q \equiv_{h^*} q'$ if and only if $h^*(q) = h^*(q')$. This equivalence relation satisfies the following two properties:

1. if $q \equiv_{h^*} q'$, then $\delta^*(f, q) \equiv_{h^*} \delta^*(f, q')$ if both are defined

2. if $q \equiv_{h^*} q'$, then $\theta^*(q) = \theta^*(q')$ and $(\theta \cup \theta')(q) \sqsubseteq \theta^*(q)$

Note that $\bowtie$ is the minimal equivalence relation satisfying these two conditions, so that $q \bowtie q'$ only if $q \equiv_{h^*} q'$.

We can now proceed to prove the theorem at hand. We first show that $F \sqcup F'$ is defined if F and F' are bounded. If F'' is an upper bound for F and F', then $\theta^*(q)$ (defined above) is an upper bound for the set $\{(\theta \cup \theta')(q') \mid q' \bowtie q\}$ because $q \bowtie q'$ only if $q \equiv_{h^*} q'$. Thus $\theta^{\bowtie}(q) = \bigsqcup\{(\theta \cup \theta')(q') \mid q' \bowtie q\}$ must be defined, because $\langle \mathsf{Type}, \sqsubseteq \rangle$ is a bounded complete partial order. Hence $F \sqcup F'$ is defined.

It now remains to verify that $F \sqcup F'$ is a least upper bound. To see that $F \sqcup F'$ is an upper bound, consider the morphisms $h: Q \to (Q \cup Q')/_{\bowtie}$ and $h': Q' \to (Q \cup Q')/_{\bowtie}$ defined by $h(q) = [q]_{\bowtie}$ and $h'(q) = [q]_{\bowtie}$, respectively. It is straightforward to verify that these are indeed morphisms by considering the definition of $\bowtie$. Consider the case of $h: Q \to (Q \cup Q')/_{\bowtie}$. First, we have $h(\bar{q}) = [\bar{q}]_{\bowtie}$ by definition. We also have $\theta(q) \sqsubseteq \theta^{\bowtie}(h(q))$, because $\theta^{\bowtie}(h(q)) = \theta^{\bowtie}([q]_{\bowtie}) = \bigsqcup\{(\theta \cup \theta')(q') \mid q' \bowtie q\}$. Finally, we have $h(\delta(f, q)) = [\delta(f, q)]_{\bowtie} = \delta^{\bowtie}(f, [q]_{\bowtie}) = \delta^{\bowtie}(f, h(q))$. Thus h is a morphism. An identical argument shows that h' is also a morphism.

Finally, to show that $F \sqcup F'$ is a least upper bound, we construct a morphism from $F \sqcup F'$ to an arbitrary upper bound. Suppose $F'' = \langle Q'', \bar{q}'', \theta'', \delta'' \rangle$ is an upper bound of F and F' with the morphisms $h: Q \to Q''$ and $h': Q' \to Q''$ as above. We define the required morphism $j: (Q \cup Q')/_{\bowtie} \to Q''$ in terms of the function h^* defined above in terms of h and h' by setting $j([q]_{\bowtie}) = h^*(q)$. This function is well defined because if $q \bowtie q'$, then $h^*(q) = h^*(q')$ by the minimal way in which we defined $\bowtie$. To see that j is indeed a morphism, we need to verify the three properties of morphisms. First, we know that $j([\bar{q}]_{\bowtie}) = h^*(\bar{q}) = h(\bar{q}) = \bar{q}''$ because h is a morphism. Secondly, it is clear that $\theta^{\bowtie}([q]_{\bowtie}), \sqsubseteq \theta''(h^*(q))$ because the second condition above ensures $\theta^{\bowtie}([q]_{\bowtie}) = \bigsqcup\{(\theta \cup \theta')(q') \mid q' \bowtie q\} \sqsubseteq \theta''(h(q)) = \theta''(h^*(q))$. Finally, we have $j(\delta^{\bowtie}(f, [q]_{\bowtie})) = j([\delta(f, q)]_{\bowtie}) = h^*(\delta(f, q)) = h(\delta(f, q)) = \delta''(f, h(q)) = \delta''(f, h^*(q))$ if $q \in Q$ because h is a morphism. A similar argument applies if $q \in Q'$.   □

This theorem tells us that our unification operation combines the information in two consistent feature structures into a single result, which is the most general feature structure that contains all of the information in both inputs.

Consider the following examples of unification:

(21) $\begin{bmatrix} \mathbf{agr} \\ \text{PER:} [\, \mathbf{1st} \,] \end{bmatrix} \sqcup \begin{bmatrix} \mathbf{agr} \\ \text{NUM:} [\, \mathbf{sing} \,] \end{bmatrix} = \begin{bmatrix} \mathbf{agr} \\ \text{PER:} [\, \mathbf{1st} \,] \\ \text{NUM:} [\, \mathbf{sing} \,] \end{bmatrix}$

$$(22) \quad \begin{bmatrix} \text{sign} \\ \text{SBJ:} \begin{bmatrix} \text{agr} \\ \text{PER:}[\,\text{1st}\,] \end{bmatrix} \\ \text{PRD:} \begin{bmatrix} \text{agr} \\ \text{NUM:}[\,\text{plu}\,] \end{bmatrix} \end{bmatrix} \sqcup \begin{bmatrix} \text{sign} \\ \text{SBJ:}[\,\bot\ \boxed{1}\,] \\ \text{PRD:}[\,\boxed{1}\,] \end{bmatrix} = \begin{bmatrix} \text{sign} \\ \text{SBJ:} \begin{bmatrix} \boxed{6}\ \text{agr} \\ \text{PER:}[\,\text{1st}\,] \\ \text{NUM:}[\,\text{plu}\,] \end{bmatrix} \\ \text{PRD:}[\,\boxed{6}\,] \end{bmatrix}$$

$$(23) \quad \begin{bmatrix} \bot \\ \text{F:}[\,\boxed{1}\ \bot\,] \\ \text{G:}[\,\boxed{1}\,] \end{bmatrix} \sqcup \begin{bmatrix} \bot \\ \text{F:} \begin{bmatrix} \bot \\ \text{H:}[\,\boxed{2}\ \bot\,] \end{bmatrix} \\ \text{G:}[\,\boxed{2}\,] \end{bmatrix} = \begin{bmatrix} \bot \\ \text{F:} \begin{bmatrix} \boxed{3}\ \bot \\ \text{H:}[\,\boxed{3}\,] \end{bmatrix} \\ \text{G:}[\,\boxed{3}\,] \end{bmatrix}$$

The last equation is significant in that it shows how cyclic structures can arise from the unification of acyclic ones.

It is worth pointing out that there is a most general feature structure with respect to the information ordering, given by:

$$(24) \quad \bot_{\mathcal{F}} = [\,\bot\,]$$

It is easy to see that $\bot_{\mathcal{F}} \sqsubseteq F$ for any feature structure $F \in \mathcal{F}$ as can be verified by considering the morphism which maps the root and only node of $\bot_{\mathcal{F}}$ to the root of F.

While we have arbitrary finite joins of consistent feature structures, we do not have arbitrary infinite joins. Simply consider the sequence:

$$(25) \quad \bot_{\mathcal{F}} \sqsubseteq \begin{bmatrix} \bot \\ f{:}[\,\bot\,] \end{bmatrix} \sqsubseteq \begin{bmatrix} \bot \\ f{:} \begin{bmatrix} \bot \\ f{:}[\,\bot\,] \end{bmatrix} \end{bmatrix} \sqsubseteq \cdots$$

Even though any finite subset of this sequence can be unified, the sequence as a whole fails to have a least upper bound because the obvious candidate would be infinite. On the other hand, this set of feature structures is bounded by:

$$(26) \quad \begin{bmatrix} \bot\ \boxed{1} \\ f{:}[\,\boxed{1}\,] \end{bmatrix}$$

The reason that there is no least upper bound is that every element of the following descending sequence is an upper bound, and the sequence as a whole does not have a meet:

$$(27) \quad \begin{bmatrix} \bot\ \boxed{1} \\ f{:}[\,\boxed{1}\,] \end{bmatrix} \sqsupseteq \begin{bmatrix} \bot \\ f{:} \begin{bmatrix} \bot\ \boxed{1} \\ f{:}[\,\boxed{1}\,] \end{bmatrix} \end{bmatrix} \sqsupseteq \begin{bmatrix} \bot \\ f{:} \begin{bmatrix} \bot \\ f{:} \begin{bmatrix} \bot\ \boxed{1} \\ f{:}[\,\boxed{1}\,] \end{bmatrix} \end{bmatrix} \end{bmatrix} \sqsupseteq \cdots$$

Aït-Kaci (1984) and Moshier (1988:57) have developed efficient algorithms for carrying out unification that rely on efficient representations of equivalence classes in terms of pointers. Their algorithms are closely related to the algorithm of Martelli and Montanari (1982) for term unification, which was extended to the cyclic Prolog II case by Jaffar (1984). The complexity of unification is near linear, being $\mathcal{O}(ack^{-1}(n) \cdot n)$ where n is the combined size of the feature structures being unified and where ack^{-1} is the inverse of Ackermann's function. Paterson and Wegman (1978) introduce a truly linear algorithm for the unification of acyclic terms, but its representation of terms by means of doubly linked lists to handle the acyclicity requirement on true first-order terms introduces a costly constant overhead, which far outweighs $ack^{-1}(n)$ for any realistic n.

Chapter 4

Attribute-Value Descriptions and Satisfaction

In this chapter we introduce the logical attribute-value language that we employ to describe feature structures. Our description language is the same (in the sense of containing exactly the same descriptions) as that of Rounds and Kasper (1986), but following Pollard (in press) our interpretations are based on our feature structures rather than the ones provided by Rounds and Kasper. One way to look at the language of descriptions is as providing a way to talk about feature structures; the language can be displayed linearly one symbol after another and can thus be easily used in implementations. Other researchers, namely Johnson (1987, 1988), Smolka (1988) and King (1989), use similar, but much more powerful, logical description languages and take a totally different view of the nature of interpretations or models for these languages. The main difference in their descriptions is the presence of general description negation, implication, and variables. The interpretations they use are based on a domain of objects with features interpreted as unary partial functions on this domain. In the system we describe here, we view feature structures themselves as partial objects; descriptions are just a particularly neat and tidy notation for picking them out. Our view thus corresponds to Aït-Kaci's treatment of his Ψ-terms, which were also taken to be partial descriptions of empirical objects. Johnson (1988:72), on the other hand, is at pains to point out that he does not view feature structures as partial models or descriptions of total linguistic objects, but rather as total objects themselves. For instance, he interprets the absence of a feature in a feature structure corresponding to a linguistic object as signaling that the feature is not present in the object being described. To handle partial information, Johnson employs an attribute-value logic related to, but much stronger than, the one we shortly introduce.

To get at the notion of "total" information, we develop a notion of maximal feature structures that represent maximal consistent amounts of information. But we do not take these objects to represent total information about an object in the real world in absolute terms, since it is unlikely that a cognitive agent would ever have total information about an object other than relative to some fixed stock of concepts, which is often referred to as a *scheme of individuation*

(see Landman 1986 and Barwise 1989 for more on the relation between partial
information and schemes of individuation). The schemes of individuation we
have chosen to classify objects are based on atomic properties, which we call
types, and on functional features that determine aspects of objects.

The well-formed expressions of our attribute-value description language are
taken to describe feature structures. We define a logical notion of satisfaction
that derives from thinking of feature structures as models of the descriptions
that describe them. In the next section, we discuss a complete axiomatization of
the logic of feature structures. With the soundness and completeness theorems
we prove for this logic with respect to the feature structure interpretation, it
is reasonable to think solely in terms of the logic as is urged by King (1989).
Höhfeld and Smolka (1988) adopt this view and take the basic requirement for
an attribute-value logic to be the existence of normal forms. They then show
in a very general way how to apply such logics in constraint logic programming
(CLP) systems and in context-free grammars (Smolka 1989). On the other hand,
feature structures correspond more closely to the kinds of data structures that
are actually used in artificial intelligence and automated reasoning tasks and
form an interesting domain of study in and of themselves. Viewed from this
perspective, our feature structures might be seen to be nothing more than
efficient encodings of normal forms of a particular attribute-value logic. But in
most respects, our logic was chosen to match the feature structures rather than
the other way around, since feature structures are known to provide efficient
data structures for the representation of partial information and for pattern-
matching applications.

Description Language

We begin by providing a formal definition of the set of well-formed formulas of
our logic, which we call *descriptions*, and then go on to provide an intuitive explanation of their intended interpretations. This definition of descriptions over
a domain of types was provided originally by Pollard (in press), but corresponds
directly to the original Rounds-Kasper description language where atoms were
taken to be descriptions.

Definition 4.1 (Descriptions)
The set of descriptions *over the collection* Type *of types and* Feat *of features is
the least set* Desc *such that:*

- $\sigma \in$ Desc *if* $\sigma \in$ Type

- $\top \in$ Desc

- $\pi{:}\phi \in$ Desc *if* $\pi \in$ Path, $\phi \in$ Desc

- $\pi_1 \doteq \pi_2 \in$ Desc *if* $\pi_1, \pi_2 \in$ Path

- $\phi \wedge \psi, \phi \vee \psi \in$ Desc *if* $\phi, \psi \in$ Desc

The most basic kind of description we have is a simple type σ. Such a description applies to objects which are of the type σ. Note that since $\bot \in$ Type, $\bot$ is a description. $\bot$ describes any feature structure, while $\top$, which must be explicitly defined to be a description, is not satisfied by any feature structure. We could have chosen not to include $\top$ directly, but rather introduced it as an abbreviation for some unsatisfiable description. Alternatively, if we had required Type to be complete, we would have had a top element in Type. A description of the form $\pi : \phi$ applies to objects whose value for the path π satisfies the description ϕ. A description of the form $\pi_1 \doteq \pi_2$ is taken to mean that the value of the object that you get by following the path π_1 is token identical to the object that you get by following the path π_2.

We employ the usual notation for the conjunction and disjunction of descriptions and interpret them in the usual way. As a matter of notational ease, we assume that : is right associative, so that $\pi_1 : \pi_2 : \phi$ abbreviates $\pi_1 : (\pi_2 : \phi)$; that the conjunction operator $\wedge$ binds more tightly than the disjunction $\vee$, so that $\phi \vee \psi \wedge \chi$ means $\phi \vee (\psi \wedge \chi)$; and, finally, that the feature selection operator : binds more tightly than the logical operators, so that $f : \phi \wedge \psi$ is the same as $(f : \phi) \wedge \psi$. We also use the usual set conjunction notation $\bigwedge \{\phi_1, \ldots, \phi_n\}$ for $\phi_1 \wedge \phi_2 \wedge \cdots \wedge \phi_n$, due to the fact that our logical operations of conjunction and disjunction are associative and commutative, as should be obvious from the definition of satisfaction below. Note that we omit parentheses in multiple conjunctions and disjunctions for the same reason. Similarly, we use the notation $\bigvee \Phi$ for the disjunction of the elements in a finite set $\Phi \subseteq$ Desc of descriptions. Note that our description language does not allow any general negative or implicative descriptions to be expressed. We later introduce inequations of the form $\pi_1 \not\doteq \pi_2$, which state that the two paths have values that are distinct.

Satisfaction

Now that we have a logical description language, we define a satisfaction relation between feature structures and descriptions. Our definition is identical to that provided by Pollard (in press).

Definition 4.2 (Satisfaction)
The satisfaction *relation* $\models$ *between feature structures and descriptions is the least relation such that:*

- $F \models \sigma$ *if* $\sigma \in$ Type *and* $\sigma \sqsubseteq \theta(\bar{q})$

- $F \not\models \top$ *for any* $F \in \mathcal{F}$

- $F \models \pi : \phi$ *if* $F @ \pi \models \phi$

- $F \models \pi_1 \doteq \pi_2$ *if* $\delta(\pi_1, \bar{q}) = \delta(\pi_2, \bar{q})$

- $F \models \phi \wedge \psi$ *if* $F \models \phi$ *and* $F \models \psi$

- $F \models \phi \vee \psi$ *if* $F \models \phi$ *or* $F \models \psi$

$$F = \begin{bmatrix} \text{sentence} \\ \text{SUBJ:} [\boxed{1}\,\text{john}\,] \\ \text{OBJ:} [\boxed{2}\,\text{john}\,] \\ \text{PRED:} \begin{bmatrix} \text{prop} \\ \text{REL:sees} \\ \text{AGT:} [\boxed{1}\,] \\ \text{PAT:} [\boxed{2}\,] \end{bmatrix} \end{bmatrix}$$

$F \models$ **sentence**

$F \models$ **phrase** if **phrase** $\sqsubseteq$ **sentence**

$F \models$ (SUBJ $\doteq$ PRED AGT)

$\qquad \wedge$ (PRED:(PAT:**john**))

$F \models$ (PRED:PAT:**bill**) $\vee$ (PRED REL:**sees**)

$F \models$ PRED:(REL:**sees** $\wedge$ OBJ:**john**)

$F \models$ (SUBJ:**john**) $\wedge$ (OBJ:**john**)

$F \not\models$ SUBJ $\doteq$ OBJ

$F \not\models$ SUBJ $\doteq$ PRED PAT

Figure 4.1. Satisfaction Example.

The satisfaction conditions in are nothing more than the formal parallel of the intuitive explanation of our descriptions. Taking the definition case by case, we have a feature structure F satisfying a type σ just in case the type of F (the type assigned to its root) is equally as specific as or more specific than σ, which we express formally as $\sigma \sqsubseteq \theta(\bar{q})$. A feature structure F satisfies a description $\pi:\phi$ just in case its value for the path π satisfies ϕ. A feature structure F models a structure sharing constraint $\pi_1 \doteq \pi_2$ just in case the object you get by following the path π_1 from the root of F is token identical to the object you get by following π_2. Thus it is not enough to have values for π_1 and π_2 which are alphabetic variants to satisfy a description $\pi_1 \doteq \pi_2$; the values must be identical. Disjunction and conjunction are interpreted classically. This means that a feature structure satisfies $\phi \vee \psi$ just in case it satisfies ϕ or it satisfies ψ, and it satisfies $\phi \wedge \psi$ just in case it satisfies both ϕ and ψ.

We now provide some examples of satisfaction. Consider Figure 4.1, which depicts a simple representation for the semantics of the sentence *John sees John*, where the two Johns are not known to be identical. The behavior of the last three descriptions is significant. Even though all of the paths SUBJ, OBJ, PRED AGT, and PRED PAT have values of type **john**, they are not identical. This is because we interpret the atomic symbols in Type as properties that may be applicable to more than one distinct individual in the empirical domain. The co-indexing in attribute value matrices, or, equivalently, the structure sharing in feature structures, indicates that the shared paths have a token-identical value and not just the same type.

We now turn our attention to model-theoretic concerns that arise from our definition of satisfaction. In the next section, we turn our attention to proof-theoretic matters and provide a complete axiomatization of the logic of feature structures. In later chapters, we characterize the logical behavior of feature structures with the addition of inequations, types and extensionality conditions.

We assume the usual definitions for validity, satisfiability and logical equivalence. First of all, it is useful to have a notation for the set of all feature structures which satisfy a description ϕ, which we denote by $Sat(\phi)$, where:

(1) $Sat(\phi) = \{F \in \mathcal{F} \mid F \models \phi\}$

We assume the usual definitions for validity, satisfiability and logical equivalence:

Definition 4.3 (Logical Notions)

Suppose $\phi, \psi \in$ Desc are descriptions. Then:

- ϕ *is* satisfiable *if and only if $Sat(\phi) \neq \emptyset$*

- ϕ *is* valid *if and only if $Sat(\phi) = \mathcal{F}$*

- ϕ *and ψ are* logically equivalent, *$\models \phi \equiv \psi$, if and only if $Sat(\phi) = Sat(\psi)$*

Informally, a description is satisfiable if there is some feature structure which satisfies it, a description is valid if every feature structure satisfies it, and two descriptions are logically equivalent if they are satisfied by exactly the same feature structures. Note that we have overloaded our $\models$ operator in the standard way: in the case $F \models \phi$ it means that F satisfies ϕ, and in $\models \phi \equiv \psi$ it means that ϕ and ψ are logically equivalent. Our axiomatizations allows us to characterize syntactically the conditions under which two descriptions are logically equivalent. In the chapters that follow, we relativize these notions to well-typed feature structures, those meeting the extensionality conditions, and extended feature structures that include a notion of inequality, which we use to model the description language extended with inequations.

Our first major result concerning satisfiability is that it is monotonic with respect to the information content of feature structures. That is, if a feature structure satisfies a description, then any extension of it also satisfies the description. The importance of this result was first noted in the context of PATR-II (Pereira and Shieber 1984), and proved for a system with descriptions similar to ours, but without type ordering, by Rounds and Kasper (1986). Pollard (in press) noted that it holds for the feature structures, descriptions, and notion of satisfaction which he developed, and that we present here.

Theorem 4.4 (Monotonicity)

If $F \models \phi$ and $F \sqsubseteq F'$, then $F' \models \phi$.

Proof: All of the satisfaction conditions are monotonic, and simply require the existence of certain structure within a feature structure. All of this structure is preserved in extensions.   □

Our notion of monotonicity is that if a feature structure satisfies a description, then adding more information (by unification, for instance) results in a feature structure that still satisfies the description. This allows us to solve constraints incrementally; if a feature structure satisfies a description, then adding more information to the feature structure does not jeopardize this satisfaction.

The logics studied by Johnson, Smolka, and King are not monotonic in the sense of Theorem 4.4, due to their classical treatments of description negation and implication. Most notably, a feature structure F with no value for a feature f satisfies $\neg(f : \bot)$, but an extension of F that does provide a value for f satisfies this description. To take an example from GPSG (Gazdar et al. 1985:246), which also included description negation and implication, consider the feature co-occurrence restriction in (2) (translated into our notation):

(2)   INV: $+$ $\longrightarrow$ (AUX: $+$ $\wedge$ VFORM: **fin**)

Now consider the feature structures in (3):

$$
(3) \quad
\begin{bmatrix}
\bot \\
\text{AUX:} [\,\text{-}\,] \\
\text{VFORM:} [\,\mathbf{prp}\,]
\end{bmatrix}
\sqsubseteq
\begin{bmatrix}
\bot \\
\text{INV:} [\,+\,] \\
\text{AUX:} [\,\text{-}\,] \\
\text{VFORM:} [\,\mathbf{prp}\,]
\end{bmatrix}
$$

The more general structure in (3) does not satisfy INV: $+$ and hence does satisfy the implicational feature co-occurrence restriction in (2) under the classical interpretation of implication. On the other hand, the more specific structure in (3) does satisfy INV: $+$, but does not satisfy the description (AUX: $+$ $\wedge$ VFORM: **fin**), and hence fails to satisfy the restriction in (2). This is a prime example of monotonicity failure in attribute-value logics with implications. The monotonicity theorem is the basis of the further results in this section that provide unique finite representation of the satisfiers of a description. Such a monotonicity condition is quite useful for efficient implementations of unification-based grammars, as is discussed by Pereira (1987).

We next consider the behavior of descriptions without disjunctions. It turns out that these descriptions stand in a close relationship to the feature structures themselves. In particular, every satisfiable non-disjunctive description is satisfied by a most general feature structure (which is unique up to alphabetic variance). Let NonDisjDesc be the collection of descriptions without disjunctions.

Theorem 4.5 (Non-Disjunctive Most General Satisfier)

There is a partial function MGSat: NonDisjDesc $\rightarrow$ $\mathcal{F}$ such that:

$F \models \phi$ *if and only if MGSat(ϕ) $\sqsubseteq$ F*

Proof: Suppose that ϕ is a consistent non-disjunctive description. We provide an inductive proof that there is a most general satisfier for ϕ. For the purposes of our induction, we order the descriptions by the number of features that show up in them, and in cases of descriptions with the same number of features, by the number of conjunctions they contain. The most basic case is that in which ϕ is simply a type symbol. In this case we have:

$$MGSat(\sigma) = \begin{bmatrix} \sigma \end{bmatrix}$$

Such a description cannot be inconsistent.

We next have a number of cases for path sharing descriptions. The most trivial case is that in which both paths are empty. In this case we have:

$$MGSat(\epsilon \doteq \epsilon) = \begin{bmatrix} \bot \end{bmatrix}$$

Next, we consider the case of cycles. We have:

$$MGSat(\epsilon \doteq f_1 \cdots f_n) = \begin{bmatrix} \boxed{1}\ \bot \\ f_1: \begin{bmatrix} \bot \\ f_2: \cdots \begin{bmatrix} \bot \\ f_n: \begin{bmatrix} \boxed{1} \end{bmatrix} \end{bmatrix} \end{bmatrix} \end{bmatrix}$$

We can reduce a more general path equation involving cycles, such as $\pi_1 \doteq \pi_1 \pi_2$, to $\pi_1 : (\epsilon \doteq \pi_2)$, which has exactly the same satisfaction conditions, and then apply the inductive hypothesis, as shown below.

We make a similar move in taking:

$$MGSat(f_1 \cdots f_n \doteq g_1 \cdots g_m) = \begin{bmatrix} \bot \\ f_1: \begin{bmatrix} \bot \\ f_2: \cdots \begin{bmatrix} \bot \\ f_n: \begin{bmatrix} \boxed{1}\ \bot \end{bmatrix} \end{bmatrix} \end{bmatrix} \\ g_1: \begin{bmatrix} \bot \\ g_2: \cdots \begin{bmatrix} \bot \\ g_m: \begin{bmatrix} \boxed{1} \end{bmatrix} \end{bmatrix} \end{bmatrix} \end{bmatrix}$$

We now turn to the inductive cases. The first concerns descriptions that describe path values. In this case we have:

$$MGSat(f_1 \cdots f_n : \psi) = \begin{bmatrix} \bot \\ f_1: \begin{bmatrix} \bot \\ f_2: \cdots \begin{bmatrix} \bot \\ f_n: MGSat(\psi) \end{bmatrix} \end{bmatrix} \end{bmatrix}$$

The fact that $MGSat(\psi)$ exists follows from the inductive hypothesis.

Our final case concerns conjunctions, in which we have:

$$MGSat(\phi \wedge \psi) = MGSat(\phi) \sqcup MGSat(\psi)$$

Suppose that $F \models \phi \wedge \psi$. Then $F \models \phi$ and $F \models \psi$. So by the inductive hypothesis we conclude that $MGSat(\phi) \sqsubseteq F$ and $MGSat(\psi) \sqsubseteq F$. But $MGSat(\phi) \sqcup MGSat(\psi)$ is the most general such element. Thus the description $\phi \wedge \psi$ is satisfiable if and only if $MGSat(\phi) \sqcup MGSat(\psi)$ exists.

The result then follows from monotonicity, since $MGSat(\phi)$ is minimal, and every feature structure which extends $MGSat(\phi)$ also satisfies ϕ. $\square$

Thus $MGSat(\phi)$ is defined if and only if ϕ is a satisfiable non-disjunctive description, and if $MGSat(\phi)$ is defined, then it produces the most general satisfier of ϕ. Another way of looking at the most general satisfier theorem is that the collection $Sat(\phi)$ of satisfiers of a description can be given by:

(4) $Sat(\phi) = \{F \mid MGSat(\phi) \sqsubseteq F\}$

This makes it obvious that the satisfiers of a description form a principal filter in the subsumption ordering of feature structures (recall that a principal filter in a poset $\langle S, \leq \rangle$ is a set $\{x \in S \mid y \leq x\}$ generated by some y). Furthermore, the result of $MGSat(\phi)$ must be unique up to alphabetic variance.

Following a result of Moshier (1988), we can show that any feature structure can be picked out by means of a description in the sense that every feature structure is the most general satisfier of some non-disjunctive description. This is not quite so easy as it sounds due to the existence of cyclic feature structures. We need to introduce Moshier's method for selecting the paths that show up in the description of a feature structure with cycles. Suppose we fix a feature structure $F = \langle Q, \bar{q}, \theta, \delta \rangle$. A path π is said to be *direct* if it is not the case that $\pi = \pi_1 \pi_2 \pi_3$ for some $\pi_2 \neq \epsilon$ such that $\delta(\pi_1, \bar{q}) = \delta(\pi_1 \pi_2, \bar{q})$. A path π is said to be a *hook* if every proper prefix of π is direct. A path in a feature structure that is not a hook is said to be *redundant*. Let $Hooks(F)$ be the collection of hooks in the feature structure F. Note that even a cyclic feature structure has only a finite number of hooks, although there may be an infinite number of redundant paths. The following theorem is essentially an extension of the result found in Moshier (1988:43). In words, the theorem says that for every feature structure there is a description such that the feature structure is an alphabetic variant of the most general satisfier of the description.

Theorem 4.6 (Describability)

If $F \in \mathcal{F}$ is a feature structure, then there is a disjunction-free description $Desc(F) \in \mathsf{NonDisjDesc}$ such that:

$$F \sim MGSat(Desc(F))$$

Proof: Fix a feature structure $F = \langle Q, \bar{q}, \delta, \theta \rangle$. Then we set:

$$Desc(F) = \bigwedge\{\pi \doteq \pi' \mid \pi, \pi' \in Hooks(F),\ \delta(\pi, \bar{q}) = \delta(\pi', \bar{q})\} \land$$
$$\bigwedge\{\pi{:}\sigma \mid \pi \in Hooks(F),\ \theta(\delta(\pi, \bar{q})) = \sigma\}$$

Since Π is finite, we are assured that $Desc(F)$ is in fact a description. Note that $F \models Desc(F)$, because it satisfies each of the conjuncts. Now suppose that $F' \models Desc(F)$. We then must have $F' \models \pi \doteq \pi'$ if $F \models \pi \doteq \pi'$ for irredundant π, π' and $F' \models \pi{:}\sigma$ if $\theta(\delta(\pi, \bar{q})) = \sigma$. This is enough to show that $F \sqsubseteq F'$. Thus F is a most general satisfier of ϕ and hence an alphabetic variant of $MGSat(\phi)$. $\square$

Much of the information in $Desc(F)$ is redundant, but $Desc(F)$ has nice closure properties that are useful in proving the completeness of the equational proof system we define in the next section. In particular, the set of hooks is *prefix closed* so that if $\pi_1\pi_2$ is a hook of F, then so is π_1. When we introduce descriptive normal forms in the next section, it will be obvious that $Desc(F)$ is in such a normal form.

Having characterized the behavior of non-disjunctive descriptions, we now consider the general case in which disjunctions may be present. The first thing to notice is that disjunction can be adequately modeled as a form of non-determinism; trying to find a satisfier for a disjunctive description involves finding a satisfier to one of the disjuncts. This corresponds to the pure notion of OR-non-determinism in logic programs, which is particularly efficient and straightforward to implement with parallel architectures. The fact that descriptions are finite means that an arbitrary description has a finite set of most general satisfiers because it can have at most finitely many disjunctions. A similar result was first proved by Rounds and Kasper (1986).

Theorem 4.7 (Disjunctive Most General Satisfiers)

There is a total function MGSats mapping descriptions to sets of pairwise incomparable feature structures such that $F' \models \phi$ if and only if $F \sqsubseteq F'$ for some $F \in MGSats(\phi)$.

Proof: We proceed by induction on the total number of disjunctions in ϕ. In the base case, suppose that ϕ contains no disjunctions. We can then set:

$$MGSats(\phi) = \begin{cases} \{MGSat(\phi)\} & \text{if } \phi \text{ is satisfiable} \\ \emptyset & \text{otherwise} \end{cases}$$

Obviously $F' \models \phi$ if and only if there is some $F \in MGSats(\phi)$ such that $F \sqsubseteq F'$ because $F \in MGSats(\phi)$ if and only if $F = MGSat(\phi)$.

For the inductive step, suppose $\phi = \psi \vee \xi$. Then set:

$$MGSats(\psi \vee \xi) = Min(MGSats(\psi) \cup MGSats(\xi))$$

where, in general, $Min(S)$ is taken to be the collection of minimal elements of S. We can now see that $F \models \phi$ if and only if $F \models \psi$ or $F \models \xi$. Suppose that $F' \models \psi$ (an analogous argument applies if $F \models \xi$). Then by the induction hypothesis, there is an element $F \in MGSats(\psi)$ such that $F \sqsubseteq F'$. Now since $MGSats(\psi \vee \xi)$ is defined to be the minimal elements of $MGSats(\psi) \cup MGSats(\xi)$, there is an element $F'' \in Min(MGSats(\psi) \cup MGSats(\xi))$ such that $F'' \sqsubseteq F$, and hence $F'' \sqsubseteq F'$. $\qquad\qquad\qquad\square$

Of course, the elements of $MGSats(\phi)$ are unique up to alphabetic variance. This result gives us the following characterization of $Sat(\phi)$:

$$(5) \quad Sat(\phi) = \{F' \in \mathcal{F} \mid F \sqsubseteq F' \text{ for some } F \in MGSats(\phi)\}$$
$$= \bigcup_{F \in MGSats(\phi)} \{F' \in \mathcal{F} \mid F \sqsubseteq F'\}$$

Thus $Sat(\phi)$ can be seen to be a finite union of principal filters in the subsumption ordering of the feature structures.

Proof Theory

Now that we have a handle on the notion of satisfaction, we turn to a syntactic characterization of the notion of logical equivalence. Recall that two descriptions are logically equivalent if and only if they have the same set of satisfiers. The obvious question to ask now that we have a logic is whether or not this logic has a sound and complete axiomatization. Luckily, Rounds and Kasper (1986) provided a sound logic for feature structures that was nearly complete (they missed only an extensionality axiom, which we discuss in the chapter on extensionality), and Pollard (in press) later extended this logic to the case of ordered types. In this section we present an exposition of Pollard's logic, which is complete for the feature structure interpretations we provided in the last section, which in turn were based on the notion of feature structure in Pollard and Moshier (1990).

Our logic is purely equational in that the only descriptions it contains are equations between attribute-value descriptions. In general, an *equation* is of the form $\phi \Leftrightarrow \psi$ where $\phi, \psi \in$ Desc (of course, $\phi \Leftrightarrow \psi$ is just a convenient notation for the ordered pair $\langle \phi, \psi \rangle$). We let Eq be the collection of all such equations. We now endeavor to present a more or less standard sequent-based version of equational logic. In particular, we consider a theory generated by a set of axioms, which is derived by applying the standard deduction schemes for equality to the axioms. If $\Delta \subseteq$ Eq and $\phi \in$ Eq, then $\Delta \vdash \phi$ is said to be a *deduction rule*. As usual, we write $\vdash \phi \Leftrightarrow \psi$ for $\emptyset \vdash \phi \Leftrightarrow \psi$ and say that $\vdash \phi \Leftrightarrow \psi$ is an *axiom*. When presenting axiomatizations, we even omit the $\vdash$. Our deduction rules are standard in the sense that they show how to soundly reason from a set Δ of premises to a conclusion ϕ. We say that a set $T \subseteq$ Eq of equations is *closed* under a deduction rule $\Delta \vdash E$ if $\Delta \subseteq T$ implies $E \in T$.

The particular deduction rules we employ ensure that $\Leftrightarrow$ behaves like an equivalence relation in that it is required to be reflexive, symmetric and transitive. The only new twist that is introduced in the context of attribute-value logics comes from the fact that we do not have any variables. Instead, paths do an analogous job. We are able to state the standard substitution schemes by cases, as there are so few to consider. We also use *deduction schemes* rather than deduction rules.

Definition 4.8 (Equational Deduction Schemes)

The equational logic deduction rules are instances of the following schemes:

$$\vdash \phi \Leftrightarrow \phi \qquad\qquad\qquad\qquad\qquad\qquad \text{(Reflexivity)}$$

$$\{\phi \Leftrightarrow \psi\} \vdash \psi \Leftrightarrow \phi \qquad\qquad\qquad\qquad \text{(Symmetry)}$$

$$\{\phi \Leftrightarrow \psi, \psi \Leftrightarrow \xi\} \vdash \phi \Leftrightarrow \xi \qquad\qquad\qquad \text{(Transitivity)}$$

$$\{\phi \Leftrightarrow \phi', \psi \Leftrightarrow \psi'\} \vdash (\phi \wedge \psi) \Leftrightarrow (\phi' \wedge \psi') \qquad \text{(Conjunctive Substitutivity)}$$

$$\{\phi \Leftrightarrow \phi', \psi \Leftrightarrow \psi'\} \vdash (\phi \vee \psi) \Leftrightarrow (\phi' \vee \psi') \qquad \text{(Disjunctive Substitutivity)}$$

$$\{\phi \Leftrightarrow \phi'\} \vdash \pi{:}\phi \Leftrightarrow \pi{:}\phi' \qquad\qquad\qquad \text{(Path Value Substitutivity)}$$

The first set of schemes ensures that $\Leftrightarrow$ is an equivalence relation, and the substitutivity schemes allow logically equivalent descriptions to be freely substituted within a description. The general substitution scheme for standard equational logic is as follows:

(6) $\{\phi \Leftrightarrow \phi'\} \vdash \psi \Leftrightarrow \psi[\phi \mapsto \phi']$ (General Substitutivity)

We take $\psi[\phi \mapsto \phi']$ to be the result of replacing every occurrence of ϕ in ψ with ϕ'. Since we do not have any quantifiers or variables, there are no complications to attend to concerning free and bound variables. We could replace our individual substitutivity schemes with the general substitutivity scheme.

We say that the *theory* generated by a set $\mathcal{D} \subseteq$ Eq of equational axioms is the least set $\mathbf{Th}(\mathcal{D})$ containing $\mathcal{D}$ and closed under the equational deduction rules. We can provide two equivalent definitions of $\mathbf{Th}(\mathcal{D})$, one in terms of least fixed points and one in terms of proofs.

Theorem 4.9

$\mathbf{Th}(\mathcal{D}) = \bigcup_{n \in \omega} \mathbf{Th}^n(\mathcal{D})$ *where:*

- $\mathbf{Th}^0(\mathcal{D}) = \mathcal{D}$

- $\mathbf{Th}^{n+1}(\mathcal{D}) = \mathbf{Th}^n(\mathcal{D}) \cup \{E \mid \Delta \subseteq \mathbf{T}^n(\mathcal{D}), \Delta \vdash E$ *is an equational rule*$\}$

Proof: This is an instance of Tarski's classic fixed point argument. We first show that $\mathbf{Th}(\mathcal{D})$ is closed under the deduction rules and contains $\mathcal{D}$. It contains $\mathcal{D}$ because $\mathcal{D} = \mathbf{Th}^0(\mathcal{D}) \subseteq \mathbf{Th}(\mathcal{D})$. So suppose $\Delta \vdash E$ is an equational rule and $\Delta \subseteq \mathbf{Th}(\mathcal{D})$. Then $\Delta \subseteq \mathbf{Th}^n(\mathcal{D})$ for some n because Δ must be finite. Thus $E \in \mathbf{Th}^{n+1}(\mathcal{D})$ and hence $E \in \mathbf{Th}(\mathcal{D})$.

To show that $\mathbf{Th}(\mathcal{D})$ is the least such set containing $\mathcal{D}$ and closed under the deductional rules, we show that for any such set $\mathcal{T}$ containing $\mathcal{D}$ and closed under the equational deduction rules, we have $\mathbf{Th}(\mathcal{D}) \subseteq \mathcal{T}$. We do this by showing that $\mathbf{Th}^n(\mathcal{D}) \subseteq \mathcal{T}$ for every $n \in \omega$ by induction on n. Obviously, $\mathbf{Th}^0(\mathcal{D}) = \mathcal{D} \subseteq \mathcal{T}$. Now suppose that $\mathbf{Th}^n(\mathcal{D}) \subseteq \mathcal{T}$. Then we must have $\mathbf{Th}^{n+1}(\mathcal{D}) \subseteq \mathcal{T}$ because the only elements in $\mathbf{Th}^{n+1}(\mathcal{D})$ that are not in $\mathbf{Th}^n(\mathcal{D})$ are those that follow from one of the equational deduction rules and hence must be in $\mathcal{T}$ if $\mathbf{Th}^n(\mathcal{D}) \subseteq \mathcal{T}$. Thus, since each $\mathbf{Th}^n(\mathcal{D}) \subseteq \mathcal{T}$, we must have $\mathbf{Th}(\mathcal{D}) \subseteq \mathcal{T}$. □

We can now formalize the notion of a proof in the usual way. Intuitively, a proof is a sequence of equations which are either instances of an axiom scheme or derived from earlier equations in the sequence by applications of the deduction schemes.

Definition 4.10 (Proof)

The sequence $E_1, \ldots, E_n$ is a proof of the equation E_n from the axioms $\mathcal{D} \subseteq$ Eq, if for every E_i either $E_i \in \mathcal{D}$ is an axiom or $(\Delta \vdash E_i)$ is an equational deduction rule for some $\Delta \subseteq \{E_1, \ldots, E_{i-1}\}$.

We write $\vdash_{\mathcal{D}} E$ if there is a proof of E from $\mathcal{D}$ and say that E is *provable* from or a *theorem* of $\mathcal{D}$. We have the following standard technical lemma relating provability from and membership in the theory generated by a set of equational axioms. That is, a description is provable from a set of axioms if and only if it is a member of the theory generated by that set of axioms.

Theorem 4.11

$\vdash_{\mathcal{D}} E$ *if and only if* $E \in \mathbf{Th}(\mathcal{D})$.

Proof: We first show that if $E_1, \ldots, E_n$ is a proof of E_n, then $E_n \in \mathbf{Th}(\mathcal{D})$. We can show this by induction. $E_1 \in \mathbf{Th}(\mathcal{D})$ because it must be the case that $E_1 \in \mathcal{D}$ or E_1 is an instance of the reflexivity deduction rule (which is an axiom). Then if $E_i \in \mathbf{Th}(\mathcal{D})$ it should be obvious that $E_{i+1} \in \mathbf{Th}(\mathcal{D})$ because $\mathbf{Th}(\mathcal{D})$ is closed under the equational deduction rules and contains $\mathcal{D}$, and E_{i+1} is either in $\mathcal{D}$ or follows by applying a deduction rule to elements already known to be in $\mathbf{Th}(\mathcal{D})$.

Conversely, suppose $E \in \mathbf{Th}(\mathcal{D})$. Then we can construct a proof of E from $\mathcal{D}$. We proceed by induction on n. Obviously, if $E \in \mathbf{Th}^0(\mathcal{D}) = \mathcal{D}$, then there is a trivial proof of E. So suppose as an induction hypothesis that if $E' \in \mathbf{Th}^n(\mathcal{D})$, then there is a proof of E'. Now if $E \in \mathbf{Th}^{n+1}(\mathcal{D})$, then either $E \in \mathbf{Th}^n(\mathcal{D})$ and hence has a proof, or is a result of applying the rule $\Delta \vdash E$ where $\Delta \subseteq \mathbf{Th}^n(\mathcal{D})$. But each equation in Δ must have a proof by the induction hypothesis, so that concatenating all of these proofs and tacking E onto the end is a proof of E. $\square$

We now provide a complete axiomatization of the logical behavior of feature structures. This axiomatization is only a slight variant of the axiomatization of feature structures developed by Pollard (in press). We separate the presentation of the axioms into those for bounded distributive lattices, those for path equations, those for path values, and, finally, those for types. We let $\mathcal{E}_{\mathcal{F}}$ stand for the collection of axioms generated by these axiom schemes. Thus we write $\vdash_{\mathcal{E}_{\mathcal{F}}} \phi \Leftrightarrow \psi$ if it is possible to prove the equation $\phi \Leftrightarrow \psi$ from the axioms given below using the equational deduction schemes.

1. Distributive Lattices with $\top$ and $\bot$

    (a) Top
    $$\phi \vee \top \Leftrightarrow \phi \qquad \phi \wedge \top \Leftrightarrow \top$$

    (b) Bottom
    $$\phi \vee \bot \Leftrightarrow \bot \qquad \phi \wedge \bot \Leftrightarrow \phi$$

    (c) Commutativity
    $$\phi \vee \psi \Leftrightarrow \psi \vee \phi \qquad \phi \wedge \psi \Leftrightarrow \psi \wedge \phi$$

    (d) Associativity
    $$(\phi \vee \psi) \vee \xi \Leftrightarrow \phi \vee (\psi \vee \xi) \qquad (\phi \wedge \psi) \wedge \xi \Leftrightarrow \phi \wedge (\psi \wedge \xi)$$

    (e) Idempotency
    $$\phi \vee \phi \Leftrightarrow \phi \qquad \phi \wedge \phi \Leftrightarrow \phi$$

(f) Absorption

$$(\phi \vee \psi) \wedge \phi \Leftrightarrow \phi \qquad (\phi \wedge \psi) \vee \phi \Leftrightarrow \phi$$

(g) Distributivity

$$\phi \wedge (\psi \vee \xi) \Leftrightarrow (\phi \wedge \psi) \vee (\phi \wedge \xi) \qquad \phi \vee (\psi \wedge \xi) \Leftrightarrow (\phi \vee \psi) \wedge (\phi \vee \xi)$$

2. Path Equations

(a) Trivial Reflexivity

$$\bot \Leftrightarrow (\epsilon \doteq \epsilon)$$

(b) Restricted Reflexivity

i. $(\pi_1 \pi_2 \doteq \pi_3) \Leftrightarrow (\pi_1 \pi_2 \doteq \pi_3) \wedge (\pi_1 \doteq \pi_1)$

ii. $\pi : \bot \Leftrightarrow \pi \doteq \pi$

(c) Symmetry

$$\pi_1 \doteq \pi_2 \Leftrightarrow \pi_2 \doteq \pi_1$$

(d) Transitivity

$$\pi_1 \doteq \pi_2 \wedge \pi_2 \doteq \pi_3 \Leftrightarrow \pi_1 \doteq \pi_2 \wedge \pi_2 \doteq \pi_3 \wedge \pi_1 \doteq \pi_3$$

(e) Restricted Substitutivity

i. $\pi_1 \doteq \pi_2 \wedge \pi_1 : \phi \Leftrightarrow \pi_1 \doteq \pi_2 \wedge \pi_2 : \phi$

ii. $\pi_1 \doteq \pi_2 \wedge \pi_3 \doteq \pi_1 \pi_4 \Leftrightarrow \pi_1 \doteq \pi_2 \wedge \pi_3 \doteq \pi_2 \pi_4$

3. Path Values

(a) Path Concatenation

$$\pi_1 : (\pi_2 : \phi) \Leftrightarrow \pi_1 \pi_2 : \phi$$

(b) Inconsistency Propagation (Top "Smashing")

$$\pi : \top \Leftrightarrow \top$$

(c) Logical Path Distributivity

$$\pi : \phi \wedge \pi : \psi \Leftrightarrow \pi : (\phi \wedge \psi) \qquad \pi : \phi \vee \pi : \psi \Leftrightarrow \pi : (\phi \vee \psi)$$

(d) Equation Path Distributivity

$$\pi : (\pi_1 \doteq \pi_2) \Leftrightarrow \pi \pi_1 \doteq \pi \pi_2$$

4. Types

(a) Consistent Type Conjunction

$$\sigma \wedge \tau \Leftrightarrow \rho \qquad [\text{if } \sigma \sqcup \tau = \rho]$$

(b) Inconsistent Type Conjunction

$$\sigma \wedge \tau \Leftrightarrow \top \qquad [\text{if } \sigma \sqcup \tau \text{ does not exist}]$$

A few comments are in order on this axiomatization. The first group of axioms capture the fact that conjunction and disjunction display the logical behavior of a distributive lattice with top and bottom elements. Conjunction behaves exactly as the dual of disjunction according to the axioms. The description ⊤ represents inconsistent information, while its dual, ⊥, represents the lack of information. ⊤ is an identity for disjunction while ⊥ is the identity for conjunction.

Next consider the axioms for path equations. The reflexivity axioms just ensure that any path that is defined is equivalent to itself. The trivial reflexivity axiom accounts for the empty path, which has a value for every feature structure. The restricted reflexivity axioms account for paths introduced by path equations and those introduced by value descriptions. The transitivity and symmetry axioms just ensure that structure sharing is an equivalence relation. The substitutivity axioms account for the purely extensional behavior of paths by stating that a path used in a path equation or value description can be replaced by any equivalent path.

The first axiom for path values states that the appearance of an inconsistency at any level of substructure guarantees the inconsistency of the whole. This carries out what Aït-Kaci dubbed the "smashing" of inconsistent Ψ-terms into one representative labeled ⊤. The second pair of axioms states that conjunctions and disjunctions distribute over paths, and the last equation guarantees that path equations also distribute over paths.

The last set of axioms captures the restrictions placed on feature structures by the type hierarchy. We treat type conjunction as type unification in our logic. There is an implicit assumption here that pairs of types which have no explicitly specified join are logically inconsistent and are thus equated with ⊤. It is important to note that we do not interpret type disjunction in the logic as generalization (meet) in the type hierarchy. Generalizations might lose information as we saw in the chapter on type hierarchies. Instead, we have a much more discriminating logic based on the non-deterministic definition of disjunction in the satisfaction definition. This behavior is characterized by the equations for disjunction as a distributive lattice operation. Our notion of disjunction is based on the logical treatment of Kasper and Rounds (1986, 1990). Pollard and Moshier (1990) provide an extensive discussion of the relation between disjunction and generalization, part of which we summarize below in the chapter on domain theoretic approaches to feature structures.

We next show that our logic is sound over the class of feature structures. That is, if two descriptions are provably equivalent, then they must be logically equivalent in that they describe exactly the same collection of feature structures.

Theorem 4.12 (Soundness)

If $\vdash_{\mathcal{E}_{\mathcal{F}}} \phi \Leftrightarrow \psi$, *then* $\models \phi \equiv \psi$.

Proof: It suffices to go through the various axioms and show that if a feature structure satisfies the left hand side of an equation, then it satisfies the right hand side and conversely. We provide some examples, and leave the rest to the reader.

Consider the distributive lattice axioms. These follow from the way in which we have defined conjunction and disjunction. For instance, to show that

$F \models \phi \vee \bot$ iff $F \models \phi$, it suffices to note that $F \models \bot$ for any feature structure F. The commutative, associative and idempotent laws are all straightforward. Distributivity is not much harder. Suppose that $F \models \phi \wedge (\psi \vee \xi)$. Then $F \models \phi$ and $F \models (\psi \vee \xi)$, so that $F \models \psi$ or $F \models \xi$. Suppose $F \models \psi$, then $F \models \phi \wedge \psi$ so that $F \models (\phi \wedge \psi) \vee (\phi \wedge \xi)$ and similarly if $F \models \xi$.

The path equality axioms are also straightforward. Trivial reflexivity is automatic since every feature structure F is defined at the empty path, and hence is such that $F@\epsilon = F@\epsilon$. Suppose $F \models \pi:\phi$. Then $F@\pi$ must be defined so that $F \models \pi \doteq \pi$, so restricted reflexivity holds. Symmetry and transitivity are straightforward again due to the fact that the order of paths in path equations does not come into the satisfaction definitions. Consider the first case of restricted substitutivity and suppose that $F \models \pi_1 \doteq \pi_2 \wedge \pi_1:\phi$. Then since $F@\pi_1 = F@\pi_2$, and $F@\pi_1 \models \phi$, we must have $F@\pi_2 \models \phi$ and hence $F \models \pi_2:\phi$.

The path value axioms are equally straightforward. The first follows from the fact that $F \models \pi_1:(\pi_2:\phi)$ if and only if $F@\pi_1 \models \pi_2:\phi$ if and only if $(F@\pi_1)@\pi_2 \models \phi$ if and only if $F@\pi_1\pi_2 \models \phi$. The second axiom follows because there is no feature structure which satisfies $\top$ and hence none that could satisfy $\pi:\top$, since if $F \models \pi:\top$, then $F@\pi \models \top$, which is impossible. The distributivity of conjunctions and equalities is easy to verify. For instance, $F \models \pi:(\pi_1 \doteq \pi_2)$ if and only if $F@\pi \models \pi_1 \doteq \pi_2$ if and only if $(F@\pi)@\pi_1 = (F@\pi)@\pi_2$ if and only if $F@\pi\pi_1 = F@\pi\pi_2$ if and only if $F \models \pi\pi_1 \doteq \pi\pi_2$.

The sort axioms are somewhat more subtle. For instance, if $F \models \sigma \wedge \tau$, then $F \models \sigma$ and $F \models \tau$, so that the sort of the root of F is more specific than either σ or τ, which means it must be more specific than their least upper bound or join. Similarly, if no such join exists, the conjunction is not satisfiable. $\quad\square$

Note that we cannot characterize disjunction soundly in terms of the inheritance hierarchy, because it is possible to have $F \models (\sigma \sqcap \tau)$ without having $F \models \sigma$ or $F \models \tau$. The relation between disjunction and inheritance is discussed more deeply in the context of knowledge representation systems by Borgida and Etherington (1989) and for feature structures by Pollard and Moshier (1990).

We now take up the problem of finding a normal form for our descriptions. The fact that we are able to put our descriptions into a disjunctive normal form allows us to test their equivalence effectively. Before tackling descriptions with disjunctions, we first consider the case of non-disjunctive descriptions. Like most normal form theorems, ours is rather technical in its details.

Definition 4.13 (Descriptive Normal Form)

A description ϕ is in descriptive normal form *iff $\phi = \top$ or:*

$$\phi = (\pi_1:\sigma_1 \wedge \cdots \wedge \pi_n:\sigma_n) \wedge (\rho_1 \doteq \rho_1' \wedge \cdots \wedge \rho_m \doteq \rho_m')$$

where:

- *$\{\pi_i \mid 1 \leq i \leq n\}$ is the set of hooks of ϕ indexed so that $\pi_i \neq \pi_j$ if $i \neq j$*

- *the $\sigma_i \in$ Type are maximal such that $\vdash_{\mathcal{E}_{\mathcal{F}}} \phi \Leftrightarrow \phi \wedge \pi_i:\sigma_i$*

- *$\rho_i \doteq \rho_i'$ occurs uniquely in ϕ if $\vdash \phi \Leftrightarrow \phi \wedge \rho_i \doteq \rho_i'$ and $\rho_i, \rho_{i'}$ are hooks*

Remember that a hook is a path which does not contain any cyclic proper prefixes. Also note that the set of hooks is prefix closed so that if $\pi_1\pi_2$ is a hook, then so is π_1. Recall that a path which is not a hook is said to be redundant. We can define hooks syntactically by saying that π is a hook if we do not have $\pi = \pi_1\pi_2\pi_3$ for some $\pi_2 \neq \epsilon$ such that:

(7) $\vdash_{\mathcal{E}_{\mathcal{F}}} \phi \Leftrightarrow \phi \wedge \pi_1\pi_3 \doteq \pi_1\pi_2\pi_3$

We use hooks in our normal form theorem in the same way that we used them in the describability theorem. Also note that in the second condition on normal forms, we assume $\pi_i \neq \pi_j$ rather than requiring that $\pi_i \doteq \pi_j$ does not hold, which is quite different. It may be the case that $\pi_i \doteq \pi_j$ for two hooks π_i and π_j such that $\pi_i \neq \pi_j$. Also note that if $\sigma_i \in$ Type, then $\sigma_i \neq \top$.

Theorem 4.14 (Non-Disjunctive Normal Form)

If $\phi \in$ Desc is a description with no disjunctions, then there is a descriptive normal form description $NF(\phi)$ such that:

$$\vdash_{\mathcal{E}_{\mathcal{F}}} \phi \Leftrightarrow NF(\phi)$$

Proof: We show how to effectively construct $NF(\phi)$ from ϕ in a way that preserves provable logical equivalence.

First, it is necessary to convert ϕ to a form containing two conjuncts, the first of which only contains descriptions of the form $\pi:\sigma$, and the second of which only contains descriptions of the form $\rho \doteq \rho'$. To see that this is possible, we define a simple rewriting system that uses axioms of $\mathcal{E}_{\mathcal{F}}$ to transform descriptions according to the following provable equivalences applied left to right:

$$\sigma \Leftrightarrow \epsilon:\sigma$$
$$\pi:\pi':\phi \Leftrightarrow \pi\pi':\phi$$
$$\pi:(\pi' \doteq \pi'') \Leftrightarrow \pi\pi' \doteq \pi\pi''$$
$$\pi:(\phi \wedge \psi) \Leftrightarrow \pi:\phi \wedge \pi:\psi$$

Repeated application of these equivalences and the transitivity scheme results in conjuncts of the desired form, which can then be rearranged into two groups using the schemes for the commutativity and associativity of conjunction.

Next, we trim the conjunct that consists of descriptions of the form $\pi:\sigma$ so that it consists of only irredundant paths occurring uniquely. First note that to reduce any duplicate path entries we can use the logical equivalence:

$$\vdash_{\mathcal{E}_{\mathcal{F}}} \pi:\sigma \wedge \pi:\tau \Leftrightarrow \pi:\gamma$$

where $\gamma = \sigma \sqcup \tau$ if it exists, and $\gamma = \top$ otherwise. If at any stage during the construction of $NF(\phi)$ we arrive at $\top$, we can simply stop, since $NF(\phi) = \top$ in this case. Now suppose that we have a redundant path value description of the form $\pi = \pi_1\pi_2\pi_3$ for some non-empty π_2 such that $\vdash_{\mathcal{E}_{\mathcal{F}}} \phi \Leftrightarrow \phi \wedge \pi_1\pi_2\pi_3 \doteq \pi_1\pi_3$. We can then replace $\pi_1\pi_2\pi_3:\sigma$ with $\pi_1\pi_3:\sigma$ by using the restricted substitutivity axiom. The repeated application of this process leads to a non-redundant set of paths, since every redundant path can be eliminated. Similarly, to make sure that the set of paths is prefix closed and hence contains all of the hooks, we know that $\vdash_{\mathcal{E}_{\mathcal{F}}} (\pi\pi':\sigma) \Leftrightarrow (\pi:\bot) \wedge (\pi\pi':\sigma)$, by applying both restricted reflexivity axioms, and thus all of the necessary prefixes can be added.

We can use the same sort of rules to reduce the set of path equivalences to those involving only non-redundant paths. This is because if π is redundant, then $\pi = \pi_1\pi_2\pi_3$ for some non-empty π_2 such that $\vdash_{\mathcal{E}_{\mathcal{F}}} \phi \Leftrightarrow \phi \wedge \pi \doteq \pi_1\pi_3$, so that we have $\vdash_{\mathcal{E}_{\mathcal{F}}} \pi \doteq \rho \Leftrightarrow \pi_1\pi_3 \doteq \rho$.

Next, we add all of the information into the path descriptions that can be gained from the path equivalences. That is, if $\pi \doteq \pi'$ is a conjunct, then we replace $\pi:\sigma \wedge \pi':\sigma'$ with $\pi:\tau \wedge \pi':\tau$, where $\tau = \sigma \sqcup \sigma'$ if this exists and $\tau = \top$ otherwise. Since there is only a finite number of equivalences, this process stabilizes after a finite number of iterations.

Now, if the final result of this process contains an occurrence of $\top$, then the whole description is equivalent to $\top$ by applying the rules for $\top$. If the result does not contain $\top$, then it is in descriptive normal form, because we have made sure that all of the conditions were met one by one. The main thing to verify is that we cannot derive any more specific sorts in our path value descriptions. But this is obvious, because we have allowed the rules that could extend these sorts to apply until they could not provide any more information. $\quad\square$

Of course, the normal form produced is unique up to the order of conjuncts.

There are alternative ways in which normal forms could be defined. First, we could replace a description of the form $\pi:\sigma$ with one of the form $f_1:(f_2:(\cdots(f_n:\phi)))$ if $\pi = f_1 f_2 \cdots f_n$, by applying the path concatenation axiom. Thus our logic would be just as expressive if we allowed only descriptions of the form $f:\phi$ and not those of the form $\pi:\phi$. Alternatively, it follows from the normal form theorem that we could have restricted descriptions of the form $\pi:\phi$ to the case $\pi:\sigma$ in which σ was a type.

We are now in a position to provide a completeness result for the non-disjunctive portion of our logic. Completeness entails that if two descriptions are logically equivalent, then they are provably equivalent.

Theorem 4.15 (Non-Disjunctive Completeness)

If ϕ and ψ are non-disjunctive and $\models (\phi \equiv \psi)$, then $\vdash_{\mathcal{E}_{\mathcal{F}}} (\phi \Leftrightarrow \psi)$.

Proof: In case ϕ and ψ are unsatisfiable, then both $\vdash_{\mathcal{E}_{\mathcal{F}}} \phi \Leftrightarrow \top$ and $\vdash_{\mathcal{E}_{\mathcal{F}}} \psi \Leftrightarrow \top$, so that $\vdash_{\mathcal{E}_{\mathcal{F}}} \phi \Leftrightarrow \psi$ by transitivity.

Now suppose that ϕ is satisfiable, and that:

$$NF(\phi) = (\pi_1:\sigma_1 \wedge \cdots \wedge \pi_n:\sigma_n) \wedge (\rho_1 \doteq \rho_1' \wedge \cdots \wedge \rho_m \doteq \rho_m')$$

We can use this normal form to get at $MGSat(\phi)$ by defining a feature structure $F = \langle \{\pi_1, \ldots, \pi_n\}/\doteq, [\epsilon]_{\doteq}, \delta, \theta \rangle$ such that:

- $\delta(f, [\pi]_{\doteq}) = [\pi'f]_{\doteq}$ where $\pi \doteq \pi'$ is in $NF(\phi)$ and $\pi'f \in \{\pi_1, \ldots, \pi_n\}$

- $\theta([\pi_i]_{\doteq}) = \sigma_i$

In this definition, we are thinking of the occurrences of $\pi \doteq \pi'$ as determining an equivalence relation over the set of hooks. Thus we take $\{\pi_1, \ldots, \pi_n\}/_{\doteq}$ to be the set of hooks modulo this equivalence, and $[\pi]_{\doteq} = \{\pi' \mid \pi \doteq \pi'\}$ to be the equivalence class generated by π consisting of all of the hooks equivalent to π. We must first show that F is a feature structure. Note that $\doteq$ as defined by the clauses of the normal form is an equivalence relation over the paths given. This means that δ is well defined, because if $[\pi]_{\doteq} = [\pi']_{\doteq}$, then $\delta(f, [\pi]_{\doteq}) = \delta(f, [\pi']_{\doteq})$. By the same kind of reasoning we can see that if $[\pi]_{\doteq} = [\pi']_{\doteq}$, then $\pi : \sigma$ and $\pi' : \sigma$ show up as clauses for some σ in a normal form, because the occurrence of different sorts at the end of shared paths would lead to a contradiction of the sort maximality condition in normal forms, so that $\theta([\pi]_{\doteq}) = \theta([\pi']_{\doteq}) = \sigma$. This means that F is a feature structure.

Now by the way that we have defined F, we obviously have $F \models \phi$, because F satisfies each conjunct of $NF(\phi)$. F is also the most general such satisfier of ϕ, because reducing any sort or removing any node or arc from F would leave some clause of $NF(\phi)$ unsatisfied. Thus $F \sim MGSat(\phi)$ is an alphabetic variant of the most general satisfier of ϕ. Because ψ also has a normal form, if we suppose that $NF(\phi) \neq NF(\psi)$, then $MGSat(\phi) \not\sim MGSat(\psi)$, and hence $\not\models \phi \equiv \psi$. Thus if $\models \phi \equiv \psi$, then $\vdash_{\mathcal{E}_{\mathcal{F}}} NF(\phi) \Leftrightarrow NF(\psi)$, and hence we can conclude $\vdash_{\mathcal{E}_{\mathcal{F}}} \phi \Leftrightarrow \psi$ by transitivity. $\square$

Notice that this result has the most general satisfier theorem as an immediate consequence. We presented the most general satisfier theorem on its own earlier, since the constructive proof that we gave there is more natural and closer to the details of a sensible satisfaction algorithm. Unification is the important operation in conjunctive descriptions, whereas disjunctions cause non-determinism by inducing a branch in the space in which the search for a satisfier is being conducted.

We can now extend our result to the general case of descriptions possibly containing disjunctions by defining a normal form for these descriptions.

Theorem 4.16 (Disjunctive Normal Form)

For every description ϕ, there is a disjunctive normal form *description:*

$$DNF(\phi) = \phi_1 \vee \cdots \vee \phi_n$$

such that each ϕ_i is in descriptive normal form and:

$$\vdash_{\mathcal{E}_{\mathcal{F}}} \phi \Leftrightarrow DNF(\phi)$$

Proof: We can use the following axioms from left to right to push all of the disjunctions to the top level:

$$\phi \wedge (\psi \vee \xi) \Leftrightarrow (\phi \wedge \psi) \vee (\phi \wedge \xi)$$
$$\pi : (\phi \vee \psi) \Leftrightarrow \pi : \phi \vee \pi : \psi$$
$$\phi \vee \top \Leftrightarrow \phi$$

We are thus left with a description of the form $\phi'_1 \vee \cdots \vee \phi'_n$ which is logically equivalent to ϕ. Each of the ϕ'_i can then be put into descriptive normal form using the substitution rule for disjunction. $\square$

This now gives us two ways to decide whether or not two descriptions are logically equivalent: we can compute their most general satisfiers or we can compute their normal forms. Of course these two approaches are not really distinct. One way to think of the most general satisfiers is as a particularly compact way of representing the disjuncts of a normal form description.

We pull a useful corollary out of this theorem that says that any two inconsistent descriptions have the same normal form, namely ⊤.

Corollary 4.17 (Equivalence of Inconsistent Descriptions)

If ϕ is an unsatisfiable description, then $\vdash_{\mathcal{E}_{\mathcal{F}}} \phi \Leftrightarrow \top$.

A consequence of the disjunctive normal form theorem is a general completeness result for our logic:

Theorem 4.18 (Completeness)

If $\models \phi \equiv \psi$, then $\vdash_{\mathcal{E}_{\mathcal{F}}} \phi \Leftrightarrow \psi$.

Proof: If $\nvdash_{\mathcal{E}_{\mathcal{F}}} DNF(\psi) \Leftrightarrow DNF(\phi)$, then there must be a disjunct of $DNF(\phi)$ which is more general than some disjunct of $DNF(\psi)$, or vice versa. Because we can read the most general satisfiers directly from $DNF(\phi)$ in the same way that we can read the most general satisfier from $NF(\phi)$, we would have $MGSats(\phi) \neq MGSats(\psi)$, so that $\nvDash \phi \equiv \psi$. □

Part II

Extensions

Chapter 5

Acyclic Feature Structures

In this chapter we consider acyclic feature structures and their axiomatization. In standard first-order logic resolution theorem provers (see Wos et al. 1984 for an overview), it is necessary to make sure that when a variable X is unified with a term t, there is no occurrence of X in t. This is the so-called *occurs check* and dates back to Robinson's (1965) original algorithm for unification. Without the occurs check, resolution produces unsound inferences. The problem with the occurs check is that it is often expensive to compute in practical unification algorithms. Unification algorithms have been developed with built-in occurs checks that are linear (Paterson and Wegman 1978) and quasi-linear (Martelli and Montanari 1982), but the data structures employed for computing the occurs check incur a heavy constant overhead (Jaffar 1984). Rather than carry out the occurs check, implementations of logic programming languages like Prolog simply omit it, leading to interpreters and compilers which are not sound with respect to the semantics of first-order logic and may furthermore cause the interpreters to hang during the processing of cyclic structures which are accidentally created. Rather than change the interpreters, the move made in Prolog II (Colmerauer 1984, 1987) was to change the semantics to allow for *infinite rational trees*, which correspond to the infinite unfoldings of the terms that result from unifications of a variable with a term that contains it. Considering the pointer-based implementation of unification (Jaffar 1984, Moshier 1988), infinite trees are more naturally construed as finite graphs containing cycles. For example, the result of unifying X and $f(a, X)$ would be a record structure whose function symbol f points to the symbol table entry for f and whose second argument value pointer points back to itself. The alternative representations are presented in Figure 5.1. The cyclic graph representation in Figure 5.1(b) is the natural one that we have been considering for feature structures. We now consider what must be done to get rid of cycles, if that is the desired behavior of the system. In the PATR-II system (Pereira and Shieber 1984) and the system developed by Rounds and Kasper (1986), it was assumed that the feature structures were (directed) acyclic graphs. Thus cycles were not allowed. Moshier (1988) modified their treatment to allow for the possibility of cycles. The equational logic models of Johnson (1988), Smolka (1988), and

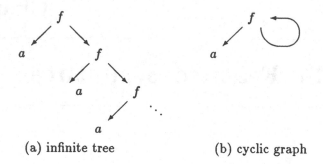

(a) infinite tree   (b) cyclic graph

Figure 5.1. Representations of X in $X = f(a, X)$.

King (1989), on the other hand, allowed cycles in general, although Johnson (1988:50) showed how acyclicity could be axiomatized in his system.

To begin, we must update the definition of feature structures.

Definition 5.1 (Acyclic Feature Structure)

$F = \langle Q, \bar{q}, \theta, \delta \rangle$ is a cyclic *feature structure if there is a non-empty path π and a node $q \in Q$ such that $\delta(\pi, q) = q$, and acyclic otherwise.*

Let $\mathcal{AF}$ denote the set of acyclic feature structures.

Because the acyclic feature structures are a strict subset of the feature structures, we do not have to change our definition of path values, subsumption, satisfaction, and so on. These operations remain well-defined for acyclic feature structures. On the other hand, unification changes slightly in that unifications that would produce cycles should now fail. Luckily, the collection of acyclic feature structures still admits finite bounded joins. This means that any pair of acyclic feature structures which can be extended to a common acyclic feature structure can be extended to a least such structure.

Theorem 5.2 (Acyclic Unification)

If F and F' are acyclic feature structures with an acyclic upper bound, then $F \sqcup F'$ is acyclic.

Proof: If $(F \sqcup F')$ contains a cycle, then any F'' such that $F \sqsubseteq F''$ and $F' \sqsubseteq F''$ must also be such that $(F \sqcup F') \sqsubseteq F''$. Hence F'' must contain a cycle. Thus F and F' have an acyclic upper bound if and only if $(F \sqcup F')$ is acyclic.   □

In practice, unifying acyclic feature structures amounts to applying an occurs check during or after the unification process. Paterson and Wegman's (1978) linear algorithm uses doubly-linked lists to keep track of the subterms of a term (or similarly, the substructures of a feature structure). The occurs check then simply amounts to making sure that no term ever becomes a subterm of itself.

We can relativize our semantics to acyclic feature structures in the obvious way, by interpreting everything relative to $\mathcal{AF}$. In particular, we let $Sat_{\mathcal{AF}}(\phi) = Sat(\phi) \cap \mathcal{AF}$, and then write $\models_{\mathcal{AF}} \phi \equiv \psi$ if and only if $Sat_{\mathcal{AF}}(\phi) = Sat_{\mathcal{AF}}(\psi)$. We can relativize our notions of satisfiability and validity in a similar manner.

When relativizing our semantics to acyclic feature structures, it is still the case that every satisfiable non-disjunctive description that is satisfied by some acyclic feature structure is satisfied by a most general acyclic feature structure. In fact, we can even use the same function $MGSat$ to find it. We simply inspect $MGSat(\phi)$ and if it is cyclic, then ϕ cannot be satisfied by an acyclic feature structure, since every feature structure that satisfies it extends $MGSat(\phi)$ and hence contain a cycle.

Theorem 5.3 (Acyclic Most General Satisfiers)

$MGSat(\phi) \in \mathcal{AF}$ *for every* $\mathcal{AF}$-*satisfiable non-disjunctive description* ϕ.

Proof: The proof goes through exactly as before, but with acyclic feature structure unification replacing feature structure unification. In particular, whenever a cycle is encountered, the construction of the most general satisfier fails rather than constructing the cyclic satisfier. If a cycle is encountered in the construction of the most general satisfier, it is not possible to construct a feature structure that satisfies the description, as every satisfier must extend the most general satisfier and hence contains a cycle. ☐

This leads to the fact that the most general satisfiers theorem for possibly disjunctive descriptions goes through just as before. Obviously monotonicity is still preserved, because we are only considering a particular subset $\mathcal{AF} \subseteq \mathcal{F}$ of the feature structures.

We can provide an axiomatization of the acyclic feature structures by the addition of a single axiom scheme to our axiomatization of feature structures. We let $\mathcal{E}_{\mathcal{AF}}$ be the collection of axioms generated from the axiom schemes for feature structures in $\mathcal{E}_{\mathcal{F}}$ and the instances of the following axiom scheme (numbered in sequence with previous axioms):

5. Acyclicity

    (a) $\pi_1 \pi_2 \doteq \pi_1 \Leftrightarrow \top$ [π_2 non-empty]

Intuitively, this axiom allows us to derive a contradiction, represented by $\top$, whenever we can derive the fact that there is a cycle. This cycle can be arbitrarily embedded; the acyclicity axiom is equivalent to the axiom:

(1) $\pi_1 : (\pi_2 \doteq \epsilon) \Leftrightarrow \top$ [π_2 non-empty]

The equivalence stems from the fact that $\pi_1 \pi_2 \doteq \pi_1 \Leftrightarrow \pi_1 : (\pi_2 \doteq \epsilon)$ is an instance of the path sharing distributivity axiom.

The acyclicity axiom is enough to completely characterize the logical behavior of acyclic feature structures. Recall that we write $\vdash_{\mathcal{E}_{\mathcal{AF}}} \phi \Leftrightarrow \psi$ if we can prove $\phi \Leftrightarrow \psi$ from the axioms in $\mathcal{E}_{\mathcal{AF}}$.

Theorem 5.4 (Acyclic Soundness and Completeness)

$\models_{\mathcal{AF}} \phi \equiv \psi$ *if and only if* $\vdash_{\mathcal{E}_{\mathcal{AF}}} \phi \Leftrightarrow \psi$.

Proof: Soundness is obvious by the definition of acyclicity, which simply parallels the acyclicity axiom.

For completeness there are two cases to consider, depending on whether the descriptions are satisfiable or unsatisfiable with respect to the acyclic feature structures. Unsatisfiability with respect to the acyclic structures can arise in one of two ways. The first is when they are unsatisfiable with respect to the possibly cyclic feature structures. In this case, the description would be provably equal to ⊤ using only axioms in $\mathcal{E}_{\mathcal{F}}$. The other possibility is that the most general satisfier contains a cycle. In this case, we can derive the normal form, and it contains a path sharing description of the form $\pi_1 \pi_2 \doteq \pi_1$ for some non-empty π_2, in which case the normal form can be converted to ⊤ using the acyclicity axiom scheme.

Now suppose that the descriptions are satisfiable. In this case, their logical equivalence can be proven using only axioms in $\mathcal{E}_{\mathcal{F}}$ because they have equivalent normal forms.   □

Although we cannot yet adequately model first-order terms because we have considered neither appropriateness nor extensionality, we need to assume acyclicity to model them in the proper way.

Chapter 6

Appropriateness and Typing

Up to now, our presentation of feature structures has been fairly standard. In particular, our feature structures are identical to the finite sorted feature structures introduced by Pollard and Moshier (1990) and axiomatized by Pollard (in press). In terms of the informational ordering that they produce, our feature structures (modulo alphabetic variance) are nothing more than a notational variant of the Ψ-terms of Aït-Kaci (1984, 1986) (modulo tag renaming and top "smashing," with a bounded complete partial order of types). The important thing to note about the feature structures is that although we allowed a combination of primitive information with type symbols and structured information in terms of features and their values, there was no notion of typing; arbitrary labelings of directed graphs with type symbols and features were permissible.

In this chapter we introduce our notion of typing for feature structures, which is based on the notion of typing introduced informally by Pollard and Sag (1987:38) for the HPSG grammar formalism. Pollard and Sag introduced appropriateness conditions to model the distinction between features which are not appropriate for a given type and those whose values are simply unknown. Note that since appropriateness is defined as a relation between types and features, we say both that types are appropriate for features or that features are appropriate for types. We have already seen how the type symbols themselves are organized into a multiple inheritance hierarchy and how information from the types interacts with information encoded structurally in terms of features and values. In this chapter, we introduce a notion of appropriateness in which we require that every type be specified only for the features for which it is appropriate, and allow types to provide restrictions on the values of their features. We require our appropriateness conditions to respect the inheritance hierarchy in that there must be a least type at which a feature is introduced, and also require that if a feature is appropriate for a type that it is appropriate for all of its subtypes. In HPSG, for instance, there is a type for linguistic signs with two subtypes for words and phrases. Signs are appropriate for phonological (or orthographic), syntactic, and semantic features. Thus words and phrases must also allow values for these attributes. But phrases introduce an additional feature for their daughters, which is used to represent information about constituent structure. Viewed from this perspective, our appropriateness specifications carry out the task originally delegated to feature co-occurrence restrictions in GPSG (Gazdar et al. 1985, Gazdar et al. 1988).

Our system is object-oriented according to the criteria set forward by Cardelli and Wegner (1985). The analogy with functional programming languages comes from thinking of feature structures as our data objects and thinking of features as unary functions over these objects. The criteria posed by Cardelli and Wegner are that there be a *strong* notion of typing (every object must come with a type), *data abstraction* (objects are only accessed using their named functions and their implementation details are hidden from the user), and *inheritance-based polymorphism* (functions defined for one type are also applicable to subtypes). Inheritance-based polymorphism is a particular kind of *universal* (as opposed to ad hoc) polymorphism, typically referred to as *inclusion* or *vertical* polymorphism. Polymorphism is referred to as universal if the same basic operation (or code) can be applied to every type of object over which the operation is defined. *Ad hoc* polymorphism, on the other hand, takes two forms. The first uses type *coercion* to convert an object of one type to another type so that an operation can be applied to it (such as the operation which converts an array to a pointer, or a pointer to an integer in the C programming language). Another form of ad hoc polymorphism is *overloading*, in which the same symbol stands for a number of different operations and is simply ambiguous in a way which must be determined by the compiler. Usually universally polymorphic functions apply to an infinite number of data types, but our system is particularly simple in that we assume a finite number of types from the outset. Universal polymorphism is usually divided into inclusion polymorphism of the sort we provide here, and *parametric polymorphism*, which we do not support. An instance in which parametric types would be useful is in representing different kinds of lists. The way to encode lists in our system is to define a type **list** for lists with two subtypes, **ne-list** and **e-list** for non-empty and empty lists, respectively. A non-empty list would have values for the features HEAD and TAIL, which would represent the first element of a list and the remainder of the list, respectively. The tail value would be required to be an object of type **list**, whereas the head value would be unrestricted (or equivalently, restricted to the universal type, $\perp$). Thus **e-list** is playing the role of the atom *NIL* in Lisp, and **ne-list** is playing the role of the *CONS* or dotted pair constructor, though in Lisp there is not a type restriction on the tail (*CDR*) of a list. In applications of feature structures such as HPSG, there are usually many different kinds of lists that are used, such as lists of phonological tokens representing utterances, lists of categories representing information about complements, and so on. It would be nice to have a parametric version of the list type, say **list**(α), for which the parameter (type variable) α ranged over types which represent the kinds of elements in the list (see, for example, Mycroft and O'Keefe (1984) or Pollard (1990)). That is, **list**(α) would have subtypes **e-list** and **ne-list**(α) and the head value of a feature structure of type **ne-list**(α) would have to be of type α. While it would not be impossible to define a notion of parametric polymorphism within our framework, we exclude it for two reasons. The first has to do with our intuitions about the appropriate factorization of information between the types and the feature structures. With parametric polymorphism, hierarchical unification that should be handled with feature structures could be fully captured using only parametric types (and nothing else). This is because parametric types are naturally modeled by (possibly higher-order) terms with respect to their ordering; type equations that then arise from trying to provide types for objects of unknown types are then carried out by unification to find minimal well-typings. With parametric types, this unification could take over the job of feature structure unification. The second reason is purely technical and is due to the fact that parametric types present problems for type inference in the case of cyclic feature structures if parametric types are not themselves allowed to be cyclic. Simply consider what the value for α would have to be for the following list:

(1)
$$\begin{bmatrix} \boxed{1} \, \text{list}(\alpha) \\ \text{HEAD:} [\boxed{1}] \\ \text{TAIL:} [\boxed{1}] \end{bmatrix}$$

In finding a minimal type for which this is well-typed we would most likely attempt to unify α and $\text{list}(\alpha)$, leading either to an infinite regress or a cyclic parametric type. Another problem for typing cyclic structures comes from an example like:

(2)
$$\begin{bmatrix} \boxed{1} \, \sigma(\alpha) \\ \text{F:} [\boxed{1}] \end{bmatrix}$$

If the appropriateness constraint was that the value of an f for a type $\sigma(\alpha)$ object had to be of type $\sigma(\sigma(\alpha))$ we would run into an infinite loop trying to find a minimal type for the feature structure in (2).

We present two notions of typing, one of which is more restrictive than the other. In the less restrictive version, we simply require that every feature that occurs is appropriate and takes an appropriate value. A feature structure which meets this less restrictive condition is said to be *well-typed*. In the more restrictive version, we require the converse so that every feature which is appropriate must be present. A well-typed feature structure meeting the more restrictive condition is said to be *totally well-typed*. Both of our type schemes are *strong* in this sense that they require every feature structure to come with a type.

Both of our notions of typing support a well-defined operation of type inference. This means that given a non-disjunctive logical description of a feature structure, which might be impoverished in terms of its type specifications, a unique (up to alphabetic variance) most general (totally) well-typed feature structure can be inferred. This means that we can maintain our representation of the satisfiers of descriptions using well-typed most general satisfiers.

The variety of type inference we provide for descriptions of our logic should be contrasted with systems that perform a much more general form of type inference in which the type scheme itself is inferred from a program or grammar specification, thus allowing the user to avoid considering types altogether. We require the user to fully specify the system of types; our type scheme does not accept an untyped grammar or program and deduce a type system that is consistent with it. Of course, any of the methods in the section on constructing type inheritance hierarchies may be used to specify the type hierarchy. These more general forms of type inference have been investigated in the context of Prolog (Mishra 1984, Xu and Warren 1988), but are not really tractable in the present context. The reason is that appropriateness as we conceive of it is not decidable in grammar formalisms such as PATR-II or HPSG (in the form presented by Pollard and Moshier (1990) without appropriateness constraints). This result follows from the relevant version of the halting problem for these grammars, which states that it is not generally possible to decide whether or not any given category can be assigned to some string. We prove these undecidability results in the chapters on applications of feature structures.

There are good reasons for requiring the user to follow such a rigorous type discipline, some theoretical and some practical. We consider a number of these reasons. When engineering a knowledge representation system, coding a logic program or writing a natural language grammar, untyped systems are usually organized by the designer into implicit categories. The incorporation of a typing system enforces these conventions and detects errors that come from misspellings, misplaced constraints, or other violations of the type system. The benefit of this is that simple error checking can be performed, but this may be a drawback in small applications. The system presented here is a true generalization of untyped feature structure or term unification systems in that a single type can be defined which is appropriate for all features and allows these features to take arbitrary values. This kind of degenerate typing models the situation in the untyped case. Explicitly providing a tight definition of the types involved in a program makes the program more structured and hence easier to understand and debug. Enforcing a strict type discipline ensures that type conventions that were implicit in untyped systems are not accidentally violated. Another major benefit of typed systems is that they allow memory to be managed in an efficient manner. With the types defined beforehand by the user, compact representations for feature structures can be determined at compile time. For instance, instead of using unordered lists of feature-value pairs as is usual in implementations of feature structures, positional encodings or record structures can be used to encode feature values with consequent reductions in both access time when searching through lists of features and the amount of memory that needs to be allocated for pointers to represent these lists. Similarly, when the type of a feature structure is known, the amount of memory that is needed to represent it can be determined and efficiently allocated or recovered. One of the standard benefits of typing, data abstraction, is not really an issue in the case of feature structures, since there is really only one kind of underlying data structure, the feature structure. The only real abstraction we derive is that we know exactly which features might be defined for any given type of feature structure and need not be concerned with their internal representation as lists or record structures.

Before going on to provide a formal characterization of our type scheme, we review the brief history of type systems for feature structures. The first feature structure unification-based grammar systems, Functional Unification Grammar (FUG) (Kay 1979, 1984, 1985) and PATR-II (Shieber et al. 1983, Shieber 1984), suffered from the problem that every object was either an atom, and thus could not be defined for any features at all, or it was a feature structure and thus could take values for completely arbitrary collections of features. This led to problems in both generation and analysis, as unwanted features could always be added to a feature structure. The standard instance of this problem occurs in generation when an attempt is made to generate a phrase meaning that John sneezed, and the string *John sneezed Bill* is generated because the addition of an object does not cause a failure. To get around this problem, a special built-in atom **none** was added to FUG which was assigned as the value of "undefined" features. The systems of feature structures developed by Kasper and Rounds (1986) and Moshier (1988) and the Ψ-terms of Aït-Kaci (1984) were also untyped in this sense and suffered from the same shortcomings.

Elhadad (1990) introduced an extension to FUG in which the user was allowed to specify a simple type hierarchy without multiple inheritance (basically a tree) and to specify for each type which features were appropriate for it. A preprocessor then added in the atomic value **none** for all of the features which were not appropriate for a given type. Although the system behaves as a typed system from the point of view of the user, it does not provide an adequate solution to the typing problem because the "undefined" features and their **none** values have to be carried around like excess baggage at run time. Because of this, a system with a large number of features would incur a significant amount of overhead. The system also behaved strangely in that subtypes could not be made appropriate for more features, but had to be defined for the same or fewer features. This was because the **none** declarations were inherited as if they were value restrictions. This runs counter to the notion of function inheritance in object-oriented type specifications, in which a function defined for a type is always defined for any subtype. A similar notion of typing to that of Elhadad was devised by Langholm (1989), who introduced a notion of *negative extended* feature structures. The negation at stake here allowed a set of features to be attached to each node of a feature structure with the interpretation that no extension of the feature structure could be defined for these features. This approach suffers from the same drawbacks as Elhadad's, being only marginally more efficient.

The Lexical Functional Grammar (LFG) formalism (Kaplan and Bresnan 1982) added special completeness and coherence conditions, which were adopted because of the schematic nature of their constituent structure (C-structure) rules. To prevent intransitive verb from occurring with direct objects, feature structures representing the semantics of an intransitive verbs were required to have their subject feature filled (*completeness*), but not their object feature (*coherence*). This was not a systematic solution to the problem of appropriateness and was only applied to their F-structures to capture the notion of grammatical function and its relation to phrase structure.

To get around the difficulties faced by these general-purpose unification formalisms, the Generalized Phrase Structure Grammar (GPSG) formalism of

Gazdar et al. (1985, 1988) employed a notion of *feature co-occurrence restriction* (FCR). For instance, to avoid getting a subcategorization feature on a maximal projection, an FCR of the form [BAR: 2] $\supset$ ¬[SUBCAT] was used. The interpretation of this FCR is that if the bar-level feature BAR had a value of 2, then the subcategorization feature SUBCAT was undefined. To prevent a verb form from appearing on a nominal category, the FCR [VFORM] $\supset$ [+V, −N] was used. The range of possible FCRs in GPSG was very broad and heterogenous, being used not only to restrict appropriateness conditions but also particular values embedded arbitrarily deeply in a structure. The language in which FCRs were stated was quite expressive and included disjunction, implication, and negation and also a modal operator to allow them to operate arbitrarily deep into a structure (see Kracht 1988 and Reape 1991) for further connections to modal logic). Luckily, it was fairly easy to see that the issue of whether or not a feature structure met an FCR was decidable in polynomial time (Gazdar et al. 1988). The problem with the GPSG notion of FCR was primarily that the collection of feature structures meeting all of the FCRs was not particularly well behaved. In particular, there is no guarantee of a unique unifier (least upper bound) for two consistent feature structures. Another problem with the FCRs of GPSG was that they did not truly form a type theory in the usual sense, but just carved out an arbitrary set of feature structures for consideration by the grammar. GPSG also did not allow unbounded recursion in feature values, resulting in a finite collection of admissible feature structures. Finally, GPSG represented arbitrary categories as trees and did not allow re-entrant structures. Tomita and Knight (1987) refer to these tree-based systems as *pseudo-unification* grammars. There was simply not a GPSG tree-based feature structure that could represent exactly the information contained in our description $\pi \doteq \pi'$, but only feature structures that met the description by virtue of having type identical structures for the sub-trees arrived at by following the paths π and π' from the root.

Moshier (1988) modified the notion of atom found in the previously mentioned formalisms to allow atoms to label arbitrary feature structures. Pollard and Moshier (1990) then defined a system in which these atoms were ordered according to their specificity. This resulted in the collection of data objects which we have called feature structures. Working from the perspective of frame-based knowledge representation systems, Aït-Kaci (1984, 1986) defined a notion of Ψ-term which is similar to the systems of Pollard and Moshier, especially when considering Moshier and Round's (1987, Moshier 1988) definition of abstract feature. The Ψ-terms modulo top "smashing" and tag renaming formed an informational ordering isomorphic to the finite feature structures of Pollard and Moshier, which are just our feature structures. But all of these systems did nothing to alleviate the problem of inappropriate features showing up where they did not belong.

One of the earliest systems of feature structures that was truly typed was that developed by Calder (1987, Moens et al. 1989) in the context of Unification Categorial Grammar (UCG) (Zeevat et al. 1987), which was developed independently of, but with surprising parallels to HPSG (see below). Calder was motivated by the problems faced by FUG and LFG in requiring certain features to be absent in some situations, and also by the problems faced in developing a consistent and well-structured large-scale grammar in an untyped system. Under Calder's type scheme, a set of declarations was given that independently specified the features that were appropriate for each type and which values were appropriate for each feature. This allowed UCGs to be translated into term unification grammars and efficiently implemented in Prolog. The drawback of Calder's system was that there was no mechanism for unique type inference, though an algorithm was given for compile-time type checking to make sure that no explicit type conflicts ever arose in a feature structure. Of course, Calder's system, being compiled into Prolog, did not allow cyclic feature structures or negation and incorporated the Prolog notion of extensional identity conditions. It also did not take into account inheritance-based polymorphism that comes from ordering the types according to specificity.

To provide theoretical foundations for Head-driven Phrase Structure Grammar (HPSG), Pollard and Sag (1987) provided the first notion of feature structures incorporating multiple inheritance and appropriateness conditions. Unfortunately, their presentation was not formalized. For instance, they do not state precise conditions on the inheritance hierarchy, but obviously have multiple inheritance in mind. Furthermore, they do not state precise conditions on appropriateness, though they explicitly state that types should pick out their appropriate features and place restrictions on their values. They also explicitly allow types to introduce features not inherited from their supertypes and place additional restrictions on the values of features that they do inherit. One way to view the present work is as an attempt to flesh out the informal presentation of Pollard and Sag (1987).

A formal foundation for HPSG was developed by King (1989). Starting from the logical framework of Smolka (1988), King chose to partition the domain of feature structures into a number of disjoint maximally specific types, which he called *species*. More general types were then specified as sets of species. We discussed the formalization of King's type hierarchy in the chapter on generating inheritance hierarchies. Appropriateness was then specified for each of his species in terms of the features that were appropriate for it and the set of possible value species that they could take. The notion of speciation employed by King could be employed in the present context as a methodology for specifying particular kinds of inheritance hierarchies and appropriateness conditions.

Only fairly recently, proposals have been put forward for providing a type mechanism for Prolog. The two major branches of this research can be traced to Mishra (1984) and Mycroft and O'Keefe (1984), respectively. In Mishra's system, regular tree automata specify monomorphic type schemes which can be inferred from totally untyped Prolog programs. Our type scheme is broadly similar to Mishra's in that we place weak restrictions on the form of feature structures that are allowable in terms of feature structures themselves. Also, there is no way in either Mishra's system or ours to specify information such as the fact that the value of two features has to be of the same type without specifying what that type is (of course, the addition of parametric polymorphism would remedy this omission). The major difference between our system and Mishra's is that we require the user to specify the types explicitly rather than writing untyped programs and allowing a compilation stage to infer the intended type scheme, as is done in programming languages such as ML (Milner 1978). The major drawback to inferring type schemes from untyped programs in a unification-based logic context is that it can be done only by using very weak methods which do not provide a very good approximation of the meaning of the program. The work following Mishra's has been directed toward uncovering better algorithms for automatically inferring type schemes from programs that provide closer approximations to the meanings of programs. The basic ideas behind these schemes is that a type system should provide an approximation to the success set of a predicate in that a predicate only succeeds on inputs that are well-typed.

With quite different goals in mind, Mycroft and O'Keefe (1984) define a method for user-specified type schemes based on parametric polymorphism. Smolka (1988b), in developing a typed logic programming language, extends the work of Mycroft and O'Keefe by adding inclusion polymorphism based on notions derived from order-sorted algebra (Meseguer et al. 1987). Our notion of typing is slightly different from theirs in that we carry around data structures which wear their types on their sleeves in the sense that our feature structures consist of an "ordinary" feature structure paired with a type symbol. This approach is termed *semantic* by Smolka (1988b), because the underlying notion of untyped unification is changed to account for the contribution of the type information. Smolka's approach to typing is very powerful in that it allows both inclusion polymorphism with multiple inheritance and also parametric polymorphism with type functions and variables.

Our notion of typing probably shares the most with the approach to automated theorem proving taken by Walther (1985, 1988), which is based on order-sorted unification. An order-sorted algebra is like an ordinary multi-sorted algebra in that it partitions the carrier (the set of objects over which the operations are defined) into overlapping sorts and allows these sorts to be organized into a multiple inheritance hierarchy. Rather than just providing a simple arity in a signature (which is the algebraic equivalent of a type scheme), each function must specify the type of each of its arguments and the types of its result. The restrictions on signatures for order-sorted algebras which ensure that unification is well defined and produces a unique minimum resulting term are similar to the restrictions we place on our type hierarchies and appropriateness conditions, which are our analogue of (sorted) algebraic signatures. One significant difference between order-sorted algebra and our type system is that we do not have a positional encoding of features and do not require all of the subtypes of a type to have the same number of arguments or features. Another major difference stems from the fact that appropriateness conditions in order-sorted algebras can provide value restrictions for a function which vary with respect to the sorts of its arguments (Meseguer et al. 1987). For instance, a one-place function symbol f can be required to have a value of type τ_1 for an argument of type σ_1 and required to have a value of type τ_2 for an argument of type σ_2. We cannot exactly model this form of type inference in our system;

the best we can do is provide two different (possibly comparable) types with different appropriateness conditions. An interesting line of future research, begun by Reape (1989), would be to study the analogue of allowing equational axioms to be "built in" rather than employing the feature structure analogue of the totally free algebra (see Plotkin 1972, Walther 1986, Meseguer et al. 1987, Gallier and Isakowitz 1988, Siekmann 1989).

Finally, it should be noted that our definition of types is very similar to the notions of inheritance hierarchies with roles that are used in associative inheritance-based knowledge representation systems (Brachman 1979). The primary application of semantic networks in artificial intelligence is in constructing hybrid reasoning systems. A number of such systems, all of which have descended from KL-ONE (Brachman and Schmolze 1985), have emerged in recent years, the most notable among them being KRYPTON (Brachman et al. 1983), KL-TWO (Vilain 1985), KANDOR (Patel-Schneider 1984), NIKL (Moser 1983), LOOM (Mac Gregor 1988, 1990), BACK (Luck et al. 1987, Nebel 1988) and CLASSIC (Borgida et al. 1989, Brachman et al. 1991). The common ground among these systems is that they employ structures like semantic networks to determine a conceptual scheme, or *terminological* system, that can be used for reasoning. These systems all employ an operation of *classification*, the purpose of which is to decide where an object can be placed in the conceptual hierarchy based on what is known about it. In some respects, classification is like our notion of type inference, but is usually much more powerful in terms of the kinds of inferences that it is allowed to perform. It is usually assumed that the process of classifying an object is efficiently computable, or decidable at the very least (Brachman 1979, Brachman and Schmolze 1985, Schmidt-Schauß 1989, Brachman and Levesque 1984, Patel-Schneider 1984, Nebel 1988). Once a conceptual hierarchy is in place, it is used to make statements about domain objects in the *assertional* component of the representation system. The assertional component of systems such as LOOM or KRYPTON allows statements to be made with the concepts introduced in the terminological component by means of a first-order-logic-like language in which the predicates are replaced by concepts. The connections between the kind of representation of feature structures that we allow here and the terminological knowledge representation systems currently gaining favor in the artificial intelligence community is an area that deserves a significant amount of attention in the future (see Aït-Kaci 1984, 1986, Kasper 1989, Nebel and Smolka 1989), especially in the light of systems with very restrictive terminological components such as CLASSIC, whose basic operations and language look very similar to our description language and unification, subsumption, and type inference operations.

Appropriateness

We now turn our attention to the presentation of our system for specifying appropriateness conditions on types. Recall that our appropriateness conditions are meant to specify the features that are appropriate for each type and provide

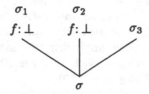

Figure 6.1. Unacceptable Appropriateness Conditions.

restrictions on their values in a way that respects the inheritance hierarchy. We model appropriateness conditions with a partial function *Approp* mapping features and types to types, where $Approp(f, \sigma)$ specifies the most general type of value that the feature f can have for an object of type σ. Before saying more about what it means to be well-typed, we provide a definition of just what kinds of functions can serve as appropriateness specifications.

Definition 6.1 (Appropriateness Specification)

An appropriateness specification *over the inheritance hierarchy* $\langle$Type, $\sqsubseteq$ $\rangle$ *and features* Feat *is a partial function Approp*: Feat $\times$ Type $\rightarrow$ Type *that meets the following conditions:*

- (Feature Introduction)
  for every feature $f \in$ Feat, there is a most general type $Intro(f) \in$ Type such that $Approp(f, Intro(f))$ is defined

- (Upward Closure / Right Monotonicity)
  if $Approp(f, \sigma)$ is defined and $\sigma \sqsubseteq \tau$, then $Approp(f, \tau)$ is also defined and $Approp(f, \sigma) \sqsubseteq Approp(f, \tau)$

We consider the clauses of this definition in order. The first clause, feature introduction, is to ensure that type inference (defined below) is well-defined. In particular, it ensures that if all we know about a feature structure is that it has a value for the feature f, which we might learn if we were told only that it satisfied the description $f: \perp$, then we would need to be able to determine the most general type that such a feature structure might have. The obvious choice is the most general type for which that feature is defined, and $Intro(f)$ is that type. Without the existence of such a most general type, we would not be able to derive a most general satisfier for the description $f: \perp$. By the feature introduction condition we are assured that if a feature structure F of type σ is defined for the feature f, then $Intro(f) \sqsubseteq \sigma$. For instance, consider what would happen with a type σ with subtypes σ_1, σ_2, and σ_3. Now suppose that the feature f was appropriate for σ_1 and σ_2, but not σ_3. We depict this situation in Figure 6.1. We have simply assumed that the feature f is typed to $\perp$ throughout. The appropriateness conditions occur under the types in the diagram. With this assumption, we would not be able to find a most general satisfier for the description $\sigma \wedge f: \perp$. The type of the most general satisfier

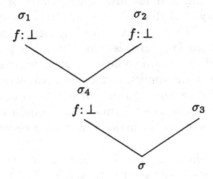

Figure 6.2. Acceptable Appropriateness Conditions.

would have to be either σ_1 or σ_2, but we would not be able to determine which. This could lead to a great deal of non-determinism solely because of the appropriateness conditions. To rule out this possibility, we assume that for every feature there is a most general type for which it is appropriate. To achieve the logical behavior of the example, we would instead need to break σ down into subtypes σ_4 and σ_3, with σ_4 further divided into the subtypes σ_1 and σ_2. Then we could assume that σ_4 was the minimal type at which f was introduced and this would allow us to infer that the type of the most general feature structure which satisfied $\sigma \wedge f: \perp$ was σ_4. This situation is illustrated in Figure 6.2. The general solution outlined in Figure 6.2 seems reasonable if we consider more concrete cases. For instance, suppose σ_1 and σ_2 in Figure 6.1 stood for cats and dogs respectively, and the feature f was for the favorite meat of the animal. If the type σ was simply for mammals, it would be unnatural to force the type σ to be appropriate for favorite meat. Instead, the solution in Figure 6.2 can be adopted in which the new type σ_4 stands for meat-eating animals. Now σ_3 might consistently be the type of horses or simply the generic type of vegetarian animal.

Note that another way of specifying the feature introduction condition would be to assume that the types appropriate for any given feature were closed under meets, as this would allow us to define $Intro(f)$ by:

(3) $Intro(f) = \bigsqcap \{\sigma \in \mathsf{Type} \mid Approp(f, \sigma) \text{ defined}\}$

The second condition we place on the appropriateness specification is that it be upward closed and monotonic (in its type argument) with respect to value specifications. This captures our intuitive notion of subtyping, as it requires any feature that is appropriate for a type to also be appropriate for all of its subtypes and to provide restrictions on values at least as strict as all of their supertypes, as is standard in object-oriented type systems. Thus it should be obvious that the two conditions taken together ensure that the set of types $\{\sigma \mid Approp(f, \sigma) \text{ is defined}\}$ appropriate for a given feature f forms a principal filter generated by $Intro(f)$ (of course, every filter in a finite BCPO is principal).

In addition to requiring that features appropriate for a type are also appropriate for every subtype of that type, we allow subtypes to place stronger restrictions on the value of features than were imposed on their supertypes. An example from programming languages is that addition is guaranteed to provide a floating point value when applied to floating point numbers, but is known to provide an integer value when applied to integers. An example from linguistics would be that the major category feature of a sign would be known to be a category, but the major feature of a nominal sign would be guaranteed to be some nominal category, whereas the major feature of a verbal sign would always be a verbal category.

The easiest way in which an actual system could allow a user to specify appropriateness conditions would be simply to allow features to be attached to arbitrary types in the inheritance hierarchy and to place arbitrary restrictions on their values. Then inheritance closure could be performed to derive an appropriateness specification in which a feature would be taken to be appropriate for a type if it was appropriate for any of its supertypes. This is very similar to the kind of reasoning introduced by Fahlman (1979) in the context of his NETL inheritance-based knowledge representation system. The value restriction on a feature at a type could be determined by simply unifying the restrictions on all of its supertypes. If there is a most general type at which every feature is introduced, this is guaranteed to produce an appropriateness specification. To ensure that there is such a most general type at which every feature is introduced, the dual of inheritance could be performed so that features were taken to be appropriate for the meet of all of the types for which they are appropriate, with a value restriction determined by taking the meet of all of the restrictions on their subtypes. This strategy could also be employed when embedding an IS(NOT)A hierarchy into a bounded complete partial order.

Well-Typed Feature Structures

We place more stringent conditions on the structure of appropriateness specifications when we come to discuss static typing, but the present conditions are adequate for our notions of well-typing and total well-typing. We now present our formal definition of what it means to be well-typed.

Definition 6.2 (Well-Typedness)

A feature structure $F = \langle Q, \bar{q}, \theta, \delta \rangle$ is said to be well-typed *if whenever $\delta(f, q)$ is defined, $Approp(f, \theta(q))$ is defined, and such that $Approp(f, \theta(q)) \sqsubseteq \theta(\delta(f, q))$.*
Let $\mathcal{TF}$ be the collection of well-typed feature structures.

The well-typedness condition can be recast in terms of our graph-based notation for feature structures as saying that if $q: \sigma \xrightarrow{f} q': \sigma'$ in F, then $Approp(f, \sigma) \sqsubseteq \sigma'$. This requires every feature to be defined for a type for which it is appropriate and provide a value that is at least as specific as the most general type that is appropriate. Note that this does not require any features to be defined; it only restricts the arcs that are present in a feature structure to be appropriate.

We are now in a position to provide an approximation to the atoms used in PATR-II and by Rounds and Kasper (1986); an atom is just a type which is not appropriate for any features. What makes our atoms slightly different is that we have intensional identity conditions; it is possible to have more than one copy of an atom in a feature structure. Thus we can only create atoms that are like the *non-singleton* (copyable) sorts of Smolka (1988). We show how to model uncopyable atoms when we come to discuss identity conditions and intensionality. Our feature structures can also be modeled in the type system by assuming that $Approp(f, \sigma) = \bot$ for every $f \in$ Feat and $\sigma \in$ Type. Every feature structure is well-typed under these appropriateness conditions.

The first thing to note about our type scheme is that it admits a natural notion of type inference. To make this more precise, we say that a feature structure F is *typable* if there is a well-typed feature structure F' such that $F \sqsubseteq F'$. The import of type inference is that if a feature structure is typable, we can find the most general well-typed extension of it.

Theorem 6.3 (Type Inference)

There is a partial function $TypInf : \mathcal{F} \to T\mathcal{F}$ such that for $F \in \mathcal{F}$, $F \sqsubseteq F'$ for $F' \in T\mathcal{F}$ if and only if $TypInf(F) \sqsubseteq F'$.

Proof: Suppose that F contains an arc $q : \sigma \xrightarrow{f} q' : \sigma'$ such that $Approp(f, \sigma)$ is not defined. We must then replace the type σ on q with a more specific type τ such that $Approp(f, \tau)$ is defined. By feature introduction, we know that $Intro(f) \sqsubseteq \tau$, and if the result is to extend F, then we must have $\sigma \sqsubseteq \tau$. But since we want to extend F minimally, we take $\tau = \sigma \sqcup Intro(f)$ if it is well-defined. If the join does not exist, we cannot extend F to a well-typed feature structure as there is no way to extend the type on q in such a way that f is appropriate.

Now suppose that F contains an arc $q : \sigma \xrightarrow{f} q' : \sigma'$ such that $Approp(f, \sigma)$ is defined, but $Approp(f, \sigma) \not\sqsubseteq \sigma'$. Then by the same reasoning as above, we must replace σ' with $\sigma' \sqcup Approp(f, \sigma)$, if it is defined, because this is the minimal value to which we can extend σ' so that the result is appropriate. If the join is not defined, then F is not typable.

We can simply iterate this update process until a join fails or we reach a well-typed feature structure. The iteration must terminate as there only finitely many nodes in F and only finitely many types that extend the type of each node. When the iteration terminates (without any of the joins being undefined), the result must be well-typed, as every feature is appropriate and takes an appropriate value. $\square$

The idea behind type inference is that we iteratively increase types locally until all features and their values are well-typed.

Our type inference function *TypInf* displays a range of useful properties which are worth singling out and providing with a name. These properties are really just the finite portion of the requirements for a domain-theoretic closure operator (see the chapter below on domain theory for more details and a more general result along these lines).

Definition 6.4 (Inference Procedure)

A partial function $Cl: D \rightarrow D$ on a partial order $\langle D, \leq \rangle$ is said to be an inference procedure *if for all $d, d' \in D$, we have:*

- *if $d \leq d'$ and $Cl(d')$ is defined, then $Cl(d)$ is also defined*
  and such that $Cl(d) \leq Cl(d')$ (Monotonicity)

- *$d \leq Cl(d)$ if $Cl(d)$ is defined*   (Increasing)

- *$Cl(Cl(d)) = Cl(d)$ if $Cl(d)$ is defined*   (Idempotency)

Note that the monotonicity condition requires an inference procedure to be defined for a downwardly closed set of objects. In our case, this means that if a feature structure is typable, then so is any generalization of it.

Theorem 6.5 (Inference Procedure)

The function $TypInf: \mathcal{F} \rightarrow \mathcal{F}$ is an inference procedure.

Proof: Suppose that F' is typable so that $TypInf(F)$ is defined, and also suppose that and $F \sqsubseteq F'$. Then by the definition of typability, F is also typable, and hence $TypInf(F)$ is defined by our typability theorem. The second half of the monotonicity condition is obviously satisfied because if $F \sqsubseteq F'$, then the minimal well-typed feature structure which extends F' is at least as specific as the minimal well-typed feature structure which extends F, and hence $TypInf(F) \sqsubseteq TypInf(F')$.

To see that $TypInf$ is increasing, simply notice that $TypInf(F)$ is defined by unifying additional information into F.

It can be seen that $TypInf$ is idempotent by its definition; we stop adding information to F and are left with $TypInf(F)$ only when our iterative procedure cannot contribute any additional information. Thus $TypInf(TypInf(F)) = TypInf(F)$ where $TypInf(F)$ is defined.   □

In what follows, we have cause to examine a number of inference procedures defined similarly to $TypInf$. These other inference procedures can all be shown to be such using arguments analogous to those used for $TypInf$.

Before surveying the benefits of having a type inference procedure, we take the time to note that we can factor $TypInf$ into a two-stage process. We let $TypDom: \mathcal{F} \rightarrow \mathcal{F}$ be the part of the $TypInf$ procedure that raises types so that all of their features are appropriate. That is, in $TypDom(F)$ it is always the case that if $\delta(f, q)$ is defined, then $Approp(f, \theta(q))$ is defined. We then let $TypRan: \mathcal{F} \rightarrow T\mathcal{F}$ be the procedure that takes an output from $TypDom$ and raises all of the values so that if $\delta(f, q)$ is defined, then $Approp(f, \theta(q)) \sqsubseteq \theta(\delta(f, q))$. We can define each of these functions by iterating the relevant steps in the proofs of the type inference theorem. The result is a pair of inference procedures.

Theorem 6.6

The functions $TypDom: \mathcal{F} \rightarrow \mathcal{F}$ and $TypRan: TypDom(\mathcal{F}) \rightarrow TypDom(\mathcal{F})$ are inference procedures.

The significance of these inference procedures is the following corollary to our type inference theorem:

Corollary 6.7 (*TypInf* Factorization)

TypInf = TypRan ∘ TypDom.

Proof: Once we have ensured that all of the features are appropriate using *TypDom*, *TypRan* simply raises the types of values. Because our appropriateness conditions are monotonic, this never results in a feature becoming inappropriate. □

The computationally attractive feature of this factorization of work in type inference is that the work of *TypDom* can be carried out at compile time, due to the fact that we can distribute the operation of *TypDom* over joins.

Theorem 6.8 (*TypDom* Distributivity)

If $F \sqcup F'$ is defined, then:

$$TypDom(F \sqcup F') = TypDom(F) \sqcup TypDom(F')$$

Proof: It suffices to note that:

$$TypDom(F \sqcup F') = TypDom(TypDom(F) \sqcup TypDom(F'))$$
$$= TypDom(F) \sqcup TypDom(F')$$

The reason for this is that the application of *TypDom* to the unification of two feature structures to which *TypDom* has been applied is redundant because of the monotonicity of the appropriateness conditions. □

A simple inductive argument suffices to show that *TypDom* can be cashed out at compile time. First of all, we must assume as a base case that every feature structure we begin with in a computation has had *TypDom* applied to it. We can guarantee that this holds at compile time by simply applying *TypDom*. If we then assume that if at any stage of the computation we have only feature structures drawn from $TypDom(\mathcal{F})$, then we know that the result of carrying out additional unifications does not take us outside of $TypDom(\mathcal{F})$, because if $F, F' \in TypDom(\mathcal{F})$ and $F \sqcup F'$ exists (in $\mathcal{F}$), then $F \sqcup F' \in TypDom(\mathcal{F})$. Thus, at the next stage of computation, we still have only feature structures drawn from $TypDom(\mathcal{F})$.

We now consider the consequences of the fact that we can perform type inference. Just as in the case of acyclic feature structures, the collection of well-typed feature structures is just a subset of the feature structures, so that our definitions of path value, satisfaction and subsumption do not need to be changed. The first fact that is worth noting is that unification is still well-defined when we restrict attention to the partial order of well-typed feature structures under subsumption. That is, for every pair of well-typed feature structures which are consistent with respect to $\mathcal{TF}$, there is a most general well-typed feature structure that extends them both. Thus finite consistent joins

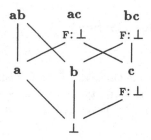

Figure 6.3. Type Hierarchy Where Unification Does Not Preserve Typability.

exist in the collection of well-typed feature structures ordered by subsumption. To compute the well-typed unification of two well-typed feature structures, it suffices to compute their unification in the ordinary way and then apply type inference to the result.

Theorem 6.9 (Well-Typed Unification)

If F, $F' \in \mathcal{TF}$ are well-typed feature structures, then $F'' \in \mathcal{TF}$ is such that $F \sqsubseteq F''$ and $F' \sqsubseteq F''$ if and only if $TypInf(F \sqcup F') \sqsubseteq F''$.

Proof: We know that $F \sqsubseteq F''$ and $F' \sqsubseteq F''$ if and only if $F \sqcup F' \sqsubseteq F''$ by the feature structure unification theorem. We also know that $F'' \in \mathcal{TF}$ is such that $F \sqcup F' \sqsubseteq F''$ if and only if $TypInf(F \sqcup F') \sqsubseteq F''$ by the type inference theorem. Taken together, these facts imply the result.   □

   Unfortunately, the combination of our type inference procedure *TypInf* and our appropriateness conditions is not enough to guarantee that if $F, F' \in \mathcal{F}$ are typable, then $F \sqcup F'$ is also typable. Pollard (personal communication) has provided a counterexample with the type inheritance hierarchy and appropriateness conditions in Figure 6.3. In this case, *TypInf* displays the following behavior:

(4) $TypInf(\begin{bmatrix} \mathbf{a} \\ \text{F:}[\perp] \end{bmatrix}) = \begin{bmatrix} \mathbf{ac} \\ \text{F:}[\perp] \end{bmatrix}$

(5) $TypInf(\begin{bmatrix} \mathbf{b} \\ \text{F:}[\perp] \end{bmatrix}) = \begin{bmatrix} \mathbf{bc} \\ \text{F:}[\perp] \end{bmatrix}$

(6) $TypInf(\begin{bmatrix} \mathbf{a} \\ \text{F:}[\perp] \end{bmatrix} \sqcup \begin{bmatrix} \mathbf{b} \\ \text{F:}[\perp] \end{bmatrix}) = TypInf(\begin{bmatrix} \mathbf{ab} \\ \text{F:}[\perp] \end{bmatrix})$ is undefined

Thus we have an example in which $TypInf(F)$, $TypInf(F')$ and $F \sqcup F'$ (in $\mathcal{F}$) are all well-defined, but $TypInf(F \sqcup F')$ is undefined.

From a procedural point of view, it does not matter how type inference is interleaved with unification. This follows immediately from the well-typed unification theorem.

Corollary 6.10 (Lazy Type Inference)

If $F, F' \in \mathcal{F}$, then $TypInf(TypInf(F) \sqcup F') = TypInf(F \sqcup F')$.

The identity we assume is the standard one for partial functions; either both sides must be undefined or they must both be defined and equal. This result yields:

(7) $\quad TypInf(TypInf(F) \sqcup TypInf(F')) = TypInf(F \sqcup F')$

(8) $\quad TypInf(TypInf(F \sqcup F') \sqcup F'') = TypInf(F \sqcup F' \sqcup F'')$

Using the well-typed unification theorem, we can now go on to show that every non-disjunctive description that can be satisfied by a well-typed feature structure is satisfied by a most general such structure.

Theorem 6.11 (Well-Typed Most General Satisfiers)

For every non-disjunctive description $\phi \in \mathsf{Desc}$ and well-typed feature structure $F \in \mathcal{TF}$, we have $F \models \phi$ if and only if $TypInf(MGSat(\phi)) \sqsubseteq F$.

Proof: From our most general satisfier theorem, we know that $F \models \phi$ for a feature structure $F \in \mathcal{F}$ if and only if $MGSat(\phi) \sqsubseteq F$. Furthermore, we know that $MGSat(\phi) \sqsubseteq F'$ for a well-typed $F' \in \mathcal{TF}$ if and only if $TypInf(MGSat(\phi)) \sqsubseteq F'$. Combining these facts gives us our result. □

Again, the well-typed most general satisfiers theorem ensures that for arbitrary (possibly disjunctive) descriptions we can find a finite set of most general well-typed satisfiers. We can just apply the type inference operation *TypInf* to the elements of $MGSats(\phi)$.

Just as in the case of acyclic feature structures, we can relativize our logical notions to well-typed feature structures. In particular, we let $Sat_{\mathcal{TF}}(\phi) = Sat(\phi) \cap \mathcal{TF}$ and write $\models_{\mathcal{TF}} \phi \equiv \psi$ if and only if $Sat_{\mathcal{TF}}(\phi) = Sat_{\mathcal{TF}}(\psi)$.

We now provide a pair of axiom schemes that characterize logical equivalence with respect to the well-typed feature structures. These axiom schemes correspond to the basic operations of our type inference algorithm. The first says that a feature structure must be of a type specific enough to have every feature for which it is defined, and the second says that the value of every feature must be of the appropriate type for the type of feature structure in which it is defined. We let $\mathcal{E}_{\mathcal{TF}}$ consist of the axioms for feature structures in $\mathcal{E}_{\mathcal{F}}$ along with all of the instances of the following axiom schemes:

6. Well-typedness

    (a) $f : \perp \Leftrightarrow f : \perp \wedge Intro(f)$

    (b) $\sigma \wedge f : \perp \Leftrightarrow \sigma \wedge f : Approp(f, \sigma)$ [$Approp(f, \sigma)$ defined]

Intuitively, the first well-typedness axiom says that the existence of a feature f is enough to infer that we are dealing with a type at least as specific as $Intro(f)$. The second axiom says that if we have a type σ which is appropriate for f and provides a value for f, then the value it provides is at least as specific as that required by the appropriateness conditions. This second axiom may not seem quite strong enough, but the first axiom ensures that we raise the type at any given point enough so that it is appropriate for f. Also, the fact that we can derive $\vdash_{\mathcal{E}_\mathcal{F}} f\!:\!\tau \Leftrightarrow f\!:\!\tau \wedge f\!:\!\bot$ and $\vdash_{\mathcal{E}_\mathcal{F}} f\!:\!\tau \wedge f\!:\!\sigma \Leftrightarrow f\!:\!\tau \sqcup \sigma$ is enough to tell us that we can raise the sort specified as the value for f so that it is appropriate using the second axiom for well-typedness. In particular, we can derive:

(9) $\vdash_{\mathcal{E}_{T\mathcal{F}}} \sigma \wedge f\!:\!\tau \Leftrightarrow \sigma \wedge f\!:\!(\tau \sqcup Approp(f,\sigma))$

Finally, it should be noted that we can derive $\top$ if we are dealing with a description that cannot be satisfied by a well-typed feature structure. The application of inferences using our well-typedness axioms can be made to exactly parallel our type inference algorithm. Thus if there is a subdescription $\sigma \wedge f\!:\!\bot$ derived at some point, and it is impossible to extend σ to some τ such that $Approp(f,\tau)$ is defined, then by applying the first axiom above we can derive:

(10) $\vdash_{\mathcal{E}_{T\mathcal{F}}} Intro(f) \wedge \sigma \Leftrightarrow \top$

It is now straightforward to prove that our axiomatization is sound and complete; we simply need to note that our axiomatization correctly captures our notion of type inference, which we know to characterize the well-typed feature structures.

Theorem 6.12 (Well-Typed Soundness and Completeness)

$\models_{T\mathcal{F}} \phi \equiv \psi$ *if and only if* $\vdash_{\mathcal{E}_{T\mathcal{F}}} \phi \Leftrightarrow \psi$.

Proof: Soundness is obvious from our definition of well-typedness.

To show that the logic is complete, we note that the axioms $\mathcal{E}_\mathcal{F}$ are complete for the feature structures and that the axioms in $\mathcal{E}_{T\mathcal{F}}$ allow us to exactly parallel a step in the type inference procedure. More precisely, if $F \in \mathcal{F}$ is well-typable, then we can show that $\vdash_{\mathcal{E}_{T\mathcal{F}}} Desc(F) \Leftrightarrow Desc(TypInf(F))$. To see this, it is only necessary to note that the updates that are carried out in our procedural characterization of $TypInf$ can be simulated using our axioms for well-typedness.   □

Nothing changes in the case of acyclicity; the acyclicity axioms and well-typedness axioms completely determine the logic of acyclic well-typed feature structures.

Totally Well-Typed Feature Structures

Now that we have considered our notion of well-typedness, we turn our attention to our total well-typedness conditions. The intuition is that a feature structure is totally well-typed if and only if every feature for which it is defined is appropriate and takes an appropriate value and furthermore, every feature which is appropriate must be given a value. The well-typedness conditions do not require any features to exist, but the total well-typedness conditions require as many features as are appropriate to be given values at every node. Thus our well-typed feature structures are more conducive to applications in which many features are appropriate for any given sort, but when there is usually very little known about their values at intermediate stages during a computation. In many applications, totally well-typed feature structures typically arise as the results of successful computations. One instance of this is the HPSG grammar formalism, in which a well-formed sign is totally well-typed; all of the features that are appropriate are given values throughout the structure.

We now present a formal definition of our total well-typedness conditions.

Definition 6.13 (Total Well-Typedness)

$F = \langle Q, \bar{q}, \theta, \delta \rangle \in \mathcal{F}$ is totally well-typed if and only if it is well-typed and if $q \in Q$ and $f \in$ Feat are such that $Approp(f, \theta(q))$ is defined, then $\delta(f, q)$ is defined.

Let TTF be the collection of totally well-typed feature structures.

This parallels our intuitive explanation of total well-typedness. We say that a feature structure $F \in \mathcal{F}$ is *totally typable* if and only if there is some $F' \in TTF$ such that $F \sqsubseteq F'$.

Unlike the situation with type inference, there are cases in which a feature structure is totally typable but has no most general totally well-typed extension. For instance, consider a type specification for representing family members in which a type **pers** for people is assumed to be appropriate for a feature FATHER representing that person's father and restricts its value to be a person, so that $Approp(\text{FATHER}, \textbf{pers}) = \textbf{pers}$ (of course, we could have a more fine-grained hierarchy in which a father had to be of the subtype **man** of **pers**). For instance, consider the following feature structure:

$$(11) \quad \begin{bmatrix} \textbf{pers} \\ \text{NAME:} [\, \textbf{mary} \,] \\ \text{FATHER:} \begin{bmatrix} \textbf{pers} \\ \text{NAME:} [\, \textbf{bill} \,] \end{bmatrix} \end{bmatrix}$$

The structure in (11) is meant to represent the situation in which there is a person named Mary whose father is a person named Bill. Assuming that the types **mary** and **bill** are appropriate for the feature NAME, then the structure in (11) is well-typed. But it is not totally well-typed because the feature FATHER is also appropriate for the node representing the person named Bill, but no value is specified for it. In the simplest case, consider what would happen if we tried to construct a totally well-typed extension of the following simple feature structure:

$$(12) \quad [\, \textbf{pers} \,]$$

We would be led to consider the infinite sequence of structures in Figure 6.4, where we have abbreviated the feature FATHER to FTH. Surprisingly, the feature

$$\left[\,\text{pers}\,\right],\ \begin{bmatrix}\text{pers}\\\text{FTH:}\left[\,\text{pers}\,\right]\end{bmatrix},\ \begin{bmatrix}\text{pers}\\\text{FTH:}\begin{bmatrix}\text{pers}\\\text{FTH:}\left[\,\text{pers}\,\right]\end{bmatrix}\end{bmatrix},\ \dots$$

Figure 6.4. Ascending Chain of Approximate Satisfiers.

$$\begin{bmatrix}\boxed{1}\,\text{pers}\\\text{FTH:}\left[\boxed{1}\right]\end{bmatrix}\sqsupseteq\begin{bmatrix}\text{pers}\\\text{FTH:}\begin{bmatrix}\boxed{1}\,\text{pers}\\\text{FTH:}\left[\boxed{1}\right]\end{bmatrix}\end{bmatrix}\sqsupseteq\begin{bmatrix}\text{pers}\\\text{FTH:}\begin{bmatrix}\text{pers}\\\text{FTH:}\begin{bmatrix}\boxed{1}\,\text{pers}\\\text{FTH:}\left[\boxed{1}\right]\end{bmatrix}\end{bmatrix}\end{bmatrix}\sqsupseteq\cdots$$

Figure 6.5. Descending Chain of Well-Typed Satisfiers.

structure in (12) is totally typable. For instance, consider the following feature structure:

(13) $\begin{bmatrix}\boxed{1}\,\text{pers}\\\text{FATHER:}\left[\boxed{1}\right]\end{bmatrix}$

The problem is that there is not a most general totally well-typed feature structure extending the structure in (12) (when we consider infinite feature structures in the chapter on domains, we see that the most general totally well-typed feature structure extending the one in (12) is infinite, and thus not a member of $\mathcal{F}$). The totally well-typed feature structure in (13) is merely the most specific in an infinitely descending chain of totally well-typed feature structures extending the structure in (12). This chain is displayed in Figure 6.5. Consequently, there is not a most general totally well-typed satisfier of simple descriptions such as **pers** ∧ NAME: **sue** ∧ FATHER FATHER NAME: **bill**. Thus the set of totally well-typed feature structures satisfying a non-disjunctive description is not guaranteed to be a principal filter (but it is a filter, because meets preserve well-typedness). Of course, if we ruled out the incestuous situation in which a person was his or her own ancestor, say by restricting attention to the acyclic feature structures, the simple feature structure in (12) would not have any totally well-typed extension. To distinguish the case in which a feature structure is totally typable from one in which it has a most general well-typed extension, we provide the following definition.

Definition 6.14 (Finite Total Typing)

If F is typable and there is a least well-typed extension of F, then F is said to be finitely totally typable.

Luckily, we can exactly identify the conditions under which a feature structure is totally typable, but not finitely totally typable. These conditions have to do with certain kinds of loops in the appropriateness conditions. We define

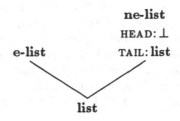

Figure 6.6. Lists: Inheritance and Appropriateness.

a *substructure requirement* relation $SubReq \subseteq \mathsf{Type} \times \mathsf{Type}$ over features as the most general relation such that:

(14) • $SubReq(\sigma, \tau)$ if $Approp(f, \sigma) = \tau$ for some $f \in \mathsf{Feat}$

  • $SubReq(\sigma, \gamma)$ if $Approp(\sigma, \tau)$ and $SubReq(\tau, \gamma)$ for some $\tau \in \mathsf{Type}$

The idea here is that if $SubReq(\sigma, \tau)$, then every totally well-typed feature structure of type σ is required to have a substructure of type τ. We thus have $SubReq(\sigma_0, \sigma_n)$ if and only if there is a sequence of features $f_1, \ldots, f_n$ and types $\sigma_0, \ldots, \sigma_n$ such that $Approp(f_{i+1}, \sigma_i) = \sigma_{i+1}$ for $i < n$. If there is a type σ such that $SubReq(\sigma, \sigma)$, then we say that $Approp$ contains an *appropriateness loop*. There are no appropriateness loops in $Approp$ if and only if $SubReq$ is anti-reflexive (by definition of anti-reflexivity). This condition of not having any loops is usually assumed in the terminological component of inheritance-based reasoning systems such as KL-ONE, LOOM or CLASSIC. But note that these systems provide an additional layer of constraints which are not required to satisfy the loop-free conditions. We consider general recursive constraint systems (which admit loops of the kind prohibited by the type system) in a later chapter after we have completed our study of feature structures.

The conditions we need to enable type inference can be easily stated as requiring acyclicity in the directed graph corresponding to all of the ISA and role restriction links. In the applications of these terminological systems to reasoning about individuals, conditions such as acyclicity are usually lifted; we make an analogous move when we come to define constraint systems over feature structures in the final chapter.

The loop-free condition on appropriateness specifications would seem at first to be too restrictive as it would appear to rule out any kind of recursive feature structures in which a structure of one type has a substructure of the same type. This is necessary in applications such as HPSG in which a phrase might have a head daughter which is also a phrase. In the simplest case, we would want to represent lists as structures that allow lists as substructures. But consider the definition of (a portion of) a type hierarchy for representing arbitrary lists in Figure 6.6. In the diagram in Figure 6.6 there is a type **list** for lists with two subtypes **ne-list** and **e-list** taken to represent non-empty and empty lists respectively. An empty list does not have any features appropriate for it, whereas we have $Approp(\text{HEAD}, \textbf{ne-list}) = \perp$, so that heads of non-empty lists can be anything, and $Approp(\text{TAIL}, \textbf{ne-list}) = \textbf{list}$, so that the tails of non-empty lists must be lists. Significantly, we do not require that the tails of lists be lists; a list might be empty and thus not have a tail. Thus there are no appropriateness loops in the appropriateness conditions and inheritance hierarchy in Figure 6.6. On the other hand, it is perfectly acceptable to have a list that has a list as a substructure, as in the totally well-typed feature structure:

$$(15) \quad \begin{bmatrix} \textbf{ne-list} \\ \text{HEAD:} \begin{bmatrix} \textbf{john} \end{bmatrix} \\ \text{TAIL:} \begin{bmatrix} \textbf{ne-list} \\ \text{HEAD:} \begin{bmatrix} \textbf{ran} \end{bmatrix} \\ \text{TAIL:} \begin{bmatrix} \textbf{e-list} \end{bmatrix} \end{bmatrix} \end{bmatrix}$$

The structure in (15) represents the list $\langle \textbf{john}, \textbf{ran} \rangle$ in the standard way. Thus we do not have to forfeit the ability to represent recursive structures when we eliminate appropriateness specifications with loops.

If we restrict our attention to appropriateness specifications without loops we are always able to find most general totally well-typed extensions of totally typable feature structures.

Theorem 6.15 (Total Type Inference)
If Approp contains no loops, then there is a total function Fill:$\mathcal{TF} \rightarrow \mathcal{TTF}$ such that $F \in \mathcal{TF}$, $F' \in \mathcal{TTF}$, and $F \sqsubseteq F'$ if and only if Fill(F) $\sqsubseteq F'$.

Proof: *Fill* is defined by iterating the following step until the result is totally well-typed:

> select a node q with a type σ such that $Approp(f, \sigma)$ is defined but $\delta(f, q)$ is undefined, and then add an arc:
>
> $$q : \sigma \xrightarrow{\ f\ } q' : Approp(f, \sigma)$$
>
> where q' is a new node that does not occur elsewhere in the structure.

The key to the correctness of this procedure is that the arcs added by the above iteration never interact with what is already in F to begin with. Thus the features and values in F remain well-typed after the application of *Fill*. The iteration terminates because there are no appropriateness loops and thus only a finite number of new paths must be added to each node in F. The totally well-typed structure that is created is known to be most general because all of the arcs that were added needed to be added to satisfy the total well-typedness conditions. $\Box$

The significance of total type inference really becomes apparent when we consider the following corollary, which shows us how to start with an arbitrary feature structure and compute its most general totally well-typed extension.

Corollary 6.16

If Approp contains no loops and $F \in \mathcal{F}$, then $F \sqsubseteq F'$ for some $F' \in TTF$ if and only if $Fill(TypInf(F)) \sqsubseteq F'$.

Proof: Firstly, if $TypInf(F)$ is not defined, then F is not typable and hence not totally typable. The minimality of $Fill(TypInf(F))$ is just a result of the minimality of $TypInf(F)$ and the result of *Fill*. □

It can easily be seen that *Fill* fits our general definition of an inference procedure in the last section. Of course, the way we have defined it, *Fill* should only be applied to well typed feature structures in $TypInf(\mathcal{F})$.

Theorem 6.17

The partial functions $Fill: TypInf(\mathcal{F}) \rightarrow TypInf(\mathcal{F})$ and $Fill \circ TypInf: \mathcal{F} \rightarrow \mathcal{F}$ are inference procedures.

Proof: Obviously $Fill(F) \sqsubseteq Fill(F')$ if $Fill(F')$ is defined, and $F \sqsubseteq F'$; all of our conditions for adding information to F to derive $Fill(F)$ are monotonic. Because we only add information to F to produce $Fill(F)$, it should also be obvious that $F \sqsubseteq Fill(F)$ if $Fill(F)$ is defined. Furthermore, *Fill* can be seen to be idempotent by the fact that it is defined by iterating a procedure until closure.

Exactly the same reasoning applies to $Fill \circ TypInf$ for monotonicity and increasingness. For idempotency, we need only to note that if F is well-typed, then $Fill(F)$ is also well-typed if it is defined. Thus $Fill(TypInf(Fill(TypInf(F)))) = Fill(Fill(TypInf(F))) = Fill(TypInf(F))$. □

Note that in this last proof, we had to do some extra work to ensure that the composition of two inference procedures was itself an inference procedure. In general, composing inference procedures results in a function which meets the monotonicity and increasing conditions in the definition of an inference procedure, but may fail to be idempotent. On the other hand, interleaving the steps in the definition of a pair of inference procedures usually results in an inference procedure, but one in which termination conditions may be more difficult to decide. For instance, we could have defined a new type inference procedure *TotTypInf* by interleaving the steps in the definition of *Fill*, *TypDom* and *TypRan*.

It should now be obvious that if there are no appropriateness loops, a feature structure is typable if and only if it is totally typable. But as we have seen, if there are appropriateness loops, it may be possible for F to be totally typable and $Fill(F)$ to be undefined (in which case, application of the procedure for computing *Fill* would go into an infinite loop). Surprisingly, although a feature structure may be totally typable, but not finitely totally typable (that is, it has a well-typed extension, but no least such), we can show that a feature structure is totally typable if and only if it is typable with respect to arbitrary appropriateness conditions possibly containing loops.

Theorem 6.18 (Total Typability)

A feature structure $F \in \mathcal{F}$ is totally typable if and only if it is typable.

Proof: We define a total function $FillCyc: \mathcal{TF} \to \mathcal{TTF}$, which is a slight variant of *Fill* by iterating the following step until a totally well-typed feature structure is created:

> select a node q with a type σ such that $Approp(f, \sigma)$ is defined but $\delta(f, q)$ is undefined, and then if there is a node $q'': \tau$, where $Approp(f, \sigma) \sqsubseteq \tau$ add the arc $q: \sigma \xrightarrow{f} q'': \tau$. Otherwise create a new node q' of type τ and add an arc $q: \sigma \xrightarrow{f} q': Approp(f, \sigma)$.

Now we can easily show that $FillCyc(TypInf(F))$ is totally well-typed and is defined if and only if $TypInf(F)$ is defined. First, $FillCyc$ terminates because at most n new nodes can be created where n is the number of types in Type. This is because only one node of each type needs to be added; each subsequent arc created can then point to an existing node of the appropriate type. Only a finite number of new arcs are added after this point because there are only a finite number of nodes and a finite number of features appropriate for the type of each node. The result of $FillCyc(TypeInf(F))$ is totally well typed because every feature that is appropriate must be defined and have an appropriate value, because all of the values supplied by $TypInf(F)$ are appropriate, and $FillCyc$ only adds appropriate values and only stops when all appropriate features are defined. $\square$

There are two appealing variants of this theorem, which both unfortunately turn out to be false. As we have already seen, it is possible for a feature structure to be totally typable, but have no most general well-typed extension, and thus not be finitely totally typable. The closest we can come is an immediate corollary to the total type inference theorem.

Corollary 6.19

If Approp contains no loops, then a feature structure is typable with respect to Approp if and only if it is finitely totally typable with respect to Approp.

Proof: The result follows from the fact that *Fill* is a total function if *Approp* is loop free. $\square$

Secondly, the total type inference theorem would not apply if we were to restrict our attention to feature structures without cycles; the proof crucially relies on the construction of cyclic structures.

By slightly modifying the procedure outlined in the proof of the total typability theorem we can prove that the collection of totally well-typed extensions of a given feature structure can be enumerated.

Theorem 6.20 (Totally Well-Typed Enumerability)

The set of totally well-typed feature structures extending a feature structure is recursively enumerable.

Proof: We define a non-deterministic procedure $NFillCyc: TF \rightarrow TTF$ which is only a slight modification of $FillCyc$. The only difference is that $NFillCyc$ makes a non-deterministic choice between adding a new node and having a new arc point back to an existing node.

Now if F' is a totally well-typed extension of F, then it must extend one of the totally well-typed structures generated by this procedure. $\qquad\square$

If we are dealing with an appropriateness specification without loops, we are able to use our total type inference procedure $Fill \circ TypInf$ to produce the least upper bound in TTF of two totally well-typed feature structures.

Theorem 6.21 (Totally Well-Typed Unification)

If Approp is loop-free and $F, F', F'' \in TTF$, then $F \sqsubseteq F''$ and $F' \sqsubseteq F''$ if and only if $Fill \circ TypInf(F \sqcup F') \sqsubseteq F''$.

Proof: Identical to the proof of the existence of well-typed unifiers. $\qquad\square$

Just as for $TypInf$, the order in which we perform unifications and $Fill$ operations does not matter. Thus we have:

Corollary 6.22 (Lazy Total Type Inference)

If $F \in TF$, then $Fill \circ TypInf(Fill \circ TypInf(F) \sqcup F') = Fill \circ TypInf(F \sqcup F')$.

Thus we can postpone total type inference as long as is desired during processing.

We now move on to consider the logical behavior of totally well-typed feature structures. Just as before, we need not alter our definitions of subsumption or satisfaction, but we let $Sat_{TTF}(\phi) = Sat(\phi) \cap TTF$ and say that ϕ and ψ are logically equivalent with respect to TTF and write $\models_{TTF} \phi \equiv \psi$ if and only if $Sat_{TTF}(\phi) = Sat_{TTF}(\psi)$. We relativize our notion of consistency and satisfiability to the totally well-typed feature structures, saying that $F, F' \in TTF$ are TTF-consistent if and only if there is a $F'' \in TTF$ such that $F \sqsubseteq F''$ and $F' \sqsubseteq F''$, and saying that $\phi \in$ Desc is TTF-satisfiable if and only if $Sat_{TTF}(\phi) \neq \emptyset$. We again go through our basic logical results and see that they can all be relativized to the totally well-typed feature structures.

We begin with most general satisfiability.

Theorem 6.23 (Most General Satisfier)

If our appropriateness conditions are loop free, then for non-disjunctive descriptions $\phi \in$ Desc and totally well-typed feature structures $F \in TTF$, we have $F \models \phi$ if and only if $Fill \circ TypInf(MGSat(\phi)) \sqsubseteq F$.

Proof: As in the case of total typing, $F \models \phi$ if and only if $MGSat(\phi) \sqsubseteq F$ and $F \in TTF$ and $F \models \phi$ if and only if $Fill \circ TypInf(MGSat(\phi)) \sqsubseteq F$. $\qquad\square$

Of course, just as before, this can be extended to descriptions ϕ with disjunctions by applying $Fill \circ TypInf$ to each member of $MGSats(\phi)$.

A corollary to the total typability theorem is that a description is satisfiable by a well-typed feature structure if and only if it is satisfiable by a totally well-typed feature structure.

Corollary 6.24 (Satisfiability)

A description $\phi \in$ Desc is $\mathcal{TF}$-satisfiable if and only if it is $\mathcal{TTF}$-satisfiable.

Proof: If ϕ is satisfiable by $F \in \mathcal{TF}$, then by the total typability theorem we know that since F is typable there is a totally well-typed $F' \in \mathcal{TTF}$ such that $F \sqsubseteq F'$. By monotonicity, we have $F' \models \phi$. The converse result is immediate because $\mathcal{TF} \subseteq \mathcal{TTF}$, and hence $Sat_{\mathcal{TF}}(\phi) \subseteq Sat_{\mathcal{TTF}}(\phi)$. $\qquad\qquad$ $\square$

Of course, this result relies solely on our ability to create cyclic structures and no longer holds if we restrict our attention to the acyclic case, in which it is possible to have structures like that in (12), which are typable but not totally typable. On the other hand, the result holds for acyclic structures if we further restrict our attention to the case in which there are no appropriateness loops.

We now consider a complete axiomatization of the totally well-typed feature structures. We let $\mathcal{E}_{\mathcal{TTF}}$ be the collection of axioms in the axiomatization $\mathcal{E}_{\mathcal{TF}}$ of the well-typed feature structures along with instances of the following axiom scheme:

7. Total Well-Typedness

$\qquad$ (a) $\sigma \Leftrightarrow \sigma \wedge f : \bot$ $\qquad\qquad\qquad\qquad\qquad$ [if $Approp(f, \sigma)$ defined]

This axiom simply requires every feature which is appropriate for σ to be given some value in a feature structure of type σ. That is, describing an object as being of type σ provides the same information as describing the object as being of type σ and having a value for the feature f if f is an appropriate feature for objects of type σ. The axioms in $\mathcal{E}_{\mathcal{TF}}$ guarantee that the value of the feature f is an appropriate one for an object of type σ.

Again, we can prove directly that the resulting logic is sound and complete. Note that this soundness and completeness result applies even to appropriateness specifications with loops. This makes the proof slightly more complicated as it must be modified to account for the fact that we are no longer guaranteed to have finite normal forms of the variety we previously enjoyed. As usual, we begin with the non-disjunctive case, which has the disjunctive case as an immediate corollary.

Theorem 6.25 (Non-Disjunctive Soundness and Completeness)

If $\phi, \psi \in$ NonDisjDesc, then $\models_{\mathcal{TTF}} \phi \equiv \psi$ if and only if $\vdash_{\mathcal{E}_{\mathcal{TTF}}} \phi \Leftrightarrow \psi$.

Proof: Soundness is obvious, since any well typed feature structure of type σ provides a definition for any f for which it is appropriate.

Suppose that $\models_{\mathcal{TF}} \phi \equiv \psi$. There are two cases to consider, depending on whether ϕ and ψ are $\mathcal{TTF}$-satisfiable.

First suppose that both ϕ and ψ are unsatisfiable. By the satisfiability theorem, we know that ϕ and ψ are $\mathcal{TTF}$-satisfiable if and only if they are $\mathcal{TF}$-satisfiable. Thus by the completeness of $\mathcal{E}_{\mathcal{TF}}$ with respect to $\mathcal{TF}$, we have $\vdash_{\mathcal{TF}} \phi \Leftrightarrow \top$ and $\vdash_{\mathcal{TF}} \psi \Leftrightarrow \top$ and hence $\vdash_{\mathcal{TF}} \phi \Leftrightarrow \psi$. Since $\mathcal{E}_{\mathcal{TF}} \subseteq \mathcal{E}_{\mathcal{TTF}}$, we immediately have $\vdash_{\mathcal{TTF}} \phi \Leftrightarrow \psi$.

It remains to consider the case in which ϕ and ψ are satisfiable. In this case, let $\phi' = Desc(TypInf(MGSat(\phi)))$ and $\psi' = Desc(TypInf(MGSat(\psi)))$. By the completeness of $\mathcal{E}_{T\mathcal{F}}$, and the fact that $\mathcal{E}_{T\mathcal{F}} \subseteq \mathcal{E}_{TT\mathcal{F}}$ we know $\vdash_{TT\mathcal{F}} \phi \Leftrightarrow \phi'$ and $\vdash_{TT\mathcal{F}} \psi \Leftrightarrow \psi'$. Now we can apply the total type inference axioms to ϕ' in a way that mimics the application of *Fill* to $TypInf(MGSat(\phi))$ so that we can prove $\vdash_{\mathcal{E}_{TT\mathcal{F}}} \phi' \Leftrightarrow \phi' \wedge \psi'$, and similarly for ψ'. If this were not possible in both cases, we could find a satisfier for ϕ which did not satisfy ψ or vice versa. $\quad\square$

To continue to stress the effects of acyclicity, completeness would no longer hold under the restriction to acyclic feature structures due to the fact that we would have $T\mathcal{F}$-unsatisfiable descriptions which were not provably equivalent to $\top$. An example of this is provided in the case of (12), where the description **person** would not be satisfiable by any acyclic totally well-typed feature structure. The reason that we could not prove that it was equivalent to $\top$ is that when using the axioms in $\mathcal{E}_{TT\mathcal{F}}$ to mimic *Fill*, we would continue to add consistent information to the descriptions without ever arriving at a contradiction. An alternative suggested by Carl Pollard (personal communication) would be to add an axiom scheme of the following form:

$$(16) \quad \sigma \Leftrightarrow \top \qquad\qquad\qquad [\text{if } SubReq(\sigma, \sigma)]$$

Recall that $SubReq(\sigma, \sigma)$ holds if every feature structure of type σ is required to have a substructure of type σ which can be reached by following a non-empty path. While we do not have $\models_{TT\mathcal{F}} \sigma \Leftrightarrow \top$ due to the distinction between total typability and finite total typability, this axiom would solve our termination problems with *Fill* cycling endlessly on sorts with appropriateness loops.

As usual, we can use the disjunctive normal form theorem for our description language to show completeness and soundness for the full logic with disjunctions:

Theorem 6.26 (Total Soundness and Completeness)

$\models_{TT\mathcal{F}} \phi \equiv \psi$ *if and only if* $\vdash_{TT\mathcal{F}} \phi \Leftrightarrow \psi$.

Some comments are now in order concerning the relative utility of the total as opposed to the simple well-typedness conditions. In the first place, there is really no change with respect to satisfiability, so if we are only interested in settling issues of consistency or satisfiability, we might as well stick to the less restrictive conditions. On the other hand, if we are interested in applying compilation techniques to provide record-based implementations of feature structures, we might just as well use the total well-typedness conditions since we are likely to allocate a pointer for the value of each appropriate feature for any given type. The well-typing conditions are more appropriate if we are doing a significant amount of work with very sparse feature structures at intermediate stages of our computations, as the requirement that every appropriate feature be present may add in a significant amount of information which does not affect the issue of consistency or satisfiability. In the next section, when we consider static typing, we see another dimension along which we can distinguish our two type schemes.

Static Typing

In this section we explore the conditions which must be imposed on the appropriateness specifications to ensure that we can carry out static type checking and inference. A type system is said to be *static* if all of the type inference and type checking can be done at compile time. Due to the fact that types can always be determined before data objects are created, static type schemes can actually be more efficient than their untyped counterparts. In fact, this is often the reason for employing static type schemes in languages like C or Pascal. In the case of feature structures, to achieve static typing, we consider how we can restrict the appropriateness conditions so that the unification of well-typed feature structures is also a well-typed feature structure. This is basically the strategy followed by Mycroft and O'Keefe (1984), who considered a parametrically typed version of Prolog in which all of the type checking was done at compile time and the ordinary SLD-resolution mechanism was applied at run time to compute answers to queries. In their system, if a program was well typed, then answering a well-typed query could never result in the construction of an ill-typed term. They proved this result by showing that the application of a resolution inference step to a well-typed sequence of goals resulted in a new sequence of goals which was also well-typed. The way we achieve static typing is by restricting the appropriateness conditions in such a way that the unification of well-typed structures is guaranteed to produce a well-typed result.

The most straightforward way in which we can achieve static typing is by requiring that the appropriateness specification be a constant function for every feature. This would mean that a feature f is always allowed to have the same type of value regardless of the type of feature structure for which it is defined. To make this more precise, we say that an appropriateness function is *constant* if for every $f \in$ Feat and $\sigma, \tau \in$ Type we have $Approp(f, \sigma) = Approp(f, \tau)$ if both are defined.

Theorem 6.27 (Constant Appropriateness)

If Approp is a constant appropriateness specification, and $F, F' \in \mathcal{TF}$ are well-typed feature structures, then $F \sqcup F' \in \mathcal{TF}$ is well-typed.

Proof: The result follows immediately from the fact that if we are unifying two feature structures of types σ and τ, the result is a feature structure of type $\gamma = \sigma \sqcup \tau$. Thus we are assured that γ is appropriate for all of the features for which both σ and τ are appropriate. This follows directly from the upward closure of the appropriateness conditions and the fact that $\sigma \sqsubseteq \sigma \sqcup \tau$ and $\tau \sqsubseteq \sigma \sqcup \tau$ in general. If the value restriction is a constant, then if the restriction is met in both of the original structures, it is satisfied in the unification, as all of the types in the unified structure are at least as specific as they were in the originals.   □

The reason that this result does not hold for the totally typed feature structures is that the result of unifying a feature structure of type σ and τ can produce a feature structure of type γ that is appropriate for features that are not appropriate for either σ or τ. In the case of well-typing, these features do not need to be defined in the result, but to satisfy the requirements of total well-typing they must be defined. To get around this problem, the basic unification algorithm would have to be modified slightly so that whenever two nodes were identified and their types were replaced by their join, if more features are introduced by the type of their result, then these features must be given their minimal values. We can add in values for the features which are introduced as appropriate by means of unification using *Fill*. Recall that all *Fill* does is add in features which are not defined; it does not affect existing features or their values. This fact allows us to derive a corollary to the constant appropriateness theorem.

Corollary 6.28 (Total Constant Appropriateness)

If Approp is a constant appropriateness specification without loops, and $F, F' \in TTF$ are totally well-typed feature structures, then $Fill(F \sqcup F') \in TTF$ is totally well-typed.

Thus we need only to fill in values for features which are introduced as a result of unification and do not need to perform any other type inference when we have totally typed feature structures and a constant appropriateness function.

In practice, it is not always desirable to have constant appropriateness specifications. We thus consider a more subtle condition on appropriateness specifications that ensures that the result of applying *Fill* to the unification of two totally well-typed feature structures results in a totally well-typed feature structure.

Definition 6.29 (Join Preservation)

An appropriateness specification is said to preserve joins if for all types $\sigma, \tau \in$ Type such that $\sigma \sqcup \tau$ exists we have:

$$
Approp(f, \sigma \sqcup \tau) = \begin{cases} Approp(f, \tau) & \text{if } Approp(f, \sigma) \text{ and} \\ \quad \sqcup\, Approp(f, \sigma) & \quad Approp(f, \tau) \text{ are defined} \\ Approp(f, \tau) & \text{if only } Approp(f, \tau) \text{ is defined} \\ Approp(f, \sigma) & \text{if only } Approp(f, \sigma) \text{ is defined} \\ unrestricted & \text{otherwise} \end{cases}
$$

Of course, a constant appropriateness function always preserves joins in this way. For those familiar with continuous functions on BCPOs (which we define below in the chapter on domains), we note the following:

Corollary 6.30

If Approp preserves joins, $f \in$ Feat, and $D_f = \{\sigma \mid Approp(f, \sigma) \text{ defined}\}$, then the total function $Approp_f : D_f \to$ Type defined by $Approp_f(\sigma) = Approp(f, \sigma)$ is continuos.

We know that D_f is itself a BCPO because it is a principal filter in Type; its generator is $Intro(f)$, the least type appropriate for f. But note that the converse does not hold. It is possible for $Approp_f$ to be continuous on D_f for

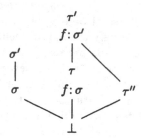

Figure 6.7. Continuous but not Join-Preserving *Approp*.

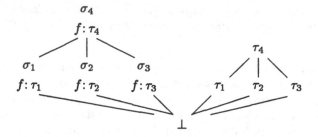

Figure 6.8. Join-Preserving Appropriateness Conditions.

every f without *Approp* preserving joins. This is because of the second and third conditions in the join preservation theorem, which apply to the situation in which only one of the joined types is in the domain of *Approp$_f$*. An example of a continuous *Approp$_f$* that does not preserve joins is given in Figure 6.7. In particular, we have $\tau \sqcup \tau'' = \tau'$, but not $Approp(f, \tau') = Approp(f, \tau)$.

The purpose of preserving joins is to make sure that if we take two totally well-typed feature structures, one of which is of type σ and one of which is type τ, and unify them to produce a feature structure of type $\sigma \sqcup \tau$, then their value for the feature f, if it is defined, is of the appropriate type, which might be required to be more specific than it was required to be for either σ or τ. For instance, the inheritance hierarchy and appropriateness conditions in Figure 6.8 preserve joins. The inheritance hierarchy in Figure 6.9, on the other hand, does not preserve joins. The reason that joins are not preserved is that:

(17) $Approp(f, \sigma_1) \sqcup Approp(f, \sigma_2) = \tau_1 \sqcup \tau_2 = \tau_{1,2}$
         $\neq Approp(f, \sigma_1 \sqcup \sigma_2) = Approp(f, \sigma_4) = \tau_4$

Theorem 6.31 (Join Preservation)

If Approp is an appropriateness specification without loops that satisfies the join preservation condition and, if $F, F' \in TTF$ are totally well-typed feature structures, then $Fill(F \sqcup F') \in TTF$ is also totally well-typed.

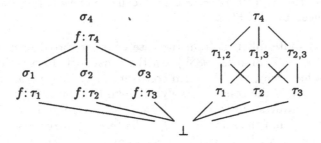

Figure 6.9. Non-Join-Preserving Appropriateness Conditions.

Proof: There are four cases to consider, corresponding to the clauses in the definition of join preservation when unifying two feature structures of types σ and τ. First suppose that both $Approp(f, \sigma)$ and $Approp(f, \tau)$ are defined. Then their values for f must be at least as specific as $Approp(f, \sigma)$ and $Approp(f, \tau)$, so that the result of the unification has a value for f which is at least of type $Approp(f, \sigma) \sqcup Approp(f, \tau)$, thus ensuring that it is appropriate for the type of their result, $\sigma \sqcup \tau$, for which $Approp(f, \sigma \sqcup \tau) = Approp(f, \sigma) \sqcup Approp(f, \tau)$. Second suppose that only $Approp(f, \sigma)$ is defined. The value for f in the result is the same as its value in the feature structure of type σ, since f is inappropriate for τ. By join preservation, we know that the value supplied by the structure of type σ is appropriate for the result because we have $Approp(f, \sigma \sqcup \tau) = Approp(f, \sigma)$. The third case is identical to the second with the roles of σ and τ reversed. Finally, consider the case in which neither $Approp(f, \sigma)$ or $Approp(f, \tau)$ are defined. Then *Fill* provides an appropriate value in the result.

This argument holds for arbitrary nodes which get identified in F and F' as a result of their unification.   □

An interesting corollary to the join preservation unification theorem arises from restricting our attention to the situation in which subtypes do not introduce additional features that were not present on their (non-bottom) supertypes. The resulting totally typed feature structures resemble (possibly cyclic) functional terms in which there is an inheritance ordering on the term constructors and in which the term constructors place restrictions on the types of their arguments. In particular, we insist that if two (non-bottom) sorts are comparable, then they have the same appropriate features. In this case, we do not need to apply *Fill* to the result of a unification, as no additional features ever get introduced on joins.

Corollary 6.32

Suppose Approp preserves joins and is such that if $\sigma \sqsubseteq \tau$ and $\sigma \neq \perp$, then $Approp(f, \sigma)$ if and only if $Approp(f, \tau)$ for all $f \in$ Feat. Furthermore, if $F, F' \in TTF$ are consistent and totally well-typed, then $F \sqcup F' \in TTF$ is totally well-typed.

Proof: In this case, $Fill(F \sqcup F') = F \sqcup F'$ because no new appropriate features can be introduced by $F \sqcup F'$. $\square$

This is actually quite different from the case of order-sorted term unification (Meseguer et al. 1987, Smolka 1988b). In the order-sorted case, the sorts are ordered into a hierarchy, and the term constructors are given "arities," which determine the sort of the result of applying them to terms. In the case of so-called *regular* signatures, the sort of the term $f(t_1, \ldots, t_n)$ would be determined by the "arity" of f and the sorts of the t_i. The term constructors, such as f in this case, are not themselves provided with an explicit ordering.

The conditions under which the previous corollary holds can actually be relaxed somewhat to the situation in which the unification of two types does not introduce any new features.

Corollary 6.33

Suppose Approp preserves joins and whenever $Approp(f, \sigma \sqcup \tau)$ is defined, then $Approp(f, \sigma)$ or $Approp(f, \tau)$ is defined. Then, if $F, F' \in TT\mathcal{F}$ are consistent, $F \sqcup F' \in TT\mathcal{F}$.

Chapter 7

Inequations

Up until this point, we have considered only how to state positive facts about feature structures in terms of existing features, values and structure sharing. In this chapter we consider how to encode negative information by means of inequations.

Inequations and Negation

Before studying inequations, we briefly consider stronger forms of negation which have been previously proposed for feature structures and logical terms. Johnson (1987, 1988), Smolka (1988), and King (1989) all allow descriptions of the forms $\neg\phi$ and $\phi \rightarrow \psi$ when ϕ and ψ are descriptions and give these constructions classical interpretations. In particular, Johnson (and those following him) assumed that:

(1) $F \models \neg\phi$ if and only if $F \not\models \phi$

As we stated in the chapter on descriptions, the main drawback in classical treatments of negation is that the resulting system is not monotonic, so that it is possible to have $F \models \neg\phi$ and $F \sqsubseteq F'$ and $F' \not\models \neg\phi$. From a processing perspective, this would mean that we would no longer be able to characterize a non-disjunctive description in terms of a most general satisfying feature structure. A standard way to implement systems with this kind of negation is to factor the positive and negative constraints, find a most general satisfier for the positive constraints, and make sure that it does not violate any of the negative constraints. Then when new information is found, the same factorization occurs, the new positive information is unified with the old positive information represented as a feature structure, and the result is checked to see that it does not conflict with any of the old or new negative constraints. This results in a blend of syntactic and semantic representations of information; positive information is represented semantically in terms of feature structures, whereas negative information is maintained as a syntactic description. Karttunen (1984) suggested this implementation technique, in one of the earliest attempts to treat negation in an extension of the PATR-II formalism. To get around this problem, Smolka (1989) introduced a notion of normal form that applies to negative descriptions with a classical interpretation.

Moshier and Rounds (1986), on the other hand, chose to employ a description negation operator, but provided it with an intuitionistic interpretation. First, a set $\mathcal{G} \subseteq \mathcal{F}$ of feature structures was picked out to which the descriptions were taken to apply. We have shown a few sensible ways of doing this in terms of our various type schemes. Then a notion of satisfaction was defined relative to the set $\mathcal{G}$ of feature structures, in which a feature structure F satisfied $\neg\phi$ with respect to $\mathcal{G}$ if every $F' \in \mathcal{G}$ such that $F \sqsubseteq F'$ was such that $F' \not\models \phi$. Thus a feature structure satisfied a negative constraint $\neg\phi$ just in case it could not be extended to a feature structure (in $\mathcal{G}$) that satisfied ϕ. This move preserved the crucial property of monotonicity that ensures that if $F \models \phi$ and $F \sqsubseteq F'$, then $F' \models \phi$. The reason that interpretation had to be done relative to a distinguished set $\mathcal{G}$ of feature structures was that otherwise it would be impossible to satisfy a description such as $\neg(f\colon \bot)$, which asserts that the feature f has no value. This is because it is always possible to extend a feature structure not defined for f to one that is defined for f. Our notion of typing allows us to express a similar constraint in a much more natural way. Even though the system of Moshier and Rounds is monotonic, it still does not admit unique most general satisfiers; there may be multiple distinct minimal satisfiers of a non-disjunctive description. Langholm (1989) presents a variant of Moshier and Rounds's intuitionistic logic for negation. Another interesting treatment of general negation was provided by Dawar and Vijay-Shanker (1989, 1990), who chose to interpret satisfaction in the feature structure analogue of Kleene's strong three-valued logic. Thus there were three possibilities: a feature structure could satisfy a description, it could satisfy the negation of a description, or its satisfaction of a description could remain undecided until further information was obtained.

Our interpretation of negation most closely follows the treatment of negation in constraint logic programming systems (see Colmerauer 1984 or Lassez et al. 1986). In Prolog II, it is possible to state that two terms are equivalent, which causes ordinary unification. Alternatively, it is also possible to state that two terms are not equivalent, by means of an inequation such as $f(a, X) \neq f(Y, b)$. The import of these inequations is that they ensure that the two terms that are stated to be different never become identical after the inequation is encountered. The process of unification must be updated to handle the inequations. In general, the equations are solved in the usual way by producing most general unifiers, and then redundant inequations (those between two terms with a different function symbol) are removed and the set of inequations is converted to a simplified form (Colmerauer 1984). The surprising thing about inequations is that this seemingly restricted version of negation has been found to be sufficient to represent most of the useful varieties of negation that are actually found in logic programs, including applications to the control of search such as the extra-logical cut operator (Colmerauer 1987).

Inequations are useful from the point of view of linguistic applications as they are a natural way to represent restrictions on pronominal binding. In fact, Pereira (1987) gives the example of:

(2)   OBJ FORM: **reflexive** $\lor$ $\neg$(SUBJ REF $\doteq$ OBJ REF)

The intuitive reading of this constraint is that the object of a clause must be a reflexive pronoun, or the subject referent and the object referent must be distinct. We are able to naturally capture this constraint by replacing the negated equation in the second disjunct with the inequation in (3):

(3)   SUBJ REF $\neq$ OBJ REF.

The other application for which negation has often been proposed is the specification of agreement features for verbs in English (and other languages) which are finite but not third singular, as in (4):

(4) $\neg$(PERSON: **third** $\land$ NUMBER: **sing**)

This common example (Karttunen 1984, Pereira 1987, Moshier and Rounds 1987, Pollard and Sag 1987, Guenthner 1988, Dawar and Vijay-Shanker 1989) is very misleading because its intended interpretation can be captured by means of a finite disjunction, namely:

(5)   PERSON: (**first** $\lor$ **second**) $\lor$ NUMBER: **plural**

Thus the kind of example in (4) is often referred to as "abbreviatory" negation since it is not adding power to the system that was not already there without negation, but simply providing more compact representations of descriptions that might otherwise involve a large number of disjunctions. As all of the systems for which general description negation have been proposed are untyped, this is not the interpretation that the negated description in (4) receives. For instance, the feature structure in (6) would satisfy the description in (4):

(6) $\begin{bmatrix} \bot \\ \text{NUMBER:} [\textbf{potato}] \end{bmatrix}$

Thus the constraint that the person feature has to be filled with an appropriate value must also be stated in these systems, resulting in a restatement of something like the description in (5). Of course, this would not be a problem for our typed system if we were to admit general description negations. On the other hand, with a typed system such as ours, or the one used in HPSG, there is a much more natural treatment of the intended interpretation of this constraint in (5). Specifically, we could include a type in the inheritance hierarchy that stood for agreement features and give it two subtypes, one for non-third singular agreement bundles and another for third-singular agreement bundles. This approach is spelled out more fully in the chapter on inheritance hierarchies, and in particular, in Figure 2.5.

Inequated Feature Structures

We only treat negative descriptions which state that two paths are not shared. The standard problem when treating these kinds of inequations is that if we consider the standard interpretation involving feature structures or first-order terms, there would be multiple distinct most general satisfiers for an inequation (Lassez et al. 1986). We thus follow the implementational lead of Karttunen (1984) and update our notion of feature structure before considering the interpretation of inequations. This move is similar to the one that was made in Prolog II (Colmerauer 1984), when attention was shifted from simple sets of equations, which could always be represented by a most general unifier if the equations were consistent, to a representation involving reduced sets of equations factored into positive and negative components. The intuition behind our extension is that an inequated feature structure consists of an ordinary feature structure with an additional inequality relation between the nodes which are known to be distinct.

Definition 7.1 (Inequated Feature Structure)

An inequated feature structure *is a quintuple* $F = \langle Q, \bar{q}, \theta, \delta, \not\leftrightarrow \rangle$, *where* $\langle Q, \bar{q}, \theta, \delta \rangle$ *is a feature structure and where* $\not\leftrightarrow \subseteq Q \times Q$ *is an anti-reflexive and symmetric* inequality *relation.*

Let $\mathcal{IF}$ *be the collection of inequated feature structures.*

The interpretation of the inequality relation $\not\leftrightarrow$ on the nodes of an inequated feature structure is intended to be that the two nodes cannot be equivalent. Thus we require the inequality relation to be symmetric and anti-reflexive. The notation we use for inequated feature structures is as in (7):

$$(7) \quad \begin{bmatrix} \textbf{sent} \\ \text{SUBJ:} \begin{bmatrix} \textbf{np} \\ \text{SEM:} [\,\textbf{ref}\,\boxed{1}\,] \end{bmatrix} \\ \text{OBJ:} \begin{bmatrix} \textbf{np} \\ \text{SEM:} [\,\textbf{ref}\,\boxed{2}\,] \end{bmatrix} \\ \boxed{1} \not\leftrightarrow \boxed{2} \end{bmatrix}$$

We have simply indexed the nodes that are inequated and listed the inequalities below all of the feature value information. We can define the operation $F @ \pi$ for $F = \langle Q, \bar{q}, \theta, \delta, \not\leftrightarrow \rangle$ just as before with the additional restriction of the inequality relation to the nodes in $F @ \pi$.

Inequated feature structures provide a very weak notion of inequality indeed. In particular, it is also possible for two nodes to be of inconsistent types or have an explicit inequality between their values for some feature and not have an inequality between them. In the next section, we consider a stronger version of inequality that allows us to make these kinds of inferences and organizes the inequated feature structures into equivalence classes based on the amount of negative information that they represent.

We define the notion of subsumption for inequated feature structures as the natural generalization of our original definition of subsumption.

Definition 7.2 (Inequated Subsumption)

$F = \langle Q, \bar{q}, \theta, \delta, \not\leftrightarrow \rangle$ subsumes $F' = \langle Q', \bar{q}', \theta', \delta', \not\leftrightarrow' \rangle$, $F \sqsubseteq F'$, *if and only if there is a total function* $h : Q \to Q'$, *called a* morphism *such that:*

- $h(\bar{q}) = \bar{q}'$

- $\theta(q) \sqsubseteq \theta'(h(q))$ *for every* $q \in Q$

- $h(\delta(f, q)) = \delta'(f, h(q))$ *if* $\delta(f, q)$ *is defined*

- *if* $q \not\leftrightarrow q'$, *then* $h(q) \not\leftrightarrow h(q')$

The only difference between this notion of subsumption and our original one is that we require all of the existing inequations to be preserved.

This notion of subsumption obviously defines a pre-ordering of the inequated feature structures because the identity function is a morphism as is the composition of morphisms. We define the notion of *alphabetic variants* just as we did before, setting $F \sim F'$ if and only if $F \sqsubseteq F'$ and $F' \sqsubseteq F$. Obviously, alphabetic variance is an equivalence relation because subsumption is a pre-ordering.

It is actually quite straightforward to show that the collection of inequated feature structures admits consistent finite joins, which can again be defined in terms of unification. We define the notion of consistency as usual, saying that two inequated feature structures $F, F' \in \mathcal{IF}$ are *consistent* if there is an inequated feature structure $F'' \in \mathcal{IF}$ that extends them both, so that $F \sqsubseteq F''$ and $F' \sqsubseteq F''$. For convenience, we present the complete definition of unification for inequated feature structures.

Definition 7.3 (Inequated Unification)

Suppose $F \sim \langle Q, \bar{q}, \theta, \delta, \not\leftrightarrow \rangle$ *and* $F' \sim \langle Q', \bar{q}', \theta', \delta', \not\leftrightarrow' \rangle$ *are such that* $Q \cap Q' = \emptyset$. *Let* $\bowtie$ *be the least equivalence relation on on* $Q \cup Q'$ *such that:*

- $\bar{q} \bowtie \bar{q}'$

- $\delta(f, q) \bowtie \delta(f, q')$ *if both are defined and* $q \bowtie q'$

The unification *of* F *and* F' *is then defined to be:*

$$F \sqcup F' = \langle (Q \cup Q')/_{\bowtie}, [\bar{q}]_{\bowtie}, \theta^{\bowtie}, \delta^{\bowtie}, \not\leftrightarrow^{\bowtie} \rangle$$

where:

- $\theta^{\bowtie}([q]_{\bowtie}) = \bigsqcup \{ (\theta \cup \theta')(q') \mid q' \bowtie q \}$

- $\delta^{\bowtie}(f, [q]_{\bowtie}) = \begin{cases} [\delta(f, q)]_{\bowtie} & \text{if } q \in Q \\ [\delta'(f, q)]_{\bowtie} & \text{if } q \in Q' \end{cases}$

- $[q]_{\bowtie} \not\leftrightarrow^{\bowtie} [q']_{\bowtie}$ *if and only if* $q'' \not\leftrightarrow q'''$ *for some* $q'' \bowtie q$ *and* $q''' \bowtie q'$

if all of the joins in the defininition of $\theta^{\bowtie}$ *exist and* $\not\leftrightarrow^{\bowtie}$ *is anti-reflexive.* $F \sqcup F'$ *is undefined otherwise.*

Theorem 7.4 (Inequated Unification)

If $F, F' \in \mathcal{IF}$ are consistent inequated feature structures, then $F \sqcup F'$ is such that $F \sqsubseteq F''$ and $F' \sqsubseteq F''$ for $F'' \in \mathcal{IF}$ if and only if $F \sqcup F' \sqsubseteq F''$.

Proof: Firstly, the result is obviously an inequated feature structure, because the inequality relation is symmetric and anti-reflexive and we know that the rest forms a feature structure because of the feature structure unification theorem.

Secondly, it follows from the proof the unification theorem that if:

$$\langle Q, \bar{q}, \theta, \delta, \not\leftrightarrow \rangle \sqcup \langle Q', \bar{q}', \theta', \delta', \not\leftrightarrow' \rangle = \langle Q'', \bar{q}'', \theta'', \delta'', \not\leftrightarrow'' \rangle$$

then:

$$\langle Q, \bar{q}, \theta, \delta \rangle \sqcup \langle Q', \bar{q}', \theta', \delta' \rangle = \langle Q'', \bar{q}'', \theta'', \delta'' \rangle$$

It only remains to verify that $\not\leftrightarrow''$ is most general. But every inequality in $\not\leftrightarrow''$ is forced by an inequality in either $\not\leftrightarrow$ or $\not\leftrightarrow'$. This could be verified more formally using the same line of argumentation as in the proof of the feature structure unification theorem. $\square$

To provide a syntactic method for describing inequalities, we add *path inequations* to our logical description language. Thus we define the set IDesc of *inequated descriptions*, which contains path inequations, with the same clauses as we used to define Desc and an additional type of basic description:

(8) $\pi_1 \not\approx \pi_2 \in$ IDesc if $\pi_1, \pi_2 \in$ Path

We then define a new notion of satisfaction between inequated feature structures and inequated descriptions using the same clauses as our original definition of satisfaction for every kind of description other than an inequation, and with the additional clause in (9) to handle inequations:

(9) $\langle Q, \bar{q}, \theta, \delta, \not\leftrightarrow \rangle \models \pi_1 \not\approx \pi_2$ if and only if $\delta(\pi_1, \bar{q}) \not\leftrightarrow \delta(\pi_2, \bar{q})$

Thus an inequated feature structure satisfies a description just in case its positive part satisfies the positive part of the description, and every path inequation is mirrored semantically by an inequality in the satisfying structure.

The resulting satisfiability relation is monotonic.

Theorem 7.5 (Inequated Monotonicity)

For $F, F' \in \mathcal{IF}$ and $\phi \in$ IDesc, if $F \models \phi$ and $F \sqsubseteq F'$, then $F' \models \phi$.

Proof: Our original satisfiability relation was monotonic, and the additional condition for the satisfiability of inequalities only requires the existence of inequalities. $\square$

Just as before we are able to combine this monotonicity result with the existence of unifiers to find most general (up to alphabetic variance) satisfiers for non-disjunctive descriptions.

Theorem 7.6 (Inequated Most General Satisfiers)

For every nondisjunctive $\phi \in \mathsf{IDesc}$ there is a $IMGSat(\phi) \in \mathcal{IF}$ such that $F \models \phi$ if and only if $IMGSat(\phi) \sqsubseteq F$.

Proof: We can construct our most general satisfiers just as we did in the case for atomic descriptions without inequations. To find the most general satisfier of an inequation, we simply construct the paths to which they refer and add an explicit inequality for the values of these paths. For instance, in the acyclic case we would have:

$$IMGSat(f_1 \cdots f_n \not\doteq g_1 \cdots g_m) = \begin{bmatrix} \bot \\ f_1: \begin{bmatrix} \bot \\ f_2: \cdots \begin{bmatrix} \bot \\ f_n: [\boxed{1}\,\bot] \end{bmatrix} \end{bmatrix} \\ g_1: \begin{bmatrix} \bot \\ g_2: \cdots \begin{bmatrix} \bot \\ g_m: [\boxed{2}\,\bot] \end{bmatrix} \end{bmatrix} \\ \boxed{1} \not\doteq \boxed{2} \end{bmatrix}$$

We can then use unification to combine the most general satisfiers of conjuncts just as we did before. The result satisfies the description and is most general. The result then follows from monotonicity. □

We can define satisfiability and logical equivalence just as before. We can then turn to the task of axiomatizing the behavior of our inequalities. We let $\mathcal{E}_{\mathcal{IF}}$ consist of the axioms in $\mathcal{E}_{\mathcal{F}}$ along with all of the instances of the following schemes:

8. Path Inequations

   (a) Symmetry
   $$\pi_1 \not\doteq \pi_2 \Leftrightarrow \pi_2 \not\doteq \pi_1$$

   (b) Inconsistency
   $$\pi \not\doteq \pi \Leftrightarrow \top$$

   (c) Subpath Definition
   $$\pi_1\pi_2 \not\doteq \pi_3 \Leftrightarrow \pi_1\pi_2 \not\doteq \pi_3 \wedge \pi_1: \bot$$

   (d) Restricted Substitutivity
   $$\pi_1 \doteq \pi_2 \wedge \pi_3 \not\doteq \pi_1\pi_4 \Leftrightarrow \pi_1 \doteq \pi_2 \wedge \pi_3 \not\doteq \pi_2\pi_4$$

   (e) Path Value Distributivity
   $$\pi: (\pi_1 \not\doteq \pi_2) \Leftrightarrow \pi\pi_1 \not\doteq \pi\pi_2$$

The axiom of symmetry states that the order in which an inequation is presented is irrelevant. The inconsistency axiom is the one that allows us to derive inconsistencies when we attempt to state that a path does not have the same value as itself. This is the only way in which inequations can lead to inconsistencies. Of course, there are many ways in which we can derive a description $\pi \not\doteq \pi$

from descriptions that do not explicitly contain a contradictory inequation. The subpath definition axiom states that if we have stated that two paths are non-identical, then it must be the case that both are defined. This parallels our construction in the most general satisfiability theorem. In other treatments of negation, such as the classical approach, one of the ways in which a negated equality such as $\neg(\pi_1 \doteq \pi_2)$ could be satisfied was by not even having a path π_1 or π_2. We are taking a much more constructive approach in which even inequations entail the existence of paths. This is similar to the three-valued treatment of Dawar and Vijay-Shanker (1990), in which the satisfaction of an inequation by a feature structure is undefined (the third value) if the paths do not exist in the feature structure. The restricted substitutivity axiom is like our other restricted substitutivity axioms in that it allows the substitution of equivalent subpaths in an inequation. Finally, the path value distributivity axiom is like our other path distributivity axiom in that it allows us to move a path value descriptor into or out of an inequation. By using these axioms together with the ones that we already have in $\mathcal{E}_{\mathcal{F}}$, we can derive equivalences such as that in (10), which follows from restricted substitutivity, inequation inconsistency, and inconsistency propagation:

(10) $\vdash_{\mathcal{E}_{\mathcal{IF}}} \pi_1 \not\doteq \pi_2 \wedge \pi_1 \doteq \pi_2 \Leftrightarrow \top$

Similarly, we have the result in (11) from restricted substitutivity:

(11) $\vdash_{\mathcal{E}_{\mathcal{IF}}} \pi_1 \doteq \pi_2 \wedge \pi_1 \not\doteq \pi_3 \Leftrightarrow \pi_1 \doteq \pi_2 \wedge \pi_2 \not\doteq \pi_3$

We can use this new axiomatization to derive a normal form result for descriptions that involve inequations. We simply convert the positive part of a description to a normal form as before and separate out all of the inequations, removing the ones that do not hold between hooks.

Definition 7.7 (Inequated Descriptive Normal Form)

A description $\phi \in$ IDesc with no disjunctions is in inequated descriptive normal form if and only if $\phi = \top$ or $\phi = \phi' \wedge \psi$, where ϕ' is in descriptive normal form, and ψ consists of a conjunction of inequations between hooks such that if $\pi_1 \not\doteq \pi_2$ is in ψ, then $\pi_2 \not\doteq \pi_1$ is also in ψ, and furthermore, there is no inequation $\pi \not\doteq \pi$ in ψ.

It is straightforward to show that every inequated description without disjunctions is provably equivalent to one in inequated descriptive normal form.

Theorem 7.8 (Inequated Descriptive Normal Form)

If $\phi \in$ IDesc is an inequated description with no disjunctions, then there is an inequated descriptive normal form description $INF(\phi)$ such that:

$$\vdash_{\mathcal{E}_{\mathcal{IF}}} \phi \Leftrightarrow INF(\phi)$$

Proof: We can use the path distributivity axiom to move all of the inequations to the top level, and the associativity and commutativity axioms to separate out the inequations. We can then convert the conjunct not containing any inequations to normal form and reduce all of the inequations to inequations between hooks using the path substitutivity axioms. If during this process we can derive an inequation stating that a hook is distinct from itself, we can derive the inconsistent description $\top$ and hence convert the whole description to $\top$. $\square$

We can define a disjunctive normal form for inequated descriptions just as we did for descriptions without inequations, by simply using the distributivity axioms to push all of the disjunctions up to the top level and converting all of the individual disjuncts to descriptive normal form.

We are now in a position to show that our axiomatization is sound and complete over the inequated feature structures.

Theorem 7.9 (Inequated Soundness and Completeness)

$\vdash_{\mathcal{E}_{\mathcal{IF}}} \phi \Leftrightarrow \psi$ *if and only if* $\models_{\mathcal{E}_{\mathcal{IF}}} \phi \equiv \psi$.

Proof: Soundness is again obvious by the definition of inequated feature structures.

Completeness can be proven directly by converting a description to disjunctive normal form and simply reading off the most general satisfiers from the normal form disjuncts as before. $\square$

One interesting theorem concerning inequations is a direct generalization of a result found in the Prolog II literature (Colmerauer 1984, Lassez et al. 1986) and concerns the so-called *independence* of inequations.

Theorem 7.10 (Independence of Inequations)

The description $\phi \wedge \xi_1 \wedge \cdots \wedge \xi_n$, *where* ϕ *contains no inequations and each* ξ_i *is of the form* $\pi_i \neq \pi'_i$, *is satisfiable if and only if* $\phi \wedge \xi_i$ *is satisfiable for* $1 \leq i \leq n$.

Proof: It is only necessary to note that there are no axioms that allow inequations to interact with one another to produce further equations or inequations, and a description is satisfiable if and only if its normal form is not $\top$. The result can also be proven by semantic means by noting that the most general satisfier for the description is built up by finding the most general satisfier for ϕ and then adding the inequalities derived from the inequations in ξ_i. $\square$

So far, we have only discussed inequations and inequality in the context of intensional untyped systems of feature structures. It is straightforward to combine inequations and either the well-typedness or total well-typedness conditions. In both cases, we simply make the positive part of the inequated feature structure respect the typing conditions and make sure that we never have an inequality holding between a node and itself. Later we see that the combination of inequations and extensionality conditions leads to some subtle and interesting results.

Fully Inequated Feature Structures

We now turn our attention to a much stronger notion of inequality that allows us to derive many more inequations in certain contexts. In particular, we have

$$\begin{bmatrix} \mathbf{c} \\ \text{F}: \begin{bmatrix} \mathbf{d} \\ \text{H}: [\boxed{1}] \end{bmatrix} \\ \text{G}: \begin{bmatrix} \mathbf{d} \\ \text{H}: [\boxed{2}] \end{bmatrix} \\ \boxed{1} \not\approx \boxed{2} \end{bmatrix} \sqsubseteq \begin{bmatrix} \mathbf{c} \\ \text{F}: \begin{bmatrix} \boxed{3}\,\mathbf{d} \\ \text{H}: [\boxed{1}] \end{bmatrix} \\ \text{G}: \begin{bmatrix} \boxed{4}\,\mathbf{d} \\ \text{H}: [\boxed{2}] \end{bmatrix} \\ \boxed{1} \not\approx \boxed{2}, \; \boxed{3} \not\approx \boxed{4} \end{bmatrix}$$

Figure 7.1. Proper Subsumption of Informationally Equivalent Structures.

left a great deal of intensionality in our system due to the fact that we can have nodes in a negative feature structure which can never be unified but do not have explicit inequalities between them. For instance, suppose that the types **a** and **b** are inconsistent. Then the two negative feature structures in (12) stand in a strict subsumption relation but really represent the same amount of information.

$$(12) \quad \begin{bmatrix} \mathbf{c} \\ \text{F}: [\,\mathbf{a}\,] \\ \text{G}: [\,\mathbf{b}\,] \end{bmatrix} \sqsubseteq \begin{bmatrix} \mathbf{c} \\ \text{F}: [\boxed{1}\,\mathbf{a}] \\ \text{G}: [\boxed{2}\,\mathbf{b}] \\ \boxed{1} \not\approx \boxed{2} \end{bmatrix}$$

So far, there is nothing that allows us to infer that two feature structures of incompatible types can never be equated. It is implicit in our notion of unification that they cannot be unified, but we are still left with distinct inequated feature structures representing what turns out to be exactly the same information. This behavior can arise in other ways as well. For instance, consider the case of the proper subsumption displayed in Figure 7.1: In the case of the more general inequated feature structure in Figure 7.1, the values of the features F and G cannot be unified because the values of the paths F H and G H are known to be distinct in light of the inequality $\boxed{1} \not\approx \boxed{2}$. The more specific of the structures in Figure 7.1 simply makes explicit with an inequality the impossibility of the feature values for F and G becoming unified.

At first blush, it might seem that the cases considered in (12) and Figure 7.1 are the only ways in which this kind of behavior can surface. These two cases could be accounted for by means of the following axiom schemes:

9. **Extended Inequation**

   (a) **Type Incompatibility**

   $$\pi_1 : \sigma \wedge \pi_2 : \tau \;\Leftrightarrow\; \pi_1 \neq \pi_2 \wedge \pi_1 : \sigma \wedge \pi_2 : \tau \qquad [\text{if } \sigma \sqcup \tau \text{ undefined}]$$

   (b) **Feature Incompatibility**

   $$\pi_1 f \neq \pi_2 f \;\Leftrightarrow\; \pi_1 \neq \pi_2 \wedge \pi_1 f \neq \pi_2 f$$

These axiom schemes certainly account for the examples at hand. The type incompatibility axiom would allow us to conclude in the case of (12) that F $\neq$ G

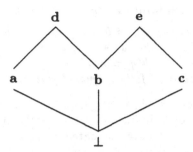

Figure 7.2. Problematic Inheritance Hierarchy for Full Inequation.

$$\begin{bmatrix} \bot \\ \text{I:} \begin{bmatrix} \bot \\ \text{F:} [\boxed{1}\, b] \\ \text{G:} [\boxed{1}] \end{bmatrix} \\ \text{J:} \begin{bmatrix} \bot \\ \text{F:} [a] \\ \text{G:} [c] \end{bmatrix} \end{bmatrix}$$

Figure 7.3. Inequated Feature Structure without Ground Extension.

because we have F: a and G: b and know that a and b are inconsistent and hence a⊔b is undefined. The second case is covered by the feature incompatibility axiom, because we would be able to infer that F ≠ G from the fact that F H ≠ G H.

Unfortunately, with the existence of more intricate type hierarchies, the same kinds of problems can surface in much more subtle ways. For instance, consider the type hierarchy in Figure 7.2 and the inequated feature structure in Figure 7.3. In this case, it is impossible to unify the path values for I and J, but both the paths I F and J F and the paths I G and J G are assigned consistent types. In particular, the type b of the path I F is consistent with the type a of the path J F, and the type b of path I G is also consistent with the type c of path J G. But it is not possible to unify the path values for I and J because all of the types are not consistent together; the explicit equation between J F and J G would require that ⊔{a, b, c} be defined, which is not the case.

Before going on to present a deduction scheme that provides exactly the notion of inequation we are after, we consider what it would mean for an inequated feature structure to behave in a fully inequated way. What we mean by saying that a feature structure is fully inequated is that if two nodes in the structure cannot be unified, then they should have an explicit inequality between them. Since we have not defined what it would mean to unify two nodes, we can state the criteria in terms of morphisms.

Definition 7.11 (Fully Inequated Feature Structure)

An inequated feature structure $\langle Q, \bar{q}, \theta, \delta, \not\leftrightarrow \rangle$ *is said to be* fully inequated *if two nodes* $q, q' \in Q$ *are such that* $q \not\leftrightarrow q'$ *if there is no* $\langle Q', \bar{q}', \theta', \delta', \not\leftrightarrow' \rangle$ *and morphism* $h: Q \rightarrow Q'$ *such that* $h(q) = h(q')$.

Let $\mathcal{FIF}$ *be the collection of fully inequated feature structures.*

We can now verify the fact that the more general inequated feature structures in (12) and Figure 7.1 are not fully inequated. Similarly, the problematic feature structure in Figure 7.3 is not fully inequated. The crucial point is that in a fully inequated feature structure, if two nodes cannot be consistently equated in any extension of the structure, then they must be explicitly inequated by an inequality. We cast the definition of fully inequated feature structure somewhat differently. If $F = \langle Q, \bar{q}, \theta, \delta, \not\leftrightarrow \rangle$ is an inequated feature structure, we define F_q to be the substructure of F rooted at q. More precisely, we take:

(13) $F_q = F @ \pi$ if $\delta(\pi, \bar{q}) = q$

Corollary 7.12

Suppose $F = \langle Q, \bar{q}, \theta, \delta, \not\leftrightarrow \rangle$ *is an inequated feature structure. Then* F *is fully inequated if and only if for every pair* $q, q' \in Q$, *we have* $q \not\leftrightarrow q'$ *if and only if* $F_q \sqcup F_{q'}$ *is undefined in the collection* $\mathcal{IF}$ *of ordinary inequated feature structures.*

Proof: If $F_q \sqcup F_{q'}$ were defined, then there would be a morphism h from F to $F \sqcup MGSat(\pi \doteq \pi')$, for $\delta(\pi, \bar{q}) = q$ and $\delta(\pi', \bar{q}) = q'$, where $h(q) = h(q')$.

Conversely, if there was a morphism h from F to F' such that $h(q) = h(q')$, then $F_q \sqcup F_{q'} \sqsubseteq F'_{h(q)}$.   □

We actually use this more constructive characterization of full inequation in developing an inference procedure for inequations.

It turns out that our inequated feature structures are sufficient representations for fully inequated feature structures in the sense that every inequated feature structure can be uniquely extended to a most general fully inequated feature structure.

Theorem 7.13

There is a total function $FIneq: \mathcal{IF} \rightarrow \mathcal{FIF}$ *such that for any* $F \in \mathcal{IF}$ *and* $F' \in \mathcal{FIF}$, *we have* $F \sqsubseteq F'$ *if and only if* $FIneq(F) \sqsubseteq F'$.

Proof: Suppose $F = \langle Q, \bar{q}, \theta, \delta, \not\leftrightarrow \rangle \in \mathcal{IF}$ is an inequated feature structure. The procedure for computing $FIneq(F)$ is quite straightforward and consists of iterating the following step:

> select $q, q' \in Q$ such that $F_q \sqcup F_{q'}$ is not defined and add $q \not\leftrightarrow q'$ and $q' \not\leftrightarrow q$ to $\not\leftrightarrow$.

We are guaranteed to reach a unique result from this non-deterministic procedure because our process of adding inequalities is fully monotonic; any inequality that can be added at one stage of the iteration can be added at any later stage. Thus we are guaranteed not to lose information based on the order in which we select elements of Q for inequality testing. The resulting inequality relation $\not\doteq$ is symmetric and anti-reflexive because $F_{\mathbf{Q}\pi} \sqcup F_{\mathbf{Q}\pi}$ is always defined. The result is obviously the most general extension of F that is fully inequated because only necessary inequalities were added. $\qquad\qquad\qquad\square$

Our full inequation procedure *FIneq*, like the type inference procedures, is an inference procedure and can be proven to be such in the same way.

Theorem 7.14

The function FIneq:$\mathcal{IF} \rightarrow \mathcal{IF}$ is an inference procedure.

Just as before, the existence of an inference procedure for full inequations allows us to prove that least upper bounds exist for finite consistent sets of fully inequated feature structures.

Theorem 7.15 (Fully Inequated Unification)

If $F, F' \in \mathcal{FIF}$ are $\mathcal{FIF}$-bounded and $F'' \in \mathcal{FIF}$, then $F \sqsubseteq F''$ and $F' \sqsubseteq F''$ if and only if $FIneq(F \sqcup F') \sqsubseteq F''$.

As an immediate corollary, we see that full inequality does not alter the satisfiability of a description:

Corollary 7.16 (Fully Inequated Satisfiability)

A description ϕ is $\mathcal{IF}$-satisfiable if and only if it is $\mathcal{FIF}$-satisfiable.

Proof: Follows immediately from the totality of *FIneq*. $\qquad\qquad\square$

We are also able to use *FIneq* to find most general satisfiers for $\mathcal{FIF}$-satisfiable descriptions without disjunctions.

Theorem 7.17 (Fully Inequated Most General Satisfiers)

If $\phi \in \mathsf{IDesc}$ is a description without disjunctions, then $F \in \mathcal{FIF}$ is such that $F \models \phi$ if and only if $FIneq(IMGSat(\phi)) \sqsubseteq F$.

Of course, this allows us to find sets of most general satisfiers for arbitrary descriptions in IDesc by defining a disjunctive normal form resulting from distributing disjunctions to the top level of a description.

We now present a syntactic characterization of the fully inequated feature structures. Unlike before, simple conditions on an axiom scheme do not suffice. Instead, we employ the inequation axioms in $\mathcal{E}_{\mathcal{IF}}$ and the following deduction scheme:

10. Full Inequation

    (a) $\{\phi \wedge \pi \doteq \pi' \Leftrightarrow \top\} \vdash \phi \wedge \pi{:}\bot \wedge \pi'{:}\bot \Leftrightarrow \phi \wedge \pi \not\doteq \pi'$

We let $\mathcal{E}_{\mathcal{FIF}}$ be the result of adding the instances of this deduction scheme to $\mathcal{E}_{\mathcal{IF}}$, our axiomatization of inequated feature structures. In particular, we allow instances of the full inequation deduction scheme in our proofs. It should be noted that we need the conjuncts $\pi: \perp$ and $\pi': \perp$ in the consequent of the deduction scheme because we want only to add inequations between paths that are already defined. This is because of the way in which we have interpreted inequations as requiring the paths that are inequated to exist. We would not want full inequation to start adding paths to feature structures because they were inappropriate; this would simply cause failure. For instance, if f is a feature that is not appropriate for σ, then we would be able to prove that:

(14) $\quad \sigma \wedge f \doteq f \Leftrightarrow \top$

We would not then want to be able to deduce from this that $f \not\doteq f$, because we also have:

(15) $\quad \sigma \wedge f \not\doteq f \Leftrightarrow \top$

This is because it is simply impossible to have an f feature defined for a feature structure of type σ.

Another alternative would be to use all of the instances of the consequent of this deduction scheme for which we could prove the antecedent from the axioms in $\mathcal{E}_{\mathcal{IF}}$. That is, we would consider all of the instances of the following axiom:

10. Full Inequation (continued)

(b) $\quad \phi \wedge \pi: \perp \wedge \pi': \perp \Leftrightarrow \phi \wedge \pi \not\doteq \pi' \qquad\qquad$ [if $\vdash_{\mathcal{E}_{\mathcal{IF}}} \phi \wedge \pi \doteq \pi' \Leftrightarrow \top$]

We let $\mathcal{FIF}_2$ be the result of adding all of the instances of the above axiom to $\mathcal{IF}$. We now show that the two alternatives for full inequation produce exactly the same collection of theorems.

Theorem 7.18

$\vdash_{\mathcal{E}_{\mathcal{FIF}}} \phi \Leftrightarrow \psi$ *if and only if* $\vdash_{\mathcal{E}_{\mathcal{FIF}_2}} \phi \Leftrightarrow \psi$.

Proof: If $\vdash_{\mathcal{E}_{\mathcal{FIF}_2}} \phi \Leftrightarrow \psi$, then it is clear that $\vdash_{\mathcal{E}_{\mathcal{FIF}}} \phi \Leftrightarrow \psi$. Every instance of an axiom in $\mathcal{FIF}_2$ can be proven using the deduction scheme in $\mathcal{FIF}$.

Conversely, suppose that $\vdash_{\mathcal{E}_{\mathcal{FIF}}} \phi \Leftrightarrow \psi$. We show by induction on the number of applications of the full inequation deduction scheme that $\vdash_{\mathcal{E}_{\mathcal{FIF}_2}} \phi \Leftrightarrow \psi$. The result holds trivially if the number of applications is 0, because the axioms in $\mathcal{E}_{\mathcal{FIF}}$ are a subset of those in $\mathcal{E}_{\mathcal{FIF}_2}$. We assume by induction that the result holds for every equation which can be proven from $\mathcal{E}_{\mathcal{FIF}}$ using n or fewer applications of the deduction scheme. Now suppose that we can prove $\phi \Leftrightarrow \psi$ from $\mathcal{E}_{\mathcal{FIF}}$ using $n + 1$ applications of the deduction scheme. Furthermore, suppose that the last application of the deduction scheme was of the form:

$$\{\phi \wedge \pi \doteq \pi' \Leftrightarrow \top\} \vdash \phi \wedge \pi: \perp \wedge \pi': \perp \Leftrightarrow \phi \wedge \pi \not\doteq \pi'$$

Then it must be the case that $\phi \wedge \pi \doteq \pi' \Leftrightarrow \top$ is provable using n or fewer applications of the deduction scheme. Thus it is also provable using the axioms in $\mathcal{FIF}_2$. We can apply the axioms of $\mathcal{FIF}_2$ to ϕ to derive a ϕ' such that $\vdash_{\mathcal{IF}} \phi' \wedge \pi \doteq \pi' \Leftrightarrow \top$ from $\mathcal{IF}$. Thus we can derive $\phi \wedge \pi: \perp \wedge \pi': \perp \Leftrightarrow \phi \wedge \pi \not\doteq \pi'$ from the full inequation axiom scheme in $\mathcal{FIF}_2$. $\qquad\square$

In the case of the axiom scheme in $\mathcal{E}_{\mathcal{FIF}_2}$ it is clear how we are bootstrapping ourselves from the axiomatization of the inequated feature structures up to the fully inequated feature structures. On the other hand, the deduction scheme in $\mathcal{E}_{\mathcal{FIF}}$ is more appealing in that it does not rely on the definition of provability in the weaker logic $\mathcal{E}_{\mathcal{IF}}$. The equivalence that we have just proved makes the choice a matter of taste.

The deduction scheme for full inequation is quite powerful and allows us to derive all of the axioms concerning inequations other than the inconsistency axiom and the subpath definition axiom. In particular, restricted substitutivity, symmetry, and inequation distributivity are all dispensable in the presence of the full inequation scheme. Similarly, the extended inequation axioms can be easily proven using the full inequation deduction scheme.

Just as before, we can use the full inequation deduction scheme in an obvious way to parallel the behavior of *FIneq*, our function that extends an inequated feature structure to a fully inequated one. As usual, we put $\models_{\mathcal{FIF}} \phi \equiv \psi$ if and only if for every $F \in \mathcal{FIF}$ we have $F \models \phi$ if and only if $F \models \psi$.

Theorem 7.19 (Fully Inequated Soundness and Completeness)

$\vdash_{\mathcal{E}_{\mathcal{FIF}}} \phi \Leftrightarrow \psi$ *if and only if* $\models_{\mathcal{FIF}} \phi \equiv \psi$.

Proof: As usual, soundness is obvious from the definition of fully inequated feature structures.

Completeness follows from the completeness of $\mathcal{E}_{\mathcal{IF}}$ and the fact that full inequation allows us to parallel the operation of the *FIneq* function. □

We have discussed inequation and full inequation starting from the feature structures. It is straightforward to combine typing or total typing to the inequated or fully inequated feature structures, with or without cycles. The results are predictable in each case. The situation is much more subtle when we come to consider the extensionality conditions presented in the next chapter.

Chapter 8

Identity and Extensionality

In this chapter we take up the identity conditions that are imposed on feature structures and their substructures and conclude that this is the most significant difference between feature structures and first-order terms. We then consider how more term-like identity conditions may be imposed on feature structures by enforcing extensionality conditions which identify feature structures on the basis of their feature values. Cycles pose interesting issues for determining identity conditions and we study two forms of extensionality which differ in how they treat cyclic feature structures. In the weaker system, feature structures are identified if their feature values are shared. In the stronger system, which mimics the identity conditions of Prolog II, a variant of Aczel's (1988) bisimulations are used to define identity conditions.

Identity in Feature Structures

In standard treatments of feature structures, such as those of Pereira and Shieber (1984) and Rounds and Kasper (1986), it is assumed that there are two types of feature structures: atoms, which do not take values for any features, and feature structures, which can take values for arbitrary collections of features. The standard models of these structures employ directed graphs with atoms labeling some subset of the terminal nodes (nodes without any feature arcs going out of them). It is also usually assumed that there can only be one copy of any atom in a feature structure, so that if we know that a path π_1 leads to an atom a and a path π_2 leads to the same atom a, then the two paths must be structure shared. In Rounds and Kasper's treatment, this is enforced by requiring the type assignment function to be one to one. Pereira and Shieber included an axiom to account for this behavior, whereas Kasper and Rounds' (1990) axiomatization was incomplete due to its omission. Moshier (1988) presented a rather different version of feature structures in which sort symbols were allowed to be attached to arbitrary nodes rather than restricting them to terminals. Additionally, Moshier changed the identity conditions so that a single sort symbol might be attached to more than one node in a single feature structure. Smolka (1988) partitioned the atoms according to whether they were copyable or not. What we do in this section can be seen as extending

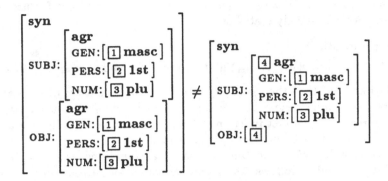

Figure 8.1. Non-Identical Feature Structures with Identical Feature Values.

Smolka's idea of partitioning atoms according to their copyability to arbitrary types.

Unlike the requirement for atoms, nodes which represent feature structures are usually modeled intensionally, so that it is possible for all of the features of two nodes in a feature structure to have token-identical values without the feature structures being identified. For instance, if we were only dealing with two features F and G, we might have the distinct feature structures in Figure 8.1. What is strange about this example is that the top level values for SUBJ and OBJ are such that they have the same values for all of their possible features, namely, PERS, NUM, and GEN, without being identified.

We claim that the reason for this is that these theories were untyped; in natural applications of such an untyped system, the situation in which every feature was shared would not arise. Just because a node representing a word, for instance, shared its phonology, syntax, and semantics attributes with another node representing a word was not enough to identify them because there was no way to say that these were the only appropriate features for words. It would always be possible to add irrelevant features such as daughters to a representation of a word without inconsistency.

Logical terms, on the other hand, limit the number of possible arguments (or appropriate features) from the outset; each term constructor (function or relation symbol) comes with an arity which determines how many arguments it takes. Two terms are identified if they have the same constructor and have identical values for all of their arguments. A theory of functions is said to be *extensional* if two functions are identified if they produce the same result for every input (Barendregt 1981). Extensionality of two functions over the same domain D can be captured logically by an axiom of the form:

(1) $(\forall x \in D)[f(x) = g(x)]$ if and only if $f = g$ (Extensionality)

This amounts to extensionality in the underlying set theory if sets are being used to construct functions (Kunen 1980). By analogy, we can think of term constructors as being fully extensional. The identity condition for first-order functional terms is usually stated as:

(2)   (Term Identity)

$$f(t_1, \ldots, t_n) = g(u_1, \ldots, u_m) \text{ iff } f = g, \ n = m, \text{ and } t_i = s_i \text{ for } 1 \leq i \leq n$$

It should be noted that the identity $f = g$ is symbol identity; to be identical, two term constructors must be the same symbol. It is assumed that every symbol represents a distinct function. This is the so-called totally free algebra construction, which is useful in both logic and algebra.

We are thinking of our feature structures as functions and their features as arguments in what follows, as in LFG (Bresnan and Kaplan 1982), which varies from the approach of Johnson (1988) and Smolka (1988), which views features as functions and feature structures as arguments. In this way, a feature structure, as a partial function, provides a value for all of the features for which it is defined. One way of formalizing a functional approach is provided by taking the collection of feature structures to be a solution for **FS** in:

(3) $\mathbf{FS} = \mathsf{Atom} \cup (\mathsf{Feat} \rightarrow \mathbf{FS})$

From this perspective, it is clear that the (partial) functions in $(\mathsf{Feat} \rightarrow \mathbf{FS})$ must be taken to be intensional; a non-atomic feature structure modeled by a function is not identified solely by the values it provides for features. The intensionality is essentially due to the fact that we cannot identify feature structures which are alphabetic variants. Distinct alphabetic variants can act as values for distinct paths in a feature structure without their being identified.

Extensionality

We are able to recover the extensional behavior of terms when desired by treating our types analogously to term constructors. The reason that this is possible is that we have specified the appropriate features for each type. We simply add more information to our type specification that determines the types which should behave extensionally. It turns out that in the case of cyclic structures, there are two sensible approaches that can be taken to extensionality. Both only make sense when defined relative to a given appropriateness specification. The first is based on the standard notion of extensionality and requires two feature structures which are labeled with the same extensional type and share all of their appropriate features to be identical. The stronger version of extensionality is based on the notion of extensionality in the non-well-founded set theory of Aczel (1988). For acyclic feature structures, the two definitions are identical. We consider each in turn.

Definition 8.1 (Extensionality Specification)

An extensionality specification *over an inheritance hierarchy* $\langle \mathsf{Type}, \sqsubseteq \rangle$ *is an upward closed set* $\mathsf{ExtType} \subseteq \mathsf{Type}$.

The types $\mathsf{IntType} = \mathsf{Type} \setminus \mathsf{ExtType}$ *are said to be* intensional.

Remember that upward closure means that if $\sigma \in$ ExtType and $\sigma \sqsubseteq \tau$, then $\tau \in$ ExtType. The upward closure condition on extensional types is assumed to make sure that if enough information is available to uniquely identify an object, then adding more type information does not take away this identifiability. This opens up the possibility of having two distinct sets of features uniquely identify feature structures of a particular type. For instance, consider the case in which we have extensional types σ_1, σ_2, and τ such that $\sigma_1 \sqsubseteq \tau$ and $\sigma_2 \sqsubseteq \tau$, with only the feature f_1 appropriate for σ_1 and only f_2 appropriate for σ_2. A feature structure of type τ is uniquely determined by either its value for f_1 or its value for f_2. For instance, consider the interpretation in which σ_1 represents the class of drivers and σ_2 the class of students, with f_1 picking out the driver's license number and f_2 the student identification number. In this case, individuals in the class of driving students ($\tau = \sigma_1 \sqcup \sigma_2$) might be uniquely identified by either their student identification number (f_1) or their driver's license number (f_2). Inconsistency follows if an attempt is made to employ two feature structures with identical student identification numbers and with distinct driver's license numbers. But in potential applications, a student identification number or name alone might not be enough to uniquely identify an individual, even when taken together, since more than one person might have the same name, and more than one university might assign a given identification number. But the combination of a student identification number and university might be sufficient information to uniquely identify an individual, assuming that any given university does not assign the same identification number to different individuals. This could be expressed using an extensional type appropriate for features representing the student identification number and university.

In relational databases, it is usually assumed that there is a unique identifying field for a record structure representing some object. For instance, every employee might be given an employee number, and parts might be given inventory numbers, invoices assigned invoice numbers, and so on. One way to think of our extensional types is as generalizing this condition in two ways. The first thing to notice is that if an extensional type is appropriate for more than one feature, then it is the combination of feature values that uniquely identifies objects of that type, as in the example of university and university-specific identification number above. The second generalization comes in that we can assume two orthogonal identifiers for a given individual, as in the case of the driver's license number and student identification number example. This occurs when two consistent types are both extensional; feature structures of both types can be identified by the features of either extensional type. Of course, it is always possible to assume that the set of minimal extensional types is pairwise inconsistent, and that each is only appropriate for a single feature to fully recover the unique identifier restrictions often placed on relational databases.

We now provide a definition of feature structures that meet the extensionality conditions. We assume that we are considering at least the collection of well-typed feature structures, as extensionality only makes sense in the context of appropriateness conditions and that we have fixed an appropriateness specification, a type hierarchy, and the collection of extensional types.

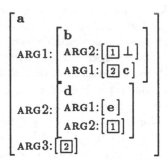

Figure 8.2. Encoding of $a(b(X, c), d(e, X), c)$.

Definition 8.2 (Extensional Feature Structure)

$F = \langle Q, \bar{q}, \theta, \delta \rangle \in \mathcal{TF}$ *is extensional if and only if* $q = q'$ *whenever* $\tau \in$ ExtType, $\tau \sqsubseteq \theta(q)$, $\tau \sqsubseteq \theta(q')$, *and* $\delta(f, q) = \delta(f, q')$ *for all* f *appropriate for* τ.

Let $\mathcal{ETF}$ *be the collection of extensional well-typed feature structures, and* $\mathcal{ETTF}$ *be the extensional totally well-typed feature structures.*

The definition of extensionality is complicated somewhat by the fact that we have allowed non-maximal types to be extensional. To paraphrase the conditions, we are simply requiring two substructures of an extensional feature structure to be identical if they share a common extensional supertype and assign identical values to all of the features appropriate for this extensional supertype.

We can now capture the logical behavior of the atoms of PATR-II or Rounds and Kasper (1986) and the copyable atoms of Smolka (1988) by considering extensional types which are not appropriate for any features. Thus we finally have enough power to form a collection of feature structures isomorphic to most of those that have been studied previously. To capture the rest of the logical behavior of PATR-II structures, it is simply necessary to treat the atoms as just described and allow a single intensional type which is appropriate for every feature. Both the atoms and the feature structure type are subtypes of the bottom element.

We can also now capture the behavior of first-order terms of the kind used in logic programming languages and automatic theorem-proving systems. For each term constructor of arity n we simply assume an extensional type appropriate for the features ARG1, ARG2, ..., ARGn. We assume that these types are are pairwise incomparable and that there is an additional least type $\perp$ appropriate for no features, which we assign as the type of variables. Since there is a maximal arity for any finite set of term constructors, we only need a finite number of features. We then represent a term as a feature structure of the type of the term's constructor and with features assigned to the value of the representations of the term's arguments. We then assume that two occurrences of the same variable indicate structure sharing in the feature structure. We thus encode a

$$\begin{bmatrix} \textbf{false} \\ \text{CONTEXT:} [\, c_1 \,] \\ \text{ARG:} \begin{bmatrix} \boxed{1}\ \textbf{false} \\ \text{CONTEXT:} [\, c_2 \,] \\ \text{ARG:} [\, \boxed{1} \,] \end{bmatrix} \end{bmatrix}$$

Figure 8.3. Contextualized Liar Encoding.

term such as $a(b(X, c), d(e, X), c)$ as in Figure 8.2. The important thing to note in this representation is that all of the subterms which would be considered identical are explicitly shared. This is what actually happens in the pointer-based representations of terms, when the constructor of a term is represented by a pointer into a symbol table (Maier and Warren 1988). Without this sharing, we would not have an extensional feature structure. Since the term c has no arguments, it is of arity 0 and hence the type c is appropriate for no arguments, so that any two occurrences of it trivially share all of their appropriate features and must be identified. Of course, we could have used our encoding of lists to represent the arguments of a term, and this is often done in implementations of Prolog (Maier and Warren 1988).

We now reconsider the feature structures (5) and (8) from Chapter 3, which we took to represent the semantic content of the liar sentence and its negation in (4) and (7), respectively. We repeat these feature structures for convenience:

$$(4) \quad \begin{bmatrix} \textbf{false} \\ \text{ARG:} \begin{bmatrix} \boxed{1}\ \textbf{false} \\ \text{ARG:} [\, \boxed{1} \,] \end{bmatrix} \end{bmatrix} \sqsubseteq \begin{bmatrix} \boxed{1}\ \textbf{false} \\ \text{ARG:} [\, \boxed{1} \,] \end{bmatrix}$$

If we were to assume that **false** was extensional and only appropriate for ARG, then the more general of these strongly well-typed feature structures would not be extensional. The reason is that the top-level structure and the feature structure that is the value for the top-level structure at ARG have identical values for all of their appropriate features and would thus have to be identified to achieve extensionality. If we do not want this identification given our representation of propositions, then we must assume that **false** is an intensional type. It should be noted that this is not the approach taken by Barwise and Etchemendy (1987), who used the extensional non-well-founded set theory of Aczel (1988) to represent the liar sentences. The trick they used can actually be generalized to a wide variety of situations involving extensionality. What they did was to assume an additional argument to represent a contextual feature which would be different for the sentence and embedded sentence in the denial of the liar. This would produce a representation something like that given in Figure 8.3. In this situation, even if **false** is extensional, the distinct substructures representing propositions are not identified because they have incompatible values for the feature CONTEXT.

$$
\left[\begin{array}{l}
t \\
\text{F:} \left[\begin{array}{l} \boxed{1}\ s \\ \text{H:} [\boxed{1}] \end{array} \right] \\
\text{G:} \left[\begin{array}{l} \boxed{2}\ s \\ \text{H:} [\boxed{2}] \end{array} \right]
\end{array} \right]
$$

Figure 8.4. Non-Identified Substructures with Identical Unfoldings.

We now turn our attention to modeling the kinds of logical terms used in logic programming languages such as Prolog II and Prolog II. We claim that the main difference between feature structures and logical terms (as they are normally defined) is their treatment of extensionality. To properly model the terms in a logic programming language (with the occurs check) we have to assume that we are dealing with only acyclic feature structures. It appears at first that we would be able to model the terms used in Prolog II (Colmerauer 1984) by simply dropping the restriction that our feature structures be acyclic. But this does not quite work due to the representation in Prolog II of cyclic terms as their infinite tree unfoldings. Our extensionality conditions are not quite strong enough to identify feature structures that have the same unfoldings into infinite trees. Simply consider the feature structure in Figure 8.4. In this structure, the values for the features F and G are alphabetic variants and thus have the same unfoldings to infinite trees. But even if we assume that the type s is extensional and only appropriate for the feature H, we are not forced to identify the two substructures because they do not have identical values for all of their features. We return shortly to the more strict version of extensionality which can be used provide an adequate model for the terms (or tree structures) of Prolog II.

Following our previous pattern, we now describe the unification and logical behavior of the class of extensional feature structures. As before, the results all hinge on a form of extensionality inference that allows us to represent the satisfiers of arbitrary non-disjunctive descriptions by means of a most general satisfier. We first consider the case of the extensional well-typed feature structures in $\mathcal{ETF}$. We say that a well-typed feature structure $F \in \mathcal{TF}$ can be *extensionalized* if there is an extensional well-typed feature structure $F' \in \mathcal{ETF}$ to which it can be extended so that $F \sqsubseteq F'$. Somewhat surprisingly, not every well-typed feature structure can be extensionalized. The problem arises in the case mentioned above when there is an extensional type with a subtype with additional features. For instance, suppose we have an extensional type σ appropriate only for F with a subtype τ which is also appropriate for G. Now suppose that the types ρ and ρ' are incompatible. Suppose for convenience that there is a type γ which is appropriate for H and J and that none of the types place restrictions on the values of their appropriate features. Then the well-typed feature structure in Figure 8.5 is not extensionalizable. The extensionality condition would require that the values for the features J and H be

$$
\begin{bmatrix}
\gamma \\
\text{H:} \begin{bmatrix} \tau \\ \text{F:} [\boxed{1}\ \bot] \\ \text{G:} [\rho] \end{bmatrix} \\
\text{J:} \begin{bmatrix} \tau \\ \text{F:} [\boxed{1}] \\ \text{G:} [\rho'] \end{bmatrix}
\end{bmatrix}
$$

Figure 8.5. Un-Extensionalizable Well-Typed Feature Structure.

shared because they are assigned to the subtype τ of σ and share values for all of the appropriate features of σ. We now present a procedure to carry out the extensionalization of a feature structure and halt with failure if the feature structure is not extensionalizable.

Theorem 8.3 (Extensionality)

There is a partial function $Ext: \mathcal{TF} \to \mathcal{ETF}$ such that if $F \in \mathcal{TF}$ and $F' \in \mathcal{ETF}$ are such that $F \sqsubseteq F'$, then $Ext(F) \sqsubseteq F'$.

Proof: To carry out extensionalization, we iterate the following step:

> select a pair of nodes assigned a common extensional supertype and sharing all appropriate feature values and identify them.

By the identification of two nodes, we mean unifying the feature structures rooted at these nodes. This process either fails or produces a unique most general result. We must be careful to apply type inference to the result of unifying the two nodes; this is because the result of unification might produce more specific types which require more specific values for some of their features. If the unification process fails, the feature structure we started with was not extensionalizable. This process is guaranteed to terminate as the unification and type inference procedures are known to halt for all inputs, and the extensionalization loop strictly reduces the size of the input structure. It is also guaranteed to produce the most general extension of a feature structure which is extensional, as all of the identifications in the body of the loop are necessary, and the order in which they are carried out does not affect the result. The order independence is again due to the fact that the conditions for identification of nodes is monotonic and is thus not affected by previous identifications. □

Not surprisingly given the form of its definition, we can use the same technique that we used for the type inference procedures to verify the following result.

Theorem 8.4

The function $Ext: \mathcal{TF} \to \mathcal{TF}$ is an inference procedure.

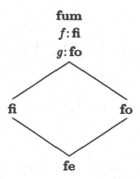

Figure 8.6. Extensionalization Loops.

We can prove a corollary to this result in the case in which every extensional type happens to be maximal.

Corollary 8.5

If every extensional type is maximal, then the inference procedure Ext:$\mathcal{TF}$ → $\mathcal{ETF}$ is total.

Proof: Two nodes are only identified if they are of the same type, so that additional type inference is not necessary. □

Of course, allowing only maximal extensional types is too restrictive to allow us to represent the case of a student driver being identified by either a driver's license number or student identification number.

As might be expected, the ramifications of extensionalization are much more subtle in the case of totally well-typed feature structures. We say that a totally well-typed feature structure $F \in \mathcal{TTF}$ can be *totally extensionalized* if there is an extensional totally well-typed feature structure $F' \in \mathcal{ETTF}$ to which it can be extended so that $F \sqsubseteq F'$. But infinite loops can be encountered in trying to extensionalize a totally well-typed feature structure that are not due to loops in the appropriateness conditions. To illustrate the problem, consider the type hierarchy, illustrated in Figure 8.6, consisting of the four types **fe**, **fi**, **fo**, and **fum** arranged so that **fe** is the bottom element and **fum** is the top element and so that **fi** and **fo** are incomparable and between the two. Now suppose that **fum** was appropriate for features f and g, where f was required to be of type **fi** and g was required to be of type **fo**. Furthermore, assume that all of the types are extensional. Consider the following totally well-typed feature structure:

(5) $\begin{bmatrix} \textbf{fum} \\ f:[\textbf{fi}] \\ g:[\textbf{fo}] \end{bmatrix}$

This structure forces the extensionalization process into an infinite loop. The problem arises because we would be forced to equate the values of f and g

because **fi** and **fo** share the extensional supertype **fe** and have identical values for all of the features appropriate for **fe**, of which there are none in this case. Thus we would unify the values for f and g, producing a result of type **fum**, which we would then totally well-type to produce the result:

$$(6) \quad \begin{bmatrix} \textbf{fum} \\ f: \begin{bmatrix} \boxed{1}\,\textbf{fum} \\ f:[\textbf{fi}] \\ g:[\textbf{fo}] \end{bmatrix} \\ g:[\boxed{1}] \end{bmatrix}$$

Repeating the extensionalization step sends us off into an infinite loop. As was the case for appropriateness loops, the feature structure in (5) is extensional-izable, but only with the additions of cycles. In this case, there is in fact a well-typed and extensional extension of the feature structure in (5), namely:

$$(7) \quad \begin{bmatrix} \boxed{1}\,\textbf{fum} \\ f:[\boxed{1}] \\ g:[\boxed{1}] \end{bmatrix}$$

But as before, there is no most general extensional totally well-typed feature structure which extends the example in (5).

One way to avoid this problem is to assume that the only extensional types are maximal. If this is the case, then we can use the same extensionalization function as before.

Theorem 8.6

If the appropriateness conditions do not contain loops and every extensional type is maximal, then the function $Ext: TTF \rightarrow \mathcal{E}TTF$ is total. Furthermore, for $F \in TTF$ and $F' \in \mathcal{E}TTF$, we have $F \sqsubseteq F'$ if and only if $Ext(F) \sqsubseteq F'$.

Proof: Simply note that type inference and value filling are not necessary because we identify two nodes only if have the same type and are identical for all of their features. $\square$

As before, the existence of an extensionalization function Ext allows us to define unification operations on the collections $\mathcal{E}TF$ and $\mathcal{E}TTF$ of extensional (totally) well-typed feature structures. We combine the results, as their proofs are identical.

Theorem 8.7 (Extensional Unification)

The least upper bound of consistent extensional well-typed feature structures can be defined by $Ext(TypInf(F \sqcup F'))$.

The least upper bound of consistent extensional totally well-typed feature structures can be defined by $Ext(Fill(TypInf(F \sqcup F')))$ if there are no loops in the appropriateness conditions and only maximal types are declared as extensional.

Proof: We present only the proof for the well-typed case as the proof for the total case is identical. We know that $TypInf(F \sqcup F')$ is the most general well-typed feature structure that extends F and F' and $Ext(TypInf(F \sqcup F'))$ is the most general extensional well-typed feature structure that extends this. Thus if $F \sqsubseteq F''$ and $F' \sqsubseteq F''$ for some $F'' \in \mathcal{ETF}$, then we must have $Ext(TypInf(F \sqcup F')) \sqsubseteq F''$.   □

This result tells us that to unify two extensional feature structures, we can take their unification, perform type inference on the result, and then extensionalization to the result of this.

We can now consider the logical behavior of the extensional (totally) well-typed feature structures. We relativize our notions of satisfiers, satisfiability and logical equivalence in the usual way to our new collection of feature structures. We can derive most general satisfiers just as we have done before by using unification.

Theorem 8.8 (Extensional Most General Satisfier)

If $\phi \in$ Desc is an $\mathcal{ETF}$-satisfiable non-disjunctive description, then $F \models \phi$ for $F \in \mathcal{ETF}$ if and only if $Ext(TypInf(MGSat(\phi))) \sqsubseteq F$.

If $\phi \in$ Desc is an $\mathcal{ETTF}$-satisfiable non-disjunctive description, there are no loops in the appropriateness conditions and only maximal types are extensional, then $F \models \phi$ for $F \in \mathcal{ETTF}$ if and only if $Ext(Fill(TypInf(MGSat(\phi)))) \sqsubseteq F$.

Proof: We again only consider the non-total case. If $F \models \phi$, then we have $MGSat(\phi) \sqsubseteq F$, and if F is well-typed and satisfies ϕ, then:

$$TypInf(MGSat(F)) \sqsubseteq F$$

and if F is also extensional and satisfies ϕ, then:

$$Ext(Fill(TypInf(MGSat(\phi)))) \sqsubseteq F \qquad\qquad □$$

As before, we can use this to derive most general satisfiers for the full set of descriptions with disjunctions. We simply find the most general satisfier for each of the disjuncts after putting the description into disjunctive normal form.

We are now ready to characterize extensionality axiomatically. The axiom scheme that we use is just the formal analogue of our extensionality condition. We let $\mathcal{E_{ETF}}$ consist of the axioms in $\mathcal{E_{TF}}$ with all of the instances of the following extensionality axiom and let $\mathcal{E_{ETTF}}$ contain the axioms in $\mathcal{E_{TTF}}$ and the instances of the extensionality axiom.

11. Extensionality

$$\pi_1 : \sigma \;\wedge\; \pi_2 : \sigma \;\wedge\; \bigwedge\nolimits_{Approp(f,\sigma)\text{ defined}} \pi_1 f \doteq \pi_2 f$$

$$\Leftrightarrow \pi_1 \doteq \pi_2 \;\wedge\; \pi_1 : \sigma \;\wedge\; \pi_2 : \sigma \;\wedge\; \bigwedge\nolimits_{Approp(f,\sigma)\text{ defined}} \pi_1 f \doteq \pi_2 f$$

$$[\text{if } \sigma \in \mathsf{ExtType}]$$

Putting this axiom into prose, it requires that if we have described a feature structure as having values for two paths (π_1 and π_2) which we know to be of an extensional type (σ) and furthermore share all of their values for appropriate features (fs such that $Approp(f,\sigma)$ is defined), then we can conclude that the two paths must be shared. This axiom covers our definition of extensionality because if $\sigma \sqsubseteq \tau$, we have:

(8) $\vdash_{\mathcal{F}} \pi : \tau \Leftrightarrow \pi : \sigma \wedge \pi : \tau$

We can use the extensionality axiom to parallel the steps used in the extensionalization procedure to allow us to derive a completeness result for the logics of extensional (totally) well-typed feature structures.

Theorem 8.9 (Extensional Soundness and Completeness)

$\models_{\mathcal{ETF(ETTF)}} \phi \equiv \psi$ *if and only if* $\vdash_{\mathcal{E}_{\mathcal{ETF(ETTF)}}} \phi \Leftrightarrow \psi$.

Proof: Soundness in both cases follows from the definition of extensionality.

Completeness follows from noting that we have completeness for $\mathcal{E}_{TF}$ and $\mathcal{E}_{TTF}$, and the instances of the extensionality axiom can be used to simulate the steps in the extensionalization procedure. $\square$

Note that it is not necessary to restrict the context of the totally well-typed extensional soundness and completeness result to the case in which no extensionalization loops can occur, such as the one seen with the hierarchy in Figure 8.6. The reason is that even though our extensionalization procedure runs into a loop, the description that causes the loop is not unsatisfiable. The extensionality axiom is strong enough to allow us to prove that two descriptions are equivalent if they are logically equivalent with respect to the extensional totally typed feature structures.

Collapsing

We now turn our attention to a more restrictive notion of extensionality which is based on Aczel's (1988) Anti-Foundation Axiom (AFA), which generalizes the standard set-theoretic notion of extensionality to handle possibly non-well-founded sets. We define our stronger version of extensionality in terms of relations which are similar to the bisimulations of Aczel (1988).

Definition 8.10 (Collapsing)

If $F = \langle Q, \bar{q}, \theta, \delta \rangle \in \mathcal{TF}$, *then an equivalence relation* $\asymp \,\subseteq Q \times Q$ *is a* collapsing *if* $q \asymp q'$ *for* $q \neq q'$ *only if:*

- *some* $\sigma \in \mathsf{ExtType}$ *is such that* $\sigma \sqsubseteq \theta(q)$ *and* $\sigma \sqsubseteq \theta(q')$
- *if* $Approp(f,\sigma)$, *then* $\delta(f,q)$ *and* $\delta(f,q')$ *are defined and* $\delta(f,q) \asymp \delta(f,q')$

A feature structure $F \in \mathcal{TF}$ *is said to be* collapsed *if and only if the only collapsing over the nodes of* Q *is trivial, so that* $q \asymp q'$ *if and only if* $q = q'$.

Let $\mathcal{CTF}$ *be the collection of collapsed well-typed feature structures and* $\mathcal{CTTF}$ *be the collection of collapsed totally well-typed feature structures.*

A feature structure which can be extended to a collapsed feature structure is said to be *collapsible*.

Suppose we have an extensional type σ which is appropriate only for a feature f. Then the feature structures F and F' in in (9) and (10) are both collapsible.

$$(9) \quad F = \begin{bmatrix} \boxed{1}\,\sigma \\ f : \begin{bmatrix} \boxed{2}\,\sigma \\ f : [\boxed{1}] \end{bmatrix} \end{bmatrix}$$

$$(10) \quad F' = \begin{bmatrix} \bot \\ h : \begin{bmatrix} \boxed{1}\,\sigma \\ f : [\boxed{1}] \end{bmatrix} \\ j : \begin{bmatrix} \boxed{2}\,\sigma \\ f : [\boxed{2}] \end{bmatrix} \end{bmatrix}$$

In the case of F, a non-trivial collapsing would put $\bar{q} \asymp \delta(f, \bar{q})$, thus identifying the nodes at the end of the paths ϵ and f. This would produce the collapsed feature structure in (11):

$$(11) \quad \begin{bmatrix} \boxed{1}\,\sigma \\ f : [\boxed{1}] \end{bmatrix}$$

For F', we could collapse the nodes at the end of the paths h and j, arriving at the collapsed feature structure in (12):

$$(12) \quad \begin{bmatrix} \bot \\ h : \begin{bmatrix} \boxed{1}\,\sigma \\ f : [\boxed{1}] \end{bmatrix} \\ j : [\boxed{1}] \end{bmatrix}$$

The first thing to note is that we have indeed strengthened our extensionality conditions.

Theorem 8.11

If $F \in TF$ is collapsed, then it is extensional.

Proof: If two distinct nodes share an extensional supertype and share all of the values for features appropriate for that supertype, then there is a collapsing which relates them. □

In general, an arbitrary well-typed feature structure with a collapsed extension has a unique such extension.

Theorem 8.12 (Collapsing)

There is a partial function $Coll: TF \rightarrow CTF$ such that if $F, F' \in TF$ are such that $F \sqsubseteq F'$ and F' is collapsed, then $Coll(F) \sqsubseteq F'$.

Proof: First note that the transitive, reflexive and symmetric closure of the union of two collapsings is also a collapsing. Thus there is a maximal collapsing of any given well-typed feature structure. We can then unify all of the nodes that are related by the collapsing and perform type inference on the result. We can then iterate this process until we reach closure. The iteration is bound to terminate because there are only a finite number of nodes to begin with. The result is the most general collapsed extension of the feature structure we began with. □

As usual, things are more subtle in the case of total typing. Just as before, an attempt to find a minimal collapsed extension of a well-typed feature structure may lead to infinite loops during the type inference stage of the collapsing process. But if we restrict our attention to the situation in which every extensional type is maximal, things go through just as before.

Corollary 8.13

If there are no appropriateness loops and every extensional type is maximal, then if $F \in TTF$, $Coll(F)$ is defined and $Coll(F) \in CTTF$.

Proof: No type inference is required during the collapsing process, since no types are ever raised. □

The nice part about this notion of collapsing is that with our representation of first-order terms as flat lattices it provides the correct identity conditions for terms in Prolog II and Prolog III, which were originally stated in terms of infinite trees (Colmerauer 1984, 1987). What we have done is assumed a canonical representation which is maximally collapsed rather than maximally unfolded.

It is actually possible to axiomatize our notion of collapsing, but the axiomatization we provide is rather inelegant, as we define it directly in terms of feature structures and collapsing rather than providing a purely syntactic characterization. We let $\mathcal{E}_{CTF}$ ($\mathcal{E}_{CTTF}$) consist of the axioms in $\mathcal{E}_{TF}$ ($\mathcal{E}_{TTF}$) and the instances of the following collapsing axiom scheme:

12. Collapsing

$$\phi \Leftrightarrow \phi \wedge \pi \doteq \pi' \quad \text{[if some collapsing on } MGSat(\phi) \text{ has } \delta(\pi, \bar{q}) \asymp \delta(\pi', \bar{q})]$$

It should be clear that this is a proper axiomatization of the collapsed feature structures because the condition we state on formulas is obviously decidable. In particular, we can compute the minimal satisfier of the description ϕ and there are only a finite number of binary relations to consider as possible collapsings over the finite set of nodes in the minimal satisfier of ϕ. Furthermore, this condition could be stated without recourse to the feature structures themselves by using the normal form theorem for descriptions and translating the notion of collapsing on the nodes of a feature structure to a relation between hooks in a normal form.

It should also be obvious that this axiomatization of the collapsed feature structures is sound and complete, simply by definition.

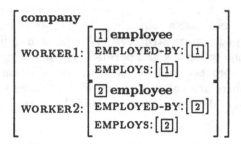

Figure 8.7. Strange Company Example.

Theorem 8.14 (Collapsed Soundness and Completeness)

$\models_{CTF(CTTF)} \phi \equiv \psi$ *if and only if* $\vdash_{\mathcal{E}_{CTF(CTTF)}} \phi \Leftrightarrow \psi$.

Finally, we consider a case brought to our attention by Carl Pollard (personal communication) in which it might be desirable to enforce the weaker extensionality axioms rather than the stronger notion of collapsing. Pollard's example involves a company in which every boss has exactly one employee and every employee is the employee of exactly one boss. In particular, this pattern should allow us to conclude from the fact that two people had the same boss and same employee that they were in fact the same person. But now consider what happens in such a company if there are two people, each of whom employs only him or herself. In particular, consider the feature structure representation of this situation in Figure 8.7. What makes this example so strange is that by using collapsing, we are able to conclude that the first and second employee are in fact identical if the type **employee** is taken to be extensional. But if we were to only use the weaker forms of extensionality inference rather than the collapsing scheme, we would not be forced to identify the two employees in this example, as their values for the EMPLOYED-BY and EMPLOYS features are not shared. Thus there seem to be cases in which the weaker notion of extensionality is preferable to collapsing. Of course, nothing prevents us from combining the two approaches to extensionality in one system.

Chapter 9

Maximality, Groundedness, and Closed World Inference

Because we think of feature structures as representing partial information, the question immediately arises as to whether the notion of total information makes sense in this framework and if so, what its relation to partial information might be. Our notions of "total" information in this chapter are decidedly relative in the sense that they are only defined with respect to a fixed type inheritance hierarchy and fixed appropriateness conditions.

Before tackling the more complicated case of feature structures, we consider the first-order terms. First-order terms can be ordered by subsumption. The maximal elements in this ordering are the ground terms, a *ground term* being simply a term without variables. It is well known that the semantics of logic programming systems and even first-order logic can be characterized by restricting attention to the collection of ground terms, the so-called *Herbrand Universe*. The reason this is true is that every first-order term is equivalent to the meet of the collection of its ground extensions (Reynolds 1970). Thus any first-order term is uniquely determined by its ground extensions. It is also interesting to note that as a corollary, a term subsumes a second term just in case its set of ground instantiations is strictly larger than the set of ground instantiations of the second term. In this chapter, we consider whether or not we can derive equivalent results for feature structures. One motivation for deriving such results is that they make life much easier when it comes time to characterize the behavior of feature structure unification-based phrase structure grammars and logic programming systems. Unfortunately, we achieve only limited success.

When we consider the analogue of the Herbrand Universe of ground terms in the collection of feature structures, we are immediately faced with a host of thorny problems. Most immediate among these issues is that with the typed feature structures there is a distinction between a maximal feature structure in the subsumption ordering and what we take to be the analogue of a ground term. A *ground feature structure* is one in which every type is maximal and all consistent substructures are shared. Complications also arise when considering extensionality and inequations. We argue that for feature structures, both extensionality and inequations are necessary to even come close to achieving a situation in which feature structures are characterized by their maximal or ground extensions.

We would like to note that the notion of maximal or ground feature structures makes sense only when we are working with some form of the closed world hypothesis. That is, we assume that a feature structure represents its set of maximal extensions. More precisely, we wish only to draw a distinction between two feature structures if they can be extended to distinct collections of maximal feature structures. Thus if we have a type σ, we assume that all of its relevant subtypes are explicitly given in the inheritance hierarchy and that all of their relevant features are detailed in the appropriateness conditions. For this kind of situation to make sense, we must not think of a non-maximal feature structure as possibly representing some extension which is not laid out in the type hierarchy and appropriateness conditions. We argue that from a closed world reasoning point of view, the appropriate notion of total information is that of a ground term. Unfortunately, we achieve only limited success in axiomatizing the situation when two descriptions are satisfied by exactly the same ground feature structures, as we have to resort to a disjunctive logic that basically expands every feature structure into the feature structures that might extend it.

Before going on to feature structures, we first consider constraints that are necessary on the type hierarchy to give us any chance of characterizing feature structures in terms of either their maximal or ground extensions. Thus our initial goal is to find a condition under which two types are identical if and only if they subsume the same maximal types. As it turns out, a necessary and sufficient condition for achieving such a maximal representation is that there are no unary branches in the type hierarchy. To make this notion of unary branching more precise, in an arbitrary partial order $\langle S, \leq \rangle$ we say t *covers* s if and only if $s \leq u \leq t$ implies $u = s$ or $u = t$. A *unary branch* is a pair s, t such that t is the only element that covers s. Note that if there is a unary branch from s to t, then there is no $t' \neq t$ such that t' covers s, but there might be an $s' \neq s$ such that t covers s'. Thus the condition has an upwards orientation. The unary branching condition rules out both of the hierarchies in Figure 9.1. For instance, even though joins exist for consistent types in both hierarchies, in the network (a) there is a unary branch from τ to ρ and in (b) from σ to τ. Note that with the unary branching condition there can be no top element in the type hierarchy (unless there is only one type).

Intuitively, the reason the unary branch prohibition turns out to be necessary is that if there was a unary branch from σ to τ, then the only way to extend a structure of type σ would be to one of type τ. Somewhat surprisingly, we can show that the unary branch condition is not only necessary, but sufficient for the representation of types in terms of their maximal extensions. We use the following notation when $\langle S, \leq \rangle$ is a partially ordered set:

(1) $Max_{\langle S, \leq \rangle}(t) = \{t' \geq t \mid t' \text{ maximal in } S\}$

We drop the subscript when the poset is obvious from context.

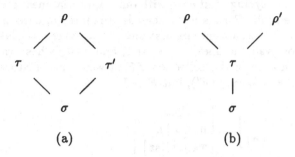

Figure 9.1. Inheritance Hierarchies Failing Unary Branch Condition.

Theorem 9.1 (Type Maximal Representation)

$\langle$Type, $\sqsubseteq\rangle$ *has no unary branching if and only if for* $\sigma, \tau \in$ Type, $\sigma = \tau$ *if and only if* $Max(\sigma) = Max(\tau)$.

Proof: First suppose that $\langle$Type, $\sqsubseteq\rangle$ has no unary branching. If $\sigma = \tau$, then obviously $Max(\sigma) = Max(\tau)$. We next show that if $\sigma \neq \tau$, then $Max(\sigma) \neq Max(\tau)$. If σ and τ are not consistent the result is obvious. So suppose that $\sigma \sqcup \tau$ exists. We proceed by induction on the maximum distance between $\perp$ and σ and τ. We know that $Max(\sigma) \cap Max(\tau) = Max(\sigma \sqcup \tau)$ because we have consistent joins. But we know that since we have no unary branches, there must be at least two direct subtypes of σ (where a direct subtype covers a type in the sense that there are no types properly between them). So suppose that ρ is a direct subtype of σ such that $\rho \neq \sigma \sqcup \tau$. The result then follows from the inductive hypothesis, since there must be at least one element in $Max(\rho)$ that is not in $Max(\sigma \sqcup \tau)$. This is enough to ensure that $Max(\sigma) \neq Max(\tau)$, since this element is in $Max(\sigma)$, but not in $Max(\sigma) \cap Max(\tau)$.

If $\langle$Type, $\sqsubseteq\rangle$ is not unary branching, then there is a unary branch from σ to τ, in which case $Max(\sigma) = Max(\tau)$. $\qquad\qquad\square$

Thus we can represent an arbitrary type in an inheritance hierarchy without unary branches by the set of its maximal subtypes. For the rest of this chapter, we suppose that we are working with a type inheritance hierarchy in which there are no unary branches, because otherwise we would have no hope of representing feature structures in terms of their maximal extensions.

We now move on to consider what other restrictions need to be enforced to give us a chance of maximal representation holding. First of all, consider the simple untyped feature structures. An untyped feature structure in $\mathcal{F}$ is maximal only if it is defined for every feature in **Feat**. It is clear that the intention of those employing feature structures, for instance in PATR-II, do not think of feature structures as representing all of their possible extensions to maximal feature structures for the simple reason that they assume an implicit type scheme whereby all of the features are not intended to co-occur. We believe that this is why the subject of maximal feature structures has not been broached before the topic of typing. But even with our appropriateness conditions, things are still not so simple. For instance, consider the familiar case in which we have the **list** type with two subtypes **ne-list** and **e-list**, where **ne-list** is appropriate for HEAD, whose value it does not restrict, and TAIL, whose value must be of type **list**. Then even in the collection $\mathcal{TF}$ of well-typed feature structures we have $Max_{\mathcal{TF}}(F) = Max_{\mathcal{TF}}(F')$, but $F \not\sim F'$, as in:

$$(2) \quad F = \begin{bmatrix} \textbf{ne-list} \\ \text{HEAD:} [\,\textbf{a}\,] \end{bmatrix} \not\sim \begin{bmatrix} \textbf{ne-list} \\ \text{HEAD:} [\,\textbf{a}\,] \\ \text{TAIL:} [\,\textbf{list}\,] \end{bmatrix} = F'$$

Unfortunately, F and F' are not alphabetic variants because although $F \sqsubseteq F'$, we do not have $F' \sqsubseteq F$. In some sense, F and F' represent exactly the same partial information, but are not alphabetic variants. Thus it is obvious that we should at least enforce the total type scheme. After all, the maximal representation result holds for first-order terms and they are totally typed in our sense.

The feature structure F in (2) is not totally well-typed, so the kind of problem in (2) simply does not arise with totally well-typed feature structures. Unfortunately, a much more subtle problem crops up even in the case of totally well-typed structures because of our notion of structure sharing. Consider the well-typed feature structures in Figure 9.2. These are examples of highly simplified structures of the variety used to represent discourse referents in HPSG (Pollard and Sag in press). Suppose that **referent** is appropriate just for the features GENDER and NUMBER. Then the structures in Figure 9.2 are both totally well-typed, assuming that **sentence** is appropriate just for SUBJECT and OBJECT. But these feature structures are obviously not alphabetic variants, as one contains strictly more structure sharing than the other. Furthermore, the more specific of the feature structures in Figure 9.2 is maximal because it cannot be consistently extended. On the other hand, the less instantiated structure in Figure 9.2 can only be extended to the more instantiated structure in Figure 9.2. Thus the structures in Figure 9.2 have the same collection of maximal extensions but are not alphabetic variants. This time we have seen that two distinct totally well-typed feature structures can represent identical information in terms of possible extensions to maximal structures. This problem arises because of the way in which we have dealt with structure sharing and its relation to subsumption.

There are two ways in which we might approach the structures in Figure 9.2, either by extensionality or by inequation. Suppose the types **referent**, **sing** and **neut** were taken to be extensional in Figure 9.2. Then if we enforced extensionality the problem in Figure 9.2 would not arise; the less instantiated of the two structures is simply not extensional and is thus ruled out on independent grounds. Note that in the case of first-order terms, every term constructor is treated extensionally, which is why these kinds of issues do not arise in that context. Similarly, in the case of Prolog II , collapsing is enforced, which again prevents violations of maximal representation. But unfortunately, considering

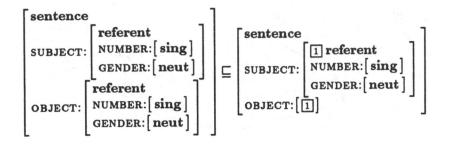

Figure 9.2. Coding Referents in HPSG.

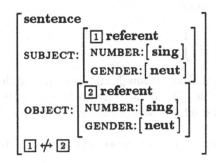

Figure 9.3. Inequated Referent Encoding.

again the example in Figure 9.2 leads us to the conclusion that the extensionality solution is not desirable in this case. In particular, in HPSG we think of feature structures as representing types of linguistic objects and just because we know two discourse referents are of the same type does not warrant the conclusion that they are identical. Thus we do not want to simply identify every maximal type-identical pair of feature structures. In this case, the only way to salvage any hope of getting a maximal representation theorem is to introduce a notion of inequation. With inequations, we see in Figure 9.3 that the extension in Figure 9.2 is not the only one possible. In particular, if two substructures are not shared in a feature structure, they may either be shared or inequated in an extension of that structure.

But even when we restrict our attention to type hierarchies without unary branches, enforce extensionality (or collapsing) where appropriate, and allow inequations in other cases, all of our problems do not go away. There are lingering problems which stem from the way in which total well-typing is defined and the nature of type inference. In particular, consider the type hierarchy and appropriateness conditions in Figure 9.4. Now consider the following totally

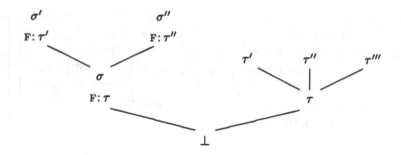

Figure 9.4. Problematic Hierarchy for Maximal Representation.

well-typed feature structures:

(3) $\quad \begin{bmatrix} \sigma \\ \text{F}:[\ \tau'\ ] \end{bmatrix} \not\prec \begin{bmatrix} \sigma' \\ \text{F}:[\ \tau'\ ] \end{bmatrix}$

It can be easily verified that although they are not alphabetic variants, the two feature structures in (3) can be extended to exactly the same maximal structures, namely, the singleton set consisting of the type σ' structure displayed in (3).

An altogether different kind of problem arises with feature structures of the following form:

(4) $\quad \begin{bmatrix} \sigma \\ \text{F}:[\ \tau'''\ ] \end{bmatrix}$

The problem with the feature structure in (4) is that it is maximal, but not in any sense grounded. In particular, the type τ''' is appropriate for the value of feature F in a type σ feature structure according to our definition. But there is something strange about the hierarchy in Figure 9.4 because it allows maximal feature structures such as that in (4) to contain non-maximal types.

Other more subtle cases exist that follow the same pattern. For instance, consider what would happen if we added a type ρ to Figure 9.4 which was appropriate for features F_1, F_2, F_3, and F_4, requiring them all to take values of type τ. Then there is no way to extend the feature structure in Figure 9.5 so that it is grounded. In this case, if we take τ', τ'' and τ''' to be extensional, then there is no way to extend the type τ in Figure 9.5 to a maximal type. Compare this with the situation illustrated in Figure 9.6. In this case, there are two ways we can extend the information in Figure 9.6, either by adding an inequality between $\boxed{4}$ and $\boxed{3}$ to recover the example in Figure 9.5 or by adding an equality between the same nodes. The problem here is that only by adding the equality can we extend the feature structure in Figure 9.6 to a feature structure in which every type is maximal. Adding the inequality leaves us with the same deadlock as in Figure 9.5.

$$
\begin{bmatrix}
\rho \\
F_1 : \begin{bmatrix} \boxed{1}\ \tau' \end{bmatrix} \\
F_2 : \begin{bmatrix} \boxed{2}\ \tau'' \end{bmatrix} \\
F_3 : \begin{bmatrix} \boxed{3}\ \tau''' \end{bmatrix} \\
F_4 : \begin{bmatrix} \boxed{4}\ \tau \end{bmatrix} \\
\boxed{4} \not\approx \boxed{1},\ \boxed{4} \not\approx \boxed{2} \\
\boxed{4} \not\approx \boxed{3}
\end{bmatrix}
$$

Figure 9.5. Ungroundable Inequated Feature Structure.

$$
\begin{bmatrix}
\rho \\
F_1 : \begin{bmatrix} \boxed{1}\ \tau' \end{bmatrix} \\
F_2 : \begin{bmatrix} \boxed{2}\ \tau'' \end{bmatrix} \\
F_3 : \begin{bmatrix} \boxed{3}\ \tau''' \end{bmatrix} \\
F_4 : \begin{bmatrix} \boxed{4}\ \tau \end{bmatrix} \\
\boxed{4} \not\approx \boxed{1},\ \boxed{4} \not\approx \boxed{2}
\end{bmatrix}
$$

Figure 9.6. Multiply Groundable Inequated Feature Structure.

It is very difficult to pinpoint the fault in these examples because the hierarchy preserves joins (and in fact, preserves meets, as well). The problem actually lies in the kinds of type inference that our system employs, which is not strong enough to conclude that any feature structure with a type τ' value for F must itself be of type σ'. It remains an open problem as to how to enhance type inference so that it can make the kinds of inferences required by hierarchies such as that in Figure 9.4. Note that a solution that only looks at the immediate subtypes of a type is not sufficient, as can be seen with the type hierarchy like that of Figure 9.4 with an extra layer of types between σ and σ' and σ''.

By brute force, we can define an operation that maps every feature structure onto the maximally specific feature structure which shares exactly the same set of maximal (or ground) instances. We do this by means of a closure operator which is defined over any partial ordering in which arbitrary non-empty meets exist.

Definition 9.2 (Maximal Closure)

If $\langle S, \le \rangle$ is closed under non-empty meets, let $CW : S \to S$ be the total closed world *function such that:*

$$
CW(x) = \bigsqcap Max_{\langle S, \le \rangle}(x)
$$

The closed world operator, as we have defined it, is not only an inference procedure, but it is also strong enough to ensure maximal representation.

Theorem 9.3 (Maximal Representation)

- $x \sqsubseteq CW(x)$

- $CW(CW(x)) = CW(x)$

- $CW(x) = CW(y)$ *if and only if* $Max(CW(x)) = Max(CW(y))$

Proof: Obviously $x \sqsubseteq y$ for every $y \in Max(x)$ and therefore, $x \sqsubseteq \bigsqcap Max(x)$.

The second result follows from the fact that $Max(CW(x)) = Max(x)$. For if there were an element $y \in Max(CW(x))$ such that $y \notin Max(x)$ this would contradict the fact that $CW(x) = \bigsqcap Max(x)$. Thus we have $CW(CW(x)) = \bigsqcap Max(CW(x)) = \bigsqcap Max(\bigsqcap Max(x)) = \bigsqcap Max(x) = CW(x)$.

The last result follows directly from the previous one.   □

Thus by restricting attention to $CW(S) = \{CW(x) \mid x \in S\}$ we have an information ordering in which the elements are identified by their maximal extensions. In particular, we can take the partial order $\langle S, \leq \rangle$ to be any of our collections of feature structures.

Of course, the same trick could be played with the ground structures. First, define the set of ground structures subsumed by F by:

(5) $Ground(F) = \{F' \mid F \sqsubseteq F' \text{ and } F' \text{ ground}\}$

By replacing *Max* with *Ground* in the definition of maximal closure to produce a notion of ground closure, we can immediately derive a ground representation theorem. But this brute force approach is rather unsatisfactory from a logical point of view as we have not shown how to axiomatize equivalence with respect to maximal (or ground) extensions.

One way to characterize the logic of ground feature structures is to consider the addition of instances of the following axioms to the total typing axioms:

13. (Type Maximality)

    $\perp \equiv \sigma_1 \vee \sigma_2 \vee \cdots \vee \sigma_n$ [if $\{\sigma_1, \ldots, \sigma_n\}$ are the maximal types]

14. (Path Separation)

    $\pi_1 {:} \perp \wedge \pi_2 {:} \perp \equiv \pi_1 \doteq \pi_2 \vee \pi_1 \neq \pi_2$

The effect of these axioms is to force every type to be replaced by one of its maximal extensions and every pair of paths defined to be either shared or explicitly inequated. Note that without inequations, there is no way to overcome the problems presented by the example in Figure 9.2 as there is no way to express conditional information directly in the logic. One way to get around this problem would be to require every maximal type to be extensional. Thus any two substructures which are unifiable become equated because every type in the result is maximal.

It makes sense to consider models in which all feature structures are ground because every path value in a ground feature structure is itself ground. Whereas it is fairly obvious that the resulting logic is sound when interpreted in a model consisting only of ground feature structures, completeness is not so direct because we have no workable notion of normal form. In particular, any given description might be satisfied by infinitely many distinct ground feature structures. The way to approach the problem is to see if equivalence satisfies an analogue of the Church-Rosser property. In particular, we would like it to be the case that if ϕ and ψ are satisfied by exactly the same set of ground feature structures, then there should be a ξ such that $\vdash \phi \equiv \xi$ and $\vdash \psi \equiv \xi$. Although we conjecture that such a result holds, we have not been able to verify it.

Part III

Alternatives

Chapter 10

Variables and Assignments

In this chapter we consider the addition of variables ranging over feature structures to our description language. It turns out that the addition of variables does not increase the representational power of the description language in terms of the feature structures which it can distinguish. Of course, this should not be surprising given the description theorem, which tells us that every feature structure can be picked out as the most general satisfier of some description. On the other hand, we can replace path equations and inequations in favor of variables and equations and inequations between variables if desirable. We prove a theorem to this effect in the latter part of this chapter. The reason that we consider variables now is that they have shown up in various guises in the feature structure literature, and are actually useful when considering applications such as definite clause programming languages based on feature structures. Our treatment of variables most closely follows that of Smolka (1988, 1989), who treats variables as part of the language for describing feature structures. Aït-Kaci (1984, 1986) also used variable-like objects, which he called *tags*. Due to the fact that he did not have a description language, Aït-Kaci had to consider variables to be part of the feature structures themselves, and then factor the class of feature structures with respect to alphabetic variance to recover the desired informational structure. We have informally introduced tags in our attribute-value matrix diagrams, but did not consider them to be part of the feature structures themselves.

We assume that we have a countably infinite collection Var of variables. Intuitively, we think of these variables as ranging over feature structures. Syntactically, they serve as descriptions. Thus we amend the definition of our description language to include the following clause:

(1) $x \in$ Desc if $x \in$ Var

This allows variables to show up arbitrarily nested within descriptions. The co-occurrence of the same variable at two locations in a description means that the feature structures described at those locations are structure shared. To carry out this development formally, we need to consider assignment functions and revise our notion of satisfaction so that it operates relative to such an assignment. More precisely, an *assignment* to the variables in Var with respect to a collection $\mathcal{G}$ of feature structures is simply a total function $\alpha: \mathsf{Var} \to \mathcal{G}$. We let Assgn be the collection of all such assignments. The use of an arbitrary collection $\mathcal{G}$ of feature structures allows us to carry out our study of variables in a way that is neutral with respect to the collection of feature structures under consideration. That is, what we have to say about variables is relevant to feature structures, well-typed feature structures, extensional feature structures, and even inequated feature structures. We can define our notion of satisfaction relative to an assignment as a relation between feature structures in $\mathcal{G}$ and descriptions with variables. In particular, we write $F \models^\alpha \phi$ if the feature structure F satisfies the description ϕ relative to the assignment α. The clauses already defined for satisfaction need only be modified so that they pass the assignment function to their recursive conditions. For example, we now have:

(2) $F \models^\alpha \phi \wedge \psi$ if $F \models^\alpha \phi$ and $F \models^\alpha \psi$

We then need an additional ground clause to account for descriptions consisting of a variable:

(3) $F \models^\alpha x$ if $\alpha(x) = F$

Thus a feature structure satisfies a variable description with respect to an assignment just in case the variable is mapped to the feature structure by the assignment.

The way in which we defined assignments and satisfaction for variables is not the only choice that makes sense in the context of feature structures. An alternative choice would have been to define an assignment relative to a feature structure to be a mapping from variables into the nodes of the feature structure. A feature structure would then be taken to satisfy a variable relative to such an assignment if its root was the image of the variable under the assignment. The reason we chose feature structures themselves rather than nodes for the images of variables under assignments is that this choice generalizes correctly to feature algebra models, which we define in the next chapter. The images of variables in the feature algebra context would have to be objects in the domain or carrier of the algebra, which more naturally correspond to feature structures themselves than to their nodes. Another reason to prefer feature structures for the images of variables is that it makes the recursive path-value satisfaction conditions more natural. We have defined satisfaction so that $F \models^\alpha \pi: \phi$ if and only if $F@\pi \models^\alpha \phi$. This condition for satisfaction would not make sense if α mapped variables in ϕ to nodes outside of $F@\pi$, and so our definition of satisfaction would need to be revised.

At this point, we can also consider two additional forms of atomic description which involve equations and inequations between variables:

(4)   • $x \mathbin{\dot{\approx}} x' \in \mathsf{Desc}$ if $x, x' \in \mathsf{Var}$

          • $x \mathbin{\dot{\not\approx}} x' \in \mathsf{Desc}$ if $x, x' \in \mathsf{Var}$

The intuitive reading of these descriptions should be obvious in that $x \mathbin{\dot{\approx}} x'$ tells us that the values of x and x' are the same, and $x \mathbin{\dot{\not\approx}} x'$ tells us that x and x' are assigned distinct values. We can formalize this notion of satisfaction as follows:

(5)   • $F \models^\alpha x \mathbin{\dot{\approx}} x'$ if and only if $\alpha(x) = \alpha(x')$

         • $F \models^\alpha x \mathbin{\dot{\napprox}} x'$ if and only if $\alpha(x) \neq \alpha(x')$

We must exercise a degree of caution in reasoning with variable equations and inequations, since it is possible to introduce variables into a description by means of an equation or inequation that do not occur elsewhere in the description. For instance, the description $(f{:}\,\sigma) \wedge (x \mathbin{\dot{\napprox}} y)$ is strange in the sense that the variables x and y are in some way disembodied. That is, we have $F \models^\alpha (f{:}\,\sigma) \wedge (x \mathbin{\dot{\napprox}} y)$ if and only if $F \models^\alpha f{:}\,\sigma$ and $F \models^\alpha x \mathbin{\dot{\napprox}} y$, which in turn is true if and only if $F@f \models^\alpha \sigma$ and $\alpha(x) \neq \alpha(y)$. Thus only the description $f{:}\,\sigma$ tells us something about what occurs in a satisfying feature structure, while $x \mathbin{\dot{\napprox}} y$ is most naturally thought of as a constraint on assignments (see Höhfeld and Smolka 1988 or Smolka 1989 for an interpretation of constraint language expressions as sets of satisfying assignments). This means that a description ϕ can independently place restrictions on both F and α in $F \models^\alpha \phi$. On the other hand, disembodied variables introduced through inequations can block satisfiability, as in the unsatisfiable description $(f{:}\,\sigma) \wedge (x \mathbin{\dot{\approx}} y) \wedge (y \mathbin{\dot{\approx}} z) \wedge (x \mathbin{\dot{\napprox}} z)$.

Of course, satisfaction is not affected by variables that do not show up in the description. Let $Vars(\phi)$ be the variables occurring in the description ϕ. It should be obvious then that we have the following result:

Theorem 10.1

If $\alpha, \alpha' \in$ Assgn are assignments such that $\alpha(x) = \alpha'(x)$ for all $x \in Vars(\phi)$, then $F \models^\alpha \phi$ if and only if $F \models^{\alpha'} \phi$.

With the addition of variables and assignments, our logical notions of satisfiability and validity need to be updated. We now define the set of satisfiers of a description with respect to an assignment α by setting:

(6) $Sat^\alpha(\phi) = \{F \mid F \models^\alpha \phi\}$

We can then define the possible satisfiers of a description by taking a union over all assignments. In particular, we set:

(7) $Sat(\phi) = \bigcup_{\alpha \in \mathsf{Assgn}} Sat^\alpha(\phi)$

Thus we have $F \in Sat(\phi)$ if and only if $F \in Sat^\alpha(\phi)$ for some assignment $\alpha \in$ Assgn. It is important to note that $Sat(\phi)$ is the set of all feature structures which could possibly be described by ϕ under some assignment, and not the (possibly smaller) set of feature structures which are described by ϕ relative to every assignment. We say that a description ϕ is *satisfiable under* an assignment α if and only if $Sat^\alpha(\phi)$ is non-empty. Similarly, we say that a description ϕ is *satisfiable* if $Sat(\phi)$ is non-empty. It should be stressed that a description is satisfiable if it is satisfiable under some assignment; a satisfiable description does not have to be satisfiable with respect to every assignment. The definition of validity also needs to be changed. We say that ϕ is *valid under* an assignment

α if and only if $Sat^\alpha(\phi) = \mathcal{G}$ and *valid* if it is valid under every assignment. The relative version of validity requires every feature structure to satisfy the description under the given assignment, while absolute validity requires validity under all assignments. Note that it may be possible for an invalid description to be valid relative to some assignments. We carry out a similar relativization of logical equivalence and say that two descriptions ϕ and ψ are *logically equivalent under* the assignment α, which we write as $\models^\alpha \phi \equiv \psi$, if and only if $Sat^\alpha(\phi) = Sat^\alpha(\psi)$. The descriptions are *logically equivalent*, written $\models \phi \equiv \psi$, if and only if they are logically equivalent under every assignment. It is worth emphasizing that two descriptions may be logically equivalent with respect to some assignment α without being logically equivalent with respect to every assignment.

We should note at this stage that it is no longer the case that satisfaction is monotonic, since we can have $F \models^\alpha \phi$ and $F \sqsubseteq F'$ and $F' \not\models^\alpha \phi$. The reason is that α might map a variable in ϕ to a substructure of F which is no longer present in F'. For instance, suppose $F \models^\alpha x$. Then we must have $\alpha(x) = F$. Now if $F \sqsubseteq F'$ and $F \neq F'$, then $F' \not\models^\alpha x$ because $\alpha(x) \neq F'$. This shows that Sat^α is not necessarily upward closed. On the other hand, we have the following upward closure result for Sat:

Theorem 10.2 (Monotonicity)

If $F \in Sat(\phi)$ and $F \sqsubseteq F'$, then $F' \in Sat(\phi)$.

Proof: Suppose that $F \sqsubseteq F'$ and $F \in Sat(\phi)$. Then there is some assignment α such that $F \in Sat^\alpha(\phi)$. We explicitly construct an α' such that $F' \in Sat^{\alpha'}(\phi)$ to show that $F' \in Sat(\phi)$. Since $F \sqsubseteq F'$, suppose that $h: Q \rightarrow Q'$ is a morphism from F to F'. We can then define α' as follows:

$$\alpha'(x) = \begin{cases} F'_{h(\bar{q}'')} & \text{if } \alpha(x) = \langle Q'', \bar{q}'', \theta'', \delta'' \rangle \in Subs(F) \\ \alpha(x) & \text{otherwise} \end{cases}$$

To unpack this last definition, we note that if α maps x to a substructure of F rooted at $\bar{q}''$, then we take the image of the root of that substructure under our morphism, which is $h(\bar{q}'')$, and define $\alpha'(x)$ to be the substructure of F' rooted at $h(\bar{q}'')$. It is straightforward to verify that $F' \models^{\alpha'} \phi$. $\square$

We now turn to the syntactic characterization of the logical equivalence of descriptions containing variables. In general, we let $\mathcal{E}^V$ be the set of axioms in $\mathcal{E}$ along with all of the instances of the following axiom schemes for variables:

15. Variables

   (a) (Variable/Path Equation Elimination)
       $$\pi: x \wedge \pi': x' \wedge x \approx x' \Leftrightarrow \pi: x \wedge \pi': x' \wedge \pi \doteq \pi'$$

   (b) (Variable/Path Inequation Elimination)
       $$\pi: x \wedge \pi': x' \wedge x \not\approx x' \Leftrightarrow \pi: x \wedge \pi': x' \wedge \pi \neq \pi'$$

(c) (Variable Elimination)

$$\pi\!:\!x \wedge \pi'\!:\!x \Leftrightarrow \pi\!:\!x \wedge \pi \doteq \pi'$$

(d) (Equation Symmetry)

$$x \mathbin{\dot{\approx}} x' \Leftrightarrow x' \mathbin{\dot{\approx}} x$$

(e) (Equation Transitivity)

$$x \mathbin{\dot{\approx}} x' \wedge x' \mathbin{\dot{\approx}} x'' \Leftrightarrow x \mathbin{\dot{\approx}} x' \wedge x' \mathbin{\dot{\approx}} x'' \wedge x \mathbin{\dot{\approx}} x''$$

(f) (Equation Reflexivity)

$$\bot \Leftrightarrow x \mathbin{\dot{\approx}} x$$

(g) (Inequation Anti-reflexivity)

$$\top \Leftrightarrow x \mathbin{\dot{\not\approx}} x$$

(h) (Inequation Substitutivity)

$$x \mathbin{\dot{\approx}} x' \wedge x \mathbin{\dot{\not\approx}} x'' \Leftrightarrow x \mathbin{\dot{\approx}} x' \wedge x' \mathbin{\dot{\not\approx}} x''$$

(i) (Path Substitutivity)

$$x \mathbin{\dot{\approx}} x' \wedge \pi\!:\!x \Leftrightarrow x \mathbin{\dot{\approx}} x' \wedge \pi\!:\!x'$$

(j) (Equation Distributivity)

$$\pi\!:\!(x \mathbin{\dot{\approx}} x') \Leftrightarrow \pi\!:\!\bot \wedge (x \mathbin{\dot{\approx}} x')$$

(k) (Inequation Distributivity)

$$\pi\!:\!(x \mathbin{\dot{\not\approx}} x') \Leftrightarrow \pi\!:\!\bot \wedge (x \mathbin{\dot{\not\approx}} x')$$

It should be kept in mind that we are attempting to axiomatize absolute logical equivalence rather than logical equivalence with respect to some fixed assignment. It should also be noted that the Path Substitutivity axiom scheme is redundant in that it can be derived from the Elimination schemes in a straightforward way. We include it here for those who wish to eliminate path equations from the description language altogether, in which case it is obviously necessary because the elimination axioms would themselves be eliminated under such a move. The equation and inequation distributivity axiom schemes are significant in that they highlight the way in which variable equations and inequations differ from all of the other descriptions. The main features of these equations and inequations is that they do not depend on their level of nesting within a description; they simply place a restriction on the assignments under which a description is satisfied independently of other considerations. But also note that $\pi\!:\!(x \mathbin{\dot{\approx}} x')$ and $\pi\!:\!(x \mathbin{\dot{\not\approx}} x')$ are treated the same way as other descriptions of the form $\pi\!:\!\phi$, and can thus only be satisfied by feature structures F defined for the path π, so that it is possible for $F@\pi$ to satisfy $x \mathbin{\dot{\approx}} x'$ or $x \mathbin{\dot{\not\approx}} x'$.

The soundness of the axiom schemes above should be obvious from our definition of satisfaction. Recall that we have $\models \phi \equiv \psi$ if and only if $Sat^{\alpha}(\phi) = Sat^{\alpha}(\psi)$ for every assignment α. For the sake of concreteness, we consider the introduction of variables in the context of inequated feature structures.

Theorem 10.3 ($\mathcal{E}^{V}_{\mathcal{IF}}$ Soundness)

If $\vdash_{\mathcal{E}^{V}_{\mathcal{IF}}} \phi \Leftrightarrow \psi$, then $\models_{\mathcal{IF}} \phi \Leftrightarrow \psi$.

As before, we proceed toward a completeness result by means of a normal form theorem. Again, we begin with the non-disjunctive case. We work with the inequated feature structures because it is the largest collection of feature structures with inequalities, and in fact, contains all of the feature structures without inequalities as a subset. Thus when we prove that every description has a disjunctive normal form with respect to the inequated feature structures, we can restrict the theorem to any of our other domains of interest.

Theorem 10.4 (Descriptive Normal Form)

For every non-disjunctive description ϕ there is a description $NF^V(\phi)$ such that $\vdash_{\mathcal{E}^V_{\mathcal{IF}}} \phi \Leftrightarrow NF^V(\phi)$, and where $NF^V(\phi) = \top$ or is of the form:

$$\phi' \wedge \pi_1 : x_1 \wedge \cdots \wedge \pi_n : x_n \wedge y_1 \dot{\approx} y_1' \wedge \cdots \wedge y_m \dot{\approx} y_m' \wedge z_1 \dot{\not\approx} z_1' \wedge \cdots \wedge z_k \dot{\not\approx} z_k'$$

where:

- ϕ' *is in descriptive normal form (as defined without variables)*

- $\pi_i : x_i$ *is a conjunct if it is derivable from ϕ, and π_i is a hook*

- $\pi \doteq \pi'$ *is a conjunct if it is derivable from ϕ, and π and π' are hooks*

- $\pi \not\doteq \pi'$ *is a conjunct if it is derivable from ϕ and π, and π' are hooks*

- $y_i \dot{\approx} y_i'$ *is a conjunct if it is derivable from ϕ, and $y_i \neq y_i'$*

- $y_i \dot{\not\approx} y_i'$ *is a conjunct if it is derivable from ϕ*

- *there is no conjunct of the form $z_i \dot{\not\approx} z_i$*

Proof: We simply use our lattice and distributivity axioms to reduce the variables to occurrences only on paths and separate out any embedded occurrences of equations or inequations. It is then straightforward to add in other path equations or inequations that arise from variable equations or inequations. Next, we can close the variable equations and inequations under our rules of inference, never adding trivial equations or variables which do not show up in ϕ. Finally, we can use our previous normal form result to put the portion without variables into descriptive normal form. □

Some remarks are in order regarding our choice of normal form. The condition that $y_i \neq y_i'$ in the clause for variable equations is enforced so that trivial equations which simply follow from reflexivity are not added to the normal forms. The deductive closure conditions on path equations and inequations simplify our later discussion of most general satisfiers. We can easily show that every formula can be put into such a disjunctive normal form using our axioms and rules of inference. We restrict our attention to inequated feature structures. As before, normal forms for other systems follow (with only slight modifications).

As usual, it is straightforward to extend our notion of descriptive normal form to disjunctive descriptions; we simply apply distributivity and then normalize each disjunct, eliminating the ones that are provably equivalent to $\top$.

We can now use our normal form theorem to show that our axiomatization is complete. As with soundness, we restrict our attention to inequated feature structures, but note that the result would still go through with the addition of appropriateness or extensionality conditions.

Theorem 10.5 ($\mathcal{E}^V_{IF}$ Completeness)

If $\models_{IF} \phi \equiv \psi$, then $\vdash_{\mathcal{E}^V_{IF}} \phi \Leftrightarrow \psi$.

Proof: As before, we can simply read the satisfiers off of the normal forms. The only difference in the present situation is that we have to add in structure sharing between nodes which are equated and furthermore, inequalities between nodes which are inequated. □

We now turn our attention to proving the fact that the addition of variables does not supply us with any additional representational power when considering the feature structures which can be picked out by means of descriptions. Our approach is to show that the collections $Sat(\phi)$ are the same whether we allow variables in ϕ or not. Recall that with the addition of variables, $F \in Sat(\phi)$ if and only if $F \models^{\alpha} \phi$ for some assignment α. Our primary result follows from the fact that we can still construct most general satisfiers of descriptions with variables, and that the sets $Sat(\phi)$ are still be upward closed. Thus $Sat(\phi)$ is still a principal filter, even though $Sat^{\alpha}(\phi)$ is not even upward closed for all ϕ.

It is important to note at this stage that we cannot construct most general satisfiers as we did before by means of a simple recursion on the structure of the description. The reason is that we have to maintain a global view of variables in which variables in two conjuncts force identity of the values that show up at those locations where the variables are found. Thus the most general satisfier of $\phi \wedge \psi$ is not the most general satisfier of ϕ unified with the most general satisfier of ψ. Simply consider the case for $\pi : x \wedge \pi' : x$. The most general satisfier for the conjunction involves a structure sharing that is not derivable from the combination of any structure sharing in the independent most general satisfiers of the conjuncts.

It should also be kept in mind what is not being stated. It is not the case that for every description there is a logically equivalent description without any occurrences of variables. The reason that we cannot fully eliminate variables in this manner is that we have maintained our substitution deduction rules, so that, for instance, if $\phi \Leftrightarrow \phi'$ and $\psi \Leftrightarrow \psi'$, then we are allowed to conclude that $\phi \wedge \psi \Leftrightarrow \phi' \wedge \psi'$. Thus we could not have $\pi \doteq \pi' \Leftrightarrow \pi : x \wedge \pi' : x$ because we do not have $\pi \doteq \pi' \wedge \pi'' : x \Leftrightarrow \pi : x \wedge \pi' : x \wedge \pi'' : x$.

We now present the most general satisfier theorem as it applies to descriptions with variables. We are able to apply the monotonicity theorem in the proof of the result, as we are looking for a most general satisfier in $Sat(\phi)$ rather than in some particular $Sat^{\alpha}(\phi)$.

Theorem 10.6 (Most General Satisfier)

If ϕ is a satisfiable description without disjunctions, then there is a most general satisfier $MGSat^V(\phi) \in \mathcal{G}$ such that $F \in Sat(\phi)$ if and only if $MGSat^V(\phi) \sqsubseteq F$.

Proof: Since we know that $Sat(\phi)$ is upward closed from the monotonicity theorem, it remains to show that $Sat(\phi)$ is generated by some most general feature structure $F \in Sat(\phi)$. To this end, we can carry out variable elimination using the elimination axioms from left to right on the normal form of F. The most general satisfier of the portion of this normal form without variables is then the most general satisfier of ϕ and hence generates $Sat(\phi)$. $\square$

This immediately leads to our new description theorem, which tells us that adding variables does not affect our representational power in terms of the collections of feature structures which can be picked out by descriptions.

Theorem 10.7 (Variable Elimination)

For every non-disjunctive description ϕ, there is a description ϕ' without variables such that $Sat(\phi) = Sat(\phi')$.

Proof: Since $Sat(\phi)$ is a principal filter, we can find its generator F and let $\phi' = Desc(F)$. It then follows from the description theorem that we have $Sat(\phi') = Sat(\phi)$. $\square$

This result tells us that variables do not add any representational power to the description language with path equations and inequations. We would now like to show that variables can be used to replace path equations and inequations in a description.

Theorem 10.8 (Path (In)Equation Elimination)

For every description ϕ without disjunctions, there exists a description ϕ' without path equations or inequations such that $Sat(\phi) = Sat(\phi')$.

Proof: First convert ϕ to normal form. Next, replace every path equation of the form $\pi \doteq \pi'$ with the conjuncts $\pi : x$ and $\pi' : x$, where x is a variable that does not yet occur elsewhere in the description. Furthermore, replace every path inequation of the form $\pi \not\doteq \pi'$ with the conjuncts $\pi : x$, $\pi' : x'$ and $x \not\approx x'$, where x and x' are variables that do not occur in the description. It should be clear that the satisfiers of the new description ϕ' constructed in this manner are the same as the satisfiers of ϕ. $\square$

In fact, this result can be strengthened to eliminate variable equations in favor of variable co-occurrence.

Theorem 10.9

For every non-disjunctive description ϕ, there is a description ϕ' without variable equations of the form $x \approx x'$ such that $Sat(\phi) = Sat(\phi')$.

Proof: Simply note that a satisfiable description $\phi \wedge x \stackrel{.}{\approx} x'$ can be replaced by ϕ', where ϕ' is the result of substituting x for x' in ϕ. □

Note that this result can be combined with the path (in)equation elimination theorem to provide descriptions with full descriptive power in the sense that they can pick out any principal filter of satisfiers without using path equations, inequations, or variable equations. Note that we cannot eliminate both variable inequations and path inequations.

Of course, all of these theorems concerning representational power can be immediately generalized to the case of descriptions possibly containing disjunctions by virtue of the distributivity of disjunction over conjunction. Together, our variable description theorems tell us that we can achieve the same effects with either path equations and inequations or variables and variable equations and inequations. The choice is primarily a matter of taste. We have chosen to emphasize the path equations and inequations, as they simplify matters to the extent that we do not need to worry about assignments.

Chapter 11

Feature Algebras

In our development up to this point, we have treated feature structures logically as models of descriptions expressed in a simple attribute-value language. In the last chapter, we extended the notion of description to include variables; in this chapter, we generalize the notion of model to partial algebraic structures. An algebraic model consists of an arbitrary collection of domain objects and associates each feature with a unary partial function over this domain. In the research of Smolka (1988, 1989) and Johnson (1986, 1987, 1990), more general algebraic models of attribute-value descriptions are the focus of attention. We pull the rabbit out of the hat when we show that our old notion of satisfaction as a relation between feature structures and descriptions is really just a special case of a more general algebraic definition of satisfaction. The feature structures constitute an algebraic model in which the domain of the model is the collection of feature structures, and the features pick out their natural (partial) value mappings. What makes the feature structure model so appealing from a logical perspective is that it is canonical in the sense that descriptions are logically equivalent if and only if they are logically equivalent for the feature structure model. In this respect, the feature structure model plays the same logical role as term models play in universal algebra. This connection is strengthened in light of the the most general satisfier and description theorems, which allow us to go back and forth between feature structures and their normal form descriptions.

We make our notion of feature algebra precise as follows:

Definition 11.1 (Feature Algebra)

A feature algebra over $\mathsf{Feat} = \{\mathrm{F}_1, \ldots, \mathrm{F}_n\}$ *and* $\langle \mathsf{Type}, \sqsubseteq \rangle$ *is a tuple* $\mathcal{A} = \langle A, \theta, f_1, \ldots, f_n \rangle$, *where:*

- A *is a collection of objects called the* carrier

- $\theta : A \to \mathsf{Type}$ *is a total* type function

- $f_i : A \to A$ *is a partial* feature value function

160

We think of the elements of the carrier A as directly representing the domain objects which the descriptions are taken to describe. The typing function θ determines the type of each object in the model. The feature value functions are what determines the interpretation of features in the description language. To bring out the feature-structure-like nature of the elements of A, if $f_i(a) = b$, then we say that a's F$_i$ is b. Note the change in font; we are making a distinction between features such as F$_i \in$ Feat, which are symbols, and partial functions such as $f_i: A \rightarrow A$, which interprets the feature F$_i$ in the feature algebra.

Feature algebras can be derived from empirical domains in straightforward ways. For instance, we could form a feature algebra whose carrier consisted of the collection of all human beings who have ever existed, in which the type function assigned each person to the location in which they were born and with features whose value for a person would be that person's father, mother, second born daughter, best friend, and immediate boss. Each of these features picks out a partial unary function over the domain of people. Another natural feature algebra would be defined for a factory in which every object in the factory was in the carrier, each object had a type that designated which area of the factory it was in, and each object had a feature corresponding to the next larger part (if any) of which it is a part. Mathematical examples can be constructed in which the carrier is the set of natural numbers, the typing function determines whether an object is even or odd, and the features compute unary algebraic functions of the numbers, such as x^2, $x - 10$, $x!$ and $1/5 * x^3 - 2x$.

It is significant to note that we have allowed our feature algebras to be intensional; it is possible for two objects a and b to be such that even if $f_i(a) = f_i(b)$ for all f_i, we might still have $a \neq b$. Of course, this situation can even arise if the types of a and b are the same, so that $\theta(a) = \theta(b)$. Thus our features and types might not be enough to distinguish between some individuals in a feature algebra.

One natural restriction to our definition would be to require the range of θ to be a subset of the maximal types, so that $\theta(a)$ would be maximal for every object $a \in A$. We do not do this because the resulting logic would be stronger than our current axiomatizations could capture. This is because it is possible to have a feature structure assgined assigned a non-maximal type which is not extendable to any maximal type due to appropriateness conflicts. For instance, suppose we had a type σ with two inconsistent subtypes σ' and σ'', and another type τ which also has two inconsistent subtypes τ' and τ''. Furthermore, suppose $Approp(f, \sigma) = \tau$, $Approp(f, \sigma') = \tau'$, and $Approp(f, \sigma'') = \tau'$. Now the description $f: \tau''$ is satisfiable by a well-typed feature structure of type σ, but not by any well-typed feature structure of a maximal type. This means that the description of such a feature structure is only satisfiable if we consider models with non-maximal types. Restricting attention to maximal types would equate the description $f: \tau''$ with the inconsistent top element, and thus considerably strengthen the existing logic. To maintain parity with the definitions for feature structures, we have allowed θ to map objects to arbitrary types.

Our interest up to now has focused on feature structures, which we can now cast as a particular feature algebra. In particular, we have looked at particular subcollections of feature structures that met certain conditions. Our algebraicization of feature structures is very general. A collection $\mathcal{G} \subseteq \mathcal{F}$ (or $\mathcal{G} \subseteq \mathcal{IF}$) of feature structures is said to be *substructure closed* if whenever $F \in \mathcal{G}$ and $F \mathord{\circ} \pi$ is defined, we have $F \mathord{\circ} \pi \in \mathcal{G}$. Thus a collection of feature structures is substructure closed just in case it contains all of the substructures of its members, so that $\mathcal{G} = \bigcup_{F \in \mathcal{G}} Sub(F)$, where $Sub(F)$ is the collection of substructures of F as before.

Definition 11.2 (Algebraicization)

The algebraicization *of a substructure closed collection $\mathcal{G} \subseteq \mathcal{F}$ of feature structures is given by $\mathcal{A}_\mathcal{G} = \langle \mathcal{G}, \Theta, \mathord{\circ} f_1, \ldots, \mathord{\circ} f_n \rangle$, where $\Theta(\langle Q, \bar{q}, \theta, \delta \rangle) = \theta(\bar{q})$, and where $\mathord{\circ} f_i(F) = F \mathord{\circ} f_i$.*

It is obvious that the algebraicization of a substructure closed collection of feature structures results in a feature algebra. The substructure closure is required to guarantee that the ranges of the partial functions $\mathord{\circ} f_i$ are subcollections of the carrier.

Lemma 11.3

If $\mathcal{G} \subseteq \mathcal{F}$ is substructure closed, then $\mathcal{A}_\mathcal{G}$ is a feature algebra.

We can generalize our notion of satisfaction in an obvious way. As we soon learn that our old notion of satisfaction between feature structures and descriptions is just a special case of the definition we are about to make, we use the same notation for satisfaction in the algebraic case.

Definition 11.4 (Algebraic Satisfaction)

If $\mathcal{A} = \langle A, \theta, f_1, \ldots, f_n \rangle$ is a feature algebra, then we define the satisfaction *relation between A and Desc to be the least such that if $a \in A$, then:*

- $a \models_\mathcal{A} \sigma$ *if $\sigma \sqsubseteq \theta(a)$*
- $a \models_\mathcal{A} f_1 \cdots f_n : \phi$ *if $(f_n \circ \cdots \circ f_1)(a) \models_\mathcal{A} \phi$*
- $a \models_\mathcal{A} f_1 \cdots f_n \doteq g_1 \cdots g_m$ *if $(f_n \circ \cdots \circ f_1)(a) = (g_m \circ \cdots \circ g_1)(a)$*
- $a \models_\mathcal{A} \phi \wedge \psi$ *if $a \models_\mathcal{A} \phi$ and $a \models_\mathcal{A} \psi$*
- $a \models_\mathcal{A} \phi \vee \psi$ *if $a \models_\mathcal{A} \phi$ or $a \models_\mathcal{A} \psi$*

The clauses of our new satisfaction definition are straightforward and we explain them briefly in order. The first clause tells us that an object a satisfies a description consisting of a type σ just in case the type assigned to a is at least as specific as σ. The second and third clauses employ partial function compositions, which we define as usual, so that:

(1) $(f_n \circ \cdots \circ f_1)(a) = b$ if and only if $f_n(f_{n-1}(\cdots f_2(f_1(a)) \cdots)) = b$

We then have a satisfying a path-value description $f_1 \cdots f_n : \phi$ just in case the successive application of the feature value functions $f_1, \ldots, f_n$ results in an object which satisfies ϕ. Similarly, an object a satisfies a path sharing $f_1 \cdots f_n \doteq g_1 \cdots g_m$ if the value of applying $f_1, \ldots, f_n$ to a is the same as that of applying $g_1, \ldots, g_m$ to a. Note that we are still assuming that path sharing is an intensional notion which requires token identity of the path values. Conjunctive and disjunctive descriptions are given their standard logical interpretation. Finally, notice that since we have defined the satisfaction relation as the least such relation meeting the given conditions, for every $a \in A$ we have:

(2) $a \not\models_A \top$

Of course, we could easily extend the relation of satisfaction between feature algebras and descriptions to include descriptions with variables. We avoid the temptation to do so, as it simply obscures the central facts concerning feature algebras.

It should now be obvious that our revised definition of satisfaction is the same as our old one when restricted to the feature algebras generated by feature structures.

Theorem 11.5

$F \models \phi$ *if and only if* $F \models_{A_{\mathcal{F}}} \phi$.

Proof: Simply note that the clauses of the definitions of $\models$ and $\models_{A_{\mathcal{F}}}$ work out to be identical. □

We now generalize some of our previous logical notions to general feature algebras. Suppose that $\mathcal{A} = \langle A, \Theta, f_1, \ldots, f_n \rangle$ is a feature algebra. We say that a description ϕ is $\mathcal{A}$-*satisfiable* if and only if there is an object $a \in A$ such that $a \models_A \phi$. We say that ϕ is simply *satisfiable* if and only if it is $\mathcal{A}$-satisfiable for some feature algebra $\mathcal{A}$. Next, we say that ϕ is $\mathcal{A}$-*valid* if and only if $a \models_A \phi$ for every $a \in A$. We drop the relativization and say that ϕ is simply *valid* if it is $\mathcal{A}$-valid for every feature algebra $\mathcal{A}$. Finally, we say that ϕ and ψ are *logically $\mathcal{A}$-equivalent*, which we write $\models_A \phi \equiv \psi$, if and only if $a \models_A \phi$ for every $a \in A$. Dropping the relativization, ϕ and ψ are *logically equivalent*, written $\models \phi \equiv \psi$ if and only if they are $\mathcal{A}$-equivalent for every feature algebra $\mathcal{A}$.

We have developed a notion of feature algebra so far that corresponds to our notion of feature structure; there has been no mention of inequation or appropriateness conditions or extensionality. While it would not be difficult to integrate type considerations with our algebraic models, it is not at all clear how inequations could be adapted. Luckily, we do not need to change our axiomatic characterization of logical equivalence, as we soon show. We begin by noting that the axioms in our axiomatization $\mathcal{E}_{\mathcal{F}}$ of the feature structures remain sound when extended to feature algebra interpretations.

Theorem 11.6 (Soundness)

If $\vdash_{\mathcal{E}_{\mathcal{F}}} \phi \Leftrightarrow \psi$, *then* $\models_A \phi \Leftrightarrow \psi$ *for every feature algebra $\mathcal{A}$.*

Proof: It is trivial to check the validity of the axiom schemes. □

On the road to completeness, we first demonstrate the canonicality of the feature structure algebra in the sense that descriptions are logically equivalent if and only if they are logically equivalent in the feature structure algebra.

Theorem 11.7 ($\mathcal{F}$ Canonicality)

$\models \phi \equiv \psi$ *if and only if* $\models_{\mathcal{A}_{\mathcal{F}}} \phi \equiv \psi$.

Proof: One direction is obvious. If $\models \phi \equiv \psi$, then $\models_{\mathcal{A}} \phi \equiv \psi$ for every feature algebra $\mathcal{A}$, including the algebra $\mathcal{A}_{\mathcal{F}}$ derived from the feature structures.

Arguing contrapositively, suppose that $\not\models \phi \equiv \psi$. Then it must be the case that ϕ and ψ have distinct normal forms by the soundness of the axioms over the feature algebra interpretations, and thus $\not\vdash_{\mathcal{E}_{\mathcal{F}}} \phi \Leftrightarrow \psi$. By the completeness of the axioms in $\mathcal{E}_{\mathcal{F}}$ for the feature structures $\mathcal{F}$, we know that we must have $\not\models_{\mathcal{A}_{\mathcal{F}}} \phi \equiv \psi$. $\qquad\Box$

In our proof, we have shown that if a logical equivalence does not hold in every feature algebra, then it does not hold in the feature structure model either. The beauty of this canonicality result is that it tells us that even if we are interested in more general feature algebra models of our description language, the feature structures suffice for logical purposes. For instance, the completeness of the axiomatization $\mathcal{E}_{\mathcal{F}}$ follows immediately.

Theorem 11.8 (Completeness)

If $\models \phi \equiv \psi$, *then* $\vdash_{\mathcal{E}_{\mathcal{F}}} \phi \Leftrightarrow \psi$.

For the sake of expository completeness, we generalize to the typed case a notion of morphism for feature algebras which is attributed to Rounds by Smolka (1989).

Definition 11.9 (Partial Morphism)

If $\mathcal{A} = \langle A, \theta, f_1, \ldots, f_n \rangle$ *and* $\mathcal{A}' = \langle A', \theta', f_1', \ldots, f_n' \rangle$ *are feature algebras, then a partial function* $h : A \to A'$ *is a* partial morphism *from* $\mathcal{A}$ *to* $\mathcal{A}'$ *if and only if:*

- *if* $h(a)$ *is defined, then* $\theta(a) \sqsubseteq \theta'(h(a))$

- *if* $h(a)$ *and* $f_i(a)$ *are defined, then* $h(f_i(a)) = f_i'(h(a))$ *with both defined*

This notion of morphism is partial in the sense that it does not need to map every element of the feature algebra. On the other hand, it is closed with respect to substructure in the sense that if it maps an object, then it maps all of the objects reachable from that object by feature value function application. We chose the term "morphism" because the identity functions are morphisms and the collection of morphisms is closed under composition, thus forming a category with the feature algebras as objects. Of course, this new notion of morphism is a true generalization of our old one.

Theorem 11.10

If $F, F' \in \mathcal{F}$ *are feature structures, then* $F \sqsubseteq F'$ *if and only if there is a partial morphism* $h : \mathcal{A}_{\mathcal{F}} \to \mathcal{A}_{\mathcal{F}}$ *on the feature algebra such that* $h(F) = F'$.

Proof: If $F \sqsubseteq F'$, then the morphism $h_Q \colon Q \to Q'$ that is defined from nodes of F to nodes of F' can be converted to a partial morphism h on the feature algebra $\mathcal{A}_{\mathcal{F}}$ by setting $h(F_q) = F'_{h(q)}$, where in general, F_q is the substructure of F rooted at q. It is easily verified that h is indeed a partial morphism.

Now suppose that there is a partial morphism h on $\mathcal{A}_{\mathcal{F}}$ such that $h(F) = F'$. Then we can construct a morphism $h_Q \colon Q \to Q'$ from the nodes of F to the nodes of F' by simply reversing the procedure we defined above. That is, we set $h_Q(q) = q'$ if G is a substructure of F rooted at q, and G' is a substructure of F' rooted at q', and $h(G) = G'$. $\qquad\qquad\square$

This result can be easily modified to require the morphism h to be total, because any feature structure for which h was previously undefined can be mapped to itself without disrupting the morphism properties. We have reason to employ this general notion of morphism in later sections on phrase structure grammars and definite clause logic programming.

We order morphisms pointwise by saying $h \sqsubseteq h'$ if and only if $h(F) \sqsubseteq h'(F)$ for every $F \in \mathcal{A}_{\mathcal{F}}$. Again, we get a notion of alphabetic variance for morphisms according to which we put $h \sim h'$ if and only if $h \sqsubseteq h'$ and $h' \sqsubseteq h$. Using this notion of alphabetic variance, we can restrict our attention to idempotent morphisms h (that is, morphisms such that $h \circ h = h$) so that $h(h(F)) = h(F)$. For any morphism h there is an alphabetic variant $h' \sim h$ such that h' is idempotent. In particular, we can simply re-name the nodes in the images of h so that if $h(F) \neq F$, then the images of h can be chosen so that if $F' \in Subs(h(F))$ is a substructure of $h(F)$, then $h(F') = F'$. This ensures idempotency. Combined with the fact that morphisms can always be taken to be total, we have the following result:

Corollary 11.11

If $F, F' \in \mathcal{F}$ are feature structures, then $F \sqsubseteq F'$ if and only if there is a total idempotent morphism h on the feature algebra $\mathcal{A}_{\mathcal{F}}$ such that $h(F) = F'$.

It should also be noted that if h and h' are morphisms, then so is $h \circ h'$. But it might be the case that both h and h' are idempotent, but $h \circ h'$ is not. In this case, the nodes in the image feature structures can be renamed so that $h \circ h'$ is idempotent.

Finally, we can characterize unification in terms of algebraic morphisms as is standard for first-order term unification, in which the unification of two terms is usually defined in terms of the least substitution for variables which makes them identical. In particular, we have the following result:

Theorem 11.12

If $F \sqcup F'$ is defined, then there is a morphism h such that $h(F) = h(F') \sim F \sqcup F'$.

Proof: Since $F \sqsubseteq F \sqcup F'$ there is a morphism h such that $h(F) \sim F \sqcup F'$. Similarly, there is a morphism h' such that $h'(F') \sim F \sqcup F'$. By node renaming, we may choose h and h' so that for every F such that $h(F) \neq F$ we have $h'(F) = F$, and for every F' such that $h'(F') \neq F'$ we have $h(F') = F'$. We then have $(h \sqcup h')(F) = h(F) \sim F \sqcup F'$ and $(h \sqcup h')(F') = h'(F') \sim F \sqcup F'$. $\quad\square$

Thus it can be seen that our notions of both subsumption and unification can be re-cast in terms of total morphisms on the algebra of feature structures.

With our generalized definition of morphism, we can provide the natural definition of *subsumption* between objects $a \in A$ for a feature algebra $\mathcal{A} = \langle A, \theta, f_1, \ldots, f_n \rangle$ by setting $a \sqsubseteq_{\mathcal{A}} a'$ if and only if there is a partial morphism $h: A \to A$ such that $h(a) = a'$. We can easily verify that our satisfaction conditions are still monotonic. We state the theorem in slightly more generality, as follows:

Theorem 11.13 (Monotonicity)

If $\langle A, \theta, f_1, \ldots, f_n \rangle$ and $\langle A', \theta', f_1', \ldots, f_n' \rangle$ are feature algebras, and $h: A \to A'$ is a partial morphism, then for every $\phi \in \mathsf{Desc}$ such that $a \models \phi$, if $h(a) \in A'$ is defined, then $h(a) \models \phi$.

Proof: A simple induction on the clauses of satisfaction suffices to show that if $a \models \phi$, then $h(a) \models \phi$. □

An immediate corollary to this result, and the reason for its name, is that satisfaction is monotonic, so that if $a \sqsubseteq_{\mathcal{A}} a'$ and $a \models \phi$, then $a' \models \phi$. This follows immediately from the definition of subsumption, since $a \sqsubseteq_{\mathcal{A}} a'$ just in case there is a morphism such that $h(a) = a'$.

Whereas it is straightforward to generalize our previous notion of subsumption to feature algebras, a generalization of unification is not forthcoming; two objects in a feature algebra might be subsumption bounded but not have a least upper bound. Thus we can see that unification is an operation that exists only in some feature algebras such as the algebra of feature structures. This should not be too surprising for those acquainted with algebra and logic; unification is normally only defined for terms in a free algebra and not for elements of an arbitrary abstract algebra.

Even though we cannot extend our notion of unification to feature algebras in general, we could continue our algebraic study of feature structures. For instance, we could define a notion of congruence relation to allow us to investigate variations of the standard algebraic isomorphism theorems. While we have not carried out this algebraic research, we believe it might shed some light on varieties of feature structures defined equationally by descriptions. This approach has already been established as an effective tool for the characterization of traditional algebraic varieties in universal unification theory (Siekmann 1989). The application of these techniques to feature structures has been initiated by Reape (1989), who studied two cases of particular interest for linguistic representations: strings and multisets.

Chapter 12

Infinite Feature Structures and Domains

In this chapter we generalize our notion of feature structure to allow for the possibility of having countably infinite collections of nodes. When we considered algebraic models in the last chapter, we implicitly allowed models with objects from which infinitely many distinct objects were accessible by iteratively applying feature value functions. In the case of feature structures as we have previously taken them, the set of substructures of a feature structure was always in one-to-one correspondence with the nodes of the feature structure and hence finite. In the case of finite feature structures, we were guaranteed joins or unifications for consistent finite sets of (finite) feature structures. We also saw examples of infinite sets of consistent finite feature structures which did not have a finite least upper bound. When we allow for the possibility of countably infinite feature structures, we have least upper bounds for arbitrary (possibly infinite) consistent sets of (possibly infinite) feature structures. In fact, the collection of feature structures with countable node sets turn out to form a pre-domain in the sense that when we factor out alphabetic variance, we are left with an algebraic countably based BCPO. Luckily, in the feature structure domain, the compact domain elements are just the finite feature structures, thus giving us a way to characterize arbitrary infinite feature structures as simple joins of finite feature structures. One benefit of such a move is that infinite or limit elements in our domains provide models for non-terminating inference procedures such as total type inference over an appropriateness specification with loops or extensionalization when non-maximal types are allowed to be extensional.

In the case of feature structures, there are two ways in which an infinite node set might arise: in terms of breadth or in terms of depth. We do not consider broad infinity, which would permit an infinite number of features to be defined for a single node. If we allow the set Feat of features to be infinite, most of our results could be extended to account for broad infinity. In particular, the resulting structure would still form a domain with the finite feature structures as compact elements. Note that a feature structure might be infinite in terms of breadth and still be bounded in the length of path for which it is defined. Deep infinity, on the other hand, can arise even if every node is only defined for a finite number of features. Of course, just being defined for an infinite number of paths does not make a feature structure infinite; it must also provide an infinite number of substructures as values of these paths. Finally, it is also possible to have an infinite feature structure which displays both broad and deep infinity.

In this chapter, we apply domain-theoretic techniques to characterize two quite different aspects of the feature structure domains we have already encountered. We begin with an application of domain theory to provide an algebraic characterization of disjunction in the description language. We already know that the finite feature structures can be used as representatives of logically equivalent classes of descriptions without disjunctions; *MGSat* and *Desc* gave us ways to move back and forth between the non-disjunctive portion of the description language and feature structures. Using a powerdomain construction due to Smyth (1978), we build a domain in which the finite objects can be used to represent classes of logically equivalent descriptions with disjunctions. The other task to which we put domain theory is in providing a uniform characterization of our various type, extensionality, and inequation inference algorithms. It turns out that they all produce closure operators on the domain of (inequated) feature structures. In general, closure operators provide a means of generating new data types in terms of known data types. Furthermore, the closure operators defined over the domain are total, whereas the corresponding operations over feature structures were often partial. From this perspective, it should be clear that we have been employing the feature structure domains $\mathcal{F}$ and $\mathcal{IF}$ as universal domains in the sense that all of our other domains can be characterized as images of effectively computable closures defined on these domains.

The material in this chapter is not crucial in what follows, but in the following chapters on applications, we often indicate where very general domain-theoretic results can be applied in lieu of the more specialized proofs that we provide. The domain-theoretic study of feature structures was originally undertaken by Pereira and Shieber (1984), who were concerned with providing an information system constructed from feature structure descriptions. They used this information system (which can be viewed through a categorical equivalence as a special kind of concrete domain) to provide a semantics for phrase structure grammar formalisms such as PATR-II (Shieber et al. 1983), which use feature structures for categories. We explain their construction in the chapter on phrase structure grammars. The Pereira and Shieber construction was tidied up and modified slightly by Moshier (1988), who considered intensional atoms that could occur on arbitrary nodes, whereas Pereira and Shieber employed extensional atoms that could only show up on terminal nodes. The most ambitious use of domains for feature structures arises in the set-valued feature structure construction of Pollard and Moshier (1990), who not only extend the domain-theoretic treatment to account for sorted atoms (our feature structures), but also to account for the semantics of the HPSG grammar formalism. Although we do not take up their notion of set-valued feature structures, we consider their semantics for HPSG in our final chapter on systems of constraint equations.

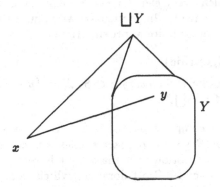

Figure 12.1. Compactness Condition.

We begin by presenting some of the standard definitions from domain theory. We begin with the fundamental notion of a directed set.

Definition 12.1 (Directed Set)

A non-empty subset $D \subseteq S$ of a partial order $\langle S, \leq \rangle$ is directed if every finite subset $E \subseteq D$ has an upper bound $x \in D$.

It is important to note that the upper bound x in the definition must come from the directed set D itself; every finite subset of D must be consistent relative to D in the sense that it has an upper bound in D. The first use to which we put the notion of directed set is in the definition of complete partial orders.

Definition 12.2 (Complete Partial Order (CPO))

A poset $\langle S, \leq \rangle$ is a complete partial order if every directed subset $D \subseteq S$ has a least upper bound $\bigsqcup D \in S$.

We are only interested in *bounded complete* CPOs, which are simply CPOs which are also bounded complete (a poset is bounded complete if all of its bounded subsets have least upper bounds). We can now pick out a special subset of a CPO whose elements play the role of generators in domains.

Definition 12.3 (Compactness)

An element x of a CPO $\langle S, \leq \rangle$ is compact or finite if for every directed $Y \subseteq S$ such that $x \leq \bigsqcup Y$, there is some $y \in Y$ such that $x \leq y$.

An element x is said to be a limit or infinite element if it is not compact.

Let $Comp(\langle S, \leq \rangle)$ be the collection of compact elements of $\langle S, \leq \rangle$.

An element x is compact if it cannot be expressed as the least upper bound of a directed set that does not contain an element greater than x. We provide an illustration of what it means for an object to be compact in Figure 12.1. A limit element x on the other hand, can be expressed as the limit of some directed set which does not contain any element as great as x. In domain theory, the focus is on orderings in which every element can be expressed uniquely in terms of the finite or compact elements. In particular, we require that every element be the least upper bound of its finite approximations.

Definition 12.4 (Algebraic)

A CPO $\langle S, \leq \rangle$ *is algebraic if for every* $x \in S$, $X = \{y \in Comp(S) \mid y \leq x\}$ *is directed and such that* $x = \bigsqcup X$.

An algebraic bounded complete partial order $\langle S, \leq \rangle$ is said to be *countably based* if the set $Comp(\langle S, \leq \rangle)$ of compact elements is countable. This gives us all we need to define the notion of domain that is required for our purposes. We choose to work in so-called Scott domains, which were originally developed by Scott because of their elegant closure properties which allowed them to be used to solve domain equations.

Definition 12.5 ((Scott) Domain)

A domain *is a countably based algebraic bounded complete* CPO.

Thus a domain is nothing more than a partially ordered set in which arbitrary bounded joins exist and, furthermore, every element can be expressed as the join of the countable set of compact elements that approximate it. The beauty of algebraic BCPOs is that we can do most of our work by only considering the finite basis. An infinite or limit structure can then be determined by enumerating the compact elements which approximate it. Since enumeration can be done computationally, this gives us a method for representing infinite structures by finite means in terms of algorithms that enumerate (codes of) their finite approximations. There is a strong duality between working in domains and working in the finite portions of domains (see Gunter and Scott in press). We are going to exploit this duality to generate domains from the ordered collections of feature structures with which we are already familiar. We can thus look at our development so far as being the finite portion of our domains. Furthermore, we exploit the morphism portion of this duality to convert our many inference procedures into domain closures.

Note that even for countably based domains, there may be a countably infinite number of domain objects. Thus directed sets might prove to be uncountable. But in the case of countably based domains, we can interchange directed sets and limits of ω-chains. An ω-*chain* is a set $X = \{x_i \mid i \in \omega\}$ of domain elements indexed by ω in such a way that $x_i \leq x_{i+1}$ for all $i \in \omega$. Thus an ω-chain is a special kind of directed set. We have the following lemma relating ω-chains and directed sets for domains.

Lemma 12.6

If X *is a directed set in the domain* $\langle D, \leq \rangle$, *then there is an* ω-*chain* $Chain(X) \subseteq Comp(D)$ *consisting only of compact elements such that* $\bigsqcup X = \bigsqcup Chain(X)$.

Furthermore, an element of D *is compact if and only if it is not the limit of any infinite* ω-*chain.*

Proof: Let $Base(X) = \{x \in Comp(D) \mid x \leq y \text{ for some } y \in X\}$. By algebraicity, we know that $\bigsqcup Base(X) = \bigsqcup X$. Since $Comp(D)$ is countable, so is $Base(X)$, so suppose $Base(X) = \{x_n \mid n \in \omega\}$. We define the chain $Chain(X)$ by setting $Chain(X) = \{y_n \mid n \in \omega\}$ where $y_n = \bigsqcup_{m<n} x_n$. We see that $\bigsqcup Chain(X) = \bigsqcup Base(X)$, because for every $x \in Chain(X)$ there is a $y \in Base(X)$ such that $x \leq y$ and for every $y \in Base(X)$ there is an $x \in Chain(X)$ such that $y \leq x$. Thus $\bigsqcup Chain(X) = \bigsqcup X$ by transitivity.

Since a chain is itself a directed set, if x is compact and $x = \bigsqcup X$ for some chain X, then $x \leq x_n$ for some element $x_n \in X$. It must then be the case that $x = x_n$, and also $x_m = x_{m+1}$ for $m \geq n$ if $x = \bigsqcup X$. Thus the chain $X = \{x_1, \ldots, x_n\}$ is finite. $\square$

This result tells us that in the case of domains, we can freely substitute ω-chains and directed sets.

We return now to our primary business of feature structures. We let $\mathcal{F}^{\omega}$ be the collection of feature structures with a countable collection of nodes. We define morphisms and consequently subsumption over the new collection of feature structures by the obvious generalization of our previous definition of morphisms. In what follows, we are only interested in feature structures up to alphabetic variance. It is usual in domain theory to define a *predomain* to be a preorder whose quotient with respect to the mutual subsumption equivalence relation is a domain.

Definition 12.7 (Predomain)

A preorder $\langle S, \leq \rangle$ is a predomain if $\langle S/_R, \leq_R \rangle$ is a domain, where the equivalence relation R is defined so that xRy if and only if $x \leq y$ and $y \leq x$, and where we set $[x]_R \leq_R [y]_R$ if and only if $x \leq y$.

We are only interested in domains, but are confronted with numerous predomains. Our strategy is to simply identify the predomains with the domains that they generate where context allows us to get away with it. This is particularly straightforward in the case of our collections of feature structures, because we have the abstract feature structures to represent equivalence classes of feature structures modulo alphabetic variance. We can extend our function Abs, which maps feature structures onto abstract feature structures, into a function Abs^{ω}, which maps a feature structure $F \in \mathcal{F}^{\omega}$ onto an abstract feature structure $Abs^{\omega}(F) = \langle \Theta_F, \approx_F \rangle$ just as before. The only difference is that now the equivalence relation $\approx_F$, which holds between paths shared in F, might not be of finite order, so that in particular, there may be an infinite number of distinct equivalence classes of paths modulo path sharing.

Of primary interest in the domain-theoretic study of feature structures is the following result, which tells us that the feature structures with possibly infinite node sets form a predomain or that they form a domain when considered modulo alphabetic variance. A result like the following was originally proved by Pereira and Shieber (1984) who used information systems to provide a concrete syntactic characterization of an appropriate domain for modelling PATR-II. We follow Pollard and Moshier (1990) in using a variation of Moshier's

(1988) abstract feature structures which accounts for type inheritance. The use of abstract feature structures makes the proof that the collection of feature structures (modulo alphabetic variance) forms a domain almost immediate.

Theorem 12.8 ($\mathcal{F}^\omega$ Domainhood)

$\langle \mathcal{F}^\omega, \sqsubseteq \rangle$ *is a domain (modulo alphabetic variance) with the countable basis* $\mathcal{F}$ *(modulo alphabetic variance) of compact elements.*

Proof: To see that $\mathcal{F}^\omega$ is a bounded complete partial order modulo alphabetic variance, simply consider the fact that arbitrary meets are defined for abstract feature structures. In particular, if we have a set of feature structures F_i indexed by elements $i \in I$, then we have:

$$\bigsqcap \{ \langle \Theta_{F_i}, \approx_{F_i} \rangle \mid i \in I \} = \langle \bigsqcap_{i \in I} \Theta_{F_i}, \bigcap_{i \in I} \approx_{F_i} \rangle$$

Recall that we define meets pointwise for the functions $\Theta_{F_i} \colon \mathsf{Path} \to \mathsf{Type}$. This shows that $\mathcal{F}^\omega$ is closed under arbitrary meets and hence closed under arbitrary bounded joins as well.

To see that $\mathcal{F}^\omega$ is a CPO, suppose $X \subseteq \mathcal{F}^\omega$ is directed. To show that X has a least upper bound, we define an abstract feature structure $\langle \Theta, \approx \rangle$ such that $\langle \Theta, \approx \rangle = Abs(\bigsqcup X)$. We do this by setting:

- $\Theta(\pi) = \bigsqcup \{ \Theta_F(\pi) \mid F \in X, \Theta_F(\pi) \text{ defined} \}$

- $\approx \ = \bigcup_{F \in X} \approx_F$

Simply notice that Θ is well-defined due to the fact that Type is a CPO and the fact that $\{ \Theta_F(\pi) \mid F \in X \}$ must itself be directed if X is directed. We work by contradiction to see that $\langle \Theta, \approx \rangle$ is in fact an abstract feature structure. For suppose that $\pi \approx \pi'$ and $\Theta(\pi) \neq \Theta(\pi')$. Then suppose (without loss of generality) that $\Theta(\pi) \not\sqsubseteq \Theta(\pi')$. Then there must be a feature structure $F \in X$ such that there is no feature structure F' such that $\Theta_F(\pi) \sqsubseteq \Theta_{F'}(\pi')$. Now since $\pi \approx \pi'$, we must have some $F'' \in X$ such that $\pi \approx_{F''} \pi'$. But since X is directed, there must be an upper bound F' for F and F'' in X. But such an F' contradicts our assertion that there is no F' such that $\Theta_F(\pi) \sqsubseteq \Theta_{F'}(\pi')$. Thus we must have $\Theta(\pi) = \Theta(\pi')$ if $\pi \approx \pi'$.

It remains to show that the finite elements in $\mathcal{F}$ are compact in $\mathcal{F}^\omega$. Suppose that $S \subseteq \mathcal{F}^\omega$ is a directed set of feature structures, and $F \in \mathcal{F}$ is a finite feature structure such that $F \sqsubseteq \bigsqcup S$. Then we can find a finite subset $S' \subseteq S$ such that $F \sqsubseteq \bigsqcup S'$ by simply choosing an element of S' for each path value and path sharing for hooks in F, of which there are at most finitely many. Then since S is directed, we must have some element $F' \in S$ such that $\bigsqcup S' \sqsubseteq F'$. But then $F \sqsubseteq F' \in S$. This shows that the elements of $\mathcal{F}$ are compact.

To show that $\mathcal{F}^\omega$ is algebraic, suppose that $F \in \mathcal{F}^\omega \setminus \mathcal{F}$ is a feature structure with a countably infinite set of nodes. Then let S be the directed set composed of finite feature structures representing every path-value pair in F and every path sharing in F. Then $\bigsqcup S = F$. Thus the BCPO $\langle \mathcal{F}^\omega, \sqsubseteq \rangle$ is both countably based and algebraic and hence a domain. $\square$

The idea behind compact and limit elements in domains can now be exemplified in terms of the feature structures. We think of an infinite or limit feature structure as one that is approximated by a sequence of finite feature structures. We can represent this infinite feature structure by finite means if we have some effective method of generating its finite approximations. An algorithm that generates the finite approximations of an infinite feature structure can be identified with that infinite structure. For instance, consider the result of the following infinite join:

$$(1) \qquad \langle \omega, 0, \theta, \delta \rangle = \begin{bmatrix} \bot \\ \mathrm{F}:[\bot] \end{bmatrix} \sqcup \begin{bmatrix} \bot \\ \mathrm{F}: \begin{bmatrix} \bot \\ \mathrm{F}:[\bot] \end{bmatrix} \end{bmatrix} \sqcup \cdots$$

where for all $n \in \omega$ we have $\delta(\mathrm{F}, n) = n+1$ and $\theta(n) = \bot$. We can best illustrate the result by:

$$(2) \qquad 0:\bot \xrightarrow{\ \mathrm{F}\ } 1:\bot \xrightarrow{\ \mathrm{F}\ } 2:\bot \xrightarrow{\ \mathrm{F}\ } \cdots \xrightarrow{\ \mathrm{F}\ } n:\bot \xrightarrow{\ \mathrm{F}\ } \cdots$$

This gives us a concrete example of how an infinite feature structure can be approximated by an infinite sequence of finite feature structures. It should also be noted that there are limit structures which subsume compact elements. For instance, the limit feature structure defined in (1) and depicted in (2) subsumes the compact feature structure:

$$(3) \qquad \begin{bmatrix} \bot \ \boxed{8} \\ \mathrm{F}: \begin{bmatrix} \boxed{8} \end{bmatrix} \end{bmatrix}$$

Notice that the BCPO $\langle \mathsf{Type}, \sqsubseteq \rangle$ also forms a domain. The domain structure on Type is not very interesting because Type is finite; any finite BCPO is trivially both countably based and algebraic and hence a domain. Furthermore, every element of a finite BCPO is compact. But the restriction to finite type hierarchies is only for convenience; it is really only necessary to require that the type inheritance hierarchy is a domain to ensure that the collection of feature structures is also a domain. Of course, operations such as type inference, which rely on iterations through types, may be significantly altered if the notion of inheritance hierarchy is generalized. We do not consider such a generalization here.

Before considering our first application, we need to consider the ideal completion construction, which shows us how to recover a representation of domains in terms of their compact elements. An ideal is a subset of a partial order that is downward closed and directed.

Definition 12.9 (Ideal)

A subset $I \subseteq S$ of a partially ordered set $\langle S, \leq \rangle$ is said to be an ideal *if:*

- *if $x, y \in I$, then some $z \in I$ is such that $y \leq z$ and $x \leq z$* (Directed)

- *if $x \in I$ and $y \in S$ is such that $y \leq x$, then $y \in I$* (Downward Closed)

Let Ideals($\langle S, \leq \rangle$) be the set of ideals of $\langle S, \leq \rangle$.

We write *Ideals(S)* for *Ideals*($\langle S, \leq \rangle$) when $\leq$ is understood. If $x \in S$ we let:

(4) $Id(x) = \{y \mid y \leq x\}$

and say that $Id(x)$ is the *principal ideal* generated by x. $Id(x)$ is simply the set of objects less than or equal to x, which is obviously an ideal.

Since ideals are sets, they can be naturally ordered by inclusion. The reason we are interested in this construction is that it always produces an algebraic CPO into which we can embed our original poset. It is standard to call $\langle Ideals(S), \subseteq \rangle$ the *ideal completion* of S. In general, the mapping from an object to its principal ideal in the ideal completion preserves not only subsumption but also all existing meets and joins.

Theorem 12.10 (Completion Embedding)

If $\langle S, \leq \rangle$ is a partial order, then the function $Id: S \rightarrow Ideals(S)$ is an order embedding from $\langle S, \leq \rangle$ to its ideal completion $\langle Ideals(S), \subseteq \rangle$ that preserves existing meets and joins so that:

- *$Id(x \sqcup x') = Id(x) \sqcup Id(x')$ if $x \sqcup x'$ is defined*

- *$Id(x \sqcap x') = Id(x) \sqcap Id(x')$ if $x \sqcap x'$ is defined*

Proof: Id is obviously one-to-one since if $x < y$, then $x \in Id(y)$ but $y \notin Id(x)$. It preserves order, since if $x \leq y$, then if $z \in Id(x)$, then $z \leq x$, so $z \in Id(y)$, so $Id(x) \subseteq Id(y)$.

To see that Id preserves existing meets, suppose that $x \sqcap y$ is defined. Then:

$$
\begin{aligned}
Id(x \sqcap y) &= \{z \mid z \sqsubseteq (x \sqcap y)\} \\
&= \{z \mid z \sqsubseteq x \text{ and } z \sqsubseteq y\} \\
&= \{z \mid z \sqsubseteq x\} \cap \{z \mid z \sqsubseteq y\} \\
&= Id(x) \cap Id(y) \\
&= Id(x) \sqcap Id(y)
\end{aligned}
$$

Showing that Id preserves existing joins is a bit more difficult. Suppose $x \sqcup y$ exists. We know $x, y \in Id(x) \sqcup Id(y) \subseteq Id(x) \cup Id(y)$ because $Ideals(S)$ is both complete and ordered by set inclusion. Furthermore, since $Id(x) \sqcup Id(y)$ is an ideal, we must have $x \sqcup y \in Id(x) \sqcup Id(y)$. Since $Id(x) \sqcup Id(y)$ is by definition the minimal ideal that extends $Id(x)$ and $Id(y)$, it must be the case that $Id(x) \sqcup Id(y) \subseteq Id(x \sqcup y)$, because $Id(x \sqcup y)$ is an ideal that extends $Id(x)$ and $Id(y)$. But since $x \sqcup y \in Id(x) \cup Id(y)$, we must have $Id(x \sqcup y) \subseteq Id(x) \sqcup Id(y)$ and hence $Id(x \sqcup y) = Id(x \sqcup y)$.   □

The primary purpose of the ideal completion is to provide joins for arbitrary directed sets of the orginal partial ordering which might not have had joins before.

Our interest in ideals is partially fueled by the following result which tells us that an algebraic CPO is uniquely determined by its compact elements.

Theorem 12.11 (Compact Representation)

Every algebraic CPO $\langle D, \leq \rangle$ *is isomorphic to the ideal completion of its compact elements, so that:*

$$\langle D, \leq \rangle \cong \langle \mathit{Ideals}(\mathit{Comp}(D)), \subseteq \rangle$$

Proof: Define a function $\phi: \mathit{Comp}(D) \to D$ by taking $\phi(I) = \bigsqcup I$. This is well defined since ideals are directed and D is a BCPO. We now need to show that ϕ is a one-to-one and onto order homomorphism. ϕ is a homomorphism since if $I \subseteq I'$, then $\bigsqcup I \leq \bigsqcup I'$. Suppose that ϕ is not one to one so that there is a pair of ideals $I, I' \in \mathit{Ideals}(\mathit{Comp}(D))$ such that $I \neq I'$ and $\bigsqcup I = \bigsqcup I'$. Without loss of generality we may suppose that $I \not\subseteq I'$, so we can take $x \in I \setminus I'$ to be an element in I not in I'. But $x \leq \bigsqcup I = \bigsqcup I'$, so since $x \in I \in \mathit{Comp}(D)$ is obviously compact there must be some $y \in I'$ such that $x \leq y$. But if this were the case, then since $x \leq y \in I'$ and I' is an ideal we would have $x \in I'$, which is a contradiction. To see that ϕ is onto suppose $x \in D$. Then $x = \bigsqcup \{y \in \mathit{Comp}(D) \mid y \leq x\}$ since D is algebraic. Now if we take the ideal $I = \bigsqcup \{Id(y) \mid y \in \mathit{Comp}(D), y \leq x\}$, then $x = \bigsqcup I = \phi(I)$. $\qquad \square$

We are finally prepared to consider our first application: the characterization of the collection of disjunctive descriptions as a domain. This application was originally developed by Pollard and Moshier (1990) who worked directly in terms of domains; Pollard (in press) makes the important connection between Pollard and Moshier (1990) and our description language. Pollard and Moshier noticed that the domain construction of Pereira and Shieber (1984) only suffices for the conjunctive portion of the domain; the generalization or meet of two feature structures did not represent their disjunction. Because feature structures are almost always used in place of the set of their extensions, it is one thing to have a choice between feature structures F and F' and quite a different thing again to have only $F \sqcap F'$. It is more often than not the case that there are F'' such that $F \sqcap F' \sqsubseteq F''$, but $F \not\sqsubseteq F''$ and $F' \not\sqsubseteq F''$. In the chapter on the type hierarchy, we saw that just this kind of behavior caused distributivity to fail for joins and meets of types. Disjunction and conjunction, on the other hand, are clearly distributive, and in fact, we have axioms to this effect. To overcome this obstacle to disjunctive representation and allow a domain-theoretic treatment of their disjunctive constraint system, Pollard and Moshier employed Smyth's (1978) upper powerdomain construction, which was designed to deal directly with finite non-determinism or disjunction. Smyth's construction is really only one of a number of domain-theoretic analogues of the powerset operation. The idea behind powerdomains is to provide informational orderings on sets of domain objects. We have already seen finite examples of both upper and (modified) lower powerdomain constructions in the section on inheritance hierarchy representations. Recall that the intuition behind Smyth's construction is that the elements of the finite sets of feature structures in the basis of the powerdomain are taken to represent non-deterministic alternatives. Thus a set $\{F_1, \ldots, F_n\} \subseteq \mathcal{F}$ of feature structures is taken to describe objects which are at least as specific as one of the F_i. This is what leads to the disjunctive reading of the upper powerdomain construction of Smyth; an object can be described with a set $\{F_1, \ldots, F_n\}$ just in case it can be described by one of the F_i in the set. The fact that we think of disjunctions as inducing non-deterministic choices means that we can apply the upper powerdomain construction to our description language in the obvious way. We provide the general construction due to Smyth first.

Definition 12.12 (Upper Powerdomain)

Suppose $\langle D, \leq \rangle$ is a domain with compact elements $Comp(D)$. Let $\mathcal{PD}(D)$ be the collection of finite subsets of pairwise incompatible elements of $Comp(D)$. For $X, Y \in \mathcal{PD}(D)$, set $X \sqsubseteq Y$ if and only if for every $y \in Y$ there is some $x \in X$ such that $x \leq y$. Then define $\mathcal{S}(\langle D, \leq \rangle) = \langle Ideals(\langle \mathcal{PD}(D), \sqsubseteq \rangle), \subseteq \rangle$ to be the upper powerdomain of D.

The idea behind the powerdomain construction is that if we start with a domain D, the compact elements of the powerdomain consist of finite sets of compact elements of the domain (or more precisely, the principal ideals in $\langle \mathcal{PD}(D), \sqsubseteq \rangle$ generated by such finite sets of compact elements). We set $X \sqsubseteq Y$ for such sets X and Y if every element of Y is at least as specific as some element of X. Under this ordering, an arbitrary subset of X would carry the same information as its set of minimal elements; thus it is only necessary to consider pairwise incomparable elements of X for $\mathcal{PD}(X)$. Note that we do not lose our original information in $\mathcal{PD}(D)$ because with the powerdomain ordering we have:

(5) $\{x\} \sqcup \{y\} = \{x \sqcup y\}$

This result can be strengthened somewhat due to the distributivity of the resulting meets and joins. We approach this generalization in two stages. We first show that the compact elements of the upper powerdomain construction form a distributive lattice.

Theorem 12.13 (Compact Distributivity)

The partial order $\langle \mathcal{PD}(D), \sqsubseteq \rangle$ is a distributive lattice.

Proof: To see that $\mathcal{PD}(D)$ is a lattice, note that if $X, Y \in \mathcal{PD}(D)$, then:

- $X \sqcap Y = Min(X \cup Y)$

- $X \sqcup Y = Min(\{X \sqcup Y \mid X, Y \in \mathcal{PD}(D), X \sqcup Y \text{ defined}\})$

The simplest way to demonstrate distributivity is to consider an alternative representation for $\langle \mathcal{PD}(D), \sqsubseteq \rangle$ in terms of an isomorphic set algebra. Consider the complete distributive lattice $\langle \mathcal{P}(D), \supseteq \rangle$ of subsets of D ordered by reverse set inclusion, where $\mathcal{P}(D)$ is the ordinary powerset of all subsets of D. Joins and meets in this powerset are given by unions and intersections respectively. We define an isomorphic embedding $\phi : \mathcal{PD}(D) \rightarrow \mathcal{P}(D)$ by assuming that for $E \in \mathcal{PD}(D)$, we have:

$$\phi(E) = \{d \in D \mid e \sqsubseteq d \text{ for some } e \in E\}$$

We then have $E \sqsubseteq E'$ if and only if $\phi(E') \subseteq E$ or equivalently, $\phi(E) \supseteq \phi(E')$. It is obvious that ϕ is one to one and hence an order isomorphism. What is important to note, though, is the following:

$$\phi(E \sqcup E') = \phi(E) \cap \phi(E')$$
$$\phi(E \sqcap E') = \phi(E) \cup \phi(E')$$

From this we can conclude that $\phi(\mathcal{PD}(D))$ ordered by reverse set inclusion has meets and joins given by intersections and unions, so that it is a set algebra isomorphic to $\langle \mathcal{PD}(D), \sqsubseteq \rangle$. Every set algebra is distributive, and hence $\mathcal{PD}(D)$ is distributive by virtue of the isomorphism we constructed. □

To generalize this distributivity result for the whole domain including limit points, we need to consider the natural extension of distributivity to the whole domain. The strongest way we can do this is by considering Heyting algebras. A *complete Heyting algebra* is a complete lattice in which finite meets distribute over infinite joins. In particular, we have:

(6) $\quad x \sqcap (\bigsqcup \{y \mid y \in Y\}) = \bigsqcup \{y \sqcap x \mid y \in Y\}$

Stone proved that the ideal completion of a distributive lattice is a Heyting algebra (see Birkhoff 1967:129).

Theorem 12.14 (Upper Powerdomain)

If $\langle D, \leq \rangle$ is a domain, then $S(\langle D, \leq \rangle)$ is a countably based complete algebraic Heyting Algebra.

Pollard and Moshier (1990) applied Stone's result to the modeling of disjunctive feature structures, a task to which we now turn.

The point of the upper powerdomain construction is that it gives us a powerful domain-theoretic handle on disjunctive constructions. Recall that for a satisfiable non-disjunctive description ϕ, we could find a most general satisfier $MGSat(\phi)$ in $\mathcal{F}$. Thus each non-disjunctive description can be identified with a compact element of $\mathcal{F}$. The beauty of $MGSat$ is the way in which it transforms description conjunction into feature structure unification, so that if $\phi \wedge \psi$ is satisfiable, we have:

(7) $\quad MGSat(\phi \wedge \psi) = MGSat(\phi) \sqcup MGSat(\psi)$

In our present situation, we can use our other operation, $MGSats$, which maps arbitrary (possibly unsatisfiable, possibly disjunctive) descriptions to the (possibly empty) finite set of their most general satisfiers. But with the Smyth construction, $MGSats(\phi)$ is a compact element of the upper powerdomain of $\mathcal{F}^\omega$. Of course, the upper powerdomain $S(\langle \mathcal{F}^\omega, \sqsubseteq \rangle)$ is fully determined by the compact elements in $\mathcal{F}$. The beauty of working in the powerdomain is that we can preserve the structure of both conjunctions and disjunctions.

Theorem 12.15 (Powerdomain Representation)

If $\phi, \psi \in$ Desc are descriptions, then:

- $MGSats(\phi \wedge \psi) = MGSats(\phi) \sqcup MGSats(\psi)$

- $MGSats(\phi \vee \psi) = MGSats(\phi) \sqcap MGSats(\psi)$

Proof: It is only necessary to work out what the meets should be in the powerdomain to see that they correspond to the way in which *MGSats* was defined:

$$
\begin{aligned}
MGSats(\phi \vee \psi) \;&=\; Min(MGSats(\phi) \cup MGSats(\psi)) \\
&=\; MGSats(\phi) \sqcap MGSats(\psi) \qquad\qquad \square
\end{aligned}
$$

Put more concisely, the powerdomain representation theorem tells us that the total most general satisfiers function $MGSats: \mathsf{Desc} \to \mathcal{S}(\langle \mathcal{F}, \sqsubseteq \rangle)$ is a morphism from the term algebra $\langle \mathsf{Desc}, \wedge, \vee \rangle$ of descriptions under disjunction and conjunction to the algebra $\langle \mathcal{PD}(\mathcal{F}), \sqcup, \sqcap \rangle$ of compact elements of the upper powerdomain of the feature structures under meet and join respectively. We already know that *MGSats* determines our notion of logical equivalence, so that $\phi \equiv \psi$ if and only if $MGSats(\phi) = MGSats(\psi)$. Let $\langle \mathsf{Desc}/_{\equiv}, \wedge, \vee \rangle$ be defined so that $[\phi]_{\equiv} \wedge [\psi]_{\equiv} = [\phi \wedge \psi]_{\equiv}$ and $[\phi]_{\equiv} \vee [\psi]_{\equiv} = [\phi \vee \psi]_{\equiv}$. The descriptions modulo alphabetic variance allow us to restate our representation theorem as the following corollary to our representation theorem:

Corollary 12.16

$\langle \mathsf{Desc}/_{\equiv}, \wedge, \vee \rangle$ *is order isomorphic to* $\langle \mathcal{PD}(\mathcal{F}), \sqcup, \sqcap \rangle$.

Proof: The function $h: \mathsf{Desc}/_{\equiv} \to \mathcal{PD}(\mathcal{F})$ defined by $h([\phi]_{\equiv}) = MGSats(\phi)$ is one to one and onto, as can be seen from the description theorem. $\square$

Note that the order has been switched in this isomorphism, so that conjunction corresponds to join and disjunction to meet. If we were to consider infinitary descriptions, we could extend this result to the whole of $\mathcal{F}^{\omega}$.

We are now ready to tackle our second application of domain theory: our characterization of our type, inequation and extensionality inference procedures as special kind of morphisms over domains. We begin with the related notions of substructure and morphism. While subdomains would be defined as preserving either arbitrary joins or directed joins, we are more interested in the subspaces of a domain, which are subposets which themselves form a domain.

Definition 12.17 (Subspace)

We say that $\langle E, \leq \rangle$ is a subspace of the domain $\langle D, \leq \rangle$ if $E \subseteq D$ and $\langle E, \leq \rangle$ is a domain.

The natural notion of morphisms over the collection of domains insists that they preserve the structure of directed joins. Such morphisms are referred to as *continuous functions* in domain theory.

Definition 12.18 (Continuity)

A function $f: S \to S'$ on complete partial orders $\langle S, \leq \rangle$ and $\langle S', \leq' \rangle$ is said to be continuous if for every directed subset $T \subseteq S$ we have:

$$f(\bigsqcup T) = \bigsqcup' f(T) = \bigsqcup' \{ f(A) \mid A \in T \}$$

Notice that only directed joins and not arbitrary bounded joins need to be preserved by continuous functions. Thus it is possible to have $f(x \sqcup y) \neq f(x) \sqcup f(y)$ for continuous f. It should also be noted that continuity is a suitable notion of morphism as the collection of continuous functions contains the identities and is closed under compositions. Furthermore, we note that every continuous function is monotonic, so that if $x \leq y$, then $\{x, y\}$ is directed so that $\bigsqcup \{x, y\} = y$ and hence:

$$(8) \quad f(x) \leq f(y) = f(\bigsqcup \{x, y\}) = \bigsqcup \{ f(x), f(y) \}$$

Our next theorem is an important representation theorem which later allows us to automatically turn our inference procedures into special kinds of continuous functions.

Theorem 12.19 (Compact Continuous Function Representation)

If $f: D \to E$ is a continuous function from the domain $\langle D, \leq \rangle$ to the domain $\langle E, \leq' \rangle$, then f is uniquely determined by its restriction to $Comp(D)$.

Proof: Because D is algebraic, we have $x = \bigsqcup \{ y \in Comp(D) \mid y \leq x \}$ for every $x \in D$. Since $\{ y \in Comp(D) \mid y \leq x \}$ is directed in general, we have:

$$f(x) = f(\bigsqcup \{ y \in Comp(D) \mid y \leq x \}) = \bigsqcup' f(\{ y \in Comp(D) \mid y \leq x \})$$

Thus the behavior of f on arbitrary $x \in D$ is fully determined by the behavior of f on the compact $y \in Comp(D)$ such that $y \leq x$. $\qquad \Box$

It should come as no surprise to those familiar with algebra that the notion of continuous function and subspace are related. We first introduce a special kind of continuous function which is modeled after standard closure operators in set theory. There is an obvious parallel between the following definition of closure and our previous definition of an inference procedure.

Definition 12.20 (Closure)

A closure operator over a domain D is a continuous function $f: D \to D$ such that for all $x \in D$:

- $f(f(x)) = f(x)$ (Idempotent)

- $x \leq f(x)$ (Increasing)

The restrictions on closures are often stated equivalently as $f \circ f = f$ and $Id_D \sqsubseteq f$, where Id_D is the identity function on D. The assumption that a closure is continuous is enough to guarantee its monotonicity; every continuous function is monotonic. The reason we are interested in closures is that they stand in a one-to-one relation with subspaces.

Theorem 12.21 (Subspace Characterization)

If $f: D \to D$ is a closure, then $f(D) = \{f(d) \mid d \in D\}$ is a subspace of D.

If $\langle E, \leq \rangle$ is a subspace of $\langle D, \leq \rangle$, then there is a unique closure $f: D \to D$ such that $E = f(D) = \{f(d) \mid d \in D\}$.

Proof: Suppose that $f: D \to D$ is a closure operation. We need to show that $f(D)$, the image of the closure, is closed under bounded joins. So suppose that $Y \subseteq f(D)$ is bounded in D. Since $Y \subseteq f(D)$, there must be some $X \subseteq D$ such that $f(X) = Y$. Furthermore, the continuity of f entails that X must also be bounded. Thus we have $f(\bigsqcup X) = \bigsqcup(f(X)) = \bigsqcup Y$ by the continuity of f.

Conversely, suppose that $\langle E, \leq \rangle$ is a subspace of $\langle D, \leq \rangle$. We define an operation $f: D \to D$ by setting $f(x) = \bigsqcap\{y \in E \mid x \leq y\}$. We must have $f(x) \in E$, because E must be closed under bounded joins. We see that f preserves directed joins and is hence continuous by noting that:

$$f(\bigsqcup X) = \bigsqcap\{y \in E \mid \bigsqcup X \leq y\} = \bigsqcup_{x \in X} \bigsqcap\{y \in E \mid x \leq y\}$$

Since we know that E is closed under bounded joins, it is closed under arbitrary meets, and hence $f(x) \in E$. If $e \in E$, then we obviously have $f(e) = e$, so that both $f(D) = E$ and $f(f(x)) = x$. Hence f is a closure operation with E as its range. To see that f is the unique closure such that $f(D) = E$, we note that if g is a closure on E such that $g(D) = E$, then f and g must agree on E, so that $g(e) = f(e)$. Furthermore, the requirements that $x \leq f(x)$ and the continuity requirement are enough to determine the action of g on the remaining elements in $D \setminus E$. $\qquad\square$

What is interesting to note from our perspective is the fact that all of the collections of feature structures that we have considered as a result of typing, extensionality, and inequation restrictions form subspaces of the domain of (inequated) feature structures. Before seeing this, we need one more result that characterizes a closure operator in terms of its effects on compact elements. Recall that f is an inference procedure if $f(f(x)) = f(x)$, $x \leq f(x)$, and $x \leq y$ implies $f(x) \leq f(y)$.

Theorem 12.22

Suppose $\langle D, \leq \rangle$ is a domain and $f: Comp(D) \to Comp(D)$ is an inference procedure. Then the function $f^*: D \to D$ defined by:

$$f^*(x) = \bigsqcup\{f(y) \mid y \leq x \text{ and } y \text{ compact}\}$$

is a closure operator.

Proof: We first show that f^* is continuous. Suppose $X \subseteq D$ is directed. Then since D is algebraic, we have:

$$
\begin{aligned}
f^*(\bigsqcup X) &= f^*(\bigsqcup\{y \in Comp(D) \mid y \leq x \text{ for some } x \in X\}) \\
&= \bigsqcup\{f(y) \mid y \in Comp(D), y \leq x \text{ for some } x \in X\} \\
&= \bigsqcup\{f^*(y) \mid y \in Comp(D), y \leq x \text{ for some } x \in X\}
\end{aligned}
$$

Thus f is continuous. To see that f^* is idempotent, simply note that if X is directed, then we have:

$$f^*(f^*(\bigsqcup X)) = f^*(\bigsqcup \{f(y) \mid y \in Comp(D), y \leq x \text{ for some } x \in X\})$$
$$= \bigsqcup \{f(f(y)) \mid y \in Comp(D), y \leq x \text{ for some } x \in X\}$$
$$= \bigsqcup \{f(y) \mid y \in Comp(D), y \leq x \text{ for some } x \in X\}$$
$$= f^*(\bigsqcup X)$$

by the fact that $f(f(y)) = f(y)$ for $y \in Comp(D)$. Finally, it is obvious that $x \leq f^*(x)$, since $f^*(x)$ is defined as a meet of objects greater than or equal to x. Thus f is a closure operator. $\square$

Of course, since closure operators are continuous, we know that they are determined by their values on compact elements. From the fact that the subspaces of a domain are determined by the closures of that domain, we see that the subspaces are determined by the inference procedures. In fact, all of our type, inequation, and extensionality inference procedures were defined as the compact components of a closure operator. In particular, the functions we are now considering include *TypDom*, *TypRan*, *TypInf*, *Fill*, *FIneq*, *Ext* and *Coll*. We first extend our partial inference procedures to continuous functions for which arguments which were previously undefined are mapped to a new $\top$ element. For instance, in the case of *TypInf*, we would have $TypInf(F) = \top$ if $F \in \mathcal{F}$ is not well-typable. We then extend this new total function to the limit (infinite) elements of $\mathcal{F}^\omega \cup \{\top\}$ in the natural way by defining a new function $TypInf^*$ as before, so that $TypInf^*(\bigsqcup S) = \bigsqcup TypInf(S)$ for directed $S \sqsubseteq \mathcal{F}$. An immediate corollary is the following:

Theorem 12.23

The following are all closure operators:

- $TypDom^* : (\mathcal{F}^\omega \cup \{\top\}) \to (\mathcal{F}^\omega \cup \{\top\})$

- $TypRan^* : (TypDom^*(\mathcal{F}^\omega) \cup \{\top\}) \to (TypDom^*(\mathcal{F}^\omega) \cup \{\top\})$

- $TypInf^* : (\mathcal{F}^\omega \cup \{\top\}) \to (\mathcal{F}^\omega \cup \{\top\})$

- $Fill^* : (TypInf^*(\mathcal{F}^\omega) \cup \{\top\}) \to (TypInf^*(\mathcal{F}^\omega) \cup \{\top\})$

- $Ext^* : (\mathcal{F}^\omega \cup \{\top\}) \to (\mathcal{F}^\omega \cup \{\top\})$

- $Coll^* : (\mathcal{F}^\omega \cup \{\top\}) \to (\mathcal{F}^\omega \cup \{\top\})$

- $FIneq^* : (\mathcal{IF}^\omega \cup \{\top\}) \to (\mathcal{IF}^\omega \cup \{\top\})$

It is easy to verify that the composition of closure operators (defined over the appropriate domains) is again a closure operator, so that, for instance, *Fill* $\circ$ *TypInf* is also a closure operator. If we had defined closures earlier, we

would have been spared a lot of trouble in proving that the images of these
closures formed subspaces of the domains that we started with. Keep in mind,
though, that continuity does not mean that the closures distribute over arbitrary joins. For instance, just because *Fill* is a closure operator does not
mean that $Fill(F \sqcup F') = Fill(F) \sqcup Fill(F')$, because $\{F, F'\}$ might not be
directed. We also saw examples where $TypInf(F)$, $TypInf(F')$, $F \sqcup F'$ and
$TypInf(F) \sqcup TypInf(F')$ were all defined, but where $TypInf(F \sqcup F')$ was undefined.

It can now be seen that we have completely cast our attribute-value logic in
the style of domains; conjunctions and disjunctions correspond to the domain
operations of meet and join and all of our subcollections of feature structures
can be seen as the images of closure operators. This accounts for the extreme
degree of redundancy in the completeness proofs in most of the sections on logic,
which can now be seen to be due to the fact that we were simply axiomatizing
various closure operators which could be composed with *MGSat* to provide
domain-theoretic treatments of the logical equivalence classes of each of our
logics.

Part IV

Applications

Chapter 13

Unification-Based
Phrase Structure Grammars

In this chapter, we consider a phrase structure grammar formalism, or more precisely, a parameterized family of such formalisms, in which non-terminal (category) symbols are replaced by feature structures in both rewriting rules and lexical entries. Consequently, the application of a rewriting rule must be mediated by unification rather than by simple symbol matching. This explains why grammar formalisms such as the one we present here have come to be known as *unification-based*. Although our presentation of unification-based phrase structure grammars is self contained, for those unfamiliar with unification-based grammars and their applications, we recommend reading Shieber's excellent introduction (Shieber 1986). Shieber lays out the fundamental principles of unification-based phrase structure formalisms along with some of their more familar incarnations, as well as providing a wide variety of linguistic examples and motivations. Another good introductory source is the text by Gazdar and Mellish (1989).

The early development of unification-based grammars was intimately connected with the development of logic programming itself, the most obvious link stemming from Colmerauer's research into Q-systems (1970) and Metamorphosis Grammars (1978). In fact, Colmerauer's development of Prolog was motivated by the desire to provide a powerful yet efficient implementation environment for natural language grammars. The subsequent popularity of Prolog led to the development of a number of so-called *logic grammar* systems. These grammar formalisms are typically variations of first-order term unification phrase structure grammars such as the Definite Clause Grammars (DCGs) of Pereira and Warren (1980), the Extraposition Grammars of Pereira (1981), the Slot Grammars of McCord (1981) and also the Gapping Grammars of Dahl and Abramson (1984, Popowich 1985). Pereira and Shieber (1987) provide an introductory survey of linguistic applications of logic grammars, while the books stemming from the *Natural Language Understanding and Logic Programming* meetings (Dahl and Saint-Dizier 1985, 1988) contain a number of applications of logic grammars to natural language processing tasks. More or less independently of the tradition in logic programming, linguists and their more computationally minded colleagues developed a number of grammar formalisms based on feature structure unification. Generalized Phrase Structure Grammars (see Gazdar et al. 1985) and Lexical Functional Grammars (see Kaplan and Bresnan 1982) are the most fully fleshed-out linguistic theories based on a mixture of phrase structure and feature structure unification (see Sells 1985 for an elegant introduction to both formalisms). At roughly the same time as linguistic formalisms began to employ various notions of feature structure unification, Kay (1979) developed Functional Unification Grammar, which was probably the earliest implementation of a general-purpose unification-based phrase structure grammar. Much of the success of unification-based grammars was due to the widely available PATR-II system of Shieber et al. (1983) which allows context-free grammar rules to be annotated by constraints on feature values.

As pointed out by Shieber (1985b), it is important to keep in mind that there are two distinct yet complementary applications for which unification-based formalisms have been developed. The difference between low-level unification-based programming environments such as PATR-II and high-level linguistic formalisms such as Lexical Functional Grammar is analogous to the difference between low-level programming languages like C and high-level languages like Prolog. Theoretically, any program that can be expressed in Prolog can also be expressed in C. In particular, a Prolog interpreter can easily be written in C. The difference between the two languages is that many useful problems are significantly easier to express using Prolog because useful features such as term unification, memory management, and depth-first search are built directly into the language. On the other hand, certain details of the underlying machine which are transparent to C, such as memory management, arrays, records, pointers, and type coercions, cannot be accessed directly from Prolog.

The Lexical Functional Grammar and Generalized Phrase Structure Grammar unification-based formalisms are analogues of high-level programming languages; their purpose is to capture linguistic generalizations in a substantive declarative linguistic theory. For a linguistic theory to be a theory rather than a programming language or abstract formalism, it must make predictions about the kinds of constructions, rules, or constraints which are found in natural languages. For instance, GPSG is designed so that it can only generate context-free languages, whereas LFG places restrictions on the grammar formalism which ensure the decidability of parsing (Kaplan and Bresnan 1982). The goal in linguistic theory is usually to develop formalisms that are as restrictive as possible and to allow details of individual grammars to be expressed as concisely as possible. On the other hand, low-level and theory-neutral programming languages such as PATR-II, Definite Clause Grammar and Functional Unification Grammar have been engineered to be as general and powerful as possible.

The primary benefit of having an abstract and general-purpose system such as PATR-II is that it allows the linguist to rapidly prototype new linguistic theories and test their behavior computationally. For instance, Shieber (1986) shows how to implement aspects of both Lexical Functional Grammar and Generalized Phrase Structure Grammars in the PATR-II formalism. Similarly, Unification Categorial Grammar (Zeevat et al. 1987), another substantive linguistic theory, is implemented as a term grammar in Prolog (Calder 1987). The ability to rapidly prototype a linguistic theory is especially important given the highly complex and subtle nature of most current linguistic theories. The existence of systems such as PATR-II has exerted a considerable influence on those adopting non-transformational approaches to linguistic theorizing. Another advantage of having a linguistic theory implemented in a system such as PATR-II is that the implementation of the linguistic theory itself constitutes a high-level programming language. While a linguist might directly code a grammar that captures facts about Swahili morphology, English syntax, or Japanese semantics in a low-level system such as PATR-II, the hope is that the same facts could be much more readily expressed in a high-level linguistic theory.

Thus the distinction between a unification-based programming system such as PATR-II and a linguistic theory such as Lexical Functional Grammar is simply one of level of abstraction. Further arguments in support of this kind of factorization in the context of inheritance-based knowledge representation systems have been made by Brachman (1979). Brachman reports that the failure to distinguish the "level of abstraction" of a construction has led to a number of avoidable confusions in the knowledge representation literature. For instance, Brachman urges us not to confuse the issue of whether an inheritance-based formalism should use roles with the issue of which roles are appropriate for a given application. Similar confusion has been avoided for the most part in the computational linguistic community primarily due to the clarity with which this distinction has been expressed in the PATR-II literature, especially by Shieber (1985b, 1986).

It should be clear from what follows that we are not proposing a particular linguistic theory, but rather developing a general-purpose grammar formalism based on our notions of feature structures. Maintaing a general perspective, we demonstrate how a unification-based phrase structure grammar formalism is determined naturally by any of our feature structure theories. In other words, we are building a general phrase structure formalism which is parameterized for the particular attribute-value logic of interest. In particular, our formalism reduces to either PATR-II or first-order term unification grammar with the appropriate choice of inheritance hierarchy, appropriateness conditions, extensional types, and attribute-value logic. Our notion of phrase-structure grammar parameterized for feature logic is similar to Höhfeld and Smolka's (1989) very general analysis of constraint logic programming.

Our concern in this chapter, as in previous chapters, is to lay out the formalism in the cleanest and most direct manner possible. In particular, we present our system non-deterministically and do not consider implementation issues such as parsing strategies, structure sharing, or backtracking. These topics have been the subject of papers and technical reports too numerous to list, especially if we were to broaden our scope to encompass the logic grammar and logic programming literature. The interested reader is urged to peruse the last ten years or so of the journal *Computational Linguistics* as well as the *ACL* and *COLING* proceedings from the same period. There have also been a number of special-purpose meetings and workshops devoted exclusively to unification-based grammar formalisms.

One interesting application of unification-based phrase structure formalisms is in designing computer language compilers. Much current compiler technology is based on attribute grammars which bear a close resemblance to the kinds of unification-based phrase structure grammars we present in this chapter (Aho, Sethi and Ullman 1988). Shieber (1989) and Moshier (1988) have studied some potential applications of feature structure based formalisms to computer languages, and the use of Prolog grammars in compiler construction is well established (Sterling and Shapiro 1986). The attractive part of the feature structure based approach is its declarative simplicity coupled with the range of ways in which it can be interpreted, a topic we take up in the sections on top-down and bottom-up parsing of unification-based grammars.

Unification Phrase Structure Grammars

As is usual in formal language theory, we work relative to a fixed a collection BasExp of *basic expressions*. The collection of *expressions* is defined to be the collection of strings of basic expressions:

(1) $\mathsf{Exp} = \mathsf{BasExp}^* = \{a_1 \cdots a_n \mid n \geq 0 \text{ and } a_i \in \mathsf{BasExp} \text{ for } 1 \leq i \leq n\}$

In general, we write arbitrary expressions over BasExp in bold face, so that by convention, $\mathbf{a} = a_1 \cdots a_n$. The expression $a_1 \cdots a_n$ is said to be of *length n*. We let ϵ be the unique string of length 0, the so-called *null string*. The binary *concatenation* operation over Exp is defined by setting:

(2) $(a_1 \cdots a_n) \cdot (b_1 \cdots b_m) = a_1 \cdots a_n b_1 \cdots b_m$

Note that concatenation is an associative binary operator, with the null string as an identity, so that:

(3)   • $\mathbf{a} \cdot (\mathbf{b} \cdot \mathbf{c}) = (\mathbf{a} \cdot \mathbf{b}) \cdot \mathbf{c}$ (Associativity)

         • $\epsilon \cdot \mathbf{a} = \mathbf{a} \cdot \epsilon = \mathbf{a}$ (Identity)

Algebraically speaking, $\langle \mathsf{Exp}, \cdot, \epsilon \rangle$ is the *free monoid* generated by BasExp. We are interested in subsets $\mathcal{L} \subseteq \mathsf{Exp}$ of expressions, which are said to be *formal languages* over BasExp. We can extend the operation of concatenation to languages, so that:

(4) $\mathcal{L} \cdot \mathcal{L}' = \{\mathbf{a} \cdot \mathbf{a}' \mid \mathbf{a} \in \mathcal{L}, \mathbf{a}' \in \mathcal{L}'\}$

In the formal development of this section, we exploit the duality between feature structures and (normal form) attribute-value descriptions. While this move is almost certain to offend purists, we feel that it leads to the cleanest and easiest possible presentation. As usual, those who feel strongly about one presentation (either feature structures or their logic) are urged to convert everything we say to their system of choice using either *MGSat* or *Desc*, as appropriate.

In our phrase structure grammar application, a feature structure (or description) is taken to represent a linguistic *category*. The most natural interpretation of a category C is as the collection of expressions which are classified as being Cs (see Gazdar 1981). Of course, such an interpretation for a category is a set of expressions and thus a formal language itself. A grammar, in our sense, provides a finite (recursive) characterization of the set of expressions of each category. The purpose in formally describing our system is to define the way in which grammars assign sets of expressions to categories. It is also worth noting at the outset that the semantics of our grammar formalism respects the informational ordering defined on feature structures by subsumption in the following sense: if an expression **a** is assigned to a category F and $F \sqsubseteq F'$, then the expression **a** is also assigned to the category F'; for a string **a** to be assigned to category F means that **a** is also assigned to every extension of F. Thus the interpretation function which maps categories onto the sets of expressions they categorize is monotonic.

The basic mechanism underlying any phrase-structure grammar is the *rewriting rule*. In our system, a *rewriting rule* is of the form $E_0 \rightarrow E_1 \cdots E_n$ where E_0 is a feature structure called the *mother* of the rule, and each *daughter* E_i for $1 \leq i \leq n$ is either a feature structure or basic expression. The interpretation of such a rule is loosely that an E_0 can consist of an expression of category E_1 followed by an expression of category E_2, ..., followed by an expression of category E_n. Note that it is possible to have $n = 0$ in a rewriting rule, and thus have no daughters on the righthand side. In such cases, we write $E_0 \rightarrow \epsilon$ to indicate that the sequence of daughters is empty. The interpretation of such a null rewriting is that the null string expression $\epsilon \in$ Exp can be categorized as an E_0. In linguistic applications such as Generalized Phrase Structure Grammar (Gazdar et al. 1985), such null productions are often used to categorize so-called *traces*. A rewriting rule is context-free in the sense that it provides an absolute characterization of categorization which cannot be overridden by other factors such as the context in which it is employed (see Gazdar 1981 for elaboration of the linguistic significance of this fact).

It is most straightforward to express our rules in terms of attribute-value descriptions with variables. As we said before, we do not specify our collection of feature structures or description language directly, as our construction generalizes over most of the feature structure systems we have presented, with the exception being inequations. It turns out to be quite complicated and messy to formalize the notion of phrase structure grammars with inequations, mainly because there may be inequations which hold across more than one category in a rule. Although equations may hold across more than one category in a rule, their effects are much more straightforward. But we should also point out that when we discuss constraint systems in Chapter 15, we will see how to add inequations to phrase structure grammars. In so doing, we do not need to change the form of the grammar rules themselves, but just the way they are interpreted.

For what we present below, we require that at least an inheritance hierarchy $\langle \text{Type}, \sqsubseteq \rangle$ of types and set Feat of features be fixed. Let Desc consist of the set of descriptions over Feat and Type and the countably infinite set Var of variables. For the time being, we only consider descriptions without inequations. Let $\mathcal{G}$ be the set of feature structures over Type and Feat and some fixed attribute-value logic axiomatization $\mathcal{E}_\mathcal{G}$. Note that fixing an attribute-value logic may require additional information about the appropriateness relation *Approp* and the set ExtType of extensional types. It must also be decided whether the descriptions may contain inequations (which we model later in the chapter on constraint systems), and which forms of type, acyclicity, and extensionality rules are to be enforced. Finally, we assume that we have some fixed set BasExp of basic expressions over which we are interested in defining formal languages. In practice, the basic expressions can be anything: abstract symbols, letters of a phonetic or orthographic alphabet or sequences of 0s and 1s. As with all formal languages, we assume the interpretation of the symbols in BasExp is a matter for the user rather than the system to decide.

Definition 13.1 (Unification Phrase Structure Grammar)

We take a unification phrase structure grammar *over* Type, Feat *and* BasExp *to be a finite set:*

$$\text{Gram} \subseteq \text{Desc} \times (\text{Desc} \cup \text{BasExp})^*$$

An element $\langle \xi_0, \langle \xi_1, \ldots, \xi_n \rangle \rangle \in \text{Gram}$ is called a *rule description* and is written as $\xi_0 \rightarrow \xi_1 \cdots \xi_n$. The phrase structure grammar in the figures Figure 13.1 and Figure 13.2, which treats a tiny fragment of English, is used as an example to illustrate our further definitions. In Figure 13.1 and Figure 13.2, we have adopted the Prolog convention of using capitalized strings of characters and numbers for variables in descriptions. In presenting phrase structure grammars in terms of descriptions, we do not need to use any path equations (or inequations); all structure sharing (and later, all inequality relations) can be expressed using variables and variable equations.

It should be kept in mind that since this grammar's purpose is purely illustrative, it is not meant to be an example of a sensible linguistic analysis. Note that we express our grammar directly in our underlying unification phrase structure formalism and do not rely on an intermediate higher-level linguistic formalism.

While grammars themselves are most easily stated in terms of descriptions, the rewriting process is most naturally captured in terms of feature structures. We exploit the correspondence between descriptions and feature structures in the following definition of rewriting rule, which allows us to treat unification phrase structure grammars as equivalent to possibly infinite sets of ordinary phrase structure rewriting rules with feature structures as non-terminals and basic expressions as terminals. This allows us to apply well known techniques

$$\text{SYN} \cdot \text{CAT: s} \wedge \text{SEM: } (X1 \wedge \text{SUBJ: } X2)$$
$$\rightarrow \quad \text{SYN: } (\text{CAT: np} \wedge \text{AGR: } X3) \wedge \text{SEM: } X2$$
$$\text{SYN: } (\text{CAT: vp} \wedge \text{AGR: } X3) \wedge \text{SEM: } X1$$

$$\text{SYN: } (\text{CAT: np} \wedge \text{AGR: } X1) \wedge \text{SEM: } (\text{DET: } X2 \wedge \text{RESTR: } X3 \wedge \text{MODS: } X4)$$
$$\rightarrow \quad \text{SYN: } (\text{CAT: det} \wedge \text{AGR: } X1) \wedge \text{SEM: } X2$$
$$\text{SYN} \cdot \text{CAT: adjseq} \wedge \text{SEM: } X4$$
$$\text{SYN: } (\text{CAT: n} \wedge \text{AGR: } X1) \wedge \text{SEM: } X3$$

$$\text{SYN} \cdot \text{CAT: adjseq} \wedge \text{SEM: e-list}$$
$$\rightarrow \quad \epsilon$$

$$\text{SYN} \cdot \text{CAT: adjseq} \wedge \text{SEM: } (\text{HEAD: } X1 \wedge \text{TAIL: } X2)$$
$$\rightarrow \quad \text{SYN} \cdot \text{CAT: adj} \wedge \text{SEM: } X1$$
$$\text{SYN} \cdot \text{CAT: adjseq} \wedge \text{SEM: } X2$$

$$\text{SYN: } (\text{CAT: vp} \wedge \text{AGR: } X1) \wedge \text{SEM: } (X2 \wedge \text{OBJ: } X3)$$
$$\rightarrow \quad \text{SYN: } (\text{CAT: sv} \wedge \text{AGR: } X1) \wedge \text{SEM: } X2$$
$$\text{SYN: scomp} \wedge \text{SEM: } X3$$

$$\text{SYN: scomp} \wedge \text{SEM: } X1$$
$$\rightarrow \quad \text{that}$$
$$\text{SYN} \cdot \text{CAT: s} \wedge \text{SEM: } X1$$

$$\text{SYN: } (\text{CAT: vp} \wedge \text{AGR: } X1) \wedge \text{SEM: } (X2 \wedge (\text{OBJ: } X3 \wedge \text{SUBJ: } X3))$$
$$\rightarrow \quad \text{SYN: } (\text{CAT: tv} \wedge \text{AGR: } X1) \wedge \text{SEM: } X2$$
$$\text{SYN: } (\text{CAT: reflex} \wedge \text{AGR: } X1)$$

Figure 13.1. Unification Phrase Structure Grammar Rule Descriptions.

for analyzing phrase structure rewriting systems.

Definition 13.2 (Rewriting Rule)

The set Rule(Gram) *of rewriting rules is such that* $E_0 \rightarrow E_1 \cdots E_n \in$ Rule(Gram) *if and only if* $\langle \xi_0, \langle \xi_1, \ldots, \xi_n \rangle \rangle \in$ Gram, *and there is an assignment* α: Vars $\rightarrow \mathcal{G}$ *such that for each* $i \leq n$:

- $E_i = \xi_i$ *if* $\xi_i \in$ BasExp

- $E_i \models^\alpha \xi_i$ *if* $\xi_i \in$ Desc

For non-trivial grammars, the set of rewriting rules is infinite. It is significant that the satisfaction relations in the definition of rewriting rule are all evaluated with respect to a common assignment α, because this ensures that structure sharing is preserved during rewriting. For instance, the rule for constructing sentences in Figure 13.1 allows us to construct the rewriting rule in Figure 13.3. In displaying this rule, we have used the same notation for structure sharing across feature structures as we used for structure sharing within feature structures (we do the same thing later for inequalities, as well). We have also carried

SYN: (CAT: **np** ∧ AGR: **sing**) ∧ SEM: **john**   →   *john*

SYN: (CAT: **det** ∧ AGR: **sing**) ∧ SEM: **every**   →   *every*

SYN: (CAT: **det** ∧ AGR: **plu**) ∧ SEM: **most**   →   *most*

SYN · CAT: **det** ∧ SEM: **the**   →   *the*

SYN: (CAT: **n** ∧ AGR: **sing**) ∧ SEM: **kid**   →   *kid*

SYN: (CAT: **n** ∧ AGR: **plu**) ∧ SEM: **kid**   →   *kids*

SYN · CAT: **n** ∧ SEM: **sheep**   →   *sheep*

SYN · CAT: **adj** ∧ SEM · REL: **tall**   →   *tall*

SYN: (CAT: **vp** ∧ AGR: **sing**) ∧ SEM · REL: **run**   →   *runs*

SYN: (CAT: **vp** ∧ AGR: **plu**) ∧ SEM · REL: **run**   →   *run*

SYN · CAT: **vp** ∧ SEM · REL: **run**   →   *ran*

SYN · CAT: **tv** ∧ SEM · REL: **hit**   →   *hit*

SYN: (CAT: **sv** ∧ AGR: **plu**) ∧ SEM · REL: **believe**   →   *believes*

Figure 13.2. Unification Phrase Structure Lexical Rule Descriptions.

out some simple type inference. We do not bother to describe the hierarchy and appropriateness conditions over which this grammar is expressed; it is apparent from the examples. It is important to note that this is not the only rule that is licensed by the rule description for constructing sequences. Any other phrase structure rule which is subsumed by a rule is also acceptable. To characterize this notion precisely, we need to consider morphisms that operate on more than one feature structure at a time, which the partial feature algebra morphisms provide for us. Recall that a total feature algebra morphism is a function $h: \mathcal{G} \to \mathcal{G}$ on the collection of feature structures such that if $h(F)$ and $h(F')$ are defined and $F \sqsubseteq F'$, then $h(F) \sqsubseteq h(F')$, and such that if $h(F)$ is defined and $F{\scriptstyle@}f$ is defined, then $h(F{\scriptstyle@}f) = h(F){\scriptstyle@}f$. As previously noted, any such function h is monotonic, so that if $F \sqsubseteq F'$, then $h(F) \sqsubseteq h(F')$. In terms of total morphisms, we can state the appropriate notion of monotonicity for rules.

Theorem 13.3 (Rule Monotonicity)

If $E_0 \to E_1 \cdots E_n \in$ Rule(Gram), and h is a total feature algebra morphism, then $h(E_0) \to h(E_1) \cdots h(E_n) \in$ Rule(Gram), where we take $h(e) = e$ if $e \in$ Exp.

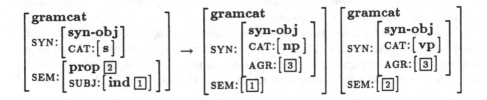

Figure 13.3. Rewriting Rule Involving Only Categories.

$$\begin{bmatrix} \textbf{gramcat} \\ \text{SYN}: [\,\textbf{scomp}\,] \\ \text{SEM}: [\,\textbf{prop}\; \boxed{1}\,] \end{bmatrix} \;\rightarrow\; \textit{that} \; \begin{bmatrix} \textbf{gramcat} \\ \text{SYN}: \begin{bmatrix} \textbf{syn-obj} \\ \text{CAT}: [\,\textbf{s}\,] \end{bmatrix} \\ \text{SEM}: [\,\boxed{1}\,] \end{bmatrix}$$

$$\begin{bmatrix} \textbf{gramcat} \\ \text{SYN}: \begin{bmatrix} \textbf{syn-obj} \\ \text{CAT}: [\,\textbf{n}\,] \\ \text{AGR}: [\,\textbf{sing}\,] \end{bmatrix} \\ \text{SEM}: [\,\textbf{kid}\,] \end{bmatrix} \;\rightarrow\; \textit{kid}$$

Figure 13.4. Rewriting Rules Involving Expressions.

Proof: If $E_0 \rightarrow E_1 \cdots E_n$, then there must be a rule $\xi_0 \rightarrow \xi_1 \cdots \xi_n$ and variable substitution α such that if $\xi_i \in \text{Exp}$, then $\xi_i = E_i$, and if $\xi_i \in \text{Desc}$, then $E_i \models^\alpha \xi_i$. Finally, $h \circ \alpha$ is such that if $E_i \models^\alpha \xi_i$, then $h(E_i) \models^{h \circ \alpha} \xi_i$. $\qquad\square$

Rules involving expressions are similarly converted into feature structure form, as seen in Figure 13.4. Linguists usually work in systems which are factored into lexical and syntactic components. Although we do not prove the result here, it is well known that any phrase structure grammar can be converted to an equivalent grammar (in the weak sense of assigning the same sets of expressions to categories) in which all rules have either a single non-terminal basic expression or a sequence of categories on their right hand sides, yielding the following two forms:

(5)   • $F_0 \rightarrow F_1 \cdots F_n$ for $F_i \in \mathcal{G}$ (Phrasal Rule)

         • $F_0 \rightarrow e$ for $F_0 \in \mathcal{G}$, $e \in \text{Exp}$ (Lexical Rule)

Grammars in this form are subsets of $(\text{Desc} \times \text{BasExp}) \cup (\text{Desc} \times \text{Desc}^*)$. In our case, the trick to the encoding is to add an additional type for each basic expression and replace every occurrence of a basic expression with a trivial one-node feature structure of that type. The lexical insertion rules then allow any such derived type symbol which represents a basic expression to be rewritten as the basic expression it represents.

It should also be noted that there is no prohibition against using disjunctions in the descriptions in Gram, but as we have set up the grammars, disjunctions are restricted to occurring in single descriptions. Of course, to eliminate disjunctions from rules may result in an exponential increase in the number of rules.

Some of our constructions are complicated by the fact that the techniques we developed to deal with subsumption and satisfaction were designed to operate on only one feature structure at a time. For instance, generating a rule from a rule description must use the same substitution for each satisfaction, and monotonicity must use the same morphism for each category in a rule. Kay (1979), in the context of FUG, developed a technique that represents a phrase structure rule as a single feature structure. The same technique is employed in PATR-II (Shieber et al. 1983) to represent rules by a single description. In particular, an arbitrary rule in the phrase structure grammar can be converted to a single description by means of the following encoding:

(6) $\quad \langle \xi_0, \langle \xi_1, \ldots, \xi_n \rangle \rangle \implies n\text{-place-rule} \wedge (0\!:\!\xi_0) \wedge (1\!:\!\xi_1) \wedge \cdots \wedge (n\!:\!\xi_n)$

Of course, this encoding requires enough natural numbers as features to encode rules. Less obviously, it is also necessary to include types for all of the basic expressions and also provide types for each arity of rule, so that the number of daughters can be determined by inspecting the resulting feature structure. The rule description for sentences is thus converted to the single description:

(7) $\quad$ **2-place-rule** $\wedge$ $0\!:\!(\text{SYN} \cdot \text{CAT}\!:\!\textbf{s} \wedge \text{SEM}\!:\!(X2 \wedge \text{SUBJ}\!:\!X3))$

$\qquad\qquad \wedge$ $1\!:\!(\text{SYN}\!:\!(\text{CAT}\!:\!\textbf{np} \wedge \text{AGR}\!:\!X4) \wedge \text{SEM}\!:\!X3)$

$\qquad\qquad \wedge$ $2\!:\!(\text{SYN}\!:\!(\text{CAT}\!:\!\textbf{vp} \wedge \text{AGR}\!:\!X4) \wedge \text{SEM}\!:\!X2)$

In general, we assume $Approp(k, n\text{-place-rule}) = \textbf{gram-obj}$ for $0 \leq k \leq n$ and is undefined otherwise, where **gram-obj** is the most specific common supertype of grammatical categories and expressions. The most general satisfier for (7) is given in Figure 13.5. A more uniform alternative to the approach of Figure 13.5 encodes the daughters of a rule by means of a head/tail encoding of lists rather than assigning each to a consecutive integer. With either encoding, we can find most general satisfiers for each compound description corresponding to a grammar rule. We already know that our operations *Desc* and *MGSat* allow us to convert back and forth between descriptions and feature structures, and we can exploit this correspondence to represent grammars either as a finite set of feature structures or descriptions. We should also note that with our variable elimination theorems, any variables occurring in the translation of a grammar rule could be eliminated. For instance, the rule in (7) for sentences could be represented as follows:

(8) $\quad$ **2-place-rule**

$\qquad \wedge$ $0 \cdot \text{SYN} \cdot \text{CAT}\!:\!\textbf{s}$ $\wedge$ $1 \cdot \text{SYN} \cdot \text{CAT}\!:\!\textbf{np}$ $\wedge$ $2 \cdot \text{SYN} \cdot \text{CAT}\!:\!\textbf{vp}$

$\qquad \wedge$ $1 \cdot \text{SYN} \cdot \text{AGR} \doteq 2 \cdot \text{SYN} \cdot \text{AGR}$

$\qquad \wedge$ $0 \cdot \text{SEM} \doteq 2 \cdot \text{SEM}$ $\wedge$ $0 \cdot \text{SEM} \cdot \text{SUBJ} \doteq 1 \cdot \text{SEM}$

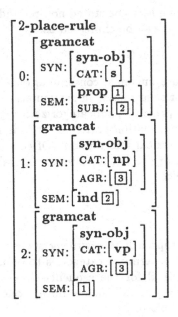

Figure 13.5. Most General Satisfier of (7).

The rule in (8) may look familiar, as it is reminiscent of the PATR-II notation for descriptions. One difference is that both the path sharing symbol $\doteq$ and path value symbol : are represented by the same symbol in PATR-II. Another difference stems from the fact that PATR-II, being untyped, must use an additional mechanism to code the number of daughters in a rule as well as the feature structure representing the mother and daughters.

Although quite natural, Kay's encoding is rather cumbersome, especially when it comes to defining the denotation of a grammar, as evident from Pereira and Shieber (1984), the first detailed semantic analysis of feature-structure-unification-based phrase structure grammars. Of course, in term unification formalisms such as Definite Clause Grammar, the rules are themselves encoded as first-order terms, so there should be nothing surprising about the possibility of doing the same in the context of grammars based on feature structures.

An interesting possibility, which is exploited in Kay's original system, but not in PATR-II, is that the entire grammar can be taken to be a single description defined as the disjunction of the descriptions of each rule. Adopting this strategy, there would be nothing to prevent us from using arbitrary (not necessarily normal form) descriptions for a grammar, in which disjunctions can be embedded at any level, including the description of individual feature structures. This possibility has been exploited (in a slightly different form) in the Head-driven Phrase Structure Grammar system of Pollard and Sag (1987), which we discuss in the chapter on constraint-based grammars below. Pollard and Sag employ a single (disjunctive) description for their grammar which allows both universal and language-specific principles to be stated non-redundantly. For instance, the phrasal component of HPSG can be expressed as:

(9) $U_1 \wedge \cdots \wedge U_n \wedge G_1 \wedge \cdots \wedge G_m$

In this example, the U_i are universal constraints on phrase structure and the G_i are language-particular constraints. In particular, the U_i express constraints such as the head-feature principle, subcategorization principles, and so forth, whereas the G_i express information particular to individual languages such as constituent ordering and lexical information. Of course, the U_i and G_i might themselves be disjunctive principles, to express constraints such as the binding principles and lexical choice.

Rewriting

We take the traditional approach to rewriting systems, extending our notion of rewriting from single non-terminal categories to sequences of categories and basic expressions. We use **E** for the sequence $E_1 \cdots E_n$, where $n \geq 0$ and $E_i \in \mathcal{G} \cup \mathsf{BasExp}$ for $1 \leq i \leq n$. We define both a one step rewriting relation and its transitive reflexive closure.

Definition 13.4 (Rewriting)

The one step rewriting *relation* $\rightarrow$ *is such that:*

- $(\mathbf{E} \cdot D_0 \cdot \mathbf{E}') \rightarrow (\mathbf{E} \cdot D_1 \cdots D_n \cdot \mathbf{E}')$ *iff* $(D_0 \rightarrow D_1 \cdots D_n) \in \mathsf{Rule}(\mathsf{Gram})$

The rewriting *relation* $\xrightarrow{*}$ *is the least such that:*

- $\mathbf{E} \xrightarrow{*} \mathbf{E}$

- $\mathbf{E} \rightarrow \mathbf{E}''$ *if* $\mathbf{E} \rightarrow \mathbf{E}'$ *and* $\mathbf{E}' \xrightarrow{*} \mathbf{E}''$.

Thus $\mathbf{E}_0 \xrightarrow{*} \mathbf{E}_n$ if and only if there is a sequence $\mathbf{E}_0 \rightarrow \mathbf{E}_1 \rightarrow \cdots \rightarrow \mathbf{E}_n$ such that $\mathbf{E}_i \rightarrow \mathbf{E}_{i+1}$ for $i < n$. Note that this definition of rewriting is "context free" in the sense that the category D_0 can be replaced by sequences of categories in a way determined only by the grammar rules and not by facts about **E** and **E**′, the context in which D_0 is rewritten.

An example of a rewriting analysis can be found in Figure 13.6. Notice that the feature structures may seem over-instantiated at first glance; the reason for this is that they are fully instantiated at every level of the tree. In particular, we do not favor either a bottom-up (from right to left during rewriting) or top-down (left to right) "flow" of information, but rather assume that the information is co-instantiated up and down the tree wherever it needs to be. In practical implementations, the information in the final rewriting sequence is assembled incrementally. We later study both top-down and bottom-up notions of rewriting and show that they provide equivalent results. Note that each of the rewritings is valid because it satisfies the appropriate rule description. An example of the satisfaction relation required for the lexical rewriting in Figure 13.6

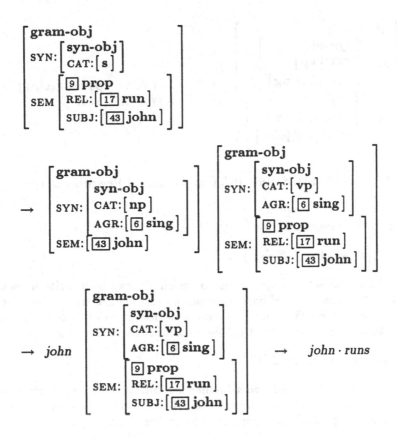

Figure 13.6. Example of Rewriting Sequence.

holds for any assignment α as shown in Figure 13.7. Also note that the other rewritings in Figure 13.6 are justified by the satisfaction relations displayed in Figure 13.8. These relations hold for any assignment α such that $\alpha(X1) = \boxed{9}$, $\alpha(X2) = \boxed{43}$, $\alpha(X3) = \boxed{6}$, where the tags represent the feature structures they tag in Figure 13.6. Although we could find less instantiated feature structures that satisfy our sentential phrase structure rule, the feature structures on the right-hand side of such a rule would not be instantiated enough to satisfy the lexical rewriting rules. Similarly, we could find less instantiated feature structures that satisfy the description of the lexical rules, but these would not be instantiated enough to satisfy the non-lexical rule descriptions. Thus the feature structures need to be instantiated enough to satisfy the rule descriptions at every stage of the rewriting process.

We think of our rewriting system as defining a collection of expressions assigned to each category. To this end, we define a function $\mathcal{L}: \mathcal{G} \to 2^{\mathsf{Exp}}$ from feature structures to sets of expressions so that $\mathcal{L}(F)$ is the set of expressions

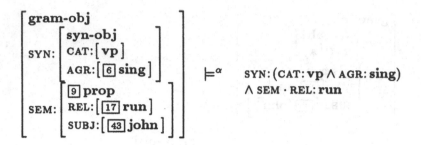

Figure 13.7. Satisfaction Relation for Lexical Rewriting of *run*.

assigned to the category F, by:

(10) $\mathcal{L}(F) = \{a \in \mathsf{Exp} \mid F \xrightarrow{*} a\}$

Thus $\mathcal{L}(F)$ is the set of expressions to which F may be rewritten, not the complete set of sequences of basic expressions and feature structures to which F may be rewritten. We can also define a notion of which categories can be assigned to a given expression, by defining a function $C: \mathsf{Exp} \to 2^{\mathcal{G}}$ by:

(11) $C(a) = \{F \in \mathcal{G} \mid a \in \mathcal{L}(F)\}$

Because our rules are closed under further instantiation, this property extends to the collection $\mathcal{L}(F)$ of expressions assigned to the category F and the collection $C(a)$ of categorizations assigned to the expression **a**.

Theorem 13.5 (Rewriting Montonicity)

If $F \sqsubseteq F'$ then:

- $\mathcal{L}(F) \subseteq \mathcal{L}(F')$

- *if $F \in C(a)$, then $F' \in C(a)$*

Proof: A simple induction on derivation length suffices in both cases.   □

Thus the set of categorizations assigned to any expression is closed under further instantiation.

Tree Admissibility

Rewriting provides a natural definition of the set of expressions assigned to the category F by a grammar. Unfortunately, in non-trivial grammars, there are derivations which only differ from one another by the order in which the expressions in a string are expanded. In (12) we have examples of two distinct

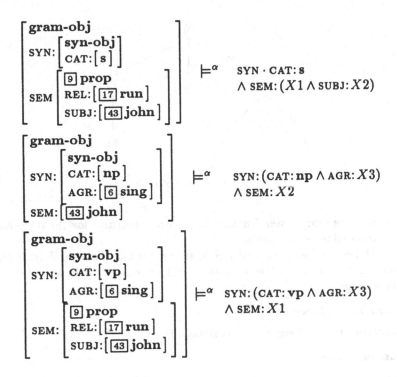

Figure 13.8. Satisfaction Relations for Category Rewriting Example.

derivations which are equivalent in all respects except for the choice between expanding E_0 or E_1 first.

(12)   • $E \rightarrow E_0\, E_1 \rightarrow a_0\, E_1 \rightarrow a_0\, a_1$

           • $E \rightarrow E_0\, E_1 \rightarrow E_0\, a_1 \rightarrow a_0\, a_1$

To remove this undesirable derivational ambiguity, we straightforwardly adopt the notion of a (phrase structure) parse tree to our unification-based setting. The notion of tree admissibility gained popularity in linguistics due to its implicit application in Lexical Functional Grammar (Kaplan and Bresnan 1982) and its more explicit formulation in Generalized Phrase Structure Grammar (Gazdar et al. 1985). At least since Chomsky (1957), trees (or notational variants of trees such as labeled bracketed strings) have been far and away the most popular data structure among linguists of all stripes for characterizing syntactic regularities. Oddly enough, even in the more recent Government-Binding theory (Chomsky 1981), the trees have remained although phrase-structure rules have been replaced by more general constraints (from X-bar theory in this case). The reason that this move seems strange is that trees are so intimately connected with phrase structure. We present a more general notion of constraint-based grammar below and remove trees from their pedestal, replac-

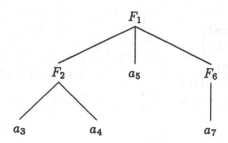

Figure 13.9. Tree Notation.

ing them with the more general notion of feature structures for the purposes of linguistic knowledge representation.

We must first define trees and the basic operations associated with them. We define a set of trees relative to a set $\mathcal{G}$ of feature structures and BasExp of basic expressions.

Definition 13.6 (Trees)

The collection Tree *of trees is the least such that:*

- BasExp $\subseteq$ Tree

- $\langle F, \langle T_1, \ldots, T_n \rangle \rangle \in$ Tree *if* $n \geq 0$, $F \in \mathcal{G}$, *and* $T_i \in$ Tree *for* $1 \leq i \leq n$.

In other words, Tree is the least solution to the equation:

(13)   Tree = BasExp $\cup$ ($\mathcal{G} \times$ (Tree*))

The reason trees are called *trees* is that they are usually pictured graphically. For instance, the rather undecipherable structure of the tree in (14) is more readily visible in the standard tree notation displayed in Figure 13.9.

(14) $\langle F_1, \langle \langle F_2, \langle a_3, a_4 \rangle \rangle, a_5, \langle F_6, \langle a_7 \rangle \rangle \rangle \rangle$

Notice that the "tree" in Figure 13.9 is oriented with its "root" toward the top and its "leaves" toward the bottom of the diagram (we make these terms more precise shortly). As it quickly grows tiresome to typeset trees in this fashion, we adopt an alternative method for displaying trees, originally due to Ades and Steedman (1982). Steedman's method displays trees in a manner similar to standard diagrams of logical proofs, where the tree in Figure 13.9 is displayed as in (15):

(15)
$$\frac{\dfrac{a_3 \ a_4}{F_2} \quad a_5 \quad \dfrac{a_7}{F_6}}{F_1}$$

The proof-like notation for trees and the implication-like notation for rules turns out not to be accidental, as we see in the next chapter on definite clause logic programs. When the categories in a tree are simple, it is often easiest to use the bracketed-string notation for trees, which encodes the tree in Figure 13.9 as:

(16) $[_{F_1} [_{F_2} a_3 a_4] a_5 [_{F_6} a_7]]$

Note that matching brackets indicate a subtree rooted at the subscript following the left bracket of the pair.

Now that we have seen what trees look like, we need some basic operations to manipulate them. The first of these is the function *Root*, which returns the *root* of a tree:

(17)   • $Root(a) = a$ if $a \in \mathsf{BasExp}$

   • $Root(\langle F, \langle T_1, \ldots, T_n \rangle \rangle) = F$

Note that the root of the tree in Figure 13.9 is F_1. At the other end of a tree, we have so-called *leaves*. The leaves of a tree T are given by the function *Leaves*, defined by:

(18)   • $Leaves(a) = \{a\}$ if $a \in \mathsf{BasExp}$

   • $Leaves(\langle F, \langle T_1, \ldots, T_n \rangle \rangle) = Leaves(T_1) \cup \cdots \cup Leaves(T_n)$

In particular, notice that if $n = 0$, then $Leaves(\langle F, \langle \rangle \rangle) = \emptyset$ by the conventional definition of empty unions. The leaves of the tree in Figure 13.9 are the members of $\{a_3, a_4, a_5, a_7\}$. In general, the leaves of a tree are always basic expressions. The leaves of a tree can be ordered from left to right to determine what is known as the *yield* of a tree, defined by:

(19)   • $Yield(a) = a$ if $a \in \mathsf{BasExp}$

   • $Yield(\langle F, \langle T_1, \ldots, T_n \rangle \rangle) = Yield(T_1) \cdot Yield(T_2) \cdots \cdot Yield(T_n)$

In the case of *Yield*, notice that if $n = 0$, then we have $Yield(\langle F, \langle \rangle \rangle) = \epsilon$. The yield of the tree in Figure 13.9 is $a_3 a_4 a_5 a_7$, which is an ordering of the leaves from left to right in a string. It is the yield of a tree that determines the expression of which it is intended to be an analysis. Many properties of trees are proved by induction on their *depth*, which measures the length of the longest path between the root and a leaf. Depth is defined by:

(20)   • $Depth(a) = 0$ if $a \in \mathsf{BasExp}$

   • $Depth(\langle F, \langle \rangle \rangle) = 1$

   • $Depth(\langle F, \langle T_1, \ldots, T_n \rangle \rangle) = 1 + Max\{Depth(T_1), \ldots, Depth(T_n)\}$

The depth of the tree in Figure 13.9 is 2.

We are finally in a position to define our notion of *parse tree*, which is intended to encode a rewriting derivation in an order-independent way. Our definition of tree admissibility is purely *local* in that it only inspects the relationship between a node and its immediate daughters in any given tree. Of course, by iteratively passing structure sharing and path value information locally, long distance constraints can be captured.

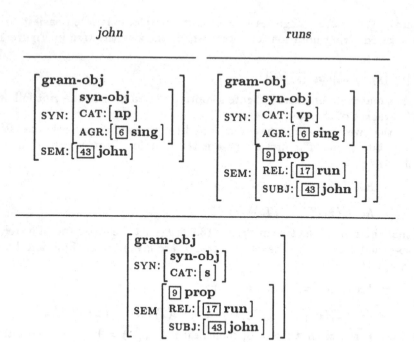

Figure 13.10. Admissible Tree Example.

Definition 13.7 (Tree Admissibility)

The set of admissible trees *with respect to the phrase structure rules* Rule *and the basic expressions* BasExp *is the least set* AdmTree *such that:*

- $a \in$ AdmTree *if* $a \in$ BasExp

- $\langle E, \langle T_1, \ldots, T_n \rangle \rangle \in$ AdmTree *if* $(E \to Root(T_1) \cdots Root(T_n)) \in$ Rule

In the terminology of Generalized Phrase Structure Grammar, a tree is admissible if every one of its so-called *local trees* is explicitly *licensed* by some rewriting rule. An admissible tree T is said to be a *parse tree* of category $Root(T)$ for the string $Yield(T)$ that it yields. An example of the admissible tree corresponding to our rewriting analysis in Figure 13.6 can be found in Figure 13.10. In particular, the structure in Figure 13.10 is the most general admissible tree with yield *john runs*.

It should be noted that although trees eliminate much of the ambiguity in the rewriting derivations, it is still possible for an expression **a** to have more than one parse tree. The existence of more than one parse tree with the same root for a single expression is referred to as a *structural ambiguity*; structural ambiguities at a syntactic level often reflect semantic ambiguities. Structural ambiguity can be demonstrated without unification when considering the ambiguous grammar for binary arithmetic expressions in Figure 13.11, which is

$$expr \rightarrow int; \quad expr \rightarrow expr \ binop \ expr; \quad expr \rightarrow unop \ expr$$

$$digit \rightarrow 0; \quad digit \rightarrow 1$$

$$int \rightarrow digit \ int; \quad int \rightarrow digit$$

$$binop \rightarrow +; \quad binop \rightarrow *; \quad binop \rightarrow \div; \quad binop \rightarrow -$$

$$unop \rightarrow -$$

Figure 13.11. Binary Arithmetic Expression Grammar.

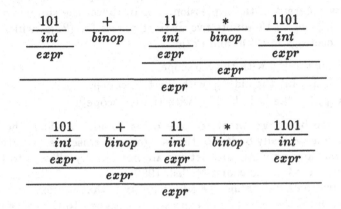

Figure 13.12. Ambiguous Parse Trees for $101 + 11 * 1101$.

defined over the non-terminals or types $expr, int, binop, unop$ and terminals or basic expressions $0, 1, +, *, \div, -$. In particular, to convert the grammar in Figure 13.11 into one of our phrase structure grammars, it is merely necessary to treat the collection of non-terminals as incomparable type symbols which are not appropriate for any features. In general, this construction shows the way in which our phrase structure grammars generalize context-free grammars. As can be seen from the grammar in Figure 13.11, expressions such as $101 + 11 * 1101$ are structurally ambiguous. The two possible parse trees for this expression are given in Figure 13.12. We have not shown the full structure of the analysis of the digit sequence as integers. Note that the integers, as digit sequences, all have unique parses. This would not be the case if we had assumed the following pair of phrase structure rules:

(21) $int \rightarrow digit \quad int \rightarrow int \ int$

With this grammar, every bracketing corresponds to a valid parse. In implementing computer languages such as Prolog or C, it is standard to have operator precedences built in to disambiguate ambiguous expressions. For instance, our expression $101 + 11 * 1101$ is unambiguously parsed as $101 + [11 * 1101]$. In

$$s \rightarrow np \quad vp \qquad np \rightarrow Bill$$
$$np \rightarrow det \quad n \qquad det \rightarrow the$$
$$n \rightarrow n \quad pp \qquad n \rightarrow kid$$
$$pp \rightarrow p \quad np \qquad p \rightarrow with$$
$$vp \rightarrow tv \quad np \qquad tv \rightarrow hit$$
$$vp \rightarrow vp \quad pp$$

Figure 13.13. Simple Ambiguous Grammar.

grammars for natural languages, structural ambiguity usually signals semantic ambiguity inherent in the expression. For instance, the simple context-free
grammar in Figure 13.13 admits two distinct parses for (22)a, which are indicated by bracketings in (22)b and (22)c:

(22) a. Fred hit the kid with the telescope.
   b. Fred $[_{vp}[_{vp}$ hit the kid] $[_{pp}$ with the telescope]].
   c. Fred $[_{vp}$ hit the $[_n [_n$ kid] $[_{pp}$ with the telescope]]].

In a unification-based grammar, on the other hand, in which the semantic
representation is typically built into the categories themselves, structural ambiguities without any semantic distinctions are not usually allowed to propagate
(see Karttunen 1984, Gazdar and Mellish 1989).

The motivation for defining tree admissibility is that it offers an alternative
characterization of the set $\mathcal{L}(F)$ of expressions assigned to the category F.

Theorem 13.8

An expression a *is such that* a $\in \mathcal{L}(F)$ *if and only if there is an admissible tree*
$T \in$ AdmTree *such that* $Root(T) = F$ *and* $Yield(T) =$ a.

Proof: Since we can think of our phrase structure grammar descriptions as
picking out a possibly infinite phrase structure grammar, we can apply the well
known relationship between trees and phrase structure rewriting (see Lewis
and Papadimitriou 1984:123–124 for further details). The full proof relies on
establishing a correspondence between trees and derivations. In particular, a
step $\mathbf{E}F_0\mathbf{E'} \rightarrow \mathbf{E}F_1 \cdots F_n\mathbf{E'}$ in a rewriting derivation corresponds to the tree
$\langle F_0, \langle T_1, \cdots, T_n \rangle \rangle$, where $Root(T_i) = F_i$ in an admissible tree and conversely. $\square$

It is significant to note that there is nothing in this result that is particular to
unification-based grammars; it holds in general for arbitrary (possibly infinite)
phrase structure grammars. We exploit this property in the next section when
we consider the bottom-up interpretation of unification-based grammars.

Denotational Semantics

We now turn our attention to an application of fix-point theory to the denotational characterization of the function $\mathcal{L}$ that maps categories F to the set

$\mathcal{L}(F)$ of expressions assigned to them. An example of an application of fix-point theory to phrase structure grammars is given by Gunter and Scott (in press) and Davey and Priestley (1990). We use $\mathcal{D}$ for our denotational equivalent of $\mathcal{L}$, so that $\mathcal{D}(F)$ is the set of categories assigned to F by the grammar in question. To simplify the inductive definition, we also assume that $\mathcal{D}$ can be applied to a basic expression.

Definition 13.9 (Phrase Structure Grammar Denotations)

The denotation *mapping* $\mathcal{D}: (\mathcal{G} \cup \mathsf{BasExp}) \to 2^{\mathsf{Exp}}$ *is the least such that:*

- $\mathcal{D}(E) = \{E\}$ *if* $E \in \mathsf{BasExp}$

- $\mathcal{D}(E_0) \supseteq \mathcal{D}(E_1) \cdot \mathcal{D}(E_2) \cdot \cdots \cdot \mathcal{D}(E_n)$ *if* $E_0 \to E_1 E_2 \cdots E_n \in \mathsf{Rule(Gram)}$

Note that the first condition states that the language corresponding to a basic expression is the singleton set consisting of that expression. The second condition tells us that if there is a rewriting rule $E_0 \to E_1 \cdots E_n$ and we can find expressions $a_i \in \mathcal{L}(E_i)$, then $a_1 \cdots a_n \in \mathcal{L}(E_0)$. In other words, if each a_i is in the denotation of E_i, then concatenating the a_is into a sequence results in an expression of category E_0.

We now show that the inductive denotation definition we have given is in fact well defined in that it produces a unique result. To do this, we explicitly construct $\mathcal{D}$ as the least fixed point of a monotonic function on a complete lattice. First, notice that the collection $(\mathsf{BasExp} \cup \mathcal{G}) \to 2^{\mathsf{Exp}}$ of functions from $(\mathsf{BasExp} \cup \mathcal{G})$ to 2^{Exp} forms a complete lattice (where we have used the notation $X \to Y$ to represent the collection of total functions from X to Y. For any set of functions $S \subseteq ((\mathsf{BasExp} \cup \mathcal{G}) \to 2^{\mathsf{BasExp}^*})$, we define $\bigsqcup S$ pointwise by setting $(\bigsqcup S)(E) = \bigcup \{\mathcal{K}(E) \mid \mathcal{K} \in S\}$. Also notice that $\mathcal{K}_\emptyset$ defined by $\mathcal{K}_\emptyset(E) = \emptyset$ is the bottom element of $((\mathsf{BasExp} \cup \mathcal{G}) \to 2^{\mathsf{BasExp}^*})$.

Definition 13.10

The function $\mathbf{L}: ((\mathsf{BasExp} \cup \mathcal{G}) \to 2^{\mathsf{BasExp}^*}) \to ((\mathsf{BasExp} \cup \mathcal{G}) \to 2^{\mathsf{BasExp}^*})$ *is defined by:*

$$\mathbf{L}(\mathcal{K})(E) = \begin{cases} \{E\} & \text{if } E \in \mathsf{BasExp} \\ \bigcup \{\mathcal{K}(E_1) \cdots \mathcal{K}(E_n) \mid E \to E_1 \cdots E_n\} & \text{if } E \in \mathcal{G} \end{cases}$$

for $\mathcal{K}: (\mathsf{BasExp} \cup \mathcal{G}) \to 2^{\mathsf{BasExp}^*}$ *and* $E \in (\mathsf{BasExp} \cup \mathcal{G})$.

As usual, the point is to define $\mathcal{D}$ as the least fixed point of $\mathbf{L}$. First note that the definition of $\mathbf{L}$ is not recursive, so there is no question as to its well-definedness. In the statement of the theorem, we let $\mathbf{L}^n(\mathcal{K})$ be the result of applying the function $\mathbf{L}$ to $\mathcal{K}$ n times, so that $\mathbf{L}^0(\mathcal{K}) = \mathcal{K}$ and $\mathbf{L}^{n+1}(\mathcal{K}) = \mathbf{L}(\mathbf{L}^n(\mathcal{K}))$.

Theorem 13.11

$\mathcal{D} = Fix(\mathbf{L}) = \bigcup_{n \in \omega} \mathbf{L}^n(\mathcal{K}_\emptyset)$.

Proof: The proof employs a direct application of Tarski's theorem (see Davey and Priestley 1990). In particular, it is easy to show by induction over $n \in \omega$ that $Fix(\mathbf{L})$ meets the conditions in the definition of PSG denotations. To show that $Fix(\mathbf{L})$ is the minimal function satisfying the conditions of PSG denotations, it is only necessary to show by induction over ω that each $\mathbf{L}^n(\mathcal{K}_\phi)$ subsumes any function which satisfies the clauses of the PSG denotation definition. □

Note that this definition is directly related to the standard denotational definition of the semantics of logic programs, as can be seen by the definition of $\mathbf{L}^n$. We exploit this fact when we use this result to derive the standard results concerning the semantics of definite clause logic programs. Again, it is important to note that there is nothing about unification-based grammars which is important for this theorem; the result holds for arbitrary phrase structure grammars.

To see the connection between $\mathbf{L}^n$ and rewriting derivations, note that an expression is an element of $\mathbf{L}^n(\mathcal{K}_\phi)$ if and only if it has a parse tree of depth at most n. This fact can be easily proved by induction over ω and leads to the following result:

Theorem 13.12

$\mathcal{D}(F) = \mathcal{L}(F)$ *for all* $F \in \mathcal{G}$.

Thus our definitions of rewriting, denotation and tree admissibility are congruent in the sense that they assign the same set of expressions to every feature structure representing a category.

Top-Down and Bottom-Up Evaluation

A distinctive feature of our presentation of feature structure unification grammars up to this point has been the way in which we require both the mother and daughter feature structures in a tree or rewriting to be instantiated enough to completely satisfy a rule description. We now turn our attention to two different ways of modeling the information flow in a rewriting analysis. We first consider a simple bottom-up interpretation of rule descriptions in which we model information as flowing from daughters to mothers in a parse tree. In particular, we derive the mother feature structure from a rule and the daughter feature structures. We then consider the reverse notion in which information flows top-down from the mother to the daughters. Under the top-down scheme, we derive the daughter feature structures from the mother feature structure. This latter method is complicated by the fact that there might be dependencies between the daughters. To model these dependencies, we need to collect composite morphisms during the rewriting process to read off the resulting root category and also to maintain dependencies between daughter categories that may be introduced by rules with structure sharing between daughters. This distinction between bottom-up and top-down analyses, and even the way in which they are modeled, is very similar to the notion of top-down (backward-chaining, operational) and bottom-up (forward-chaining, denotational) evaluation of logic programs. In fact, in the next chapter, when we turn our attention to definite clauses consisting of feature structures, we see that this analogy can be exploited to derive the standard results concerning the equivalence of top-down and bottom-up analyses of logic programs.

In both the top-down and bottom-up approaches, we exploit the analogy between our notion of morphism between feature structures and the notion of substitution of terms for variables. We define total morphisms over the collection of feature structures considered as a feature algebra (that is, monotonic functions $h: \mathcal{G} \rightarrow \mathcal{G}$ such that if $h(F)$ and $F \mathbf{o} f$ are defined, then $h(F \mathbf{o} f)$ is defined and equal to $h(F) \mathbf{o} f$). Our approaches to top-down and bottom-up derivations employ morphisms in the same way that substitutions are applied in modeling the backward-chaining and forward-chaining semantics of logic programs.

For both the top-down and bottom-up notions of rewriting, we only want to consider rules in their most general forms. As we set things up in the last section, we took Rule(Gram) to be closed under further instantiation, so that if R is a rule in Rule(Gram), and $R \sqsubseteq R'$, then R' is in Rule(Gram) as well. For this section, we define a new notion of rule which casts out all but the most general rules:

Definition 13.13 (Most General Rules)

The collection MGRule(Gram) *of* most general rules *is defined by:*

$$\text{MGRule(Gram)} = \textit{Min}(\text{Rule(Gram)})$$

where $\textit{Min}(\text{Rule(Gram)})$ *is the set of subsumption minimal rules in* Rule(Gram).

Note that MGRule(Gram) is truly minimal and thus does not necessarily coincide with the result of taking the most general satisfiers of the rule descriptions themselves, as one description in Gram might be more specific than another. On the other hand, the elements of MGRule(Gram) could be generated by first converting the rules in Gram to normal form and casting out the non-minimal ones and then taking most general satisfiers. In fact, parsers for unification-based grammar formalisms that use dynamic programming techniques (such as chart parsers) seek to cast out non-minimal analyses. In the rest of this section, we see that this move is sound due to the monotonicity of the interpretation of satisfaction as it applies to grammars. It is also important to note that since we have assumed that Gram is finite, MGRule(Gram) is also finite. In practice, this limits our search through the rule space in seeking rules to apply during an analysis.

Bottom-Up Rewriting

We begin with the bottom-up notion of rewriting in which the primary step is to apply a rule to a sequence of categories to collect them together under a single mother category whose nature is determined by the rules and categories being combined. In the bottom-up case, we are able to employ the general techniques we developed in the last section for arbitrary phrase structure grammars. When we turn to top-down rewriting, this is no longer the case. Thus we define a notion of bottom-up rule based on our collection MGRule(Gram) of most general rules. The idea is then that we can fully determine the category of an expression by working bottom-up from the basic expressions using only the most general rule instances. To do this, we employ the notion of algebraic morphisms which we studied in the chapter on feature algebras. In the definition of bottom-up rewriting, we also keep track of the morphisms that are used to generate most general instantiations of rules matching a given sequence of daughters.

Definition 13.14 (Bottom-up Rules)

The relation $\rightarrow_{bu}$ *representing* bottom-up rewriting rules *is such that:*

$$h(D_0) \rightarrow_{bu} F_1 \cdots F_n \text{ via } h$$

if and only if $(D_0 \rightarrow D_1 \cdots D_n) \in$ MGRule(Gram) *is a rule and* h *is the most general morphism such that* $h(F_i) = h(D_i)$ *for* $1 \leq i \leq n$.

The notion of bottom-up rewriting instantiates each node in a tree with only the information that can be directly gleaned from its daughters. It is important to note that we have simply defined another notion of phrase structure rule. Thus all of our general results in the previous section concerning phrase structure grammars remain valid for our new notion $\rightarrow_{bu}$ of bottom-up rewriting.

We use the collection of bottom-up rules in the standard way to define a notion of rewriting with bottom-up information flow.

Definition 13.15 (One-Step Bottom-Up Rewriting)

The bottom-up one step rewriting *relation* $\rightarrow_{bu}$ *is defined by taking:*

$$\mathbf{E} \cdot E_0 \cdot \mathbf{E}' \rightarrow_{bu} \mathbf{E} \cdot E_1 \cdots E_n \cdot \mathbf{E}' \text{ via } h$$

if and only if $E_0 \rightarrow_{bu} E_1 \cdots E_n$ *via* h.

We keep track of the morphism used in rewriting in one step because it is useful later in the proof that bottom-up and standard rewriting provide equivalent results. We do not need to keep the morphism in sequences of rewritings, so we take the transitive reflexive closure of the rewriting in one step relation.

Definition 13.16 (Bottom-Up Rewriting)

The bottom-up rewriting *relation* $\xrightarrow{*}_{bu}$ *is the least such that:*

- $\mathbf{E} \xrightarrow{*}_{bu} \mathbf{E}$

- $\mathbf{E} \xrightarrow{*}_{bu} \mathbf{E}''$ *if there is some* $\mathbf{E}'$ *such that* $\mathbf{E} \rightarrow_{bu} \mathbf{E}'$ *and* $\mathbf{E}' \xrightarrow{*}_{bu} \mathbf{E}''$

As before, we let $\mathcal{L}_{bu}(E)$ be the set of expressions assigned to E by rewriting, so that:

(23) $\mathcal{L}_{bu}(E) = \{\sigma \in \mathsf{Exp} \mid E \xrightarrow{*}_{bu} \sigma\}$

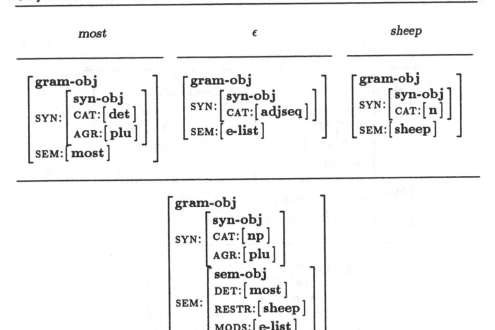

Figure 13.14. Bottom-Up Rewriting Example – Part 1.

The notion of admissible tree is defined in exactly the same way as before by requiring every local tree to be admitted by some rule. More precisely, the collection **BUAdmTree** of bottom-up admissible trees is the least set such that:

(24)   • $e \in$ **BUAdmTree** if $e \in$ **BasExp**

       • $\langle C, \langle T_1, \ldots, T_n \rangle \rangle \in$ **BUAdmTree** if $T_i \in$ **BUAdmTree** for $1 \leq i \leq n$ and $C \rightarrow_{bu} Root(T_1) \cdots Root(T_n)$

We note that the general theorem concerning the relation between admissible trees and rewriting holds for all phrase structure formalisms, so that in particular, we have $\sigma \in \mathcal{L}_{bu}(E)$ if and only if there is some tree $T \in$ **BUAdmTree** such that $Root(T) = E$ and $Yield(T) = \sigma$.

Using our sample grammar from Figure 13.1 and Figure 13.2, the instantiation pattern of bottom-up rewriting can be seen in Figure 13.14 and Figure 13.15. Note that it is actually necessary to combine the trees in the obvious way to get a full parse tree; we separated them only because a full tree would not fit across one line of text. In Figure 13.14 and Figure 13.15, it should be noted how the semantic information and agreement information flow upward from the leaves to the root. In particular, the plural agreement information on the determiner is forced to agree (interpreted as consistency or unifiability) with the agreement information on both the noun and the verb. The result of combining the plural determiner *most* with the underspecified noun *sheep* results in a plural noun phrase. If the noun had been *kid* rather than *sheep*, an attempt would

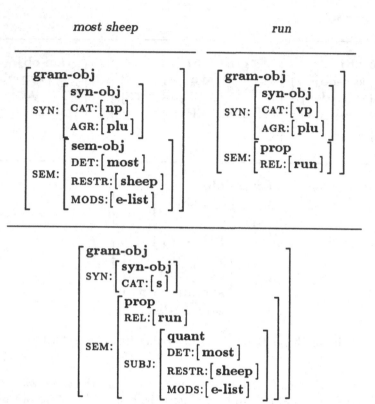

Figure 13.15. Bottom-Up Rewriting Example – Part 2.

be made to unify **sing** and **plu**, which would fail. Similarly, the noun phrase *most sheep*, being marked as plural, is forced to agree with the number of the verb phrase. It is now apparent where the semantic information which appears on the root node for the sentence originates, whereas this was unclear in our previous tree diagrams such as that in Figure 13.10. This kind of bottom-up instantiation is popular for implementations of unification-based grammars.

Finally, the notion of denotational semantics is defined in the same manner as for standard rewriting. More specifically, we take $\mathcal{D}_{bu}(E)$ to be the the set of expressions assigned to category e by taking the least function $\mathcal{D}_{bu}$ such that:

(25)   • $\mathcal{D}_{bu}(e) = \{e\}$ if $e \in \mathsf{BasExp}$

         • $\mathcal{D}_{bu}(E_0) \supseteq \mathcal{D}_{bu}(E_1) \cdots \mathcal{D}_{bu}(E_n)$ if $E_0 \rightarrow_{bu} E_1 \cdots E_n$

As our result in the last section concerning the relation between denotational definitions of categories and their interpretations in terms of rewriting hold for arbitrary phrase structure grammars combined with the fact that the bottom-up rewriting rules form a phrase structure grammar, we have $\mathcal{D}_{bu}(E) = \mathcal{L}_{bu}(E)$.

The most significant thing about this new definition of rewriting in terms of bottom-up instantiation is that it yields equivalent results to the standard notion of rewriting defined in the previous section. We separate the statement of this result into soundness and completeness components. Before stating the theorems, we note an obvious yet important lemma which relates bottom-up rewriting and standard rewriting.

Lemma 13.17

If $E_0 \rightarrow_{bu} E_1 \cdots E_n$ via h, then $E_0 \rightarrow h(E_1) \cdots h(E_n)$.

Proof: If $E_0 \rightarrow_{bu} E_1 \cdots E_n$ via h, then we know that there is a sequence $C_1, \ldots, C_n$ of categories and basic expressions and a rule $D_0 \rightarrow D_1 \cdots D_n \in$ MGRule(Gram), so that $h(D_0) = E_0$ and $h(D_i) = h(C_i)$ for $1 \leq i \leq n$. Therefore $h(E_0) \rightarrow h(E_1) \cdots h(E_n) \in$ Rule(Gram) by monotonicity, and hence by substitution of equals, $E_0 \rightarrow h(E_1) \cdots h(E_n) \in$ Rule(Gram). □

Soundness tells us that every bottom-up analysis yields a categorization which is also generated by the standard analysis.

Theorem 13.18 (Bottom-Up Soundness)

$\mathcal{L}_{bu}(E) \subseteq \mathcal{L}(E)$.

Proof: Suppose $\sigma \in \mathcal{L}_{bu}(E)$, so that $E \xrightarrow{*}_{bu} \sigma$. Then there are sequences $E = \mathbf{E}_0, \mathbf{E}_1, \ldots, \mathbf{E}_{n-1}, \mathbf{E}_n = \sigma$ and $h_0, \ldots, h_{n-1}$ such that $\mathbf{E}_i \rightarrow_{bu} \mathbf{E}_{i+1}$ via h_i for $i < n$. By the lemma relating bottom-up rewriting to standard rewriting, we know that we have $\mathbf{E}_i \rightarrow h_i(\mathbf{E}_{i+1})$. Also note that since the standard rules are monotonic, if we have $\mathbf{D} \rightarrow \mathbf{D}'$ and h is a morphism, then we also have $h(\mathbf{D}) \rightarrow h(\mathbf{D}')$. Thus a simple iteration yields:

$$\mathbf{E}_0 \rightarrow h_0(\mathbf{E}_1) \rightarrow h_1 \circ h_0(\mathbf{E}_2) \rightarrow \cdots \rightarrow h_{n-1} \circ \cdots \circ h_0(\mathbf{E}_n)$$

Furthermore, since $\mathbf{E}_n = \sigma$, we have $(h_{n-1} \circ \cdots \circ h_0)(\mathbf{E}_n) = \sigma$ by definition. Thus, since $\mathbf{E}_0 = E$, we have $\sigma \in \mathcal{L}(E)$. □

The key step in the proof is the collection of the morphisms used at each rewriting stage into composite morphisms which could be applied throughout the bottom-up rewriting to produce a standard analysis. We now turn our attention to completeness, which must be stated rather carefully, as bottom-up analyses derive only the most general categorization possible with respect to the rules which are chosen at each stage.

Theorem 13.19 (Bottom-Up Completeness)

If $\sigma \in \mathcal{L}(E)$, then there is some $E' \sqsubseteq E$ such that $\sigma \in \mathcal{L}_{bu}(E')$.

Proof: Suppose $\sigma \in \mathcal{L}(E)$ so that there is a sequence $E = \mathbf{E}_0, \ldots, \mathbf{E}_n = \sigma$ such that $\mathbf{E}_i \rightarrow \mathbf{E}_{i+1}$ for $i < n$. But if $\mathbf{E}_i \rightarrow \mathbf{E}_{i+1}$, then there is some $\mathbf{E}_i' \sqsubseteq \mathbf{E}_i$ for which bottom-up rewriting yields $\mathbf{E}_i' \rightarrow_{bu} \mathbf{E}_{i+1}$. By iteration, we can find a sequence $\mathbf{E}_0', \cdots \mathbf{E}_n'$ such that $\mathbf{E}_i' \sqsubseteq \mathbf{E}_i$ and such that $\mathbf{E}_i' \rightarrow_{bu} \mathbf{E}_{i+1}'$ for $i < n$. Let $E' = \mathbf{E}'$ so that $E' = \mathbf{E}_0' \sqsubseteq \mathbf{E}_0 = E$ and $\mathbf{E}_n = \sigma$. Thus we have $\sigma \in \mathcal{L}_{bu}(E')$ for $E' \sqsubseteq E$. □

Our completeness and soundness results tell us that:

(26) $\mathcal{L}(E) = \bigcup_{E' \sqsubseteq E} \mathcal{L}_{bu}(E')$

It should be noted that the reason that we could not make either the statement of the theorem or our proof any simpler is because we do not have the equivalent of the Herbrand representation theorem holding in general as we do in the case of first-order terms. In the semantics of Prolog, it is standard to consider only rewriting derivations consisting of ground terms. It should also be noted that the standard bottom-up analysis in logic programming terms does not employ rewriting but rather the denotational definition. Of course, in general we know that the denotational definition is equivalent to the rewriting analysis as we have cast bottom-up rewriting as a phrase structure system. Thus our result also holds when $\mathcal{D}_{bu}$ is substituted in the above for $\mathcal{L}_{bu}$, as they are identical.

Top-Down Rewriting

We now turn our attention to a notion of top-down rewriting which proceeds in the opposite direction from bottom-up rewriting. But the fact that there can be interactions between daughters under the top-down scheme leads to a slightly more complicated analysis. In this case, we must directly define the notion of sequence rewriting, which is our phrase structure analog of SLD-resolution in logic programming. Just as in SLD-resolution, we define our notion of top-down rewriting so that it collects together composite morphisms that must be applied to generate an appropriate result. This means that we are really defining a three-place relation of the form $E \rightarrow_{td} E'$ via h.

Definition 13.20 (One-Step Top-Down Rewriting)

$$\mathbf{E} \cdot E_0 \cdot \mathbf{E}' \rightarrow_{td} h(\mathbf{E}) \cdot h(D_1) \cdot \cdots \cdot h(D_n) \cdot h(\mathbf{E}') \text{ via } h$$

if and only if there is a rule $D_0 \rightarrow D_1 \cdots D_n \in \mathsf{MGRule}(\mathsf{Gram})$, *and* h *is the most general morphism such that* $h(D_0) = h(E_0)$.

Now when we take the transitive reflexive closure of the top-down rewriting relation, we must also calculate the composite morphism which must be applied to the result to get a valid rewriting according to the standard definition.

Definition 13.21 (Top-Down Rewriting)

The top-down rewriting *relation is the least relation* $\xrightarrow{*}_{td}$ *such that:*

- $\mathbf{E} \xrightarrow{*}_{td} \mathbf{E}$ *via* $\mathbf{id}$ *where* $\mathsf{id} \colon \mathcal{G} \rightarrow \mathcal{G}$ *is the identity function*

- $\mathbf{E} \xrightarrow{*}_{td} \mathbf{E}''$ *via* $h' \circ h$ *if there is some* $\mathbf{E}'$ *and morphisms* h' *and* h *such that* $\mathbf{E} \rightarrow_{td} \mathbf{E}'$ *via* h *and* $\mathbf{E}' \xrightarrow{*}_{td} \mathbf{E}''$ *via* h'

Because the effects of top-down rewriting are not local, we have not stated top-down rewriting as a phrase structure rewriting relation. Thus we cannot apply the notions of phrase structure tree or our denotational semantics definition.

But we can prove that top-down rewriting is sound and complete in the same way that we proved bottom-up rewriting is sound and complete. We take a slightly different tack in defining the language generated by top-down rewriting that accounts for the composite morphisms and set:

(27) $\mathcal{L}_{td}(E) = \{\sigma \mid E' \xrightarrow{*}_{td} \sigma \text{ via } h, \text{ and } E = h(E')\}$

Again, we use a lemma that relates top-down rewriting to standard rewriting. It is true for the same reason that the bottom-up rewriting lemma holds; if we further instantiate the mother with the morphism used, the result is sufficient to satisfy a standard rewriting rule.

Lemma 13.22

If $\mathbf{E} \rightarrow_{td} \mathbf{E}'$ *via* h, *then* $h(\mathbf{E}) \rightarrow \mathbf{E}'$.

We tackle soundness first.

Theorem 13.23 (Top-Down Soundness)

$\mathcal{L}_{td}(E) \subseteq \mathcal{L}(E)$.

Proof: Suppose $\sigma \in \mathcal{L}_{td}(E)$ so that $E' \xrightarrow{*}_{td} \sigma$ via h and $h(E') = E$. Then we have sequences $E' = \mathbf{E}_0, \mathbf{E}_1, \ldots, \mathbf{E}_n = \sigma$ and $h_0, \ldots, h_{n-1}$ such that $h = h_{n-1} \circ \cdots \circ h_0$ and $\mathbf{E}_i \rightarrow_{td} \mathbf{E}_{i+1}$ via h_i for $i < n$. By the lemma and the monotonicity of standard rewriting, we have $h_{n-1} \circ \cdots \circ h_0(\mathbf{E}_0) \rightarrow h_{n-1} \circ \cdots \circ h_1(\mathbf{E}_1) \rightarrow \cdots \rightarrow h_{n-1}(\mathbf{E}_{n-1}) \rightarrow \mathbf{E}_n$. By noting that $\mathbf{E}_0 = E'$ and $\mathbf{E}_n = \sigma$, and also noting that $h_{n-1} \circ \cdots \circ h_0 = h$ we have $E = h(E') \xrightarrow{*} \sigma$. $\square$

We now turn our attention to completeness, which is again slightly more straightforward than soundness.

Theorem 13.24 (Top-Down Completeness)

$\mathcal{L}(E) \subseteq \mathcal{L}_{td}(E)$.

Proof: Suppose $\sigma \in \mathcal{L}(E)$ so that there is a sequence $E = \mathbf{E}_0, \ldots, \mathbf{E}_n = \sigma$ such that $\mathbf{E}_i \rightarrow \mathbf{E}_{i+1}$. But if $\mathbf{E}_i \rightarrow \mathbf{E}_{i+1}$, then we can find an $\mathbf{E}'_{i+1} \sqsubseteq \mathbf{E}_{i+1}$ such that $\mathbf{E}_i \rightarrow_{td} \mathbf{E}'_{i+1}$ via h. Iterating this observation yields a sequence $\mathbf{E}'_0, \ldots, \mathbf{E}'_n$ such that $\mathbf{E}'_i \sqsubseteq \mathbf{E}_i$ and such that $\mathbf{E}'_i \rightarrow_{td} \mathbf{E}'_{i+1}$. Since $\mathbf{E}_n = \sigma$, we must have $\mathbf{E}'_n = \sigma$ and hence we have $\mathbf{E}'_i \xrightarrow{*}_{td} \sigma$. Thus we have $\sigma \in \mathcal{L}_{bu}(\mathbf{E}'_0)$ and hence $\sigma \in \mathcal{L}_{bu}(E)$ since $\mathbf{E}'_0 \sqsubseteq \mathbf{E}_0 = E$. $\square$

We now have two ways to evaluate unification-based phrase structure grammars in terms of rewriting systems which yield the same results as the standard system but do so by only instantiating the feature structures in the rewriting sequences as much as is necessary locally. When we turn to the characterization of logic programs in the next chapter, we see that these results specialize to showing that the operational semantics of logic programs are sound and complete with respect to their denotational semantics. These results also validate implementations that are based on either the top-down or bottom-up analysis scheme. In terms of grammar, top-down rewriting corresponds most closely to generation; that is, top-down rewriting answers the question of which expressions have analyses which extend a given categorization. Bottom-up rewriting, on the other hand, corresponds most closely to parsing problems in which the question is which categories correspond to a given expression.

Chapter 14

Definite Clause Programming

In this chapter we briefly show how definite clause logic programs fall out as a particular instance of unification-based phrase structure grammars. The analysis is based on the realization that parse trees for unification-based grammars bear a striking resemblance to proof trees for logic programs. More significantly, the top-down analysis of unification-based grammars generalizes the notion of SLD-resolution as it is applied in definite clause logic programming, whereas the bottom-up analysis generalizes the standard notion of denotational semantics for logic programs. The results in this chapter can be taken as a generalization of the Prolog family of programming languages (though as we have said before, we put off the analysis of inequations in grammars and hence in definite clause programs until the next chapter on constraint-resolution).

It has been noted in the past, most notably by Mukai (1985, 1987, Mukai and Yasukawa 1985), Aït-Kaci and Nasr (1986), and Höhfeld and Smolka (1988), that the idea of definite clause programming can be extended to domains other than first-order terms. In particular, the systems developed by Mukai and Yasukawa, Aït-Kaci and Nasr, and Höhfeld and Smolka employ a more or less standard notion of definite clauses with the simple modification of replacing first-order terms with various notions of feature structure. Of course, this move was preceded by extensions to Prolog from within the Prolog community itself by Colmerauer (1984), who developed Prolog II, a language based on definite clauses that allowed terms to contain cycles and also inequations. In this chapter, we generalize all of these systems by showing how any of our systems of feature structures can be used as the basis for defining a definite clause programming language. Thus we are developing a definite clause programming paradigm which is parameterized for a choice of attribute-value logic. Formally, our development does not follow the route of constraint logic programming as developed by Jaffar and Lassez (1987), though it can be viewed as an instance of the more general notion of constraint logic programming developed by Höhfeld and Smolka, though this is not how we present it. The constraint logic programming paradigm is based on the notion of constraint resolution, whereas our development is based on feature structure unification. But it should be kept in mind that it is possible to translate between the two approaches by simply considering our description language as expressing constraints and translating

215

everything we state in terms of unification into statements in terms of normalization of descriptions.

One benefit our approach shares with that of Aït-Kaci and Nasr's and also with that of Höhfeld and Smolka's is that it shows how to neatly integrate a notion of inheritance into logic programs. Our approach to typing allows us to provide a formalism which has as instances both Aït-Kaci and Nasr's system and standard Prolog. In particular, Aït-Kaci and Nasr's system falls out by assuming that every feature is appropriate for every type with no restriction on value (or simply working with an untyped system), while (standard) Prolog arises from the case in which the type hierarchy is flat, cycles are disallowed and every type is extensional. But as we mentioned in the chapter on types themselves, our notion of typing does not closely correspond to any of the type systems developed for logic programs themselves. Thus it may be treated as an alternative proposal for typing logic programs.

The motivation behind the development of definite clause programming was to provide a system that would allow logic to be used for programming purposes. But general-purpose theorem provers, such as those based on various notions of resolution, are not very well behaved operationally in the sense that their search spaces tend to explode rather quickly. The insight that led to the development of Prolog was to restrict the class of formulas that could be used in a logic program to definite implications of the form: $(\phi_1 \wedge \cdots \wedge \phi_n) \rightarrow \phi_0$, where the ϕ_i are single literals consisting of a relation applied to a number of terms. The standard (*Edinburgh Syntax*) method for representing such a clause in logic programming systems such as Prolog is as:

(1) $\phi_0 :- \phi_1, \ldots, \phi_n.$

The antecedent $\phi_1, \ldots, \phi_n$ is referred to as the *body* of the clause, while ϕ_0 is called the *head* of the clause. A *unit clause* is one in which $n = 0$, so that the body of the clause is empty. A unit clause is often abbreviated to:

(2) $\phi_0.$

Such implicative formulas are termed *definite clauses* because their consequents consist of a single positive (definite) literal, rather than a general formula involving disjunction or negation. It is common to allow disjunctions in the antecedent of a definite clause, but all such disjunctions can be converted into an equivalent set of non-disjunctive clauses by converting to disjunctive normal form. In particular, under the standard interpretation of definite clauses, a clause of the form $(\psi_1 \vee \cdots \vee \psi_n) \rightarrow \phi_0$, where the ψ_i are disjunct-free, would be equivalent to the set of clauses $\psi_i \rightarrow \phi_0$ for $1 \leq i \leq n$. The operational behavior of logic programs is then regulated by having queries or goals consist of a set of literals and the search for a solution carried out by backward chaining. In particular, the result of backward chaining is to further instantiate a goal and a clause so that the goal matches the head of a clause and then replace the goal by the body of the clause. The search for a solution halts when every goal has been instantiated with a unit clause so that the goal sequence is empty.

append
∧ ARG1: **e-list**
∧ ARG2: $X1$
∧ ARG3: $X1$.

append	:–	**append**
∧ ARG1: (HD: $X1$ ∧ TL: $X2$)		∧ ARG1: $X2$
∧ ARG2: $X3$		∧ ARG2: $X3$
∧ ARG3: (HD: $X1$ ∧ TL: $X4$)		∧ ARG3: $X4$.

Figure 14.1. **append** as a Definite Clause Program.

Definite Clause Programs

The analysis we develop in this section simply allows the literals in definite clauses to be arbitrary feature structure descriptions. With the duality between our descriptions and feature structures, another way to view our approach is as replacing first-order terms with our version of feature structures in logic programs. Before we begin, we must fix a type inheritance hierarchy and collection of features. We must also specify appropriateness conditions and the collection of extensional types if we are to enforce typing and extensionality constraints. Finally, we must fix a logic and decide which forms of extensionality and type inference are to be used. As we have said before, we put off dealing with inequations until the next chapter. We thus assume that a collection **Desc** of descriptions (including variables) has been fixed over which we define definite clause programs. We let $\mathcal{G}$ be the resulting collection of feature structures relative to a fixed choice $\mathcal{E}_{\mathcal{G}}$ of attribute-value logic.

Definition 14.1 (Definite Clause Programs)

The collection DC *of* definite clauses *is defined by* DC = Desc × Desc*. *A* definite clause program *is a finite set* Prog ⊆ DC.

We employ the standard Prolog notation and display a definite clause such as $\langle \phi_0, \langle \phi_1, \dots, \phi_n \rangle \rangle$ in the form:

(3) $\phi_0 :– \phi_1, \dots, \phi_n.$

We say that ϕ_0 is the *head* of this clause and $\phi_1, \dots, \phi_n$ is the *body*. If the body is empty, so that $n = 0$, we say that the clause is a *unit clause*. We say that a sequence $\phi_1, \dots, \phi_n$ of descriptions where $n \geq 0$ is a *goal*. Thus the body of an arbitrary (possibly unit) clause is itself a goal.

In Figure 14.1, we provide an example of a definite clause program which defines the **append** relation which holds between three lists if the third is the result of appending the first two. We assume that there are three features appropriate for **append**, ARG1, ARG2, and ARG3, all of which take values of

reverse
∧ ARG1: $(X1 ∧$ **e-list**$)$
∧ ARG2: $X1$.

reverse	:–	**reverse**	,	**append**
∧ ARG1: (HD: $X1$		∧ ARG1: $X2$		∧ ARG1: $X4$
∧ TL: $X2$)		∧ ARG2: $X4$		∧ ARG2: (HD: $X1$
∧ ARG2: $X3$				∧ TL: **e-list**)
				∧ ARG3: $X3$.

Figure 14.2. **reverse** as a Definite Clause Program.

type **list**, where we assume a HD/TL encoding of lists as before. Thus we are using features and their values to play the role of arguments in a standard logic program. In Figure 14.2, we define the **reverse** relation which holds between two lists if the second is the reversal of the first one. We assume that there are two arguments, ARG1 and ARG2 for reversing a list. Of course, with this assumption, **append** and **reverse** must have a common supertype, so that there is a minimal type for ARG1 and ARG2, but this does not pose a problem. Alternatively, we could simply assume that **append** and **reverse** are appropriate for different features, for instance by taking ARG1-REV and ARG2-REV for **reverse**.

In defining the semantics of definite clause programs, we are interested in which goals can be said to succeed. Goals are interpreted existentially, therefore we are also interested in how the goals must be further instantiated so that they can be derived from the program. Of course, unlike logic programming, in which a further instantiation corresponds to a substitution for variables, a further instantiation in the case of feature structures is represented in terms of a morphism. It is significant to notice that a definite clause program has the same definition as a phrase structure grammar without any basic expressions. On the other hand, since the body of a clause may be empty, we have the correlate of empty rewritings. We exploit this analogy to provide the semantics of our definite clause programming language. As with phrase structure grammars, we may convert our definite clause programs stated in terms of descriptions into a definite clause program stated in terms of feature structures by taking most general satisfiers. Thus if Prog is a definite clause program expressed in terms of descriptions, the collection MGRule(Prog) of minimal satisfiers of the clauses in Prog contains the same information expressed in terms of feature structures. We write elements of MGRule(Prog) in the form of definite clauses. We should note that one way in which our system differs from standard logic programs is that we allow disjunction within the description of a literal in a clause. The collection MGRule(Prog) for the program given in Figure 14.2 is given in Figure 14.3. In this figure and those that follow, we have abbreviated feature names. Note that we could have replaced the first clause of **reverse**

$$\begin{bmatrix} \textbf{reverse} \\ \text{A}1:[\boxed{1}\ \text{e-list}] \\ \text{A}2:[\boxed{1}] \end{bmatrix}.$$

$$\begin{bmatrix} \textbf{reverse} \\ \text{A}1: \begin{bmatrix} \textbf{ne-list} \\ \text{HD}:[\boxed{1}\ \bot] \\ \text{TL}:[\boxed{2}\ \text{list}] \end{bmatrix} \\ \text{A}2:[\boxed{3}\ \text{list}] \end{bmatrix} :\!\!- \begin{bmatrix} \textbf{reverse} \\ \text{A}1:[\boxed{2}] \\ \text{A}2:[\boxed{4}\ \text{list}] \end{bmatrix}, \begin{bmatrix} \textbf{append} \\ \text{A}1:[\boxed{4}] \\ \text{A}2: \begin{bmatrix} \textbf{ne-list} \\ \text{HD}:[\boxed{1}] \\ \text{TL}:[\text{e-list}] \end{bmatrix} \\ \text{A}3:[\boxed{3}] \end{bmatrix}.$$

Figure 14.3. Most General Rules for **reverse**.

with the following clause if we had assumed that e-list is an extensional type:

(4)   **reverse** $\wedge$ ARG1: **e-list** $\wedge$ ARG2: **e-list**.

Forward Chaining and Program Meaning

An attractive aspect of definite clause programs is that their semantics falls out directly from the semantics of unification-based phrase structure grammars. In particular, the bottom-up interpretation of phrase structure grammars provides the denotational, fix-point or bottom-up denotation of definite clause programs. Translating the definition of bottom-up rewriting into the present context yields:

(5)   • $\mathbf{G} \cdot h(F_0) \cdot \mathbf{G'} \rightarrow_{bu} \mathbf{G} \cdot G_1 \cdot \cdots \cdot G_n \cdot \mathbf{G'}$

if and only if there is a rule $F_0 :\!- F_1, \ldots, F_n \in \mathsf{MGRule}(\mathsf{Prog})$ and h is the most general morphism such that $h(F_i) = h(G_i)$ for $1 \leq i \leq n$. We then take $\overset{*}{\rightarrow}_{bu}$ to be the least relation such that:

(6)   • $\mathbf{G} \overset{*}{\rightarrow}_{bu} \mathbf{G}$

• $\mathbf{G} \overset{*}{\rightarrow}_{bu} \mathbf{G''}$ if some $\mathbf{G'}$ is such that $\mathbf{G} \rightarrow_{bu} \mathbf{G'}$ and $\mathbf{G'} \overset{*}{\rightarrow}_{bu} \mathbf{G''}$

We use this notion of bottom-up rewriting to define the forward-chaining semantics of logic programs. The definition is complicated slightly by the fact that we want the meaning of a logic program to be closed under further instantiation so that if G is a provable goal and $G \sqsubseteq G'$, then G' is also provable.

Definition 14.2 (Forward Chaining)

The forward-chaining *meaning* $\mathcal{M}$ *of a logic program is defined to be:*

$$\mathcal{M} = \{G \mid G' \sqsubseteq G, G' \overset{*}{\rightarrow}_{bu} \epsilon\}$$

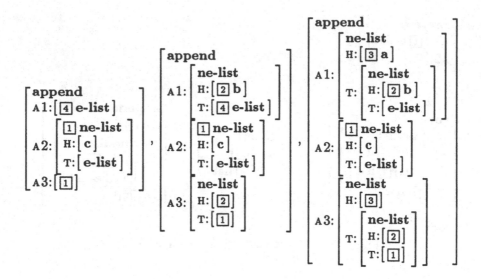

Figure 14.4. Example of Forward-Chaining Analysis.

From the results in the previous chapter on phrase structure grammars, we can state this result in slightly more familiar terms using the standard inductive (fix-point) definition of the meaning of a logic program.

Corollary 14.3

M is the least set such that:

$$G \in \mathcal{M} \; if \, G :- G_1, \ldots, G_n \in \mathsf{Rule(Prog)} \; and \; G_i \in \mathcal{M} \; for \; 1 \leq i \leq n$$

Note that in the corollary we assumed we were dealing with Rule(Prog), which by definition consists of all possible further instantiations of the clauses in MGRule(Prog). The way to think of this fix-point definition of $\mathcal{M}$ is as closing the empty set under implication. If the terms in the body of a clause are all in the meaning of the program, then the head of the clause must be in the meaning of the program. In particular, the fix-point definition of $\mathcal{M}$ is able to get off the ground because the head of every unit clause must be in the meaning of a program, because trivially every clause in its body is in the meaning of the program. Of course, we could expand out the inductive definition of $\mathcal{M}$ into a more explicit fix-point form as we did in the previous chapter.

We provide an example of the forward-chaining analysis of a logic program by means of the feature structures in Figure 14.4, each of which is in the meaning $\mathcal{M}$ of the program in Figure 14.1. The reasoning according to the fix-point definition goes as follows. The first feature structure in Figure 14.4 is in $\mathcal{M}$ because it satisfies the unit clause of the definition of **append** (under the assignment $\alpha(X1) = \boxed{1}$). The second feature structure in Figure 14.4 is in $\mathcal{M}$ because it satisfies the head of the recursive clause for **append**, whereas the first feature structure in Figure 14.4 is in $\mathcal{M}$ and simultaneously satisfies the only goal in the body of the recursive clause (under the assignment $\alpha(X1) = \boxed{2}, \alpha(X2) = \boxed{4}, \alpha(X3) = \boxed{1}, \alpha(X4) = \boxed{1}$). Finally, the last feature structure in Figure 14.4 can be shown to be in $\mathcal{M}$ by reasoning analogous to that for the second.

Of course, we already know that the forward-chaining analysis of definite clause programs, because of its definition as an instance of unification-based phrase structure grammars, is identical to the standard definition of rewriting in phrase-structure systems. In particular, an admissible tree in the standard sense for a definite clause program is such that every leaf is labeled with the empty string ϵ. In logic, such an admissible tree is referred to as a *proof tree*. Our results in the last chapter are sufficient to show that a goal G is in the meaning of a program $\mathcal{M}$ if and only if there is a proof tree rooted at G whose yield is the empty sequence ϵ. In fact, all proof trees have the empty sequence as their yield as there are no basic expressions.

In standard logic programming systems based on first-order terms, such as Prolog or even Prolog II, the term constructor (relation symbol) of a goal term must exactly match that in the head of a clause it is being resolved against. Of course, in such a matching procedure, unifying the goal against the head of a clause can cause the subgoals of the clause or other goals in the goal set to become further instantiated. Such further instantiation must occur solely by further instantiating existing variables. With our notion of inheritance built into the type system, we can match a goal against the head of a clause with a different type as long as the goal type and clause head type can be unified. This mechanism can be exploited to arrange the types that are used relationally (that is, as the types of some feature structure in a clause or goal) in an inheritance hierarchy, so that proof methods can be inherited by means of unification. Of course, this is a standard notion in inheritance-based reasoning systems such as KRYPTON (Brachman et al. 1983) and LOOM (Mac Gregor 1988), and also in many less formally developed frame-based production systems. Aït-Kaci and Nasr (1986) noticed the possibility of exploiting inheritance and incorporated it into the design of their logic programming language LOGIN, which uses data structures more or less isomorphic to our feature structures (with inheritance, but without typing, inequations, or extensionality). As Aït-Kaci and Nasr point out, the use of inheritance allows reasoning that is usually carried out by means of inference rules to be replaced by simple type inheritance. We present one of their simpler examples in Figure 14.5 and Figure 14.6. Figure 14.5 displays the information that all people like themselves, every student is a person, and John is a student, using standard logic programming techniques. In particular, notice that a rule is used to state that every person is a student. The same program in our inheritance-based notation is provided in Figure 14.6. We assume that **student** is a subtype of **person** so that **person** $\sqsubseteq$ **person**. We also assume that **likes** is appropriate for LIKER and LIKEE whereas **person** and **student** are appropriate for NAME. While this is not quite the same as Aït-Kaci and Nasr's example, it shows how we can exploit the uniformity between the data structure used to represent relations and that used to represent functions. In

$$likes(X, X) :- person(X).$$
$$person(X) :- student(X).$$
$$student(john).$$

Figure 14.5. Standard Logic Program Encoding.

standard logic programming, some special mechanism would be necessary to encode an example of the kind we used. What is important to notice about this example is that the feature structure in Figure 14.7 is in the meaning $\mathcal{M}$ assigned to the program in Figure 14.6. Quite significantly, we do not need to use another resolution inference step to infer the fact that every student is a person; the result simply follows from the definition of unification and the type inheritance hierarchy, which states that the type of students is a subtype of the type of people. Of course, in more sophisticated examples, some of which are provided by Aït-Kaci and Nasr, more use could be made of inheritance. In particular, Aït-Kaci and Nasr point out that if there are long chains of the form $p_i :- p_{i+1}$ for $0 \leq i \leq n$, then as many as n inference steps can be eliminated in favor of type inheritance. The significance of this arises when implementations of logic programs are considered in which new reference stacks are created for an inference step, which is quite costly indeed, especially as their resulting instantiations must be undone upon backtracking. In the present arrangement, this expensive inference is performed during the stage that matches a goal to the heads of clauses in the program. This step can be made quite efficient by the use of indexing techniques, such as those used for efficiently compiling Prolog programs into Warren Abstract Machine instructions (see Aït-Kaci 1990).

Backward Chaining and Program Operation

Turning now to the more well-known (abstract) operational or backward-chaining semantics of logic programs, we see that the top-down interpretation of unification-based phrase structure grammars is simply a generalization of the backward-chaining interpretation of logic programs. We repeat the portion of the definition of top-down rewriting that is relevant here. We define $\rightarrow_{td}$ by setting:

(7) $\mathbf{G} \cdot G_0 \cdot \mathbf{G'} \rightarrow_{td} h(\mathbf{G}) \cdot h(F_1) \cdot \cdots \cdot h(F_n) \cdot h(\mathbf{G'})$ via h

if and only if there is a rule $F_0 :- F_1, \ldots, F_n \in \mathsf{MGRule(Prog)}$ and h is the most general morphism such that $h(F_0) = h(G_0)$ We then take $\xrightarrow{*}_{td}$ to be the least relation such that:

(8)   • $\mathbf{G} \xrightarrow{*}_{td} \mathbf{G}$ via $\mathbf{id}$

        • $\mathbf{G} \xrightarrow{*}_{td} \mathbf{G''}$ via $h' \circ h$ if $\mathbf{G} \rightarrow_{td} \mathbf{G'}$ via h and $\mathbf{G'} \rightarrow_{td} \mathbf{G''}$ via h'

With top-down rewriting as our representation of backward-chaining analyses of logic programs, we can define the operational semantics of a logic program.

$$\text{person} \sqsubseteq \text{student}$$

$$
\begin{bmatrix}
\textbf{likes} \\
\text{LIKER:}\,[\boxed{1}] \\
\text{LIKEE:}\,[\boxed{1}]
\end{bmatrix}
:\!-\; [\boxed{1}\,\textbf{person}]\,.
$$

$$
\begin{bmatrix}
\textbf{student} \\
\text{NAME:}\,[\,\text{john}\,] \\
\text{STUD-NUM:}\,[\,\textbf{123}\,]
\end{bmatrix}.
$$

Figure 14.6. Feature Structure Definite Clause Program Encoding.

$$
\begin{bmatrix}
\textbf{likes} \\[4pt]
\text{LIKER:}
\begin{bmatrix}
\boxed{1}\,\textbf{student} \\
\text{NAME:}\,[\,\text{john}\,] \\
\text{STUD-NUM:}\,[\,\textbf{123}\,]
\end{bmatrix} \\[10pt]
\text{LIKEE:}\,[\boxed{1}]
\end{bmatrix}
$$

Figure 14.7. Consequence of Program in Figure 14.6.

Definition 14.4 (Backward Chaining)

The backward-chaining *semantics $\mathcal{O}$ of a program is given by:*

$$\mathcal{O} = \{h(\mathbf{G}) \mid \mathbf{G} \rightarrow_{td} \epsilon \text{ via } h\}$$

The reason that we do not need to close the backward-chaining definition under subsumption is that there is no restriction on the instantiation of the feature structure $\mathbf{G}$ with which we begin rewriting.

From our results in the previous chapter, we conclude that the forward- and backward-chaining semantics of definite clause programs are congruent.

Corollary 14.5

For any definite clause program Prog, *the backward-chaining and forward-chaining semantics are equivalent so that:*

$$\mathcal{O} = \mathcal{M}$$

Proof: This result falls out of our results concerning phrase structure grammars, because a definite clause program is simply a unification-based phrase structure grammar without any basic expressions. □

Consider the backward-chaining analysis of the query in Figure 14.8 with respect to the clauses given for **reverse** and **append**. The resulting composite

$$
\begin{bmatrix}
\boxed{1}\ \textbf{reverse} \\
\text{A1:}
\begin{bmatrix}
\boxed{4}\ \textbf{ne-list} \\
\text{HD:}\begin{bmatrix}\boxed{10}\ \textbf{a}\end{bmatrix} \\
\text{TL:}
\begin{bmatrix}
\boxed{9}\ \textbf{ne-list} \\
\text{HD:}\begin{bmatrix}\boxed{11}\ \textbf{b}\end{bmatrix} \\
\text{TL:}\begin{bmatrix}\boxed{6}\ \textbf{e-list}\end{bmatrix}
\end{bmatrix}
\end{bmatrix}
\end{bmatrix}
$$

Figure 14.8. Backward-Chaining Example – Query.

$$
(h_4 \circ h_3 \circ h_2 \circ h_1 \circ \text{id} \circ h_0)(\boxed{1}) =
\begin{bmatrix}
\textbf{reverse} \\
\text{A1:}
\begin{bmatrix}
\textbf{ne-list} \\
\text{HD:}\begin{bmatrix}\boxed{10}\ \textbf{a}\end{bmatrix} \\
\text{TL:}
\begin{bmatrix}
\textbf{ne-list} \\
\text{HD:}\begin{bmatrix}\boxed{11}\ \textbf{b}\end{bmatrix} \\
\text{TL:}\begin{bmatrix}\boxed{6}\ \textbf{e-list}\end{bmatrix}
\end{bmatrix}
\end{bmatrix} \\
\text{A2:}
\begin{bmatrix}
\textbf{ne-list} \\
\text{HD:}\begin{bmatrix}\boxed{11}\ \textbf{b}\end{bmatrix} \\
\text{TL:}
\begin{bmatrix}
\textbf{ne-list} \\
\text{HD:}\begin{bmatrix}\boxed{10}\ \textbf{a}\end{bmatrix} \\
\text{TL:}\begin{bmatrix}\textbf{e-list}\end{bmatrix}
\end{bmatrix}
\end{bmatrix}
\end{bmatrix}
$$

Figure 14.9. Backward-Chaining Example – Solution.

$$
\begin{bmatrix}
\textbf{reverse} \\
\text{A1:}
\begin{bmatrix}
\boxed{9}\ \textbf{ne-list} \\
\text{HD:}\begin{bmatrix}\boxed{11}\ \textbf{b}\end{bmatrix} \\
\text{TL:}\begin{bmatrix}\boxed{6}\ \textbf{e-list}\end{bmatrix}
\end{bmatrix} \\
\text{A2:}\begin{bmatrix}\boxed{2}\ \textbf{list}\end{bmatrix}
\end{bmatrix}
,\quad
\begin{bmatrix}
\textbf{append} \\
\text{A1:}\begin{bmatrix}\boxed{2}\end{bmatrix} \\
\text{A2:}
\begin{bmatrix}
\textbf{ne-list} \\
\text{HD:}\begin{bmatrix}\boxed{10}\ \textbf{a}\end{bmatrix} \\
\text{TL:}\begin{bmatrix}\textbf{e-list}\end{bmatrix}
\end{bmatrix} \\
\text{A3:}\begin{bmatrix}\boxed{3}\ \textbf{list}\end{bmatrix}
\end{bmatrix}
\quad \text{via} \quad
h_0(\boxed{1}) =
\begin{bmatrix}
\textbf{reverse} \\
\text{A1:}\begin{bmatrix}\boxed{4}\end{bmatrix} \\
\text{A2:}\begin{bmatrix}\boxed{3}\end{bmatrix}
\end{bmatrix}
$$

Figure 14.10. Backward-Chaining Example – Rewrite 1.

morphism is displayed in Figure 14.9. The steps of the rewriting are detailed starting in Figure 14.10 and concluding in Figure 14.15. In all of these figures, we have performed simple type inference and also included the relevant details of the morphisms under which the rewritings are licensed. We use these morphisms

$$
\left[
\begin{array}{l}
\textbf{reverse} \\
\text{A1:}\,[\boxed{6}\,\text{e-list}\,] \\
\text{A2:}\,[\boxed{5}\,\text{list}\,]
\end{array}
\right]
,\quad
\left[
\begin{array}{l}
\textbf{append} \\
\text{A1:}\,[\boxed{5}\,] \\
\text{A2:}
\left[
\begin{array}{l}
\boxed{7}\,\textbf{ne-list} \\
\text{HD:}\,[\boxed{11}\,\text{b}\,] \\
\text{TL:}\,[\,\text{e-list}\,]
\end{array}
\right] \\
\text{A3:}\,[\boxed{2}\,\text{list}\,]
\end{array}
\right]
,\quad
\left[
\begin{array}{l}
\textbf{append} \\
\text{A1:}\,[\boxed{2}\,] \\
\text{A2:}
\left[
\begin{array}{l}
\textbf{ne-list} \\
\text{HD:}\,[\boxed{10}\,\text{a}\,] \\
\text{TL:}\,[\,\text{e-list}\,]
\end{array}
\right] \\
\text{A3:}\,[\boxed{3}\,\text{list}\,]
\end{array}
\right]
\quad \textbf{via id}
$$

Figure 14.11. Backward-Chaining Example – Rewrite 2.

$$
\left[
\begin{array}{l}
\textbf{append} \\
\text{A1:}\,[\boxed{6}\,\text{e-list}\,] \\
\text{A2:}
\left[
\begin{array}{l}
\boxed{7}\,\textbf{ne-list} \\
\text{HD:}\,[\boxed{11}\,\text{b}\,] \\
\text{TL:}\,[\,\text{e-list}\,]
\end{array}
\right] \\
\text{A3:}\,[\boxed{2}\,\text{list}\,]
\end{array}
\right]
,\quad
\left[
\begin{array}{l}
\textbf{append} \\
\text{A1:}\,[\boxed{2}\,] \\
\text{A2:}
\left[
\begin{array}{l}
\textbf{ne-list} \\
\text{HD:}\,[\boxed{10}\,\text{a}\,] \\
\text{TL:}\,[\,\text{e-list}\,]
\end{array}
\right] \\
\text{A3:}\,[\boxed{3}\,\text{list}\,]
\end{array}
\right]
\quad \textbf{via } h_1(\boxed{5}) = [\boxed{6}]
$$

Figure 14.12. Backward-Chaining Example – Rewrite 3.

$$
\left[
\begin{array}{l}
\textbf{append} \\
\text{A1:}
\left[
\begin{array}{l}
\boxed{7}\,\textbf{ne-list} \\
\text{HD:}\,[\boxed{11}\,\text{b}\,] \\
\text{TL:}\,[\,\text{e-list}\,]
\end{array}
\right] \\
\text{A2:}
\left[
\begin{array}{l}
\textbf{ne-list} \\
\text{HD:}\,[\boxed{10}\,\text{a}\,] \\
\text{TL:}\,[\,\text{e-list}\,]
\end{array}
\right] \\
\text{A3:}\,[\boxed{3}\,\text{list}\,]
\end{array}
\right]
\quad \textbf{via } h_2(\boxed{2}) = [\boxed{7}]
$$

Figure 14.13. Backward-Chaining Example – Rewrite 4.

to track the relevant instantiations of the original goal. Although we have not used any of the inheritance-based features of our system in this rather simple example, we have started the rewriting process with a goal not all of whose arguments are instantiated. Thus the first morphism h_1 in Figure 14.10 maps the original goal onto one that also has the second argument feature ARG2 instantiated. If we had enforced total typing, ARG2 would have been required to show up in the original goal to make the result totally well typed.

$$\begin{bmatrix} \textbf{append} \\ \text{A}1\text{:}\begin{bmatrix} \textbf{e-list} \end{bmatrix} \\ \text{A}2\text{:}\begin{bmatrix} \textbf{ne-list} \\ \text{HD:}\begin{bmatrix} \boxed{10}\ \textbf{a} \end{bmatrix} \\ \text{TL:}\begin{bmatrix} \textbf{e-list} \end{bmatrix} \end{bmatrix} \\ \text{A}3\text{:}\begin{bmatrix} \boxed{8}\ \textbf{list} \end{bmatrix} \end{bmatrix} \quad \text{via} \quad h_3(\boxed{3}) = \begin{bmatrix} \textbf{ne-list} \\ \text{HD:}\begin{bmatrix} \boxed{11}\ \textbf{b} \end{bmatrix} \\ \text{TL:}\begin{bmatrix} \boxed{8}\ \textbf{list} \end{bmatrix} \end{bmatrix}$$

Figure 14.14. Backward-Chaining Example – Rewrite 5.

$$\epsilon \quad \text{via} \quad h_4(\boxed{8}) = \begin{bmatrix} \textbf{ne-list} \\ \text{HD:}\begin{bmatrix} \boxed{10}\ \textbf{a} \end{bmatrix} \\ \text{TL:}\begin{bmatrix} \textbf{e-list} \end{bmatrix} \end{bmatrix}$$

Figure 14.15. Backward-Chaining Example – Rewrite 6.

Chapter 15

Recursive Type Constraints

Until now, we have only considered relatively weak typing schemes. The only type restrictions have to do with whether or not a feature is appropriate for a type and whether it takes an appropriate value; under total typing, we additionally require every appropriate feature to take a value. We have shown that this kind of type scheme could be very simply specified in the description language by the following axioms, which can be used as a rewriting system in the direction specified in:

(1)
- $f{:}\bot \Rightarrow Intro(f)$ (Domain Typing)

- $f{:}\bot \wedge \sigma \Rightarrow f{:}Approp(f, \sigma)$ (Range Typing)

- $\sigma \Rightarrow f{:}\bot$ if $Approp(f, \sigma)$ defined   (Total Typing)

Recall that $Approp(f, \sigma) = \tau$ if τ is the most general value appropriate for the feature f in a type σ feature structure, and that $Intro(f)$ is the most general type appropriate for σ. The axioms in (1) are weak enough that type inference can be performed in linear time. In this chapter, we consider extensions of the notion of typing in which we allow types to be restricted by arbitrary descriptions. More specifically, we consider collections of constraints of the following form, where ϕ is an arbitrary description:

(2) $\sigma \Rightarrow \phi$

The intuitive idea is that a feature structure of type σ must satisfy the constraint ϕ, which is why the constraint is expressed in the form of an implication. Of course, with arbitrary descriptions, which themselves might contain arbitrary types, there is the possibility of recursive type systems. We take a feature structure to satisfy a system of such constraints if every one of its substructures satisfies the constraint on its type. It turns out that if we allow arbitrary collections of constraints such of the form of (2), it is undecidable whether a constraint system is solvable in the sense that there are feature structures which satisfy all of the constraints. The best we can do is provide a procedure to recursively enumerate the solutions to a given type system, which is exactly what we do below.

The idea of using such a strong type system dates back to Aït-Kaci's (1984) dissertation. Aït-Kaci specifically looked at the case of constraint systems defined over Ψ-terms, which form a domain isomorphic to our simple untyped feature structures. Aït-Kaci's motivation was to provide a general-purpose knowledge representation in the KL-ONE family that would be able to enforce arbitrary constraints. Following a quite different tradition in unification-based grammar formalisms and linguistic theories, Pollard and Sag (1987) introduced the Head-driven Phrase Structure Grammar (HPSG) theory. HPSG object grammars are expressed as a system of constraints on types of the form found in (2). As can be seen from the denotational presentation of the HPSG formalism in Pollard and Moshier (1990), the semantics of HPSG is very closely related to Aït-Kaci's system. Emele and Zajac (1989, 1989b, 1990, Zajac 1989) have further developed and extended Aït-Kaci's (1984, 1986) system and applied it to automatically process HPSG grammars. Not surprisingly, both the semantics of Aït-Kaci's knowledge representation formalism and the HPSG formalism are closely related to the semantics of logic programming languages, as can be seen in Carpenter, Pollard and Franz (1991) and Franz (1990). The semantics of the constraint resolution system is also related to the Functional Unification Grammar formalism of Kay (1984, 1985). In this chapter, we present a general-purpose constraint resolution system in the form of a non-deterministic rewriting system which is able to enumerate solutions to arbitrary collections of constraints over any of the feature structure systems we have introduced.

Type Constraint Systems

As with the chapters on phrase structure grammars and definite clause programming, everything we do in this chapter generalizes across all of the feature structure systems we have introduced. In particular, inequations pose no problem for our constraint resolution method. An additional benefit is that the treatment of inequations in constraint systems provides a straightforward means of characterizing the behavior of phrase structure grammars and definite clause programs with inequations. Before we begin, we must decide which collection of feature structures (or equivalently, which description logic) to use. At the very least, we need to fix a type inheritance hierarchy $\langle \mathsf{Type}, \sqsubseteq \rangle$. We might also need to fix appropriateness conditions *Approp* and decide which type inference system to employ. Similarly, we can fix a collection ExtType of extensional types and decide which form of extensionality inference and decide whether or not to allow inequations. Let Desc be the resulting collection of descriptions and $\mathcal{G}$ be the resulting collection of feature structures. A constraint system simply associates every type σ with a description ϕ in Desc.

Definition 15.1 (Constraint System)

A constraint system *is a total function* Cons: Type $\rightarrow$ Desc.

We exploit the arrangement of types by subsumption and provide a means of inheriting constraints from supertypes. One benefit of such a strategy is that we can place constraints at the appropriate level of generality in the inheritance hierarchy, much like we could define clauses at the appropriate level of generality in both our phrase structure grammar and definite clause programming applications. To perform simple monotonic multiple inheritance of constraints, we define the inherited constraint associated with each type.

Definition 15.2 (Inherited Constraint)

Cons*: Type → Desc, *the* inherited constraint *function, is given by:*

$$\text{Cons}^*(\sigma) = \bigwedge\nolimits_{\tau \sqsubseteq \sigma} \text{Cons}(\sigma)$$

Aït-Kaci (1984, 1986) presented his constraint system directly in terms of his ψ-structures, which are the analogue of our feature structures. Similarly, Pollard and Moshier (1990) define their constraint systems directly in terms of feature structures. We could have taken a constraint system to associate a finite set of feature structures with every type because in general we can translate back and forth between finite sets of feature structures and descriptions according to the most general satisfier and describability theorems.

We can provide constraint systems that characterize fairly arbitrary sorts of constraints, as was first illustrated by Aït-Kaci (1984), who tested his system by applying it to a fairly complex logic puzzle. We present an encoding of a very simple logic puzzle in Figure 15.1, where we write $\sigma \Rightarrow \phi$ if $\text{Cons}(\sigma) = \phi$. For this example we use inequations and extensionality to capture the fact that neither Jones, Smith, nor Tucker have the same kind or make of car. It should be clear from this example that the feature structure in Figure 15.2 is the only one of type **situation** which satisfies all of the constraints. Note that we have not listed all of the inequalities which hold in Figure 15.2.

We say that a feature structure is *resolved* if it satisfies the constraint system. The only complication in defining this notion arises from the fact that we require every substructure of a resolved feature structure to itself be resolved.

Definition 15.3 (Resolved Feature Structure)

We say that a feature structure $F = \langle Q, \bar{q}, \theta, \delta \rangle$ *is* resolved *if and only if:*

$$F@\pi \models \text{Cons}^*(\theta(\delta(\pi, \bar{q})))$$

for every path π *for which* $F@\pi$ *is defined.*

Recall that $F@\pi$ is just the substructure of F found at the end of the path π, while $\delta(\pi, \bar{q})$ is the node found at the end of the path π from the root $\bar{q}$ so that $\theta(\delta(\pi, \bar{q}))$ is the type of $F@\pi$. Thus a feature structure is resolved if and only if every one of its substructures satisfies the inherited constraint on its type. Note that this includes the whole feature structure itself, which is the substructure found along the empty path. Thus it can be seen that the feature structure in Figure 15.2 is resolved according to this definition.

Puzzle: There are three people, Smith, Jones, and Tucker, and each of them has a car of a different make and model. The makes represented are Buick, Ford, and Toyota, and the models are sport, coupe, and wagon. Tucker has either a wagon or a sports car made by either Buick or Ford. Smith has either a Ford or Toyota sports car. Jones has a Buick which is either a coupe or a wagon.

> **maker** $\sqsubseteq$ {**ford, buick, toyota**}
> **style** $\sqsubseteq$ {**sport, wagon, coupe**}
>
> **buick, ford, toyota, sport, wagon, coupe** $\in$ ExtType
>
> $Approp(\text{SMITH}, \textbf{situation}) = \textbf{car}$ $Approp(\text{MAKE}, \textbf{car}) = \textbf{maker}$
> $Approp(\text{JONES}, \textbf{situation}) = \textbf{car}$ $Approp(\text{TYPE}, \textbf{car}) = \textbf{style}$
> $Approp(\text{TUCKER}, \textbf{situation}) = \textbf{car}$
>
> **situation** $\Rightarrow$
> (SMITH · MAKE $\neq$ JONES · MAKE $\wedge$ SMITH · MAKE $\neq$ TUCKER · MAKE
> $\wedge$ JONES · MAKE $\neq$ TUCKER · MAKE $\wedge$ SMITH · TYPE $\neq$ JONES · TYPE
> $\wedge$ SMITH · TYPE $\neq$ TUCKER · TYPE $\wedge$ JONES · TYPE $\neq$ TUCKER · TYPE)
> $\wedge$ TUCKER: (TYPE: (**wagon** $\vee$ **sport**) $\wedge$ MAKE: (**buick** $\vee$ **ford**))
> $\wedge$ SMITH: (MAKE: (**ford** $\vee$ **toyota**) $\wedge$ TYPE: **sport**)
> $\wedge$ JONES: (MAKE: **buick** $\wedge$ TYPE: (**coupe** $\vee$ **wagon**))
>
> **car** $\Rightarrow$ (MAKE: **maker** $\wedge$ TYPE: **style**)
>
> **maker** $\Rightarrow$ (**buick** $\vee$ **ford** $\vee$ **toyota**)
>
> **style** $\Rightarrow$ (**sport** $\vee$ **wagon** $\vee$ **coupe**)

Figure 15.1. Logic Puzzle Encoding Using Constraints.

Queries and π-Resolution

We now turn our attention to the resolution of constraint equations. In particular, we are interested in solving queries consisting of additional constraints.

Definition 15.4 (Queries and Solutions)

A query is simply an arbitrary description ϕ. A feature structure F is said to be a solution *to ϕ if and only if F is resolved and satisfies ϕ.*

In the degenerate case in which the query is simply a type, the solutions to the query are just the resolved feature structures whose types are subtypes of the query type. For instance, with the logic puzzle, we were only interested in finding resolved feature structures of type **situation**. Alternatively, we could have expressed the constraint of the logic puzzle in the form of a query rather than in the constraint system itself, as Aït-Kaci (1984) did originally.

It is worth noting that, in general, the description $\perp$ is a valid query, and its solutions are exactly the resolved feature structures. Thus when we provide

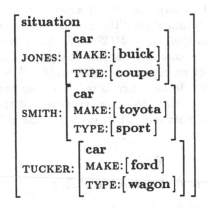

Figure 15.2. Solution to the Logic Puzzle.

methods below for enumerating solutions to arbitrary queries, we can use them for enumerating all of the resolved feature structures.

It turns out that queries can be resolved with respect to constraint equations in much the same way as logic program queries can be resolved by backward chaining with SLD-resolution. We define our resolution strategy in terms of a non-deterministic rewriting relation between feature structures. Starting with the most general satisfier(s) of the query, all of the solutions to the query can be effectively enumerated. The relation to SLD-resolution is so close that the non-deterministic choice points are even analogous. Our non-deterministic constraint resolution strategy generalizes the approach of Aït-Kaci (1984, 1986), which turns out to be just one particular method of determinizing the non-determinism in our approach. As the eventual goal of resolution is to find a feature structure all of whose substructures satisfy the constraints on their types, it is natural to proceed substructure by substructure, at each stage adding as much information to each substructure as is needed to satisfy its constraint. By iterating this process, we eventually arrive at a result which is fully resolved. We call this resolution process π-*resolution*, as we state it in terms of paths.

Definition 15.5 (π-Resolution)

We take $F \stackrel{\pi}{\Rightarrow} F \sqcup_{\mathcal{G}} (\pi \mid F')$ *if and only if* $F' \in MGSats(\mathsf{Cons}^*(\theta(\delta(\pi, \bar{q}))).$

We use the HPSG notation $\pi \mid G$ to denote the most general feature structure G' whose value at the path π is the structure G, so that $G' \mathbf{0} \pi = G$. Unpacking the definition shows that it is really quite straightforward. Starting with a feature structure F defined for the path π, we find $\tau = \theta(\delta(\pi, \bar{q}))$, the type of the substructure $F \mathbf{0} \pi$ found by following π from the root and finding a most general satisfier $F' \in MGSats(\mathsf{Conc}^*(\tau))$ of the constraint inherited by τ and unifying it into F at the path π. As we have not stated which form of type inference we are using, we may need to do some type inference to form $\pi \mid F'$. We have used $\sqcup_{\mathcal{G}}$ to stand for unification in the collection $\mathcal{G}$ of feature structures.

We have provided the interior portion of a rewriting system without present-ing either the initial or terminal conditions. When we are solving a query ϕ, we begin rewriting from an element of $MGSats(\phi)$, the collection of most general satisfiers of ϕ. This is because any resolved feature structure which satisfies ϕ must be an extension of an element of $MGSats(\phi)$. We terminate resolution when we reach a resolved feature structure. While an entire feature structure may be resolved, it makes sense to ask whether or not the substructure found at a given path is itself resolved. We can define this notion in terms of our rewriting relation.

Definition 15.6 (Resolved Path)

The path π is resolved in F if and only if $F \stackrel{\pi}{\Rightarrow} F$.

We use this definition in the following lemma which allows us to characterize when a feature structure is resolved directly in terms of the π-resolution.

Lemma 15.7 (Stable Expansion)

A feature structure F is resolved if and only if every path for which it is defined is resolved.

Proof: F is resolved just in case it satisfies the constraint on every one of its substructures. But according to the most general satisfiers theorem, $F@\pi \models$ $\text{Cons}^*(\theta(\delta(\pi, \bar{q})))$ if and only if there is some $F' \in MGSats(\text{Cons}^*(\theta(\delta(\pi, \bar{q}))))$ such that $F' \sqsubseteq F@\pi$. Now this holds if and only if $F = F \sqcup_g (\pi \mid F')$, which holds if and only if $F \stackrel{\pi}{\Rightarrow} F$.   □

In other words, a feature structure is resolved just in case it rewrites to itself along every path π.

The fundamental result of this section is that every most general solution to an arbitrary query can be found by π-resolution. First, we define a relation $\stackrel{*}{\Rightarrow}$ which is just the transitive reflexive closure of $\stackrel{\pi}{\Rightarrow}$ along arbitrary paths.

Definition 15.8 (Resolution)

The resolution relation $\stackrel{*}{\Rightarrow}$ is the least such that:

- $F \stackrel{*}{\Rightarrow} F$

- $F \stackrel{*}{\Rightarrow} F''$ if $F \stackrel{\pi}{\Rightarrow} F'$ for some π and $F' \stackrel{*}{\Rightarrow} F''$

We now state our result in terms of this rewriting relation.

Theorem 15.9 (Completeness of π-Resolution)

F is a most general solution to the query ϕ only if $F' \stackrel{*}{\Rightarrow} F$ for some $F' \in$ $MGSats(\phi)$.

Proof: We explicitly construct a rewriting sequence $H_0, \ldots, H_n$ beginning from a most general satisfier H_0 of ϕ such that $F = H_n$. To begin, suppose F is a most general solution to the query ϕ. Then since we know $F \models \phi$, we can choose some $H_0 \in MGSats(\phi)$ such that $H_0 \sqsubseteq F$. We proceed by induction under the hypothesis that each $H_i \sqsubseteq F$, which obviously holds for $i = 0$. Now if $H_i \sqsubseteq F$ and is unresolved along the path π, then we must be able to find some $H_{i+1} \sqsubseteq F$ such that $H_i \overset{\pi}{\Rightarrow} H_{i+1}$. This is because π-resolution is obviously monotonic in the sense that if $G \sqsubseteq G'$ and $G \overset{\pi}{\Rightarrow} J$, then there is a J' such that $G' \overset{\pi}{\Rightarrow} J'$ and $J \sqsubseteq J'$. Thus since $H_i \sqsubseteq F$ and $F \overset{\pi}{\Rightarrow} F$ we must have some H_{i+1} such that $H_i \overset{\pi}{\Rightarrow} H_{i+1}$ and $H_{i+1} \sqsubseteq F$. Since F is a finite feature structure, after some finite number n of resolution steps each of which strictly adds information because it works on an unresolved path, we must have $H_n = F$, as we have already seen that at every resolution stage we have $H_i \sqsubseteq F$. Also note that if $H_i \sqsubseteq F$ and $F \not\sqsubseteq H_i$ at some stage, then H_i is not a solution, because we assumed that F was a most general solution to ϕ. $\qquad\qquad\square$

Thus we can use π-resolution to completely enumerate the most general solutions to an arbitrary query by employing some form of breadth-first search strategy. Aït-Kaci used a strategy whereby the unresolved node of minimal depth from the root was always rewritten first, thus ensuring a complete search strategy. We return to a slight generalization of Aït-Kaci's search strategy below.

Note the caveat in the statement of the proof that tells us that π-resolution is only guaranteed to find most general solutions. Unlike in the case of satisfaction which was monotonic, arbitrary extensions of solutions are not necessarily solutions themselves. For instance, consider the simple case in which $\sigma \sqsubseteq \sigma' \sqsubseteq \sigma''$ and in which we have $\mathrm{Cons}(\sigma) = \sigma$ and $\mathrm{Cons}(\sigma') = \sigma''$. Then the one-node feature structure of type σ is resolved, whereas the one-node feature structure of type σ' is not resolved.

It has been the tradition in HPSG to enforce a kind of closed-world approach to resolution in which part of the constraint associated with every type is the disjunction of its immediate subtypes. This has the effect of forcing a solution to contain only maximally specific types, because anything with a non-maximal type does not satisfy the description consisting of the disjunction of its subtypes. But even after adopting this measure, we are still not guaranteed to find all of the solutions to a given constraint system. The problem that arises is similar to that which arose from total typing and that has to do with cyclic feature structures. In general, our resolution process does not consider the possible identification of substructures by unification as a means of increasing information. For instance, the appropriateness condition we considered earlier in the chapter on total typing, which requires a person to have a father who is also a person. This condition returns now to haunt us in the form of the follwoing constraint:

(3)   person $\Rightarrow$ FATHER: person

But unlike the case of total typing, we do not in general wish to rule out constraint systems which are recursive in this way. But as we also saw before, there is no finite acyclic solution to the constraint in (3), whereas the cyclic

$$\begin{bmatrix} \boxed{1}\ \textbf{person} \\ \text{FTH:}\ [\,\boxed{1}\,] \end{bmatrix} \sqsupseteq \begin{bmatrix} \textbf{person} \\ \text{FTH:}\ \begin{bmatrix} \boxed{2}\ \textbf{person} \\ \text{FTH:}\ [\,\boxed{2}\,] \end{bmatrix} \end{bmatrix} \sqsupseteq \begin{bmatrix} \textbf{person} \\ \text{FTH:}\ \begin{bmatrix} \textbf{person} \\ \text{FTH:}\ \begin{bmatrix} \boxed{3}\ \textbf{person} \\ \text{FTH:}\ [\,\boxed{3}\,] \end{bmatrix} \end{bmatrix} \end{bmatrix} \sqsupseteq \cdots$$

Figure 15.3. Descending Chain of Solutions.

$$[\,\textbf{adam}\,],\quad \begin{bmatrix} \textbf{person} \\ \text{FTH:}\ [\,\textbf{adam}\,] \end{bmatrix},\quad \begin{bmatrix} \textbf{person} \\ \text{FTH:}\ \begin{bmatrix} \textbf{person} \\ \text{FTH:}\ [\,\textbf{adam}\,] \end{bmatrix} \end{bmatrix},\ \ldots$$

Figure 15.4. Infinitely Many Most-General Solutions.

feature structure in (4) is both finite and resolved:

(4) $\quad \begin{bmatrix} \boxed{1}\ \textbf{person} \\ \text{FATHER:}\ [\,\boxed{1}\,] \end{bmatrix}$

But this does not contradict the completeness theorem for resolution, which only guarantees that π-resolution uncovers all most general solutions. As it turns out, there is no finite most general solution to the query **person** in the constraint system in (3), as can be seen with the descending chain of solutions in Figure 15.3. We will return to these cyclic conditions when we consider domain-theoretic approaches to constraints in which a most general infinite resolved feature structure can be found for the constraint in (3). Note that if we change the constraint slightly in (3) according to a biblical picture of fatherhood, we get the example in (5).

(5) $\quad$ **person** $\Rightarrow$ (**adam** $\vee$ FATHER: **person**)

In the case of (5), we get not only the cyclic solutions, but also infinitely many subsumption-incomparable finite solutions of type **person**, as shown in Figure 15.4. Note that we have abbreviated FATHER to FTH in the figures.

Although these examples show us that resolution does not find all of the solutions to a query, the solutions to a query are still recursively enumerable. This follows simply from the fact that we can enumerate all of the finite feature structures, and the issue of whether a feature structure is resolved is easily decidable as it simply reduces to a satisfaction test.

Phrase Structure with Constraints

We now turn to some more complicated applications of the π-resolution system, which lead us to conclude that arbitrary phrase structure grammars and definite clause programs can be simulated by a constraint system. Consider the cat $\sqsubseteq$ {np, vp, sv, s}

word $\sqsubseteq$ {phrase, word}

basexpr $\sqsubseteq$ {john, mary, ran, jumped, knew, thought}

$Approp$(DTR1, phrase) = $Approp$(DTR2, phrase) = sign

$Approp$(CAT, sign) = cat

$Approp$(PHON, word) = basexpr

cat $\Rightarrow$ np $\vee$ vp $\vee$ sv $\vee$ s

sign $\Rightarrow$ phrase $\vee$ word

phrase $\Rightarrow$ (CAT: s $\wedge$ DTR1: np $\wedge$ DTR2: vp)

$\qquad\qquad\vee$ (CAT: vp $\wedge$ DTR1: sv $\wedge$ DTR2: s)

word $\Rightarrow$ (CAT: np $\wedge$ PHON: (john $\vee$ mary))

$\qquad\qquad\vee$ (CAT: vp $\wedge$ PHON: (ran $\vee$ jumped))

$\qquad\qquad\vee$ (CAT: sv $\wedge$ PHON: (knew $\vee$ thought))

Figure 15.5. Simple Phrase Structure Grammar Encoding Example.

$$
\begin{bmatrix} \text{sign} \\ \text{D1:} \begin{bmatrix} \text{word} \\ \text{PH:}[\,\text{mary}\,] \end{bmatrix} \\ \text{D2:} \begin{bmatrix} \text{phrase} \\ \text{D1:} \begin{bmatrix} \text{word} \\ \text{PH:}[\,\text{thought}\,] \end{bmatrix} \end{bmatrix} \end{bmatrix}
\stackrel{\leq}{\Rightarrow}
\begin{bmatrix} \text{phrase} \\ \text{D1:} \begin{bmatrix} \text{word} \\ \text{PH:}[\,\text{mary}\,] \end{bmatrix} \\ \text{D2:} \begin{bmatrix} \text{phrase} \\ \text{D1:} \begin{bmatrix} \text{word} \\ \text{PH:}[\,\text{thought}\,] \end{bmatrix} \end{bmatrix} \end{bmatrix}
$$

Figure 15.6. Resolution of Phrase Structure Grammar Query – Part 1.

constraint system encoding of a phrase structure grammar in Figure 15.5. We assume that those types without constraints explicitly listed have themselves (or equivalently $\perp$) as their constraint. We trace the resolution behavior of the constraint system in Figure 15.5 as it applies to solve the following query:

(6)　　sign $\wedge$ DTR1 · PHON: mary $\wedge$ DTR2 · DTR1 · PHON: thought

We enforce total typing in this example, showing the results of resolution in Figures 15.6, 15.7, and 15.8. Note that we have abbreviated the daughter features; for example, DTR1 is displayed as D1. We proceed one path at a time, working outward from the root. We begin in Figure 15.6 with the most general satisfier to the query in (6). Next we resolve along the empty path, making the choice **phrase** for **sign**; the choice of **word** would have left the result untypable and is thus eliminated. But after one resolution step, the substructure at the root is not yet resolved, so we must add in enough information so that

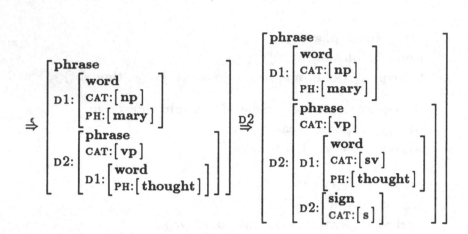

Figure 15.7. Resolution of Phrase Structure Grammar Query – Part 2.

$$
\begin{bmatrix} \text{sign} \\ \text{CAT:}[\,\text{s}\,] \end{bmatrix} \overset{\le}{\Rightarrow} \begin{bmatrix} \text{phrase} \\ \text{CAT:}[\,\text{s}\,] \end{bmatrix} \overset{\le}{\Rightarrow} \begin{bmatrix} \text{phrase} \\ \text{CAT:}[\,\text{s}\,] \\ \text{D1:} \begin{bmatrix} \text{sign} \\ \text{CAT:}[\,\text{np}\,] \end{bmatrix} \\ \text{D2:} \begin{bmatrix} \text{sign} \\ \text{CAT:}[\,\text{vp}\,] \end{bmatrix} \end{bmatrix} \overset{\text{D1}}{\Rightarrow} \begin{bmatrix} \text{phrase} \\ \text{CAT:}[\,\text{s}\,] \\ \text{D1:} \begin{bmatrix} \text{word} \\ \text{PH:}[\,\text{john}\,] \\ \text{CAT:}[\,\text{np}\,] \end{bmatrix} \\ \text{D2:} \begin{bmatrix} \text{sign} \\ \text{CAT:}[\,\text{vp}\,] \end{bmatrix} \end{bmatrix}
$$

Figure 15.8. Resolution of Phrase Structure Grammar Query – Part 3.

it satisfies the constraint on **phrase**. We choose the first disjunct and unify in its most general satisfier. Now when we proceed to type the substructure at the path DTR1, we see that it is already totally resolved in that it satisfies its constraint and all of its substructures are themselves resolved. Thus we can move on to the substructure at DTR2. Only one of the disjuncts is consistent with the information at DTR2, so we unify in its most general satisfier. As the path at DTR2 · DTR1 is already resolved, we continue with the resolution of the substructure at DTR2 · DTR2 in Figure 15.8.

The first step is to resolve **sign** to **phrase** at the root. Next, we choose the only resolution of phrase consistent with category s. Next, we combine two resolution steps, the first of which resolves the type **sign** at DTR1 to **word** and the second of which resolves **word**. Finally, we perform a similar two-step resolution at DTR2 to achieve a resolved result. Thus one most general solution to the query in (6) is given in Figure 15.9.

Unrestricted constraint systems as we have presented them here are powerful enough to encode arbitrary unification-based phrase structure grammars

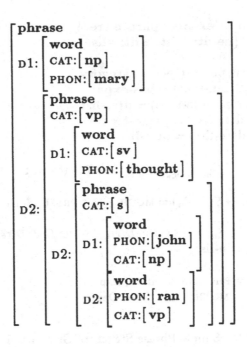

Figure 15.9. Most General Solution to Phrase Structure Grammar Query.

and definite clause programs. The trick to the encoding is to define a constraint which is only satisfied by admissible phrase structure parse trees. The encoding of definite clause programs follows from the encoding of proof trees as a restricted form of parse trees. We only directly consider the case of encoding phrase structure grammars. So suppose that Gram is a unification-based phrase structure grammar with rules of the form $\xi_0 \rightarrow \xi_1, \ldots, \xi_n$, where ξ_0 is a description, and the ξ_i are either descriptions or basic expressions. We treat every basic expression as a type and encode the grammar according to the recursive rules in Figure 15.10. The encoding is straightforward in that we use feature structures to represent parse trees in the obvious way. All parse trees have a mother category, but lexical parse trees have phonology values, and phrasal parse trees encode their subtrees using a standard head/tail encoding. We assume total type inference is operating over the appropriateness specifications, as well. Our claim is that a parse tree is admissible if and only if its encoding is a resolved feature structure of type **parse-tree**.

With the encoding in Figure 15.10, we can state a generation problem quite naturally by the query MOTH:ϕ if we want to find a parse tree whose root category satisfies the description ϕ. By encoding logic programs as phrase structure grammars, our encoding is sufficient to represent arbitrary logic programs and queries. In particular, this shows how to add inequations to logic programs, as nothing prohibits the descriptions ξ from having inequations.

parse-tree $\sqsubseteq$ {**lex-tree**, **phrase-tree**}
dtrs-list $\sqsubseteq$ {**ne-dtrs-list**, **e-dtrs-list**}

$Approp(\text{MOTH}, \textbf{parse-tree}) = \textbf{category}$
$Approp(\text{PHON}, \textbf{lex-tree}) = \textbf{bas-expr}$
$Approp(\text{DTRS}, \textbf{phrase-tree}) = \textbf{dtrs-list}$
$Approp(\text{HD}, \textbf{dtrs-list}) = \textbf{parse-tree}$
$Approp(\text{TL}, \textbf{dtrs-list}) = \textbf{dtrs-list}$

$\textbf{parse-tree} \Rightarrow \bigvee_{\xi_0 \to \xi_1 \cdots \xi_n \in \text{Gram}} CodeRule(\xi_0 \to \xi_1 \cdots \xi_n)$

$CodeRule(\xi_0 \to \xi_1 \cdots \xi_n) = \text{MOTH}\colon \xi_0 \wedge \text{DTRS}\colon CodeDtrs(\xi_1 \cdots \xi_n)$

$CodeDtrs(\xi_1 \cdots \xi_n) = \text{HD}\colon CodeDtr(\xi_1) \wedge \text{TL}\colon CodeDtrs(\xi_2 \cdots \xi_n)$
$CodeDtrs(\epsilon) = \textbf{e-list}$

$CodeDtr(e) = \text{PHON}\colon e \qquad \text{if } e \in \mathsf{Exp}$
$CodeDtr(\phi) = \text{MOTH}\colon \phi \qquad \text{if } \phi \in \mathsf{Desc}$

Figure 15.10. Simple Phrase Structure Grammar Encoding.

Theorem 15.10 (Faithful Encodings)

A generation problem for a phrase structure grammar can be reduced to a query in a constraint system determined by the grammar.

A query with respect to a definite clause program can be reduced to a query in a constraint system determined by the program.

Because we know that whether a query in a definite clause program has a solution is undecidable, we have the following immediate result.

Corollary 15.11 (Undecidability)

Whether or not a query in a constraint system has a solution is recursively enumerable, but not decidable.

Junk Slots, Definite Constraints, and Parsing

Unfortunately, the simple encoding of parse trees is not sufficient to encode arbitrary parsing problems in which we want to know which trees have a particular yield. To get around this problem, we embark on a study of how to enforce arbitrary constraints from a definite clause program on resolved feature structures in a constraint system. It is significant to note that while constraint systems are undecidable, they cannot encode arbitrary recursively enumerable collections of feature structures. In particular, it is impossible to define a type whose resolved elements consist of feature structures with only two features, both of which represent lists, and the second of which is the reverse of the first. This follows from the fact that there is a bound on the distance between feature structures which are shared due to the fact that constraints are enforced locally.

Theorem 15.12 (Locality of Constraints)

For every constraint system there is a finite bound k such that for every most general resolved feature structure F and every path π defined in F, if π is shared with some path π', then there is a path π'' shared with π such that:

$$AbsVal(Length(\pi) - Length(\pi')) \leq k.$$

Proof: This result follows from the fact that every path sharing in a most general resolved feature structure must be introduced by some constraint, and there is a finite bound k on the maximal length difference between shared paths in the constraint system. ☐

This theorem shows why we cannot have a **reverse** type. Simply consider the following feature structure:

$$(7) \quad \begin{bmatrix} \textbf{reverse} \\ \text{ARG}1: \langle \boxed{1}, \ldots, \boxed{n} \rangle \\ \text{ARG}2: \langle \boxed{n}, \ldots, \boxed{1} \rangle \end{bmatrix}$$

We use a transparent tuple notation to indicate a head/tail encoding of a list. It can be seen in (7) that the difference between size of paths to $\boxed{n}$ in ARG1 and ARG2 is directly proportional to n. This would require sharing of an unbounded distance as its arguments grew larger. To get around this problem, Aït-Kaci (1984) introduced a technique that has come to be known as *junk slots*. In particular, new features are introduced whose values are ignored, but that are used to enforce constraints on other substructures. Note that the constraint locality theorem also tells us that it is impossible to find a type whose resolved feature structures have three features which represent two lists appended together to produce a third. In Figure 15.11, we follow Aït-Kaci (1984) in using junk slots to define a type that represents appending two lists to produce a third, but also has a fourth feature whose value acts as a workspace to carry out the appending. We have followed Aït-Kaci's normal form conventions, which require every constraint to either be a disjunction of simple subtypes or a purely non-disjunctive description. Note that the constraint system in Figure 15.10 is not in such a normal form as there are general disjunctions in the constraints on phrases and lexical entries. It is a simple exercise to show that all constraint systems can be converted into this form by the use of extra type symbols to represent the disjuncts within constraints. Also note that we have included type restrictions on the values of **append**$_1$ and **append**$_2$, which could be used to choose between the disjunctive clauses of **append**. With respect to the constraint system append $\sqsubseteq$ {append$_1$, append$_2$}

$Approp(\text{LEFT}, \text{append}) = \text{list}$ $Approp(\text{RIGHT}, \text{append}) = \text{list}$
$Approp(\text{LEFT}, \text{append}_1) = \text{e-list}$ $Approp(\text{RESULT}, \text{append}) = \text{list}$
$Approp(\text{LEFT}, \text{append}_2) = \text{ne-list}$ $Approp(\text{JUNK}, \text{append}_2) = \text{append}$

append $\Rightarrow$ append$_1$ $\vee$ append$_2$

append$_1$ $\Rightarrow$ (LEFT: e-list) $\wedge$ (RIGHT $\doteq$ RESULT)

append$_2$ $\Rightarrow$ LEFT $\cdot$ HD $\doteq$ RESULT $\cdot$ HD $\;\wedge\;$ LEFT $\cdot$ TL $\doteq$ JUNK $\cdot$ LEFT
$\wedge$ RIGHT $\doteq$ JUNK $\cdot$ RIGHT $\;\wedge\;$ RESULT $\cdot$ TL $\doteq$ JUNK $\cdot$ RESULT

Figure 15.11. Junk Slot Encoding of **append** as a Constraint.

$$
\begin{bmatrix}
\textbf{append}_2 \\
\text{LEFT}: \langle a, b \rangle \\
\text{RIGHT}: \langle c, d \rangle \\
\text{RESULT}: \langle a, b, c, d \rangle \\
\text{JUNK}: \begin{bmatrix}
\textbf{append}_2 \\
\text{LEFT}: \langle b \rangle \\
\text{RIGHT}: \langle c, d \rangle \\
\text{RESULT}: \langle b, c, d \rangle \\
\text{JUNK}: \begin{bmatrix}
\textbf{append}_1 \\
\text{LEFT}: \langle \rangle \\
\text{RIGHT}: \langle c, d \rangle \\
\text{RESULT}: \langle c, d \rangle
\end{bmatrix}
\end{bmatrix}
\end{bmatrix}
$$

Figure 15.12. Resolution of **append** Query.

in Figure 15.11, we can cast the following query:

(8)
$$
\begin{bmatrix}
\textbf{append} \\
\text{LEFT}: \langle a, b \rangle \\
\text{RESULT}: \langle a, b, c, d \rangle
\end{bmatrix}
$$

The unique resolution of this query is displayed in Figure 15.12. Note that we have not listed all of the explicit structure sharing. From the resolved structure in Figure 15.12, it can be seen that the junk slot is simply being used to encode the proof tree of the append relation defined analogously to a definite clause. Viewed from another angle, the junk slots provide a work space in which

$Approp(\text{PHON}, \textbf{parse-tree}) = \textbf{expr-list}$

$CodeRule_2 \Rightarrow CodeRule \land (\text{PHON} \doteq \text{DTRS} \cdot \text{PHON})$

$CodeDtrs_2 \Rightarrow CodeDtrs$
$\qquad \land (\text{JUNK}: \textbf{append}) \land (\text{JUNK} \cdot \text{LEFT} \doteq \text{HD} \cdot \text{PHON})$
$\qquad \land (\text{JUNK} \cdot \text{RIGHT} \doteq \text{TL} \cdot \text{PHON}) \land (\text{JUNK} \cdot \text{RESULT} \doteq \text{PHON})$

Figure 15.13. Phrase Structure Grammar Encoding with Phonology.

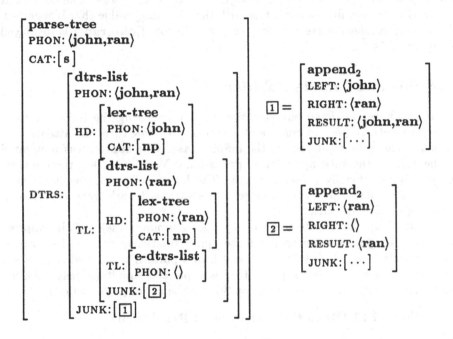

Figure 15.14. Resolution of PHON: ⟨john,ran⟩.

subgoals can be resolved. It is possible to encode multiple subgoals either by multiple junk slots or by a single junk slot whose value is a list of subgoals. Every such subgoal is resolved in the end, as every substructure in a resolved feature structure must itself be resolved.

We can use the technique of junk slots to encode arbitrary phrase structure parsing problems directly as a constraint system. This technique is used in HPSG for exactly the same reasons as we present it here: to compute the mother's phonology value in terms of the phonology values of the daughters. The revised encoding which computes phonology values is given in Figure 15.13. Note that we have simply assumed the original encoding with additional constraints to

$$[\,\text{person}\,] \overset{bf}{\Rightarrow} \begin{bmatrix} \text{person} \\ \text{FTH}:[\,\text{person}\,] \end{bmatrix} \overset{bf}{\Rightarrow} \begin{bmatrix} \text{person} \\ \text{FTH}:\begin{bmatrix} \text{person} \\ \text{FTH}:[\,\text{person}\,] \end{bmatrix} \end{bmatrix} \overset{bf}{\Rightarrow} \cdots$$

Figure 15.15. Infinite Rewriting Sequence.

pass the phonology value up the tree. In effect, the junk slot is being used to compute the yield at every stage of the tree. A parsing query can now be stated as a description of the phonology value of a parse tree. The constraint system then simply finds a parse tree with the phonology value that is specified. The unique resolved parse tree for the query (PHON: ⟨**john,ran**⟩) is displayed in Figure 15.14.

Domains and Infinite Solutions

So far, we have restricted our attention to characterizing the finite solutions to queries with respect to constraint systems. We now turn our attention to a domain-theoretic treatment of the infinite case. Our approach is motivated by the domain-theoretic approach of Pollard and Moshier (1990), though their analysis is superficially rather different. The benefit of employing domains is that we are able to produce most general solutions to arbitrary constraints, including cyclic ones such as (3).

We build up the infinite solutions by taking limits (joins) of finite approximations. To generate the proper finite approximations, we introduce a new notion of rewriting which follows a breadth-first parallel scheme whereby every node in an unresolved feature structure is expanded simultaneously. We use the abstract feature structure notation $\mathcal{P}_F$ for the set of paths defined in F.

Definition 15.13 (Breadth-First Parallel Resolution)

$F \overset{bf}{\Rightarrow} \bigsqcup_{\pi \in \mathcal{P}_F} G@\pi$ *if and only if* $F \overset{\pi}{\Rightarrow} G@\pi$ *for every* $\pi \in \mathcal{P}_F$.

Thus ¡breadth-first parallel rewriting is achieved by simply unifying the results of rewriting along every path. The result of such a rewriting in the limit is derived by unifying the feature structures found at every stage of the rewriting.

Definition 15.14 (Resolution in the Limit)

F_0 *resolves in the limit* to F, *written* $F_0 \overset{\omega}{\Rightarrow} F$, *if and only if* $F = \bigsqcup_{n \in \omega} F_n$ *and* $F_n \overset{bf}{\Rightarrow} F_{n+1}$ *for* $n \in \omega$.

Note that the join in the definition of resolution in the limit is well defined as the sequence $F_1, F_2, \ldots$ is obviously directed as it is increasing. Of course, resolution in the limit is still non-deterministic, but it can be determized with the upper-powerdomain construction (see Pollard and Moshier 1990).

$$\left[\begin{array}{l} \text{person} \\[2ex] \text{FATHER:} \left[\begin{array}{l} \text{person} \\[2ex] \text{FATHER:} \left[\begin{array}{l} \text{person} \\[1ex] \text{FATHER:}\left[\cdots\right] \end{array}\right] \end{array}\right] \end{array}\right]$$

Figure 15.16. Limit of Infinite Rewriting Sequence.

First note that if $F \stackrel{\omega}{\Rightarrow} F'$, then F' might be an infinite feature structure. Simply consider the case of (3), for which we have the infinite rewriting sequence in Figure 15.15. The limit of the infinite sequence in Figure 15.15 is given by the infinite feature structure indicated in Figure 15.16. Note that the feature structure in Figure 15.16 is more general than any of the cyclic solutions given in Figure 15.3. Furthermore, this infinite feature structure is resolved along each of its paths. We first note that the result of resolution in the limit always leads to a resolved feature structure, even if the limit is infinite.

Theorem 15.15 (Soundness of Resolution in the Limit)

If $F \stackrel{\omega}{\Rightarrow} F'$, then F' is resolved.

Proof: Suppose by way of contradiction that π is a path at which $F' = \bigsqcup_{n \in \omega} F_n$ is not resolved, where the F_i are the ones derived from the breadth-first rewriting sequence. Then there must be some F_i such that the type of the substructure along π in F_i is the same as that in F'. This is because there are only finitely many types. But then the path π is resolved in F_{i+1} and hence in F', which leads to a contradiction. □

More interestingly, it can also be shown that every most general solution to a constraint system can be found by resolution in the limit.

Theorem 15.16 (Completeness of Resolution in the Limit)

If F is a (possibly infinite) solution to the query ϕ, then some $G \in MGSats(\phi)$ is such that $G \stackrel{\omega}{\Rightarrow} H$ and $H \sqsubseteq F$.

Proof: If F is a solution to ϕ, then choose $G \in MGSats(\phi)$ such that $G \sqsubseteq F$. Since F is resolved, π-resolution is monotonic, and breadth-first parallel resolution can be simulated by a sequence of π-resolution steps, we are able to define a sequence of G_i such that $G_0 = G$, $G_i \stackrel{bf}{\Rightarrow} G_{i+1}$ and $G_i \sqsubseteq F$ for all $i \in \omega$. Thus $\bigsqcup_{i \in \omega} G_i \sqsubseteq F$. □

In particular, every most general resolved feature structure can be found by resolving the most general feature structure $\perp$ in the limit.

A generalization of Aït-Kaci's (1984, 1986) rewriting strategy, the so-called *fan-out order* can be shown to yield the same results as our breadth-first parallel resolution.

Definition 15.17 (Fan-Out Resolution)

F fan-out resolves *to F', written $F \overset{fo}{\Rightarrow} F'$, if either:*

- $F \overset{\pi}{\Rightarrow} F'$ *and π is of minimal length such that F is unresolved at π, or*

- F *is resolved and $F = F'$*

In fan-out order, we only resolve one path at a time, but always choose the path so that it is of minimal length among the unresolved paths. Suppose we define a notion of resolution in the limit using fan-out resolution, by setting:

$$(9) \quad F \overset{f-\omega}{\Rightarrow} \bigsqcup_{n \in \omega} F_n$$

if there are F_i such that $F = F_i$ and $F_i \overset{fo}{\Rightarrow} F_{i+1}$ for $i \in \omega$. Then we can show that fan-out and breadth-first parallel resolution find the same answers in the limit. The easiest way to do this is to show directly that fan-out resolution in the limit is itself sound and complete. Soundness follows by the same argument that showed breadth-first parallel rewriting to be sound. The only trick is that now each path is not immediately resolved at every stage. But since there are only finitely many features, there are only finitely many paths of any given depth from the root in any feature structure. Thus it can be shown by induction that paths of arbitrary finite depth are resolved after finitely many fan-out resolution steps. Completeness follows by a completely analogous argument to completeness for breadth-first parallel resolution.

Bibliography

Aczel, P. (1988). *Non-Well-Founded Sets*. Volume 14 of *CSLI Lecture Notes*. Chicago University Press, Chicago.

Ahlèn, S. (1989). Sorts in HPSG. Unpublished manuscript, Computational Linguistics Program, Philosophy Department, Carnegie Mellon University, Pittsburgh.

Aho, A. V., Sethi, R., and Ullman, J. D. (1986). *Compilers: Principles, Techniques and Tools*. Addison-Wesley, Reading, Massachusetts.

Aït-Kaci, H. (1984). A lattice-theoretic approach to computation based on a calculus of partially ordered types. Ph.D. thesis, University of Pennsylvania.

Aït-Kaci, H. (1986a). An algebraic semantics approach to the effective resolution of type equations. *Theoretical Computer Science*, 45:293–351.

Aït-Kaci, H. (1986b). Solving type equations by graph rewriting. In *Proceedings of the 1st International Conference on Rewriting Techniques and Applications*. Lecture Notes in Computer Science 202, 158–179. Springer-Verlag, Berlin.

Aït-Kaci, H. (1990). The WAM: A (real) tutorial. PRL Research Report 5, Digital Equipment Corporation Paris Research Laboratory, Paris.

Aït-Kaci, H., and Nasr, R. (1986a). Logic and inheritance. In *Proceedings of the 13th ACM Symposium on Principles of Programming Languages*, 219–228, St. Petersburg, Florida.

Aït-Kaci, H., and Nasr, R. (1986b). LOGIN: A logical programming language with built-in inheritance. *Journal of Logic Programming*, 3:187–215.

Barendregt, H. (1981). *The Lambda Calculus: Its Syntax and Semantics*. North-Holland, Amsterdam.

Barton, G. E., Jr., Berwick, R. C., and Ristad, E. S. (1987). *Computational Complexity and Natural Language*. MIT Press, Cambridge, Massachusetts.

Barwise, J. (1989). *The Situation in Logic*. Volume 17 of *CSLI Lecture Notes*. Center for the Study of Language and Information, Stanford.

Barwise, J., and Etchemendy, J. (1987). *The Liar: An Essay in Truth and Circularity.* Oxford University Press.

Birkhoff, G. (1933). On the combination of subalgebras. *Proceedings of the Cambridge Philosophy Society,* 29:441–464.

Birkhoff, G. (1967). *Lattice Theory.* Volume 25 of *American Mathematical Society Colloquium Publications.* American Mathematical Society, Providence, Rhode Island.

Borgida, A., Brachman, R. J., McGuinness, D. L., and Resnick, L. A. (1989). CLASSIC: A structural data model for objects. In *Proceedings of the SIG-MOD International Conference on Management of Data,* 59–67, Portland, Oregon.

Borgida, A., and Etherington, D. W. (1989). Disjunction in inheritance hierarchies. In *Proceedings of the 1st International Conference on Principles of Knowledge Representation and Reasoning,* 33–43, Toronto.

Boyer, R., and Moore, J. (1972). The sharing of structure in theorem-proving programs. In Meltzer, B., and Michie, D., editors, *Machine Intelligence 7,* 101–116. John Wiley and Sons, New York.

Brachman, R. J., Fikes, R., and Levesque, H. (1983a). Implementing KRYPTON: Integrating terminology and assertion. In *Proceedings of the 1983 National Conference on Artificial Intelligence,* 31–35, Washington, D. C.

Brachman, R. J., Fikes, R., and Levesque, H. (1983b). KRYPTON: A functional approach to knowledge representation. *IEEE Computer,* 16(10):67–73.

Brachman, R. J. (1979). On the epistemological status of semantic networks. In Findler, N., editor, *Associative Networks: Representation and Use of Knowledge by Computers,* 3–50. Academic Press, New York.

Brachman, R. J., and Levesque, H. J. (1984). The tractability of subsumption in frame-based description languages. In *Proceedings of the 1984 National Conference on Artificial Intelligence,* 34–37, Austin, Texas.

Brachman, R. J., McGuinness, D. L., Patel-Schneider, P. F., and Resnick, L. A. (1991). Living with CLASSIC: When and how to use a KL-ONE-like language. In Sowa, J., editor, *Principles of Semantic Networks.* Morgan Kaufmann, San Mateo, California.

Brachman, R. J., and Schmolze, J. G. (1985). An overview of the KL-ONE knowledge representation system. *Cognitive Science,* 9:171–216.

Calder, J. (1987). Typed unification for natural language processing. In Klein, E., and van Benthem, J., editors, *Categories, Polymorphism and Unification,* 65–72. Centre for Cognitive Science, University of Edinburgh, Edinburgh, Scotland.

Cardelli, L. (1984). A semantics of multiple inheritance. In Kahn, G., Mac-Queen, D., and Plotkin, G., editors, *Proceedings of the International Symposium on the Semantics of Data Types. Lecture Notes in Computer Science* 173, 51–67. Springer-Verlag, Berlin.

Cardelli, L., and Wegner, P. (1985). On understanding types, data abstraction and polymorphism. *Computing Surveys*, 17(4):471–522.

Carpenter, B. (1989). Phrase meaning and categorial grammar. Ph.D. thesis, Centre for Cognitive Science, University of Edinburgh, Edinburgh, Scotland.

Carpenter, B. (1990). Typed feature structures: Inheritance, (in)equations and extensionality. In *Proceedings of the 1st International Workshop on Inheritance in Natural Language Processing*, 9–13, Tilburg, The Netherlands.

Carpenter, B. (in press). Skeptical and credulous default unification with applications to templates and inheritance. In Briscoe, T., Copestake, A., and de Paiva, V., editors, *Default Inheritance Within Unification-Based Approaches to the Lexicon*. Cambridge University Press.

Carpenter, B., Pollard, C., and Franz, A. (1991). The specification and implementation of constraint-based unification grammars. In *Proceedings of the 2nd International Workshop on Parsing Technology*, 143–153, Cancun, Mexico.

Carpenter, B., and Thomason, R. (1990). Inheritance theory and path-based reasoning: An introduction. In Kyburg, Jr., H. E., Loui, R. P., and Carlson, G. N., editors, *Defeasible Reasoning and Knowledge Representation*. Volume 5 of *Studies in Cognitive Systems*, 309–344. Kluwer Academic, Dordrecht.

Chomsky, N. (1957). *Syntactic Structures*. Mouton, The Hague.

Chomsky, N. (1981). *Lectures on Government and Binding*. Foris, Dordrecht.

Chomsky, N. (1988). *Language and Problems of Knowledge*. Volume 16 of *Current Studies in Linguistics*. MIT Press, Cambridge, Massachusetts.

Chomsky, N., and Halle, M. (1968). *The Sound Pattern of English*. Harper and Row, New York.

Cohn, A. (1987). A more expressive formulation of many-sorted logic. *Journal of Automated Reasoning*, 3(2):113–200.

Cohn, P. M. (1965). *Universal Algebra*. Harper and Row, New York.

Colmerauer, A. (1970). Les systèmes-q ou un formalisme pour analyser et synthétiser des phrases sur ordinateur. Internal Report 43, Université de Montréal, Montreal.

Colmerauer, A. (1978). Metamorphosis grammars. In Bolc, L., editor, *Natural Language Communication with Computers*. *Lecture Notes in Computer Science 63*, 143–189. Springer-Verlag, Berlin.

Colmerauer, A. (1982a). An interesting subset of natural language. In Clark, K. L., and Tärnlund, S.-Å., editors, *Logic Programming*, 45–66. Volume 16 of *APIC Studies in Data Processing*. Academic Press, New York.

Colmerauer, A. (1982b). Prolog and infinite trees. In Clark, K. L., and Tärnlund, S.-Å., editors, *Logic Programming*, 1–44. Volume 16 of *APIC Studies in Data Processing*. Academic Press, New York.

Colmerauer, A. (1982c). Prolog II: Reference manual and theoretical model. Internal Report, Groupe Intelligence Artificielle, Université Aix-Marseilles II, Marseilles.

Colmerauer, A. (1984). Equations and inequations on finite and infinite trees. In *Proceedings of the International Conference on Fifth Generation Computer Systems*, 85–99, Tokyo.

Colmerauer, A. (1987). Theoretical model of prolog II. In van Caneghem, M., and Warren, D. H., editors, *Logic Programming and its Application*, 1–31. Ablex, Norwood, New Jersey.

Dahl, V., and Abramson, H. (1984). On gapping grammars. In *Proceedings of the 2nd International Joint Conference on Logic Programming*, 77–88, Uppsala, Sweden.

Dahl, V., and Saint-Dizier, P., editors (1985). *Natural Language Understanding and Logic Programming*. Volume I. North-Holland, Amsterdam.

Dahl, V., and Saint-Dizier, P., editors (1988). *Natural Language Understanding and Logic Programming*. Volume II. North-Holland, Amsterdam.

Davey, B., and Priestley, H. (1990). *Introduction to Lattices and Order*. Cambridge Mathematical Textbooks. Cambridge University Press.

Dawar, A., and Vijay-Shanker, K. (1989). A three-valued interpretation of negation in feature structure descriptions. In *Proceedings of the 27th Annual Conference of the Association for Computational Linguistics*, 18–24, Vancouver.

Dawar, A., and Vijay-Shanker, K. (1990). An interpretation of negation in feature structure descriptions. *Computational Linguistics*, 16(1):11–21.

Dörre, J., and Eisele, A. (1990). Feature logic with disjunctive unification. In *Proceedings of the 13th International Conference on Computational Linguistics*, 100–105, Helsinki.

Dörre, J., and Rounds, W. (1990). On subsumption and semiunification in feature algebras. In *Proceedings of the 19th Annual IEEE Symposium on Logic in Computer Science*, 300–310, Philadelphia.

Eisele, A., and Dörre, J. (1988). Unification of disjunctive feature descriptions. In *Proceedings of the 26th Annual Conference of the Association for Computational Linguistics*, 286–294, Buffalo.

Elhadad, M. (1990). Types in functional unification grammar. In *Proceedings of the 28th Annual Conference of the Association for Computational Linguistics*, 157–164, Pittsburgh.

Emele, M., and Zajac, R. (1989a). Multiple inheritance in RETIF. Technical Report TR-I-0114, ATR, Kyoto.

Emele, M., and Zajac, R. (1989b). RETIF: A rewriting system for typed feature structures. Technical Report TR-I-0071, ATR, Kyoto.

Emele, M. C., and Zajac, R. (1990). Typed unification grammars. In *Proceedings of the 13th International Conference on Computational Linguistics*, Helsinki.

Fages, F., and Huet, G. (1986). Complete sets of unifiers and matchers in equational theories. *Theoretical Computer Science*, 43:189–200.

Fahlman, S. E. (1979). *NETL: A System for Representing and Using Real-World Knowledge*. MIT Press, Cambridge, Massachusetts.

Flickinger, D. (1987). Lexical rules in the hierarchical lexicon. Ph.D. thesis, Stanford University, Stanford.

Flickinger, D., Pollard, C. J., and Wasow, T. (1985). Structure-sharing in lexical representation. In *Proceedings of the 23rd Annual Conference of the Association for Computational Linguistics*, 262–267, Chicago.

Franz, A. (1990). A parser for HPSG. Technical Report LCL–90–3, Laboratory for Computational Linguistics, Carnegie Mellon University, Pittsburgh.

Gallier, J. H., and Isakowitz, T. (1988). Rewriting in order-sorted equational logic. In Kowalski, R. A., and Bowen, K. A., editors, *Proceedings of the 5th International Symposium on Logic Programming*, 280–294, Seattle.

Garey, M. R., and Johnson, D. S. (1979). *Computers and Intractability: A Guide to the Theory of NP-Completeness*. W. H. Freeman and Company, New York.

Gazdar, G. (1981). On syntactic categories. *Philosophical Transactions of the Royal Society (Series B)*, 295:267–283.

Gazdar, G., Klein, E., Pullum, G., and Sag, I. (1985). *Generalized Phrase Structure Grammar*. Basil Blackwell, Oxford.

Gazdar, G., and Mellish, C. S. (1989). *Natural Language Processing in Prolog*. Addison-Wesley, Reading, Massachusetts.

Gazdar, G., Pullum, G., Carpenter, R., Klein, E., Hukari, T., and Levine, R. (1988). Category structures. *Computational Linguistics*, 14:1–19.

Gierz, G., Hofmann, I., Keimel, K., Lawson, J., Mislove, M., and Scott, D. (1980). *A Compendium of Continuous Lattices*. Springer-Verlag, Berlin.

Goguen, J., Jouannaud, J.-P., and Meseguer, J. (1985). Operational semantics for order-sorted algebra. In *ICALP '85. Lecture Notes in Computer Science* 194, 221–231. Springer-Verlag, Berlin.

Goguen, J., and Meseguer, J. (1987). Order-sorted algebra I: Partial and overloaded operations, errors, inheritance. Technical Report, SRI International, Menlo Park, California.

Goguen, J. A. (1988). What is unification? A categorical view. Computer Science Laboratory Report SRI–CSL–88–2, SRI International, Menlo Park, California.

Goguen, J. A., Thatcher, J., and Wagner, E. (1978). An initial algebra approach to the specification, correctness and implementation of abstract data types. In Yeh, R., editor, *Current Trends in Programming Methodology: Volume 4, Program Structuring*, 80–149. Prentice Hall, Englewood Cliffs, New Jersey.

Grätzer, G. (1971). *Lattice Theory: First Concepts and Distributive Lattices.* W. H. Freeman and Company, San Francisco.

Guenthner, F. (1988). Features and values 1988. Technical Report SNS–Bericht 88–40, Seminar für natürlich-sprachliche system der Universität Tübingen, Tübingen.

Gunter, C., and Scott, D. S. (in press). Semantic domains. In *Theoretical Computer Science*. North-Holland, New York.

Harman, G. (1963). Generative grammars without transformation rules: a defense of phrase-structure. *Language*, 39:597–616.

Hasida, K. (1986). Conditioned unification for natural language processing. In *Proceedings of the 11th International Conference on Computational Linguistics*, 85–87, Bonn.

Hirsch, S. (1987). PATR into Prolog. Master's thesis, Stanford University, Stanford.

Höhfeld, M., and Smolka, G. (1988). Definite relations over constraint languages. LILOG–REPORT 53, IBM – Deutschland GmbH, Stuttgart.

Holcombe, W. (1982). *Algebraic Automata Theory*. Volume 1 of *Cambridge Studies in Advanced Mathematics*. Cambridge University Press.

Huet, G. (1976). Résolution d'équations dans des langages d'ordre $1, 2, \ldots, \omega$. Ph.D. thesis, Université de Paris VII. Thèse d'État.

Jaffar, J. (1984). Efficient unification over infinite terms. *New Generation Computing*, 2:207–219.

Jaffar, J., and Lassez, J.-L. (1987). Constraint logic programming. In *Proceedings of the 14th ACM Symposium on Principles of Programming Languages*, 111–119, Munich.

Johnson, M. (1987). A logic of attribute-value structures and the theory of grammar. Ph.D. thesis, Stanford University.

Johnson, M. (1988). *Attribute-Value Logic and the Theory of Grammar*. Volume 14 of *CSLI Lecture Notes*. Center for the Study of Language and Information, Stanford.

Johnson, M. (1990a). Expressing disjunctive and negative feature constraints with first-order logic. In *Proceedings of the 28th Annual Conference of the Association for Computational Linguistics*, 173–179, Pittsburgh.

Johnson, M. (1990b). Features, frames and quantifier-free formulae. In Saint-Dizier, P., and Szpakowicz, editors, *Logic and Logic Grammars for Language Processing*. Ellis Horwood, New York.

Johnson, M. (1991). Logic and feature structures. In *Proceedings of the 12th International Joint Conference on Artificial Intelligence*, Sydney.

Johnson, M. (in press). Features and formulae. *Computational Linguistics*.

Kaplan, R., and Bresnan, J. (1982). Lexical-functional grammar: A formal system for grammatical representation. In Bresnan, J., editor, *The Mental Representation of Grammatical Relations*, 173–281. MIT Press, Cambridge, Massachusetts.

Karttunen, L. (1984). Features and values. In *Proceedings of the 10th International Conference on Computational Linguistics*, 28–33, Stanford.

Kasper, R. T. (1986). Systemic grammar and functional unification grammar. In Benson, J., and Greaves, W., editors, *Proceedings of the 12th International Systemics Workshop*.

Kasper, R. T. (1987a). Feature structures: a logical theory with applications to language analysis. Ph.D. thesis, University of Michigan, Ann Arbor, Michigan.

Kasper, R. T. (1987b). A unification method for disjunctive feature structures. In *Proceedings of the 25th Annual Conference of the Association for Computational Linguistics*, 235–242, Stanford.

Kasper, R. T. (1988a). Conditional descriptions in functional unification grammar. In *Proceedings of the 26th Annual Conference of the Association for Computational Linguistics*, 233–240, Buffalo.

Kasper, R. T. (1988b). An experimental parser for systemic grammars. In *Proceedings of the 12th International Conference on Computational Linguistics*, Budapest.

Kasper, R. T. (1989). Unification and classification: An experiment in information-based parsing. In *Proceedings of the 1st International Workshop on Parsing Technologies*, pages 1–7, Pittsburgh.

Kasper, R. T., and Rounds, W. C. (1986). A logical semantics for feature structures. In *Proceedings of the 24th Annual Conference of the Association for Computational Linguistics*, 235–242, New York.

Kasper, R. T., and Rounds, W. C. (1990). The logic of unification in grammar. *Linguistics and Philosophy*, 13(1):35–58.

Kay, M. (1979). Functional grammar. In Chiarello, C., editor, *Proceedings of the 5th Annual Meeting of the Berkeley Linguistic Society*, 142–158, Berkeley.

Kay, M. (1984). Functional unification grammar: a formalism for machine translation. In *Proceedings of the 10th International Conference on Computational Linguistics*, 75–78, Stanford.

Kay, M. (1985a). Unification in grammar. In Dahl, V., and Saint-Dizier, P., editors, *Natural Language Understanding and Logic Programming*, Volume I, 233–240. North-Holland, Amsterdam.

Kay, M. (1985b). Parsing in functional unification grammar. In Dowty, D. R., Karttunen, L., and Zwicky, A., editors, *Natural Language Parsing*, 206–250. Cambridge University Press.

King, P. (1989). A logical formalism for Head-Driven Phrase Structure Grammar. Ph.D. thesis, University of Manchester, Manchester, England.

Knight, K. (1989). Unification: A multidisciplinary survey. *ACM Computing Surveys*, 21(1):93–124.

Kracht, M. (1988). On the logic of category definitions. *Computational Linguistics*, 15(2):111–113.

Kress, G. R., editor (1979). *Halliday: System and Function in Language*. Oxford University Press.

Kunen, K. (1980). *Set Theory*. Volume 102 of *Studies in Logic and the Foundations of Mathematics*. North-Holland, Amsterdam.

Landman, F. (1986). *Towards a Theory of Information: The Status of Partial Objects in Semantics*. Volume 6 of *Groningen-Amsterdam Studies in Semantics*. Foris, Dordrecht.

Langholm, T. (1989). How to say no with feature structures. Computational Semantics Report 13, University of Oslo Mathematics Department, Oslo.

Lassez, J.-L., Maher, M. J., and Marriott, K. G. (1986). Unification revisited. Internal Report RC 12394 (55630), IBM – T. J. Watson Research Center, Yorktown Heights, New York.

Lehner, C. (in press). Typing and inheritance for natural language grammars in Prolog III. *Computational Linguistics*.

Lewis, H. R. and Papadimitriou, C. H. (1981) *Elements of the Theory of Computation*. Prentice-Hall, Englewood Cliffs, New Jersey.

Lloyd, J. W. (1984). *Foundations of Logic Programming*. Springer-Verlag, Berlin.

Mac Gregor, R. (1988). A deductive pattern matcher. In *Proceedings of the 1988 National Conference on Artificial Intelligence*, 403–408, St. Paul, Minnesota.

Mac Gregor, R. M. (1990). LOOM users manual. ISI Technical report, University of Southern California, La Jolla, California.

Maher, M. J. (1988). Complete axiomatizations of the algebras of finite, rational and infinite trees. In *Proceedings of the 3rd Annual IEEE Symposium on Logic in Computer Science*, 348–357, Edinburgh, Scotland.

Maier, D., and Warren, D. S. (1988). *Computing with Logic: Logic Programming with Prolog*. John Benjamin, Menlo Park, California.

Martelli, A., and Montanari, U. (1982). An efficient unification algorithm. *ACM Transactions on Programming Languages and Systems*, 4(2):258–282.

Maxwell, J., and Kaplan, R. (1989). An overview of disjunctive constraint satisfaction. In *Proceedings of the 1st International Workshop on Parsing Technology*, 18–27, Pittsburgh.

McCord, M. C. (1981). Slot grammars. *American Journal of Computational Linguistics*, 6:255–286.

Mellish, C. S. (1988). Implementing systemic classification via unification. *Computational Linguistics*, 14(1):40–51.

Meseguer, J., Goguen, J., and Smolka, G. (1987). Order-sorted unification. Report CSLI–87–86, Center for the Study of Language and Information, Stanford.

Milner, R. (1978). A theory of type polymorphism in programming. *Journal of Computer and System Sciences*, 17(3):348–375.

Minsky, M. (1975). A framework for representing knowledge. In Winston, P. H., editor, *The Psychology of Computer Vision*. McGraw-Hill, New York.

Mishra, P. (1984). Towards a theory of types in Prolog. In *Proceedings of the 1st International Symposium on Logic Programming*, 289–298, Atlantic City, New Jersey.

Moens, M., Calder, J., Klein, E., Reape, M., and Zeevat, H. (1989). Expressing generalizations in unification-based grammar formalisms. In *Proceedings of the 4th Meeting of the European Association for Computation Linguistics*, 66–71, Manchester, England.

Moser, M. (1983). An overview of NIKL, the new implementation of KL-ONE. In *Research in Natural Language Understanding*. BBN Technical Report 5421. Bolt, Beranek and Newman, Inc., Cambridge, Massachusetts.

Moshier, D. (1988). Extensions to unification grammar for the description of programming languages. Ph.D. thesis, University of Michigan, Ann Arbor.

Moshier, D., and Rounds, W. (1987). A logic for partially specified data structures. In *Proceedings of the 14th ACM Symposium on Principles of Programming Languages*, 156–167, Munich.

Moshier, M. A. (1989). A careful look at the unification algorithm. Unpublished manuscript, Department of Mathematics, University of California, Los Angeles.

Moss, L. S. (1990). Completeness theorems for logics of feature structures. In Moschovakis, Y. N., editor, *Proceedings of the MSRI Workshop on Logic from Computer Science*. Springer-Verlag, Berlin.

Mukai, K. (1985). Unification over complex indeterminates in Prolog. Technical Report TM-103, ICOT, Tokyo.

Mukai, K. (1987). Anadic tuples in Prolog. Technical Report TR-239, ICOT, Tokyo.

Mukai, K. (in press). A system of logic programming for linguistic analysis. In *Proceedings of the Workshop on the Semantics of Natural and Human Languages*. MIT Press, Cambridge, Massachusetts.

Mukai, K., and Yasukawa, H. (1985). Complex indeterminates in Prolog and its application to discourse models. *New Generation Computing*, 3:441–466.

Mycroft, A., and O'Keefe, R. A. (1984). A polymorphic type system for Prolog. *Artificial Intelligence*, 23(3):295–307.

Nebel, B. (1988). Computational complexity of terminological reasoning in BACK. *Artificial Intelligence*, 34(3):371–383.

Nebel, B., and Smolka, G. (1989). Representation and reasoning with attributive descriptions. IWB Report 81, IBM – Deutschland GmbH, Stuttgart.

Patel-Schneider, P. F. (1984). Small can be beautiful in knowledge representation. In *Proceedings of the IEEE Workshop on Principles of Knowledge-Based Systems*, 559–565, Denver.

Paterson, M., and Wegman, M. (1978). Linear unification. *Journal of Computer and System Sciences*, 16:158–167.

Pereira, F. C. (1987). Grammars and logics of partial information. In Lassez, J.-L., editor, *Proceedings of the 4th International Symposium on Logic Programming*, 989–1013, Melbourne.

Pereira, F. C. N., and Shieber, S. M. (1984). The semantics of grammar formalisms seen as computer languages. In *Proceedings of the 10th International Conference on Computational Linguistics*, 123–129, Stanford.

Pereira, F. C. N., and Shieber, S. M. (1987). *Prolog and Natural-Language Analysis*. Volume 10 of *CSLI Lecture Notes*. Center for the Study of Language and Information, Stanford.

Pereira, F. C. N., and Warren, D. H. D. (1980). Definite clause grammars for language analysis – a survey of the formalism and a comparison with augmented transition networks. *Artificial Intelligence*, 13(3):231–278.

Plotkin, G. (1972). Building-in equational theories. In *Machine Intelligence 7*, 73–90. Edinburgh University Press, Edinburgh, Scotland.

Pollard, C. J. (in press). Sorts in unification-based grammar and what they mean. In Pinkal, M., and Gregor, B., editors, *Unification in Natural Language Analysis*. MIT Press, Cambridge, Massachusetts.

Pollard, C. J., and Moshier, M. D. (1990). Unifying partial descriptions of sets. In Hanson, P., editor, *Information, Language and Cognition*. Volume 1 of *Vancouver Studies in Cognitive Science*. University of British Columbia Press, Vancouver.

Pollard, C. J., and Sag, I. A. (1987). *Information-Based Syntax and Semantics: Volume I, Fundamentals*, Volume 13 of *CSLI Lecture Notes*. Center for the Study of Language and Information, Stanford.

Pollard, C. J., and Sag, I. A. (in press). *Head-driven Phrase Structure Grammar*. Chicago University Press, Chicago.

Popowich, F. P. (1985). Unrestricted gapping grammars: theory, implementations and applications. Master's thesis, Simon Fraser University, Burnaby, British Columbia.

Porter, H. H. (1987). Incorporating inheritance and feature structures into a logic grammar. In *Proceedings of the 25th Annual Conference of the Association for Computational Linguistics*, 228–234, Stanford.

Reape, M. (1989). A logical treatment of semi-free word order and bounded discontinuous constituency. In *Proceedings of the 4th Meeting of the European Association for Computational Linguistics*, 103–110, Manchester, England.

Reape, M. (1990). The semantics of feature value logics: Intensionality is unnecessary. Unpublished manuscript, Centre for Cognitive Science, University of Edinburgh, Edinburgh, Scotland.

Reape, M. (1991). An introduction to the semantics of unification-based grammar formalisms. DYANA Deliverable R3.2.A, ESPRIT BR 3175, Centre for Cognitive Science, University of Edinburgh, Edinburgh.

Reynolds, J. C. (1970). Transformational systems and the algebraic structure of atomic formulas. In Michie, D., editor, *Machine Intelligence 5*, 135–151. Edinburgh University Press, Edinburgh, Scotland.

Robinson, J. A. (1965). A machine-oriented logic based on the resolution principle. *Journal of the ACM*, 12:23–41.

Rounds, W. C. (1988). Set values for unification-based grammar formalisms and logic programming. Report CSLI–88–129, Center for the Study of Language and Information, Stanford.

Rounds, W. C., and Kasper, R. T. (1986). A complete logical calculus for record structures representing linguistic information. In *Proceedings of the 15th Annual IEEE Symposium on Logic in Computer Science*, 39–43, Cambridge, Massachusetts.

Rounds, W. C., and Manaster-Ramer, A. (1987). A logical version of functional grammar. In *Proceedings of the 25th Annual Conference of the Association for Computational Linguistics*, 89–96, Stanford.

Sag, I. A., Kaplan, R., Karttunen, L., Kay, M., Pollard, C. J., Shieber, S. M., and Zaenen, A. (1986). Unification and grammatical theory. In *Proceedings of the 5th West Coast Conference on Formal Linguistics*, 238–254, Seattle.

Sag, I. A., and Pollard, C. J. (1987). Head-driven phrase structure grammar: An informal synopsis. Report CSLI–87–79, Center for the Study of Language and Information, Stanford.

Schmidt-Schauß, M. (1989). Subsumption in KL-ONE is undecidable. In *Proceedings of the 1st International Conference on Principles of Knowledge Representation and Reasoning*, pages 421–431, Toronto.

Schmolze, J., and Lipkis, T. (1983). Classification in the KL-ONE knowledge representation system. In *Proceedings of the 8th International Joint Conference on Artificial Intelligence*, 330–352, Karlsruhe, Germany.

Scott, D. S. (1970). Outline of a mathematical theory of computation. Programming Research Group Technical Monograph PRG–3, University of Oxford, Oxford.

Sells, P. (1987). *Lectures on Contemporary Syntactic Theories*. Volume 3 of *CSLI Lecture Notes*. Center for the Study of Language and Information, Stanford.

Shieber, S. M. (1984). The design of a computer language for linguistic information. In *Proceedings of the 10th International Conference on Computational Linguistics*, 362–366, Stanford.

Shieber, S. M. (1985a). Criteria for designing computer facilities for linguistic analysis. *Linguistics*, 23:189–211.

Shieber, S. M. (1985b). Using restriction to extend parsing algorithms for complex-feature-based formalisms. In *Proceedings of the 23rd Annual Conference of the Association for Computational Linguistics*, 145–152, Chicago.

Shieber, S. M. (1986). *An Introduction to Unification-Based Approaches to Grammar*. Volume 4 of *CSLI Lecture Notes*. Center for the Study of Language and Information, Stanford.

Shieber, S. M. (1989). Parsing and type inference for natural and computer languages. Ph.D. thesis, Stanford University, Stanford. Available as SRI International Technical Note 460.

Shieber, S. M., Uszkoreit, H., Pereira, F. C. N., Robinson, J., and Tyson, M. (1983). The formalism and implementation of PATR-II. In *Research on Interactive Acquisition and Use of Knowledge*. Volume 1894 of *SRI Final Report*, SRI International, Menlo Park, California.

Siekmann, J. H. (1984). Universal unification. In *Proceedings of the 7th International Conference on Automated Deduction. Lecture Notes in Computer Science* 170, 1–42. Springer-Verlag, Berlin.

Siekmann, J. H. (1986). Unification theory. In *Proceedings of the 8th European Conference on Artificial Intelligence*, Brighton, England.

Siekmann, J. H. (1989). Unification theory. *Journal of Symbolic Computation*, 7:207–274.

Smolka, G. (1988a). A feature logic with subsorts. LILOG–REPORT 33, IBM – Deutschland GmbH, Stuttgart.

Smolka, G. (1988b). Logic programming with polymorphically order-sorted types. LILOG–REPORT 55, IBM – Deutschland GmbH, Stuttgart.

Smolka, G. (1989a). Attributive concept descriptions with unions and complements. IWBS Report 68, IBM – Deutschland GmbH, Stuttgart.

Smolka, G. (1989b). Feature constraint logics for unification grammars. IWBS Report 93, IBM – Deutschland GmbH, Stuttgart. To appear in *Journal of Logic Programming*.

Smolka, G., and Aït-Kaci, H. (1989). Inheritance hierarchies: Semantics and unification. *Journal of Symbolic Computation*, 7:343–370.

Smyth, M. (1978). Power domains. *Journal of Computer Systems Science*, 16:23–36.

Sterling, L., and Shapiro, E. Y. (1986). *The Art of Prolog: Advanced Programming Techniques*. MIT Press, Cambridge, Massachusetts.

Stone, M. H. (1936). The theory of representations for boolean algebras. *Transactions of the American Mathematical Society*, 40:37–111.

Stoy, J. E. (1977). *Denotational Semantics: The Scott-Strachey Approach to Programming Language Theory*. MIT Press, Cambridge, Massachusetts.

Tomita, M., and Knight, K. (1987). Pseudo-unification and full-unification. Unpublished manuscript, Computer Science Department and Center for Machine Translation, Carnegie Mellon University, Pittsburgh.

Touretzky, D. S. (1986). *The Mathematics of Inheritance Systems*. Research Notes in Artificial Intelligence. Morgan Kaufmann, San Mateo, California.

Uszkoreit, H. (1988). From feature bundles to abstract data types: New directions in the representation and processing of linguistic knowledge. In Blasre, A., editor, *Natural Language at the Computer*, pages 31–64. Springer-Verlag, Berlin.

van Emden, M., and Kowalski, R. A. (1976). The semantics of predicate logic as a programming language. *Journal of the ACM*, 23(4):733–743.

Vickers, S. (1989). *Topology Via Logic*. Volume 5 of *Cambridge Tracts in Theoretical Computer Science*. Cambridge University Press.

Vilain, M. (1985). The restricted language architecture of a hybrid representation system. In *Proceedings of the 10th International Joint Conference on Artificial Intelligence*, 547–551, Los Angeles, California.

von Luck, K., Nebel, B., Peltason, C., and Schmiedel, A. (1987). The anatomy of the BACK system. Technical Report KIT 41, Technische Universität Berlin, Berlin.

Walther, C. (1985). A mechanical solution of Schubert's Steamroller by many-sorted resolution. *Artificial Intelligence*, 26(2):217–224.

Walther, C. (1986). A classification of many-sorted unification problems. In *Proceedings of the 8th International Conference on Automated Deduction*. *Lecture Notes in Computer Science* 230, 525–537. Springer-Verlag, Berlin.

Walther, C. (1988). Many-sorted unification. *Journal of the ACM*, 35:1–17.

Warren, D. H. (1977). Implementing Prolog – compiling logic programs I, II. Research Report 39,40, Department of Artificial Intelligence, University of Edinburgh, Edinburgh, Scotland.

Winograd, T. (1983). *Language as a Cognitive Process: Volume I, Syntax*. Addison-Wesley, Reading, Massachusetts.

Wos, L., Overbeek, R., Lusk, E., and Boyle, J. (1984). *Automated Reasoning: Introduction and Applications*. Prentice Hall, Englewood Cliffs, New Jersey.

Xu, J., and Warren, D. S. (1988). A type inference system for Prolog. In Kowalski, R. A., and Bowen, K. A., editors, *Proceedings of the 5th International Symposium on Logic Programming*, 604–619. MIT Press, Cambridge, Massachusetts.

Zajac, R. (1989). A transfer model using a typed feature structure rewriting system with inheritance. In *Proceedings of the 27th Annual Conference of the Association for Computational Linguistics*, Vancouver.

Zeevat, H., Klein, E., and Calder, J. (1987). Unification categorial grammar. In Morrill, G., Haddock, N. J., and Klein, E., editors, *Categorial Grammar, Unification Grammar and Parsing*. Volume 1 of *Edinburgh Working Papers in Cognitive Science*. Centre for Cognitive Science, University of Edinburgh, Edinburgh, Scotland.

Zobel, J. (1987). Derivation of polymorphic types for Prolog programs. In Lassez, J.-L., editor, *Proceedings of the 4th International Symposium on Logic Programming*, 817–838, Melbourne.

Index of Symbols

Index